Alternative Projections

Alternative Projections: Experimental Film in LA 1945–1980 was made possible by major grants from the Getty Foundation, the Andy Warhol Foundation for the Visual Arts, and Visions and Voices: A Humanities Initiative at the University of Southern California, and the assistance of the School of Cinematic Arts, University of Southern California.

Alternative Projections was part of Pacific Standard Time: Art in L.A. 1945–1980. This unprecedented collaboration, initiated by the Getty, brought together more than sixty cultural institutions from across Southern California in 2011 to tell the story of the birth of the L.A. art scene

Alternative Projections:
Experimental Film in Los Angeles, 1945–1980

Edited by David E. James and Adam Hyman

British Library Cataloguing in Publication Data

Alternative Projections: Experimental Film in Los Angeles, 1945–1980

A catalogue entry for this book is available from the British Library

ISBN: 9780 86196 715 5 (Paperback)

Cover design: From *Foregrounds*, by Pat O'Neill (1978), courtesy of the artist.

Published by
John Libbey Publishing Ltd, 3 Leicester Road, New Barnet, Herts EN5 5EW, United Kingdom
e-mail: john.libbey@orange.fr; web site: www.johnlibbey.com

Distributed Worldwide by **Indiana University Press**,
Herman B Wells Library – 350, 1320 E. 10th St., Bloomington, IN 47405, USA.
www.iupress.indiana.edu

Printed and bound in China by 1010 Printing International Ltd.

Contents

Acknowledgements

Bringing this book to completion has involved the efforts of many people, most fundamentally the writers of the various contributions to it, but especially our publisher, John Libbey. Without the initiative and generosity of his intervention, the work of the rest of us would not have reached this fruition. For financial assistance for publication, we thank Los Angeles Filmforum and the School of Cinematic Arts at the University of Southern California. For manuscript preparation we thank Dr. Ken Provencher.

For permission to reprint texts, the editors wish to thank the following: Robert Pike, "A Letter from the West Coast", *Film Culture* 14 (November 1957), provided courtesy of Anthology Film Archives, All Rights Reserved; Maya Deren, "Amateur vs. Professional ," *Film Culture* 39 (Winter 1965), 45–46, provided courtesy of Anthology Film Archives, All Rights Reserved; John Fles, "Personal State Meant", and *Seeing Is Believing*, © and courtesy of Michael Fles; John Fles, "Are Movies Junk", *Film Culture* 29 (Summer 1963), provided courtesy of Anthology Film Archives, All Rights Reserved; Curtis Harrington, "A Statement". *Film Culture* 29 (Summer 1963), provided courtesy of Anthology Film Archives, All Rights Reserved; Jack Hirschman, "Los Angeles Film Festival", *Film Culture* 32 (September 1964), provided courtesy of Anthology Film Archives, All Rights Reserved; Kevin Thomas, "Underground Movies Rise to the Surface", © 1967, *Los Angeles Times*, Reprinted with permission; Gene Youngblood, "Students Reflect Future of Cinema", © and courtesy of Gene Youngblood; Chick Strand, "Woman as Ethnographic Filmmaker", © and courtesy of *University Film and Video Association*; Peter Mays, *Mouse Enigma*, © and courtesy of Peter Mays.

For permissions to reproduce photographs and other material, the editors wish to thank the following: cover illustration including film strip from *Foregrounds*, © and courtesy of Pat O'Neill; photograph of Stephanie Sapienza and Adam

Hyman at the announcement of the *Pacific Standard Time* initiative, March 2009, © and courtesy of Adam Hyman; announcement postcard, *Alternative Projections* symposium, © and courtesy of "Visions and Voices: The Arts and Humanities Initiative, University of Southern California"; photograph of principal organizers, *Alternative Projections* symposium, © and courtesy of Andrew Hall/Los Angeles Filmforum; Filmforum, first calendar, © and courtesy of Terry Cannon and Filmforum; front page preview edition, *Los Angeles Free Press*, courtesy of David E. James; composite photograph, "Bob Pike Photographs Fred Leitsinger for Pike's Film, *Desire in a Public Dump* (1958)", © and courtesy of the iotaCenter; photograph of Chick Strand, © and courtesy of estate of Chick Strand; filmstrip, *Death of the Gorilla*, © and courtesy of Peter Mays; film frames from *To L.A. . . . With Lust* by Vernon Zimmerman, courtesy of Anthology Film Archives and The Film-Makers' Cooperative; Hollis Frampton's "Chili Bean Brand Blue Boys" from his *By Any Other Name* – Series 1 (1979), © Estate of Hollis Frampton; photograph of John Vicario at the screening of *Shoppers Market* at the Cinefamily, © Adam Hyman/Filmforum; photograph of the Coronet Theatre by Danny Rouzer, © and courtesy of Janet B. Rouzer; Society of Cinema Arts calendars produced by the late Raymond Rohauer, © and courtesy of Douris UK Ltd (In Administration); photograph of Stan Brakhage and Raymond Rohauer, © and courtesy of Douris UK Ltd (In Administration); photograph of Terry Cannon, © and courtesy of Judith Gordon; all photographs of *The Exiles*'s production reproduced courtesy of Milestone Film & Video and © 1961 Kent Mackenzie; all images from Ed Ruscha's *All the Buildings on Sunset Strip*, © Ed Ruscha Studios, courtesy of the artist and Gagosian Gallery; photographs of "Willie F. Herrón III and Gronk in front of the *Black and White Mural*, Estrada Courts housing project, Boyle Heights", "Instant Mural", and "Death of Fashion", all © and courtesy of Harry Gamboa, Jr.; photograph "Unused explosion for *Star Wars* by Adam Beckett", © and courtesy of the iotaCenter; photographs of Nancy Angelo, Kate Horsfield, and Candace Compton Pappas, Summer Video Program, Woman's Building, Los Angeles, 1976 by Sheila Ruth, courtesy of and © Woman's Building Image Archive, Otis College of Art and Design; photograph of Nancy Angelo's "Sister Angelica Furisosa" performance persona 1977, courtesy of and © Woman's Building Image Archive, Otis College of Art and Design; photograph of Mark Toscano working on film preservation at the Academy Film Archive, courtesy of Todd Wawrychuk and © A.M.P.A.S.; photographs of attendees at *Alternative Projections* screenings 10 October 2011, 3 December 2011, 8 January 2012, 7 January 2012, and 11 March 2012, © and courtesy of Adam Hyman.

Foreword

Adam Hyman

Los Angeles Filmforum Executive Director and Alternative Projections Project Supervisor

When I originally received a phone call from Rani Singh of the Getty Research Institute in early 2008 about the Getty's imminent "On the Record" initiative, which would entail grants to organizations for archival and research activities on the history of artistic practice in Los Angeles, I knew that Los Angeles Filmforum had to take part. Filmforum, extant since 1975, is the city's longest-running organization dedicated to artist-driven, non-commercial experimental film and video art. Such practice isn't normally included in the art spaces of galleries and museums, but it has been a vital part of the story of art in this city of film. But I also had no idea of what our project might include, as I had sent an email to the board members of Filmforum on 8 April 2008, that included a simple question: "As far as I can tell, it needs to relate to LA Art 1945–1980. Do any of you have ideas for a research or archival project that might fit … ?"

Within a week, we mustered together a letter of interest that spelled out our grand ideas: a symposium that would "include panel discussions, presentations, and screenings", "a gallery show", "a new publication", screenings, and oral histories. Although a great amount changed in the following years, it seems remarkable to me, looking at that correspondence for the first time in six years, how closely we ended up hewing to our original dreams. We named our project *Alternative Projections: Experimental Film in Los Angeles, 1945–1980*, a multi-faceted exploration of film and video created outside the Hollywood and independent narrative spheres.

I'd like to thank The Getty Foundation and its leadership, particularly Deborah Marrow, Joan Weinstein, and Nancy Micklewright, for giving us the opportunity to make all of this happen as part of *Pacific Standard Time: Art in Los Angeles, 1945–1980* (as "On the Record" was eventually renamed).

One key element of *Alternative Projections* was a symposium, a fantastic three-day event held at the School of Cinematic Arts at University of Southern California from 12–14 November 2010, made possible by the School's commitment to the project and by USC's "Visions and Voices" initiative. Sixteen papers were presented in two days, along with screenings and open discussions. The majority of these papers have been expanded and refined to create the book that you now hold, in the section called "Scholarship". These papers are preceded by multiple historical writings to give readers and scholars both a single resource for primary works and a deeper sense of the development of artists' cinematic practice in Los Angeles over thirty-five years.

From the start we intended to create a database and a set of resources that would be useful to all future scholars. We don't know of anything else like it in the artist film world, combining oral histories, film descriptions, biographies, scans of images, and more. The database and website are live and elaborate, but also ongoing projects. We invite you to use it as a resource, to explore, and it is open for more contributions. It can be found at www.alternativeprojections.com.

All this scholarly work was designed to support our exhibition, a screening series over the course of 2011–2012, as part of the larger *Pacific Standard Time* initiative. We originally proposed sixteen programs, but ended up doing twenty-eight. The large final section of this volume lists these programs and the works screened, while the website gives fuller details. An additional grant from the Andy Warhol Foundation for the Visual Arts was also essential to the exhibition series, and I'd like to thank Pamela Clapp, James Bewley, and Jackie Farrell at the Warhol for their support. Programmers, filmmakers, projectionists, distributors, and volunteers all gave us tremendous support to make the series possible. The website contains further thanks and acknowledgements to everyone who made *Alternative Projections* possible, more than I have room to include here.

The screening series concluded in May 2012, along with the other *Pacific Standard Time* exhibitions. But *Alternative Projections*, the project, continues, as we add to our database, discover new films, and make it all available to everyone interested. We believe that these films are great art and need to be seen, and we hope that everyone who sees them might carry away some of our enthusiasm. Thank you for taking a chance on these unconventional and noncommercial works of art. We invite you to share with us the delights of thirty-five years of artists' cinema from Los Angeles.

Introduction

David E. James

Alternative Projections: Experimental Film in LA 1945–1980, the project documented and elaborated here, resulted from the initiative and energy of a few individuals working with several diverse institutions in the city. Primary among the individuals were Adam Hyman and Stephanie Sapienza, who at the time of the project's inception were, respectively, executive director and board president of the Los Angeles Filmforum, an independent film screening organization founded as the Pasadena Filmforum in 1975.[1] As well as Filmforum itself, the institutions included the Getty Foundation and its *Pacific Standard Time* (PST) project, and the University of Southern California's (USC's) School of Cinematic Arts (SCA) and its "Visions and Voices" program. Though some ancillary funds were provided by SCA and Filmforum, the present volume was made possible only by the generosity of its contributors and especially of an independent British publisher, John Libbey, who undertook it after it had been rejected by a dozen US university presses. Its production, then, recapitulates the individual initiative and commitment of the kind that has sustained the century-long history of independent cinema in the city. The greatest era of that cinema is traced here in the accounts by and of specific filmmakers, curators, scholars, and administrators, and in the record of the screening series that forms its conclusion. The belatedness of this book's appearance, on the other hand, and the fact that it could only find a publisher on the other side of the globe and in another continent, testifies to the resistance still faced by the kind of cinema with which it is concerned, especially in the city that was historically the medium's capital.

Since the earliest attempts "to paint the movie red" in 1913,[2] the precariousness and marginality of all non-commodity filmmaking have always been extreme in Los Angeles, and are so especially now when forced to sail between the Scylla of what has become a monstrously inflated artworld, and the Charybdisian whirlpool of the corporate media industries. Both of these sustain massive capital investment and hence possess an equivalent social authority, while experimental film's inability to valorize capital has made it primarily an amateur pursuit. Indeed, Maya Deren, whose film *Meshes of the Afternoon*, made in Los Angeles in 1943, and which initiated and inspired the postwar US avant-garde, defined her conception of the medium in exactly these terms in her essay (reprinted below), "Amateur Versus Professional": filmmaking undertaken for love against filmmaking for money. Given Hollywood's primacy in, if not dominance over, global culture of all kinds during the twentieth century, her formulation indicates the radical importance of any practice of cinema that is inassimilable into the productive system of capital and its ideological force field. Besieged, importuned, and immediately framed – if also frequently inspired – by Hollywood, experimental filmmaking in Los Angeles may consequently claim a paradigmatic significance; undertaken at the center of industrial culture, it is the prototypical practice of resistance to it and the inauguration of emancipatory possibilities. To this extent, all those individuals and groups who between 2009 and 2014 worked to realize the various components of *Alternative Projections* played a part in experimental film's utopian project.

Alternative Projections

According to the J. Paul Getty Trust's own report, the *PST* project originated around the turn of the millennium, when scholars there perceived the danger that the historical record of the city's avant-garde art might be lost.[3] After almost a decade of preparation, in 2007 the Getty Foundation announced a competition for nearly one million dollars' worth of grants of between $50,000 and $250,000 each for "the collaborative research and planning of scholarly exhibitions related to the history of postwar art in the Los Angeles area", a project at that time called "On the Record: Art in L.A. 1945–1980".[4]

Though Filmforum had not previously been on the Getty's radar, Rani Singh, Senior Research Associate in the Department of Contemporary Art & Architecture at the Getty Research Institute and also director of the Harry Smith Archives, alerted Hyman to the announcement. A documentary filmmaker, Hyman had also been Filmforum's director since 2003, after serving as volunteer and then *de facto* house manager of the organization since 1996. Founded as a non-profit film society in 1975 by the then twenty-one year old Terry Cannon, the Pasadena Filmforum had variously prospered and barely survived under a variety of administrations, and had held screenings at a variety of locations in Los Angeles. Hyman had shown himself to be an unusually capable, ambitious, and imaginative programmer of avant-garde and other non-commercial films, reviving Filmforum's fortunes. In 2002 Filmforum found a regular home for its screenings at the American Cinematheque's restored Egyptian Theater on Hollywood Boulevard. Sapienza, the Assistant Director of the iotaCenter (a Los Angeles public benefit, non-profit arts organization founded in 1994 with a special commitment to abstract film, animation, and experimental films from West Coast artists), had recently completed her MA degree in the Moving Image Archive Studies (MIAS) program at the University of California at Los Angeles (UCLA), and was eager to find a project on which to employ her skills.

Contacted by Sapienza, Dr. Nancy Micklewright, Senior Program Officer at the Foundation, responded enthusiastically, and invited her and Hyman to apply. With Singh advising on the formulation of the historical recovery component of their project, Hyman and Sapienza consulted with Cannon and a dozen other interested filmmakers, programmers, and scholars, and on 13 April 2008, Hyman submitted the requested preliminary letter of inquiry for a Research and Planning Grant in the amount of $150,000. Filmforum's project was deemed eligible, and in her invitation to submit a formal application, Micklewright also made suggestions: the addition of art historians who would contribute both to the proposal and to a future catalogue publication; the fiscal sponsorship of some organization larger than Filmforum itself as an intermediary to distribute the funds, possibly the USC or the UCLA art department; and an increase in my role.[5]

With the assistance of Elizabeth Hesik (a filmmaker and professional grant writer who had accepted an invitation to join Filmforum's board and to assist in their general search for funding), Hyman and Sapienza assembled a research team, obtained commitments from a dozen scholars to write essays, and submitted an extremely sophisticated fourteen-page application for the Exhibition and Planning Grant, whose summary objective was "to expand understanding of how experimental filmmaking evolved in Los Angeles".[6] Along with Hyman and Sapienza, respectively Project Supervisor and Project Director, the team was comprised of myself (Coordinator – Film History), Russell Ferguson, Chair of the UCLA Department of Art (Coordinator – Art History), Mark Toscano, a film preservationist at the Academy Film Archives (Archival Coordinator); three people with connections to previous Los Angeles independent cinema organizations, namely Angelina Pike (Creative Film Society), Cannon (Filmforum), and Amy Halpern (Los Angeles Independent Film Oasis); and George Baker, another UCLA art historian. The objectives of the research and planning phase of the project were:

> (a) to collect existing information about films, artists, curators, and organizations from the archives of five selected organizations, as well as other repositories with relevant textual information; (b) to record a series of oral histories with filmmakers and curators about their

Figure 1. Stephanie Sapienza and Adam Hyman at the announcement of the *Pacific Standard Time* Initiative, March 2009.

> experiences during this time period; (c) to hold a research symposium with focused, topic-specific panels and paper presentations, which will be videotaped and archived along with the oral histories; and (d) to locate lost or forgotten avant-garde films which have not been screened in Los Angeles for many years, or are languishing in the homes or storage units of the filmmakers and their families, and to negotiate their deposit at an archival repository so they can be made available for research.

All these were understood as preliminary to the primary goal, a film screening series to take place between September 2011 and June 2012, roughly in tandem with the many exhibitions of the overall initiative, eventually renamed as *Pacific Standard Time: Art in Los Angeles, 1945–1980*. They were to be accompanied by the creation of a complementary exhibition catalogue in the forms of both a printed document and a downloadable on-line PDF, and the inclusion of scholarly and related articles and resources about the films screened on Filmforum's recently-updated website. On 28 October 2008, the J. Paul Getty Trust announced that Filmforum was one of fifteen organizations selected to receive a grant in their nearly $2.8 million awarded in an overall project that would "launch an unprecedented series of concurrent exhibitions at museums throughout Southern California highlighting the post-World War II Los Angeles art scene".[7] All the organizations were given three years to research and plan for their exhibitions.

This was not the first time that Filmforum had undertaken an ambitious program of historical recovery. In 1994, Executive Director Jon Stout had produced a festival, *Scratching the Belly of the Beast: Cutting Edge Media in Los Angeles,*

1922–94, consisting of six weeks of screenings and panel discussions.[8] But certainly it was the most ambitious, and Hyman and Sapienza's acuity, expertise – and audacity – had returned big rewards. Filmforum, whose annual operating budget at the time was a meager $20,000, was elevated to the ranks of the Los Angeles County Museum of Art (LACMA), the Museum of Contemporary Art (MOCA), the Hammer Museum, the Museum of Contemporary Art San Diego (MCASD) and other corporately-funded municipal behemoths. And on 24 April 2009, Sapienza issued a Filmforum press release announcing an award of $118,000, and summarizing the projects enumerated in the grant application.[9]

Meeting quarterly at the Academy of Motion Pictures, the research team advised and assisted Hyman and Sapienza, who commenced to coordinate the recording and transcription of the oral histories, to hire and oversee the researchers undertaking the archival projects, and to plan the research symposium. The title *Alternative Projections: Experimental Film in LA 1945–1980* was adopted, and a further application to the Getty for an Exhibition and Publication Grant was prepared. For this application, the project was fine-tuned: the time frame for the films to be screened was extended; collaborations with other screening venues, including MOCA and the Roy and Edna Disney/CalArts Theater (REDCAT), were announced; and publication plans were now specified as a grouping of some of the more developed scholarly pieces in a clustered journal volume, along with a media-rich web publication, distinct in form and branding from Filmforum's standard website, for which additional database editors had been added to the team. For the film series and this online publication, in early 2010 the Getty awarded Filmforum an additional $65,000.

Despite – or perhaps because of – the project leaders' immoderate ambition, their goals were almost entirely fulfilled. When the planning was all-but-complete, Sapienza left Los Angeles, but with Hesik taking over as Project Director, thirty-three oral histories, most of them with filmmakers but others with curators and journalists, were recorded on video, and many are now available on-line and/or have been transcribed.[10] Researchers were hired to build an archive of resources to serve future generations of scholars, leading to the creation of a searchable, internet-accessible database of information about local films, filmmakers, exhibitions, and arts organizations.[11] Initially hired to cull from multiple archives to create a comprehensive exhibition history, Alison Kozberg assumed the role of Head Researcher after Sapienza's departure, and collaborated with web designers and a team of generous volunteers to prepare the research for internet publication. Curated primarily by Hyman and Toscano, the screening series presented some three hundred films and videos (many of them restored by

Toscano) in twenty-eight programs between October 2011 and May 2012, some of them in collaboration with MOCA, Otis College of Art and Design, and other participants in the PST program.[12] The three-day research symposium had been held a year earlier in fall 2010, with most of the revised academic presentations and other materials at last assembled in the present volume constituting a form of the promised exhibition catalogue. These last two items were made possible by the co-operation of USC.

Although the Getty had initially demanded that Filmforum secure a partnership with a larger institutional fiscal sponsor, Sapienza and Hyman were unable to work with UCLA on account of the university's insistence on a reimbursement-based financial arrangement. Because this would have required a level of financial fluidity that was impossible for an organization as small as Filmforum, Sapienza was able to convince the Getty to make an exception to its normal procedures, and, in a remarkable gesture of confidence in the relatively tiny organization, it eventually relented and supplied the grant funds directly to Filmforum.[13] But Filmforum did eventually secure the collaboration of two USC institutions: the School of Cinematic Arts and Visions and Voices, a university-wide arts and humanities initiative.[14] Though USC's moving image program was best known for its affiliations with the film and television industries, it also had a history of relations with the avant-garde. As SCA's Dean Elizabeth Daley noted in her welcome to the conference, the statue of Douglas Fairbanks in the courtyard of the first of the school's imposing new buildings donated by George Lucas appropriately figured the Hollywood connections. But, she continued, the school's personnel had also included Slavko Vorkapich, one of the makers of one of the very first and most important American avant-garde films, *Life and Death of 9413 – A Hollywood Extra* (1928), and her predecessor as chair from 1949 to 1951 of what was then the film department; and its students included Gregory Markopoulos and Curtis Harrington in one era, Thom Andersen and Morgan Fisher in another – and more recently, Hyman himself. Dean Daley made the school's resources freely available, including the Norris Cinema Theater and other projection facilities and conference rooms, along with the necessary staffing. Under its managing director, Daria Yudacufski, Visions and Voices had already featured a spectrum of theatrical productions, music and dance performances, and film screenings, along with talks and presentations by artists and other speakers; it had been especially hospitable to vanguardist projects, including a few years earlier a festival of poetry and film. With a $20,000 grant from Visions and Voices, the symposium became a possibility, and, organized primarily by Hyman, Sapienza, Cannon, and myself, it was finally scheduled for the weekend of 12–14 November 2010.[15]

Figure 2. Announcement postcard, *Alternative Projections* symposium.

For the opening, Cannon curated several large vitrines containing historic posters, photographs, filmmaking artifacts, catalogues, and original artwork. These were stationed in the SCA building lobby, while the gallery contained "Side Phase Drift 1965", a restored abstract three-screen performance projection by John Whitney Jr., which was composed of sets of images that were manipulated in form, color, superimposition, and time. After the welcoming reception, the first evening, Friday, was given over to screenings in the Eileen Norris Cinema Theater of several of the seldom-seen films to be discussed in the scholarly panels, which began the next day.[16] Sapienza's call for papers had netted more than thirty proposals from scholars throughout the US, and one from as far away as Germany. Sapienza, Hyman, and the other members of the team had selected sixteen of these for presentation on four panels: three, respectively entitled, "Shoppers' Market: Exhibition, Distribution, and Canonization"; "Subcultures Scene and Seen"; and "Blurred Boundaries: Outside/Insider Filmmaking and Group Identities", on the second day; and on the third and last day, the fourth, "High Concepts: Cross Section of Art and Film". The second, Saturday, evening was given over to the present members of the recently reconstituted light show, the Single Wing Turquoise Bird: Amy Halpern, Shayne Hood, Larry Janss, David Lebrun, Peter Mays, and Michael Scroggins gathered in a panel moderated by Adam Hyman. As well as reminiscing about the Bird and announcing upcoming performances, they screened old and new work by the group, and films by the individual members.[17] After the fourth panel in the morning, the afternoon of the last day was devoted to the Los Angeles Independent Film Oasis, a screening collective organized by filmmakers from 1976 to 1981. Present for the panel moderated by Cannon were Oasis members Grahame Weinbren, Pat and Beverly O'Neill, Amy Halpern, Roberta Friedman, Morgan Fisher, and Tom Leeser.[18] Taking place in the heart of the capital of commodity culture, this congress of filmmakers, curators, scholars, and other interested people was, along with the other research components of the overall initiative, an unprecedented occasion for the retrieval of the history of non-commodity cinema in Los Angeles, a moment of freedom secured amidst – but against – alienation.[19]

Experimental Film in Los Angeles, 1945–1980

In 1943, at his apartment studio at 1245 Vine Street in Hollywood, Man Ray made a short 8mm home movie for which he and his new wife filmed each other as they informally hammed for the camera. His film *Juliet* was at once a recapitulation of the interactive surrealist cinema that he and Dudley Murphy had pioneered in Paris in the photography of their respective lovers for the avant-garde classic *Ballet mécanique* (1924) and an anticipation the use of the

Figure 3. Principal organizers, *Alternative Projections* symposium (left to right): Terry Cannon, Stephanie Sapienza, Adam Hyman, and David E. James.

same trope in underground films – Stan Brakhage's *Wedlock House: An Intercourse* (1959), for instance. It also echoed the foundational and perhaps most seminal film of the American avant-garde made the same year three miles away, also in Hollywood, and also a collaboration by two newlyweds who photographed each other: Maya Deren and Alexander Hammid's *Meshes of the Afternoon*. *Meshes*, too, had echoes of the Parisian avant-garde, especially of Luis Buñuel and Salvador Dalí's *Un chien Andalou* (1929), as well as of surrealist interludes in classic Hollywood films, including Buster Keaton's *Sherlock, Jr.* (1924); and, as in *Juliet*, in *Meshes* the main author played the main protagonist. In this, as well as in its use of multiple subjective narratives, it recalled the most celebrated US art film, Orson Welles's *Citizen Kane*, which was released two years earlier by RKO, a little more than a mile from Man Ray's apartment.

Spatially and temporally proximate, and linked by common structuring formal characteristics, these three films also limned the spectrum of possible modes of production for the subsequent art of film in Los Angeles. This variable gear articulated the pull between Deren's "amateur" and "professional" practices: at one extreme, Welles's unprecedented auteurist control over the industrial studio, not matched till the doyens of the 1970s "New Hollywood"; on the other, Man Ray's *jeu d'esprit*, made sheerly for pleasure and with recourse to only the most minimal domestic form of the cinematic apparatus; and between them, Deren's inauguration of an art cinema as a process of psychic self-realization. Inventing the genre that would be termed a "trance film", she innovated a true psychodrama in which filmmakers were "realizing the themes of their films through making and acting them".[20]

Deren's vision of film as a medium of personal self-expression independent of the theatrically distributed products of the capitalist film industry created – as Jon Stout had phrased it, in *Belly of the Beast* – became the single most important model for subsequent avant-garde cinema, and by the same terms made personal filmmaking the paradigmatic alternative to capitalist culture for the next quarter century, or for as long as cinema continued to be the world's medium in dominance. Though soon after completing *Meshes*, Deren left for New York, she frequently returned to Los Angeles to screen her works, and her recreation of cinema as the investigation of the filmmaker's own psychosexual subjectivity inspired three young filmmakers, Curtis Harrington, Kenneth Anger, and Gregory Markopoulos. All these replaced her traumatized heterosexual female protagonist with a similarly traumatized homosexual young man in films about their own psychosexual self-discovery: respectively, *Fragment of Seeking* (1946), *Fireworks* (1947), and *The Dead Ones* (1949). In his 1949 essay "Personal Chronicle: The Making of an Experimental Film" reprinted below, Harrington, also an important film historian and theorist, recognized another historical model for their work: "Only now, exactly thirty years after its production, is the lesson of *Caligari* being applied: most of the motion pictures of the experimental film movement since World War II are concerned precisely with the construction of the imaginative filmic reality – a direct extension of the creative principle of *The Cabinet of Dr. Caligari*". Reconstructing Deren's premise of the mutual imbrication of mind and medium, his phrase, "the construction of the imaginative filmic reality", specified the subjectivist expressionist basis of the strongest tradition of postwar avant-garde filmmaking.

After making their first films in the city, these three artists each differently negotiated the art-industry divide. Markopoulos categorically rejected the business. After his student works at USC, he also moved to New York and became one of the most celebrated of the underground filmmakers; but in the late 1960s he withdrew his films from distribution and left the US entirely. As Harrington's "Personal Chronicle" also reveals, he turned in the direction of carefully planned production and financial accountability in his film *Picnic* (1948) before following his hero, Josef von Sternberg – and Welles's example – by attempting to deploy his artistic ambitions and vanguardist innovations in Hollywood, what he called "The Dangerous Compromise".[21] By the mid-1950s, in "A Statement" (also reproduced below), he declared that he was "attempting to tread gingerly that hovering, swaying tightrope" across "the commercial chasm". Between these options, Anger continued his commitment to Deren's amateur mode of production in films that explored the radical sexual and other shifts that transformed youth cultures in the 1960s. Though his film about the homoeroticism of motorcycle gangs, *Scorpio Rising* (1963), was his most scandalous, like Harrington he was also concerned with subterranean investigations of the black magical arts, as Alice Hutchison's essay on their films about the artist Cameron below details. And, as Josh Guilford proposes, the result was a distinctively West Coast contribution to the New American Cinema of the 1960s.

As these various countercultures attempted to reproduce the visual experiences supplied by hallucinatory drugs, filmmakers found a vocabulary for "imaginative filmic reality" in another local tradition of experimental filmmaking that also interfaced with the film industry, the abstract animation or "visual music" begun in Los Angeles by Oskar Fischinger and the brothers John and James Whitney. The offer of a job at Paramount had allowed Fischinger to escape from Nazi Germany in the mid-1930s, and later in the decade he worked on Walt Disney's *Fantasia*. But his relations with the studios were stormy, and it was his independent work that inspired several generations of California filmmakers, as well as the composer John Cage. James Whitney mostly worked independently, making *Lapis* (1966) and other sublime abstract films inspired by, and sometimes reproducing, the meditational aspects of Asian religions. John's abstract films, on the other hand, what he called "motion graphics" were often produced in collaboration with the industry and with television, and continued the tradition of experimental filmmakers supporting their own art by working "day jobs" in the industry, especially on special effects in the way that, as Julie Turnock's essay below documents, was later most productively functional for Pat O'Neill. Though in the 1950s the Hollywood Blacklist effectively destroyed radical Socialist culture in Los Angeles, allowing the baton of avant-garde filmmaking to be taken up by New York and San Francisco, these traditions of visual music became seminal for the psychedelic freak subcultures that formed in Los Angeles in the late 1960s, especially around UCLA and the Sunset Strip. There, the trance film became the psychedelic "trip" film, a quintessentially Los Angeles genre, that also inspired what was commonly regarded as the greatest of the '60s' light shows, the Single Wing Turquoise Bird.

These and other film-based communities in Los Angeles were nurtured by pioneers who inaugurated commercial, semi-commercial, and eventually non-commercial distribution systems and public screening venues. This development too had been anticipated by Harrington and Anger, who founded the first "cooperative distribution center" for experimental films controlled by filmmakers themselves, the first such organization in the country since the days of the Workers Film and Photo Leagues. Announced by Harrington in his 1948 essay reproduced here, "Distribution Center for Experimental Films", the Creative Film Associates pre-dated by more than a decade both the Film-Makers' Cooperative in New York and the Bay Area's Canyon Cinema. In the next decade its innovations were expanded by Robert Pike, a filmmaker and historian, who founded his similarly-named distribution center, the Creative Film Society (CFS), and then by a number of more commercially-minded entrepreneurs, including Raymond Rohauer (whose career is surveyed by Tim Lanza below) and Mike Getz. Getz's Movies 'Round Midnight screenings at the Cinema Theater became the home of the late 1960s freak counterculture, and also of three festivals of experimental film, one of which was described (in the essay reprinted below) by Jack Hirschman for what had become the house organ of the New York avant-garde, the magazine *Film Culture*. The figure most responsible for re-igniting an oppositional film culture in Los Angeles from the ashes of what had been destroyed by the blacklist was John Fles. His visionary screenings at the Cinema Theater are described in his three texts printed below, one also appearing in *Film Culture*, another self-published in Los Angeles, and one never before published but only read aloud at the Cinema Theater. In his autobiography, *Mouse Enigma*, first published below, Peter Mays gives an account of the genesis of his own remarkable filmmaking amidst the world of the Cinema Theater and the culture to which Fles was dedicated.

Appearing in the mainstream *Los Angeles Times* in 1967, Kevin Thomas's essay published below on the emergent popularity of what before had been a specifically *underground* cinema indicates the unprecedented public interest in and acceptance of the avant-garde. This cultural shift was also refracted in the increasing hospitality to experimental filmmaking shown by university and art schools. Both Harrington and Markopoulos had been students at USC; but while in the 1940s they had only marginally survived there, in the 1960s, the "movie brats" took over. In his essay, Ken Eisenstein describes his recovery of a film by John Vicario, a UCLA filmmaker of the same period; while it and many other important student films were forgotten, others were greeted with apocalyptic fervor. The *Los Angeles Free Press* account (reproduced below) of student filmmaking and of George Lucas's primacy among the radical innovators by Gene Youngblood, the most committed spokesperson for the avant-garde, exhibits the utopian politics which, it was believed, they often augured: "viewing student films is like participating in a revolution".

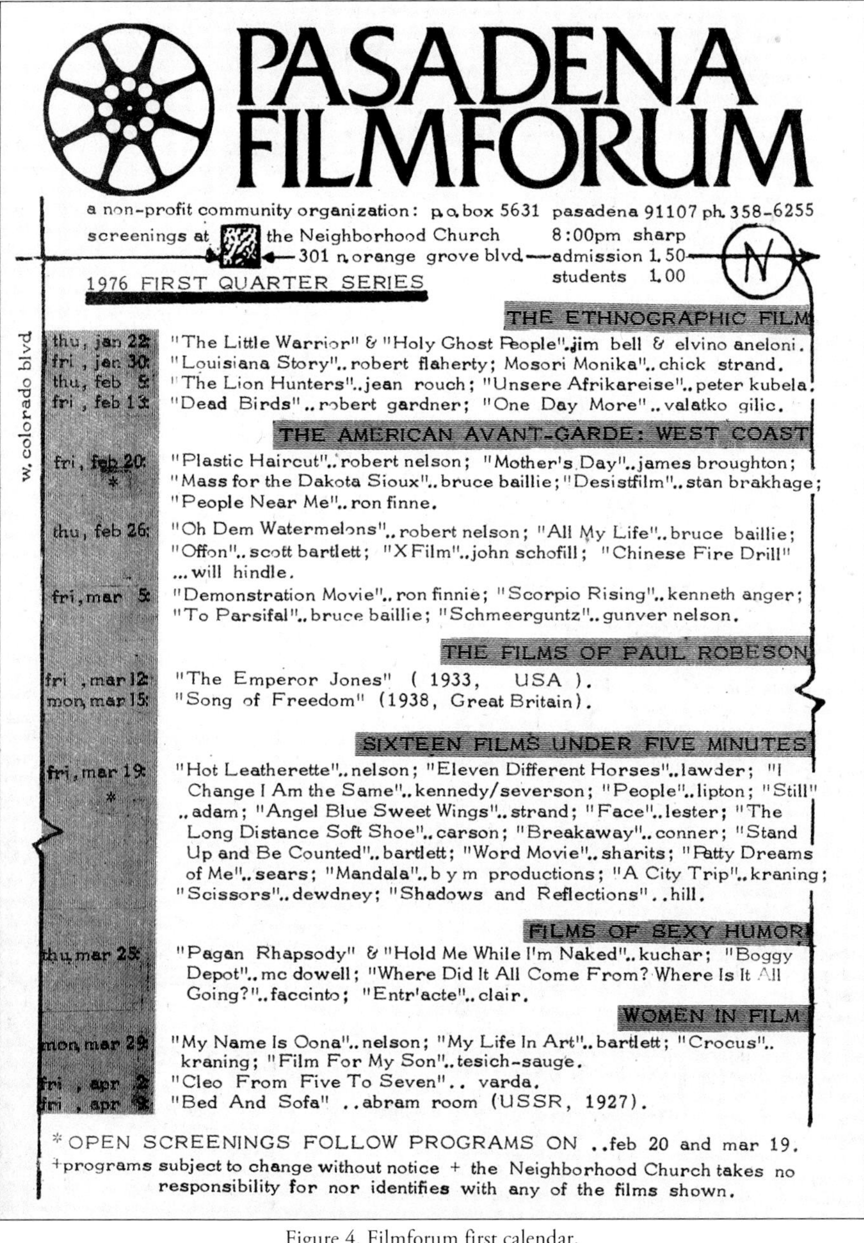

PASADENA FILMFORUM

a non-profit community organization: p.o. box 5631 pasadena 91107 ph. 358-6255

screenings at the Neighborhood Church 8:00pm sharp
301 n. orange grove blvd. — admission 1.50
students 1.00

w. colorado blvd

N

1976 FIRST QUARTER SERIES

THE ETHNOGRAPHIC FILM

thu, jan 22: "The Little Warrior" & "Holy Ghost People"..jim bell & elvino aneloni.
fri, jan 30: "Louisiana Story"..robert flaherty; Mosori Monika"..chick strand.
thu, feb 5: "The Lion Hunters"..jean rouch; "Unsere Afrikareise"..peter kubela.
fri, feb 13: "Dead Birds"..robert gardner; "One Day More"..valatko gilic.

THE AMERICAN AVANT-GARDE: WEST COAST

fri, feb 20: * "Plastic Haircut"..robert nelson; "Mother's Day"..james broughton; "Mass for the Dakota Sioux"..bruce baillie; "Desistfilm"..stan brakhage; "People Near Me"..ron finne.

thu, feb 26: "Oh Dem Watermelons"..robert nelson; "All My Life"..bruce baillie; "Offon"..scott bartlett; "X Film"..john schofill; "Chinese Fire Drill" ...will hindle.

fri, mar 5: "Demonstration Movie"..ron finnie; "Scorpio Rising"..kenneth anger; "To Parsifal"..bruce baillie; "Schmeerguntz"..gunver nelson.

THE FILMS OF PAUL ROBESON

fri, mar 12: "The Emperor Jones" (1933, USA).
mon, mar 15: "Song of Freedom" (1938, Great Britain).

SIXTEEN FILMS UNDER FIVE MINUTES

fri, mar 19: * "Hot Leatherette"..nelson; "Eleven Different Horses"..lawder; "I Change I Am the Same"..kennedy/severson; "People"..lipton; "Still"..adam; "Angel Blue Sweet Wings"..strand; "Face"..lester; "The Long Distance Soft Shoe"..carson; "Breakaway"..conner; "Stand Up and Be Counted"..bartlett; "Word Movie"..sharits; "Fatty Dreams of Me"..sears; "Mandala"..b y m productions; "A City Trip"..kraning; "Scissors"..dewdney; "Shadows and Reflections"..hill.

FILMS OF SEXY HUMOR

thu, mar 25: "Pagan Rhapsody" & "Hold Me While I'm Naked"..kuchar; "Boggy Depot"..mc dowell; "Where Did It All Come From? Where Is It All Going?"..faccinto; "Entr'acte"..clair.

WOMEN IN FILM

mon, mar 29: "My Name Is Oona"..nelson; "My Life In Art"..bartlett; "Crocus"..kraning; "Film For My Son"..tesich-sauge.
fri, apr 2: "Cleo From Five To Seven".. varda.
fri, apr 9: "Bed And Sofa" ..abram room (USSR, 1927).

* OPEN SCREENINGS FOLLOW PROGRAMS ON ..feb 20 and mar 19.
+programs subject to change without notice + the Neighborhood Church takes no responsibility for nor identifies with any of the films shown.

Figure 4. Filmforum first calendar.

Alison Kozberg's history of exhibition practices that accompanied these developments from the 1950s to the 1970s clarifies their relation to the transformed social-cultural possibilities of the period and reveals how, against received ideas, the 1970s was a golden age for avant-garde cinema in Los Angeles. By the early

1970s, the decline of the counterculture and its commercial extensions that had supported underground film created the need for non-commercial institutions. The most important of them was the Pasadena Filmforum, eventually to become the Los Angeles Filmforum, the chief agency in the present project. These and similar institutions helped sustain the new developments in avant-garde film: varieties of critical formalism more or less parallel to structural film, on the one hand, and on the other, the breakthrough to film production by sexual and ethnic minorities.

In New York, structural film emerged in the late 1960s, when painters and sculptors turned to their attention to cinema; a similar, often fraught, exchange among filmmakers and artists-who-made films also occurred in Los Angeles, most prominently perhaps in the case of Ed Ruscha, who, as Matthew Reynolds details below, made both films and cinematically-informed artworks. Otherwise, the innovations of structural film resonated most vibrantly among a group of young filmmakers in the mid-1970s who organized the Los Angeles Independent Film Oasis, notably Morgan Fisher, Roberta Friedman, Amy Halpern, Pat and Beverly O'Neill, Susan Rosenfeld, Grahame Weinbren, and David and Diana Wilson. Working together, Weinbren and Friedman produced a radically innovative oeuvre, while Weinbren himself became the group's preeminent theorist and historian. The two sides of his project are manifest below, respectively in Carlos Kase's essay on his and Friedman's films, and in Weinbren's own essay on Pat O'Neill. As Weinbren recognized, O'Neill's intuitive compositional procedures and his use of complex optical printing to articulate separate image layers in the film frames exceeded structural film's reflexive minimalism. Eventually O'Neill's technical sophistication led him to 35mm and to follow Harrington across the commercial chasm towards feature length works in which he brought the history of cinema, both Hollywood and the avant-garde, to bear on the land- and cityscapes of the West.

If the intellectual rigor of structural film marginalized it from other cultural currents in Los Angeles, the opposite was the case with developments around identity politics in both ethnic and sexual versions: respectively Native- Asian-, Latina/o-, and African American; and feminist, gay, and lesbian. Begun by African Americans' response to the racism of Griffith's *The Birth of a Nation* (1915), filmmaking on behalf of people of color had been maintained in the 1930s in the Los Angeles Workers Film and Photo League's agitational documentaries about multicultural agricultural strikes during the Depression. Destroyed by McCarthyism and the blacklist, such working-class cinemas were renewed in the late 1950s, initially by liberal whites. Most notable was a USC student, Kent Mackenzie, who made eloquent documentaries: *Bunker Hill* (1956), about the old downtown soon to be destroyed in urban development, and *The Exiles* (1961), about the Native Americans living there. The latter, examined below by Ross Lipmann, effectively inaugurated non-commercial cinema about ethnic minorities in Los Angeles.

In the aftermath of the black civil rights movements, attempts by ethnic groups to control their own representation decisively replaced such liberal projects, and Los Angeles became the single most important point of origin for African American, Asian American, and Mexican American independent cinemas in the US. Largely integrated into academic identity politics, these all originated in film schools or other state-supported institutions, the most important of which was the Ethno-Communications Program at UCLA, a pilot program begun in 1970 to teach filmmaking to young people of color. Before eventually merging with the film school proper, the program graduated several classes that established the foundation for the three distinct minority cinemas. In these, the contrary pulls between local, organic communities and the commercial industry that defined previous avant-gardes were re-engaged chronologically in the fundamentally parallel forms of production they each developed. In general, all groups began with an initial period of inexpensive, community-based, agitational documentary and/or experimental practices that emphasized a militant ethnic nationalism, and in general these were succeeded by more extended narratives and independent feature production in which the initial drive for autonomy and the rejection of the entertainment industry modulated into various kinds of negotiation, rapprochement, and eventually integration into it. But after the beginnings in the Ethno-Communication Program, cooperation or connection between the groups were limited, and at least until the mid-1980s their distinctive cultural heritages and different histories of relation to cinema and their present economic and social conditions caused each to develop distinct modes of filmmaking, each with quite different social, ideological, and aesthetic qualities, and quite different relationships to the communities they represented.

The Asian American group remained most strongly oriented towards documentary and community organization, while the African Americans directly aspired to revive the tradition of independent features and to engage with industrial production. Mexican American filmmaking oscillated between these alternatives, appearing in various forms on the peripheries of several overlapping modes of production and also engaging more extensively than the others with public policy initiatives and with television. By the end of the 1980s, all forms of ethnic cinema had crossed over to the mainstream, merging with Hollywood's cultivation of niche markets and producing specific well-known directors. Until then, the Asian American sector's preoccupation with community issues tended to subordinate the role of individuals, and few auteurs attained prominence. The most important exception was Robert Nakamura, maker of one of the first Asian American films, *Manzanar* (1971), a study of the camp where Japanese Americans were interned during World War II, and later co-director of *Hito Hata* (1980), the first Asian American feature film. The most important Chicano filmmaker was Jesús Salvador Treviño; beginning in public television, he moved to shorts and feature film production, and eventually to a Chicano-themed commercial television drama. But other Chicano groups adamantly rejected such assimilation, especially the art collective Asco, whose work between film and murals is considered below by Jesse Lerner, himself a filmmaker. Still working at UCLA and often with philanthropic support, the African American sector produced several remarkable independent feature directors, including Haile Gerima (*Bush Mama,* 1976), Charles Burnett (*Killer of Sheep*, 1977), and Larry Clark (*Passing Through*, 1977). While these male directors, especially Burnett, received substantial recognition, the women who followed them at UCLA and who often made more experimental short films did not, not even Barbara McCullough, whose masterpiece, *Water Ritual #1: An Urban Rite of Purification* (1979) and its urban context Veena Hariharan examines below.[22] Eventually labeled the "L.A. Rebellion", these black filmmakers were examined in another PST historical recovery project undertaken by the UCLA Film & Television Archive.

The situation of sexual minority cinemas was yet more complex. The trajectory of feminism in Los Angeles was profoundly inflected by the role of women in Hollywood and hence in the city's overall cultural life. So although Los Angeles was very important in the burgeoning of women's art in the early 1970s, and indeed the first Anglophone feminist film journal, *Women & Film*, was founded in Los Angeles in 1972, the dominant forms of feminist cinema in the city were not radically oppositional so much as either reformist and oriented towards the film industry; or, in the case of the avant-garde, unaffiliated amateur undertakings of the kind Deren inaugurated. Isolated endeavors within or on the edges of the industry generally took the place of the theoretical reconsideration of cinema and sexuality offered by feminist avant-gardes elsewhere. Even those women filmmakers, especially white ones, who were concerned with non-industrial film forms, often supported themselves by jobs in the industry or by teaching, and they typically worked independently of each other. The most notable was Chick Strand, a radically original pioneer in ethnographic, feminist, and compilation filmmaking. After co-founding Canyon Cinema with Bruce Baillie in the Bay Area, she studied ethnographic filmmaking at UCLA, and her first films were

LOS ANGELES FREE PRESS

INSIDE

FCC TEXT ON PACIFICA
DEATH OF A JAZZER
JOAN BAEZ LETTER

MAY 25, 1964 SAMPLE COPY OF A NEW WEEKLY TO BEGIN PUBLICATION SOON SEE PAGE 2

PURITANISM SCORES VICTORY

ALL-WOMAN JURY FINDS KEN ANGER'S ANTI-FASCIST FILM "OBSCENE"

BY SEYMOUR STERN

A filthy-minded interpretation by a city prosecuting attorney and his witnesses of a brief scene in a new, anti-Fascist film, envenomed with an hysterial appeal to an all-woman jury to find the film guilty of "obscenity", resulted, on Ma[illegible]h 13, in a verdict of "Guilty", in the latest attempt by Los Angeles police to destroy freedom of the screen.

The film is **Scorpio Rising**, written, produced and directed by Kenneth Anger. The defendant was Michael A. Getz, 25-year-old manager of the Cinema Theatre, at 1122 N. Western Avenue, Hollywood.

On March 7 the theatre was raided by members of the Hollywood Vice Squad. Getz was arrested and was charged with a lewd exhibition.

The theatre's owner, Louis K. Sher, who operates a chain of 28 film-art houses from Los Angeles to Cleveland, O., opposes all censorship and so accepted the challenge to fight the case through as many courts as necessary, until a legal victory is won and Anger's film is cleared for further exhibition.

Less than a week after **Scorpio Rising** was seized, Anger received a $10,000 grant from the Ford Foundation to make another film. The award was largely based on the superlative degree of creative know-how and technical skill evidenced here.

The Cinema Theatre

Distinguished for its laissez-faire policy of exhibition of artistic, classic, experimental, and unusual films, both domestic and foreign, and moreso, perhaps, for the Saturday-midnight showings of new product by new talent, the Cinema Theatre is the current battleground—the first major one since the bygone movie-days of the Coronet on La Cienega—in a renewed war between the reactionary forces of suppression and the radical friends of freedom over the control and future of the motion picture screen. As such it has endeared itself to one of the most film-ically-wise and intellectually vigorous audiences in America.

New Censorship Threatened

Timed to coincide with news of the verdict was a published announcement by the District Attorney's office that a "new tactic in its war on smut" was complaints right down the line" from distributor (or exhibitor) to author.

The reference was to books and booksellers, with authors or creators as the new target for suppression and punishment, the same as in the Dark Ages of medieval Europe. By implication the "new tactic", aimed at the "source of these books rather than the booksellers", would also apply to the creative source of other products as well—e.g., movie scenarists, movie directors, photographers, playwrights and others. Thus in its salacious, medieval-minded and fanatical "zeal" to widen all censorship in the Los Angeles area, the District Attorney's office emerges into the forefront of the forces which, till now, have been somewhat more prudent and moderate, or stealthier, in lending weight and substance to what Bertrand Russell has aptly termed the "myth of American freedom". In the current case of SCORPIO RISING, the unspoken motive, which has so long nurtured the everlasting "crusades" against

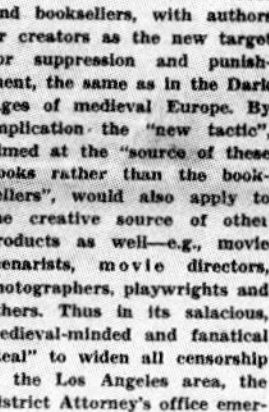

so-called "smut", is more nakedly revealed than usual: both the attack against the film and the verdict by a conservative jury are unprecedentedly significant, because they have transformed the charge of "obscenity" into a legal weapon for the suppression of political content.

Theme And Content

Vividly photographed in color, the film depicts certain aspects of Fascist-style behavior among Far Right elements of the teen-age motorcycle-cultists of the United States. Due to oversight on the director's part, it fails to establish that not all motor-cyclists are Fascist or pro-Nazi and, conversely, not all Fascists are motor-cyclists. It assumes this to be understood by the spectator—a perhaps somewhat optimistic acceptance of public political perception.

The bulk of the footage concentrates on emblems, rituals, symbols, and traumatic-style obedience to dictatorial Authority. Filmically, it builds without comment the idea that abject obedience to, and worship of, Authority for the sake of authority and of obedience, as a possible comforting sense of security, lead to cultism and, through this, to a vicarious feeling of power and triumph. This idea comes through most effectively in the sound-track of the closing sequence, when the voice of the motorcycle-Fuehrer's girl, as though in a trance, half-sings, half-wails: "I'll follow, I'll follow, I'll follow . . .," until the hypnotic mental surrender implicit in the verbal allegiance dies off in darkness and distance. And, as if this psychological, self-imposed 'loyalty oath" were not enough, there is also a continuity of visual resemblance between the faces and postures of the motorcycle-leaders to those of a familiar type of law-enforcement officer, such, for example, as the arrogant cops who break up civil rights demonstrations.

Depicted in an almost sociological, "case-history" light, the cyclist's private cult-activities reflect the real-life operations of juvenile storm-troop types of the Far Right. Except for the absence of robe and hood or other forms of "halloween"-mask, the film could as well be about the secret rituals of the Ku Klux

Finally, a brief sequence of a party, near the end, suggests, without actually showing, forms of sexual perversion as practiced by this element: i.e., buggery and homosexuality. In effect, this appears as a kind of climax or conclusion to previous ideological sequences, featuring images of Nazi flags, swastikas, Hitler, Goebbels, Goehring, Himmler, Streicher, and the Hitler-Jugend of Nazi Germany. The obscenity charge was chiefly based on a few flashes from the party scene.

Unlike 'The Wild One'

Art Seidenbaum, in a crude review of the film with crude comment, Los Angeles Times, April 20, charged the picture "with considerable crudity". But he also wrote, in part: "I am sure that what aroused the vice squad was a squalid little party, scored with homosexual overtones, that brings the cyclists off the streets . . . I wouldn't be surprised if profanity, more than obscenity, was what leapt in the eyes of

the official beholders. But profanity is not a criminal complaint." Noting that the effect of the whole is that of "the harsh echo of an honest comment", Seidenbaum likened **Scorpio Rising** to "**The Wild One** of a decade ago, in which Marlon Brando and assorted other famous talents went to feature lengths on the black leathered, booted set."

The comparison is superficial, inept, at best, because, unlike **The Wild One, Scorpio Rising** is fundamentally and above all a political essay, critically anti-Fascist. Yet the 'picked up' by at least one defense witness at the trial to the tactical disadvantage of **Scorpio Rising:** if the film was just a latter-day version or variation of **The Wild One,** then there appeared to be no need, no reason, for the objectionable material. The need, however, was absolute and indisputable in a portrait of Fascist behavior and mentality.

The Trial

The trial began on April 29, in Judge Bernard S. Selber's municipal court, and ended May 13. Jury foreman, Mrs. Anita Strobot, of North Hollywood, reported that the jury had taken four ballots before arriving at its "Guilty" verdict. It was out five hours—not long, in view of the volumes of testimony.

Here is the courtroom "cast":

Prosecution: Deputy City Attorney Warren I. Wolfe. Witnesses: Cecil Selman, an industrial photographer, of the Art Center School, who filed the original complaint; Police Sergeant Terrence Hannon of Hollywood vice; and Bud Nease, a Los Angeles Police Department photographer Warren Day, Boy Scout leader from a Methodist Church in La Crescenta; and Fred Goldstein Ph. D., a private psychiatrist.

Defense: Attorney Stanley Fleishman, who had won an earlier case, on appeal, involving a previous film, **Fireworks** also by Kenneth Anger. Witnesses: James Powers, film critic for the "Hollywood Reporter"; the Rev. Paul Sawyer, of Valley Unitarian Universalist Church; Archer Goodwin, professor of anthropology at Valley State and technical director for the Eastman Kodak Pavillion at the New York World's Fair; Colin Young, professor of cinema at UCLA and film critic for "Frontier" magazine ; Mel Sloane, professor of critic for the "Saturday Review"; Verna Fields, film cutter [El Cid, etc.]; Ruth Hirschman, drama and literature program director for KPFK; Rabbi Leonard Beerman Leo Baeck Temple; Dr. Ted Carpenter, chairman of the Department of Anthropology at Valley State and author of a 9-volume work for the Ford Foundation on communications; Jules Langsner, art critic Martin Ritt, film director [Hud, etc.], and Michael A. Getz, the defendant

Figure 5. Front page, preview edition, *Los Angeles Free Press*. This copy was preserved by Richard Whitehall, who along with Gene Youngblood wrote reviews of avant-garde films for the *Free Press*. His annotation in the right hand column clarifies that Mel Sloan was a USC cinema professor and that the omitted Arthur Knight was also a USC professor and a *Saturday Review* critic.

documentaries about women in Meso-America that brought to ethnography the expressive languages of the experimental film. The core of her subsequent work was a domestic ethnography, a series of sensuous and intimate portraits of women in Los Angeles. But since her unabashedly erotic lyricism was anathema to the dominant academic feminist theory of the 1970s and 1980s, her achievement only later received the recognition it merited. Of her several essays, the one reproduced below reveals her espousal of the feminist form of the auto-ethnography that underlay most identity-based filmmaking. Members of minority communities commonly represented their own personal subjectivity and social being, attempting to secure their own self-representation to contest what was perceived as the oppressive representation of them by others, especially by the commercial film industry.

The profile of experimental gay and lesbian cinema was somewhat higher, but again deeply entwined in industrial projects, in the case of the former, especially pornography. Its history dates back to at least 1923, when Alla Nazimova produced and starred in the independent feature, *Salomé*, whose cast was almost entirely gay and lesbian. In the years after World War II, male physique photography centered in the city provided the context for Kenneth Anger's films, which were several times prosecuted for putatively promoting homosexuality. A particularly important instance was the prosecution of Mike Getz for screening *Scorpio Rising* at the Cinema Theater. The wider cultural significance of his trial is indicated in the article in the preview edition of the very first of the underground newspapers, Art Kunkin's *Los Angeles Free Press*, by Seymour Stern. Thirty years earlier, Stern had directed *Imperial Valley* (1931), a documentary about migrant agricultural laborers in California, and in the mid-1930s had been a Soviet-sympathizing member of the Los Angeles Workers Film and Photo League. That Stern should justify Anger's film as "anti-fascist" bespeaks both the unstable semiology prized in – or forced upon – avant-garde filmmakers and the historical displacement of radical socialism into identity politics. The vitality of transgressive Los Angeles gay film culture of the 1960s is further revealed in Marc Siegel's essay on *Passion in a Seaside Slum* (Robert Wade Chatterton, 1961), a long-lost film starring Taylor Mead, while Erika Suderburg's account of the emergence of lesbian filmmaking in the 1970s demonstrates its importance for someone who was herself both a pioneer in lesbian and community filmmaking, and a scholar of both. But with the extremely rapid industrialization of pornography in the next decade, Los Angeles became the most important productive center for both heterosexual and gay porn and, as US capitalist culture became entirely pornographic, the original outlaw cinemas entered the mainstream, even to the point of matching the capital returns of Hollywood itself.

Since the period when identity politics and minority cinemas made Los Angeles the nation's most important center for progressive cinema, film has generally been replaced by analogue and digital video, developments that were well underway by 1980. Though celluloid is still the medium of preference for many filmmakers in Los Angeles, the archival and scholarly components of the *Alternative Projections* historical recovery project, as well as the screenings it made possible, concluded at this moment of unprecedentedly radical transformations of moving image culture.

Notes

1. Filmforum's extensive *Alternative Projections* website is at www.alternativeprojections.com.
2. Made by union organizer Frank E. Wolfe and released in 1913, *From Dusk to Dawn* was among the first films made specifically to counter the capitalist film industry; it envisaged the election of a socialist governor of California. Wolfe proclaimed his intentions in the essay "The Movie Revolution" in the *Western Comrade* 1.4 (July 1913): 125.
3. Pacific Standard Time's website extensively documents the exhibitions and performances it sponsored at sixty museums and programming venues, and seventy-five galleries across Southern California, concentrated in Los Angeles but also extending south to San Diego, north to Santa Barbara, and inland to Palm Springs, as well collecting retrospective analyses and evaluations of the initiative: see http://past.pacificstandardtime.org. Between September 2011 and May 2012, the Getty Center itself mounted "Pacific Standard Time: Crosscurrents in L.A. Painting and Sculpture, 1950–1970" and three other exhibitions about Los Angeles art, accompanying them with a large catalogue with five synoptic essays and more than thirty sidebars: *Pacific Standard Time: Los Angeles Art 1945–1980*, eds. Rebecca Peabody, Andrew Perchuk, Glenn Phillips, and Rani Singh (Los Angeles: The Getty Research Institute and The J. Paul Getty Museum, 2011). As well as contributing to several of the essays, Rani Singh provided an overviewed the post-war history of experimental cinema in Los Angeles in a sidebar, "In the Shadow of the Spotlight" (71).
4. http://www.getty.edu/grants/research/institutions/on_the_record_2.html, accessed 10 February 2014.
5. In the interest of full disclosure, I note that I had been a regular Filmforum attendee since its inception, and a board member since the early 1980s. Documenting the extensive history of independent, avant-garde, and radical cinemas in Los Angeles, my then-recent book, *The Most Typical Avant-Garde: History and Geography of Minor Cinemas in Los Angeles* (Berkeley: University of California Press, 2005) had demonstrated how and why the New York orientation of previous avant-garde film historiography should be replaced by the recognition of the priority of such cinema in Los Angeles. It thus anticipated the *Pacific Standard Time* project and provided an appropriate historiographical framework for it.
6. "Getty on the Record Exhibition and Planning Grant", Filmforum Archives, retrieved 8 February 2014. References immediately below are to this document.
7. "News from the Getty", Filmforum Archives, retrieved 8 February 2014.
8. *Scratching the Belly of the Beast* screened more than one hundred and seventy works, including both experimental shorts and feature films and video, roughly divided amongst guest-curated programs, roundtables and "tributes" to earlier screening and distribution organizations, including the Los Angeles Independent Film Oasis, the Creative Film Society, Visual Communications, and the Long Beach Museum of Art's artists' video project. Many of the programs were shaped by the identity politics of the time, with a strong emphasis on women's and African- and Asian American and Latina/o initiatives. It too was linked to city-wide initiatives, especially to the "Motion Picture Centennial", a celebration of the first hundred years of cinema. To accompany the festival, Filmforum produced a booklet with two dozen short essays by filmmakers, curators, and scholars: *Scratching the Belly of the Beast: Cutting Edge Media in Los Angeles, 1922–94*, ed. Holly Willis (Los Angeles: Filmforum, 1994). A significant precursor to the present volume, it is available from Filmforum.
9. http://www.facebook.com/note.php?note_id=93312091960&ref=mf.
10. These may be found at http://www.alternativeprojections.com/oral-histories. Full transcripts and DVDs are available at Los Angeles Filmforum, the Getty Research Institute, and other archives.
11. These included Alice Royer and Amy Jo Damitz (for the Creative Film Society), Peter Oleksik (for the collections of the Los Angeles Independent Film Oasis at the Smithsonian Archives of American Art), Pauline Stakelon (for

Visual Communications), and Jesse Lerner (for ASCO). A complete list of people who worked on the archival and oral history projects may be found at http://alternativeprojections.com/#ProjectName.

12. The opening show's favorable *Los Angeles Times* review included statements by Hyman and Toscano about the nature of experimental film and its overall marginalization in Los Angeles. See Jasmine Elist, "Experimental Films Offer Avant-garde Angle", *Los Angeles Times*, 6 October 2011, D6. The programs and abbreviated forms of the program notes are assembled in chapter 29 below.
13. In fact, because of the Getty's attitude to Filmforum's small size and operating costs, the initial award was given to Filmforum via UCLA. Administrative difficulties proved this form of disbursement impossible, but only after prolonged negotiations were Sapienza and Hyman able to persuade the Getty to make the funds available directly.
14. For Visions and Voices, see http://www.usc.edu/dept/pubrel/visionsandvoices/about.php.
15. The conference and its associated screenings were budgeted at $29,036.00, of which Filmforum provided $9,000.00 from the Getty funds and Visions and Voices the remainder. SCA provided at least the equivalent in in-kind contributions. USC's investment proved wise; according to Visions and Voices' own survey, the "Alternative Projection" event secured the following audience ratings: Excellent: 75.4%; Good: 21.5%: Fair 1.5%; Poor: 1.5%.
16. These were *The Wormwood Star* (Curtis Harrington, 1956), *Flesh Of Morning* (Stan Brakhage, 1956), *Passion In A Seaside Slum* (Robert Wade Chatterton, 1961), *Shoppers Market* (John Vicario, 1963), *A Painter's Journal* (Renate Druks, 1967), and *Nun And Deviant* (Nancy Angelo and Candace Compton Pappas, 1976).
17. Beginning with the only visual record of the original light show, *The Single Wing Turquoise Bird Light Show Film* (Single Wing Turquoise Bird, 1970), these were *Adagio For Jon And Helena* (Michael Scroggins, 2009), *Metamorphosis* (David Lebrun, 2010), *Yoga-Sutras* (Peter Mays, 2010), *Slum Goddess Goes To New Mexico* (Larry Janss, 2010), *Jackpot* (Shayne Hood, 1991), *Fluxus Film #22: Shout* (Jeff Perkins, 1991), *Invocation* (Amy Halpern, 1982) and, in its world premiere, *Out Of Our Depth* (Single Wing Turquoise Bird, 2010).
18. These also screened a selection of their films: *Filament (The Hands)* (Amy Halpern, 1975), *Sidewinder's Delta* (Pat O'Neill, 1976), *Presence Of Mind* (David Wilson, 1976), *Projection Instructions* (Morgan Fisher, 1976), *Four Corners* (Diana Wilson, 1978), *Murray And Max Talk About Money* (Grahame Weinbren and Roberta Friedman, 1979) and *Gratuitous Facts* (Tom Leeser, 1981).
19. In an extensive but supercilious review of the symposium, the art-critic for an alternative paper belatedly noticed that Los Angeles had "supported a thriving underground almost from the birth of the industry", and remarked that Filmforum, then in its thirty-fifth year of continuous operation, had "become a cornerstone of L.A.'s cultural identity": Doug Harvey, "Hollywood's Soft Psychedelic Underbelly: Filmforum's 'Alternative Projections' symposium draws a line from avant-garde to *Avatar*", *LA Weekly*, 11 November 2010, 42.
20. P. Adams Sitney, *Visionary Film: The American Avant-Garde in the 20th Century*, 3rd Edition (New York: Oxford University Press, 2002), 14.
21. "The Dangerous Compromise", *Hollywood Quarterly*, 3:4 (Summer 1948), 405–415.
22. Eventually labeled the "L.A. Rebellion", these black filmmakers were the subject of another PST historical recovery project. See *Emancipating the Image: The L.A. Rebellion of Black Filmmakers*, eds. Allyson Nadia Field, Jan-Christopher Horak, and Jacqueline Stewart (Berkeley: University of California Press, forthcoming).

PART I
HISTORICAL MATERIALS

Introduction

David E. James

The following texts were selected both for their intrinsic interest and as supplements to the scholarly essays. One of those by John Fles and the one by Peter Mays are published here for the first time, while the others have received little or no notice. All were written in Los Angeles except for Maya Deren's "Amateur vs. Professional", which was written after she left for New York. Unless otherwise indicated, all notes are by D.E.J.

1 Distribution Center for Experimental Films

Curtis Harrington*

The postwar revival of the experimental film movement in the United States, which Lewis Jacobs wrote about in detail in the Spring, 1948, issue of the *Hollywood Quarterly*, has resulted in the formation of a coöperative distribution center to extend the distribution of these films through film societies, universities, art museums, and galleries, and all interested groups and private individuals. The organization has been named Creative Film Associates, and represents the attempt of the film makers to get together on a coöperative basis to insure the widest possible circulation of their work.

Already available for rental from Creative Film Associates is its *Program I*, which includes *Film Exercises 4 and 5* by John and James Whitney, *Fragment of Seeking* by Curtis Harrington, *Meta* by Robert Howard, and *Escape Episode* by Kenneth Anger. Also available are a program of films by Maya Deren – *Meshes of the Afternoon*, *At Land*, *A Study in Choreography for Camera*, and *Ritual in Transfigured Time* – and Kenneth Anger's much-discussed *Fireworks*. Further releases are to be made in the near future. For the convenience of those who wish to rent an evening's program of experimental works without facing the almost impossible task of assembling a group of films from a wide variety of sources – usually, heretofore, from the individual film makers themselves – several of the films have been put together by Creative Film Associates to form a balanced, forty-five-minute program, which is available at a rental rate lower than the total of fees for each film rented separately.

Creative Film Associates has also established the Creative Film Foundation, which will attempt to preserve and make available as many of the earlier

* First published in the *Hollywood Quarterly* 3: 4 (Summer 1948): 450–451.

experimental films as may be recovered (for many of the negatives and prints of the experimental films made in the '20s and early '30s have since disappeared), or obtained through the kindness of the film makers who still own their negatives. In the latter category, the films of Man Ray – *L'Étoile de Mer*, *Emak Bakia*, *Les Mystères du Château de Dé* – and Robert Florey and Slavko Vorkapich's *Life and Death of a Hollywood Extra* are soon to be released by the foundation. A further activity of the associates has been the establishment of the Creative Film Press, which will publish a series of monographs on various aspects of the creative film.

As Lewis Jacobs concluded in his article, "the future for experimental films is more promising than ever before", and the organization of Creative Film Associates represents one of the first concrete steps taken by the film makers as a group to implement the promise by making experimental films readily available from a central source. As a nonprofit organization, developed and operated on a coöperative basis by the film makers themselves, Creative Film Associates will return all revenue from the rentals to the artists, in order to insure the production of new films. It is hoped that by this method enough films may continually be produced to create a steady supply of new works, so that film centers and other interested groups may expect to have regular experimental film showings throughout the year. This will, of course, contribute to the continued development of the cinema as an independent art form.

More detailed information about the films available from Creative Film Associates, and the activities of the organization, may be obtained by writing to Creative Film Associates, 6215 Franklin Avenue, Hollywood 28, California.

2 Personal Chronicle: The Making of an Experimental Film

Curtis Harrington*

"An art in which youth is barred from practicing freely is sentenced to death in advance. The moving picture camera should be like a fountain pen, which anyone may use to translate his soul onto paper. The 16-mm. film presents the only solution, and in this I think America should take the initiative. ... It offers an opportunity of trying for miracles."
– Jean Cocteau, "Focus on Miracles", *New York Times Magazine,* 24 October 1948.

My new film, *Picnic*, which at this writing is completed except for the sound score, is the fifth film I have made in approximately seven years. The films that go before it include a version of Poe's *The Fall of the House of Usher* (1942), *Crescendo* (1943), *Renascence* (1945), and *Fragment of Seeking* (1946). The first three were photographed on 8-mm. film, and *Renascence* was in color. Seen today in chronological sequence, they illustrate a kind of cinematic development that could take place only outside of regular commercial production and distribution.

At the beginning, my attempt was simply to film a dramatic, literary subject in

* First published in the *Hollywood Quarterly* 4:1 (Fall 1949): 42–50. In the previous issue, Harrington had published an essay arguing that "certain cinematic tendencies and ideas which are gradually gaining momentum in the commercial cinema of Europe and in the experimental cinema of the United States" had been "strongly presaged and anticipated in the films and theoretical ideas of Josef von Sternberg"; among these tendencies was Sternberg's use of "external reality ... to illustrate an inner conflict"; see "The Dangerous Compromise", *Hollywood Quarterly* 3:4 (Summer 1949): 405–406. A decade later, Robert Pike noted Harrington's similar practice, but contrasted *Picnic* with his *Fragment of Seeking* (1946). In the earlier film, he argued, "the naiveté of the visual imagery, which enforced the feeling that the film expressed the ideas and frustrations of the teenager who produced it" made it "a highly successful example of a personal cinematic statement", whereas in *Picnic*, his attempt "to become more sophisticated in his imagery ... marks the film's basic weakness and thwarts it from becoming as meaningful and powerful". *A Critical History of the West Coast Experimental Film Movement* (MA Thesis, University of California, Los Angeles, 1960), 91. Seven years after *Picnic*, Harrington had himself decided to follow von Sternberg's precedent of making art films in Hollywood and to cross the "commercial chasm" from the experimental to the industrial cinema; see "A Statement" below.

an effective "cinematic" way. Stimulated by Paul Rotha's exciting critical history of the silent cinema, *The Film till Now*, I sought to emulate the extension of the creative means of the cinema exemplified by the films he wrote about most favorably. Instead of going to a primary source, such as the Hollywood film, which seldom stirred my imagination in the direction I had elected to follow, I gathered inspiration from Rotha's account of the most remarkable efforts in the motion pictures of the past. I set out to investigate the possibilities of the medium on my own, influenced only by the suggestion of the critical essay. After *The Fall of the House of Usher* I deserted the literary subject altogether, as the later films indicate.

In retrospect it appears most significant that I was especially impressed by Rotha's comment on *The Cabinet of Dr. Caligari:* "... [it showed that] a film, instead of being realistic, might be a possible reality, both imaginative and creative ... and the mind of the audience might be brought into play psychologically". Practically without exception, film historians and critics, having noted the great historical importance of *Caligari*, pointed out that it turned out to be a dead end, an admittedly interesting but wholly isolated work leading nowhere. Only now, exactly thirty years after its production, is the lesson of *Caligari* being applied: most of the motion pictures of the experimental film movement since World War II are concerned precisely with the construction of the imaginative filmic reality – a direct extension of the creative principle of *The Cabinet of Dr. Caligari*.

The postwar experimental film movement, now gradually gaining momentum and strength, results partly from the fact that a generation has grown up to whom the motion picture is as natural a creative medium as the other, older, more well-established arts: this serves to provide the cinema, for the first time in its short history, with a group of creators unprejudiced by theatrical conventions and other distorting preconceptions of film. The growing movement also results from the fact that these young artists at last have accessible to them the means of realizing individual, independent films: the inexpensive 16-mm. equipment that was brought to a point of perfection and became fully accepted only during the recent war. It is possible now to produce the creative film and even make a small profit from its distribution through art galleries, universities, museums, and private homes; that an unexpectedly wide audience for these films exists has already been proved. Until distribution has become more stabilized, however, the individually realized film must continue to be made with an absolute minimum of means. For me the necessary restriction of means has served as a kind of challenge to my ingenuity and powers of invention. As Josef von Sternberg recently stated, "Films can be made cheaply ... the idea is to 'trick the eye'. ... Expensive details aren't any more necessary in film than details are in painting."

Picnic, which I produced in the Summer of 1948, may serve as a good example of how an experimental film may be made on the most slender of personal budgets – and at the same time with a minimum of compromise.

The first and undoubtedly the most important single step in realizing a creative film is the preparation of a detailed shooting script. This requires the film maker to have the whole film, *cut by cut*, firmly set in his mind and on paper immediately before the shooting and long before the cutting. The internal rhythms of the film must be fully planned in writing the script, so that the completed work will not suffer from unanticipated, misplaced emphasizes or unbalanced tempo. Because the budget will not allow enough footage for taking cover shots of important action in close, medium, and long shots – common practice in making a commercial film, in order to protect the director – the experimental film maker must be certain of his conception: he must see his film in detail on the screen as it will finally appear, even before he has written down the exact sequence of shots on paper.

Another primary consideration in writing the shooting script must be the settings that will be used in the film. The script must anticipate camera angles in relation to the settings that will be used. The locations for the film must, for obvious practical reasons, be chosen before the script is written, usually concurrently with the conception of the film.

The shooting scripts, even much of the inspiration for the content of both *Fragment of Seeking* and *Picnic*, grew out of photographically interesting settings with which I was familiar and to which I had easy access.

For the same reasons that every young creative writer is cautioned to write about those people and locations with which he is most familiar, I suggest that the most effective experimental film results when the film maker uses settings that he knows well. It is not necessary for him to reconstruct the city of Babylon; he can find in the settings of reality about him – his own or his neighbor's house, a garden, the ruins in a vacant lot, the desert or the mountains – the most evocative of settings, real backgrounds which will lend their aura of actuality to the imaginative event that he causes to take place in front of them. Such use of a real setting instead of one artificially constructed is necessary not only because these locations may be photographed free of charge, but, which is more important, because this essentially "documentary" approach serves to give the execution of an imaginative conception a validity which is quite impossible to obtain in any other art form: an immediate juxtaposition of reality and imagination, each lending strength to the other.

In *Picnic* I used only five basic settings: an isolated, rocky strip of beach slightly north of Malibu; a wooded area with the ruins of an exploded (faulty gas main) house nearby; a small room with only one window; a long, skyward-leading outdoor cement staircase; and the living room of an acquaintance's house. While on a Christmas trip to the Imperial Valley, I also photographed the protagonist of the film walking through desert wastes and a landscape of burnt trees; this material was then used for a visual timespace bridge in his journey from the beach to the ruins in the forest.

In content, *Picnic* begins as a genre film comedy of American middle-class life and ends as a minor tragedy in the same milieu. But in between the opening and closing sequences, with their filmically objective reality, lies the subjective adventure of the protagonist, who is caught up in a false love. His quest after the object of his love is necessarily doomed because of the influences surrounding her, reinforced by her own true nature. His love is false and empty because it is being expended on an idealized dream image rather than a reality. Recurrent images throughout the film serve to emphasize the forces of actuality, forces that also appear significantly in the subjective, entirely personal adventure. The imagery of the film is self-contained. All meanings, suggestions, symbols, and ideas are immediately present, if not always immediately perceivable (the layers of meaning must be reached, perhaps, through repeated viewings of the film, in the way that many books must be reread, or music reheard). No special outside frame of reference is required in order to understand it. Of course, already established associations with the predominantly bourgeois pastime of the picnic will serve to heighten certain aspects of the film in the minds of many spectators; this is, to a certain extent, expected and hoped for by the filmmaker. However, the fact that the film is directly inspired by certain forces in the American culture pattern – and, therefore, has a more immediate significance to Americans aware of that cultural pattern and its implications – does not, in my opinion, obviate the basic, universal validity of the images. With this and many of the other films of the postwar experimental film movement, we may once again regard the cinema as a truly international language.

Once the conception of the sequence of images that would constitute the finished film was complete and on paper, and, consequently, the settings and actors chosen, the first day's shooting was merely a matter of plunging in. The young man who had accepted the role of the protagonist (not quite realizing how arduous the task was that lay ahead of him) drove the girl who had agreed to play opposite him, my assistant, and myself to the beach location, and in a state of inevitable confusion we took the first shots, scenes that would appear somewhere

Figure 6. *Picnic*, frame enlargements.

in the middle of the completed picture. The film was processed on the following day, and when I looked at the footage I knew that I had successfully begun the actual production of a new film: both the photography and the performances were better than we had dared hope.

With this first assurance behind me, I could move ahead with more confidence; the initial plunge had not been as cold as I had braced myself for, and the sudden warmth gave me the courage to go on to attempt the realization of the more difficult scenes, scheduled to be taken in the following weeks of the all-too-short summer vacation period.

The picnic sequence itself, which we photographed next, presented the most difficulties. On a week-day afternoon, in order to avoid the possibility of a crowded beach, I had to assemble four actors, two assistants, an automobile (none of the people directly involved in the film owned a car), and a picnic lunch. I had to coordinate such details as the correct costuming of the principals. It was difficult to find two middle-aged persons (to play the parents of the protagonist and his sister) with an indulgent enough spirit to consent to spend one whole day at the seashore – especially when that day turned out to be cold and windy and, as we discovered at the last minute, the car we were to ride in had no top. However, we managed to reach the location, and I proceeded with a minimum of complications to film the rather long sequence of the picnickers' perilous descent to the beach. The first part of the afternoon was not without its hazards, however, the wind whipping sand into the picnic lunch and, more dangerously, into a relatively fragile European camera.

After we had finished shooting the picnic scene, I set out with some determination to film a scene of the protagonist falling from a rock into the sea. The shooting was delayed interminably. Falling from a rock into the sea did not, somehow, look as dangerous to me, with my legs sunk securely into dry sand, as it did to the young man who was called upon to do the falling. He saw the danger keenly. After about an hour of watching the tide and making certain that there were no jagged rocks hidden under the surf, the young man fell gracefully into the water. We really hadn't been able to see a thing beneath the foaming water, but I had felt a sort of spiritual certainty that all would be well. A breathless moment, and then his head bobbed above the surface, and he waved to us. The image had been successfully recorded.

Very late in the afternoon we walked some distance down the now entirely empty beach hunting for four men to play the discoverers of the drowned body. We came across one lonely person who told us that if we continued walking we would come to a beach party of Negroes who might volunteer their services. I rejected the idea then because the sun was sinking much too rapidly below the horizon and the shooting location was already far behind us. Later I rather wished that I had at least sought out members of the party: the pictorial stylization of four anonymous dark figures carrying on their shoulders the body of the "hero" would have contributed to the late afternoon aura of melancholy, emptiness, and death. Instead, I hurriedly placed the camera, and I, with my two assistants, carried the body while the girl operated the camera. To appear thus briefly in my film was not a gesture of vanity on my part, or of superstition (shades of Hitchcock!), but a necessary improvisation, the kind of last-minute substitution that often becomes necessary when one is confronted with limited shooting time. And yet one must not regard the necessity of changing the preconceived plan very suddenly as a wholly unfortunate factor in the production of the personal experimental film; it should be looked upon, rather, as one aspect of the reciprocal play between the film maker and his material. The artist, exerting a formalizing force upon the reality that confronts him, must seize upon the vagaries of that reality, even those that may seem distant from the original dream, and readjust them into the context of the whole. This cannot, of course, always be done with complete success, but the challenge must nevertheless be faced with a certain courage.

The next days were given over to shooting the poetic sequence staged in the ruins in the forest, the suspended, melancholy scene in the tiny room, and the delirium of the climb to the top of the perilously steep staircase. Each day's shooting presented its own peculiar problems, and each of them was in some way circumnavigated. The ruins in the forest were on a forbidden piece of property, and when the liquid smoke which gives, ideally, the aura of low-lying mists got out of control and rose in great clouds as if the forest were on fire, we were asked to leave. We returned later, however, and surreptitiously finished what we had begun. Again, the protagonist had to cry in the little room, but he could not concentrate. First we sprayed grapefruit juice into his eyes – but the effect was artificial; finally, a Spanish onion produced tears of true mourning. The scene on the staircase proved grueling, the most difficult that the protagonist had yet enacted. He bruised his legs in his agonized attempts to reach the object of his quest, and the perspiration pouring from his forehead into his eyes seemed to result from the anguish of the immobilized dreamer.

On the last afternoon we photographed the final sequence of the film: a scene within the semidarkness of a tasteless home filled with unnecessary bric-a-brac. Into this already overcrowded atmosphere we introduced, so as to make up a kind of cinematic tableau, a coffin in which the protagonist lay, the parents sitting beside it in mourning and the daughter finally revealed in the context of actuality. The room, filled with leftover flowers obtained from several florists' shops, looked curiously correct – the setting for a modern wake.

For almost a week before we photographed the coffin, I had been constructing it out of pasteboard and lining it with satin. The local casket company would not rent me one, but I had paid them a visit nevertheless to see if I could duplicate a coffin in an approximate fashion. As if I were a potential buyer they ushered me into the showroom of coffins, all open, with their elaborate satin insides spilling over the edges. In this macabre atmosphere I saw how the essentials of a casket could be reproduced quite easily for photographic purposes. The construction of the coffin, even though it was merely a "prop" of cardboard, elicited a marked response from those who happened to see it lying in my yard. This eminently false suggestion of a symbol of death had immediately assumed its own power; two persons made an elaborate pretense at being afraid even to look at the work I was doing. Since the film maker deals in effect, I could assume from this that I had once more successfully created cinematic reality with the necessary minimum of means.

The production costs for *Picnic*, which runs twenty-five minutes on the screen, were $159.45. During the production of the film I kept a carefully itemized account of the expenditures:

1,600 feet of Ansco Hypan	$106.08
6 filters, at 45 cents each	$ 2.70
Material for heroine's costume	$ 5.00
Fish net	$ 3.45
Rope	$ 0.50
Cheesecloth	$ 1.00
Liquid smoke (2 pints)	$ 5.00
Photofloods	$ 0.72
Rental equipment (extra lens and dolly)	$ 9.05
Rental of large electric fan	$ 4.00
Veiling	$ 3.75
Flowers	$ 1.50
Pasteboard for coffin	$ 1.95
Satin lining for coffin lid	$ 3.35
Transportation	$ 5.15
Miscellaneous (including dry ice, make-up, cleaning bill, food for picnic, etc.)	$ 6.25
Grand total	$159.45

I present this chronicle of the production of an experimental film not only as a generally illuminating production account, of which, I feel, there are all too few, but as a note of encouragement: with the knowledge that it *can* be done, that the writing with film of which Cocteau speaks is entirely within the realm of immediate possibility, perhaps more will set out to give their dreams plastic realization.

3 A Letter from the West Coast

Robert Pike[*]

A peculiar current of creativity is sweeping through San Francisco and Los Angeles and the results are exciting!

And there is an awareness in each city of what is happening in the other. Artists, poets, and film-makers are both writing and visiting one another. From this torrential flux of communication should come a deluge of new film ideas! The Art in Cinema Festival next year or in two years, when the first concrete results of this creativity are shown, is an exciting prospect.

Already, the new creative surge is being valuably channeled. In Los Angeles, Wallace Berman has begun a series of poetry readings by the rising poets of that city. The first evening was attended by Curtis Harrington, Cameron Parsons, Samson De Brier, and many others both interested and active in art and poetry. Berman is also starting work on his first experimental film.

And some of the early names in the experimental film movement are back at work. Curtis Harrington is completing his first film in four years: it deals with the paintings and personage of Cameron Parsons and is called *The Wormwood Star*. John Whitney, working together with Charles Eames, has just completed *Toy Trains*, and IBM has sponsored them in the making of an animated film for the 1958 Brussels Festival.

Stan Brakhage, who is emerging as the most prolific and perhaps the most controversial experimental film-maker of the decade, has recently produced three new films: *Daybreak, White Eye,* and *Loving*. He is presently in Denver, working

* First published in *Film Culture* 14 (November 1957): 9–10. Pike wrote the first substantial account of specifically West Coast experimentalism, *A Critical History of the West Coast Experimental Film Movement* (MA Thesis, University of California, Los Angeles, 1960), as well as himself making films and organizing the Creative Film Society, one of the nation's main distribution centers during the 1960s and 1970s.

Figure 7. Bob Pike photographs Fred Leitsinger for Pike's film, *Desire in a Public Dump* (1958).

on a feature-length experimental film in color. Brakhage writes, "My work has taken a new, much more difficult, direction. The three best examples of this direction are *The Wonder Ring, Nightcats,* and *Loving* .... I no longer make a film 'about' something. The statement of the film is now the result of the film's becoming."

Ten years ago in San Diego, a newspaper woman named Ettilie Wallace invented an interesting color box which she called "Kaleidolight". With the help of some friends, she created a film out of the abstract patterns formed by the color box. She showed the results to Robert Greensfelder, then head of Kinesis, in San Francisco. He introduced her to poet-artist-composer Christopher Maclaine, who offered to make a sound track for the film. The end result was *Moods in Motion*, a film released two years ago. Then, Ettilie was commissioned by the film unit of the Los Angeles chapter of the American Association for the United Nations to do another film using her "Kaleidolight" technique. This film was completed in 1956 and is called *Come In, Jupiter.* At present, Ettilie is in Los Angeles, planning further film work. Maclaine, who in 1953 made *The End*, an experimental film, is still in San Francisco and is now working on the sound track for his newly completed film *The Man Who Invented Gold*; assisting him on the score is George Abend.

Elwood Decker is an excellent example of a dormant film-maker being re-activated by the current wave of creative effort. Decker, a Los Angeles artist and art instructor, made a wonderful film, *Color Fragments*, in 1949. As its title implies, the film was actually a part of a larger film idea which was never realized, and *Color Fragments* remains as a beautiful silent suggestion of what could have been.

But just recently, as the result of the showing of the film by the Creative Film Society in Los Angeles and the general enthusiasm of the Society, Decker has become re-interested enough in his film to work on a sound track for it, and the new sound version should be ready by the end of the year.

Other active experimental film-makers on the West Coast are: Robert Pike, Flora Mock, Helene Sand Turner, Steve Clensos, and John Schmitz, all in Los Angeles; and Lawrence Jordan and Brant Sloan, in San Francisco. Oskar Fischinger (Los Angeles), the dean of abstract film-makers, is presently concentrating on his painting and is postponing his film work until the necessary funds are available. Whereas most of the other experimental film-makers work on a 16 mm., semi-amateur basis and can therefore produce films on a relatively small budget, Fischinger operates on a completely professional basis (as he should) and consequently needs large sums of money to produce his films. It is because of this financial barrier that his output of completed films has been so small since his arrival in this country in 1936. Through the years, he has begun many projects which he was forced to abandon for lack of funds. Typical of these was a project sponsored by Orson Welles: a series of abstract films dealing with early American jazz; Fischinger had already planned the sound track and the myriad drawings when the money ran out.

Although most of the new film-making activity seems to have arisen spontaneously, some of it was institutionally inspired by the restoration of the Art in Cinema Society in San Francisco and by the formation of the Creative Film Society in Los Angeles. The Art in Cinema Society, which had been relatively inactive the last two years since the death of Frank Stauffacher, has been revived by the appointment of John R. Baxter to the staff of the San Francisco Museum of Art. One of Baxter's responsibilities is the Art in Cinema Festival, and the 1957 Festival was his first effort. Although Baxter is doing a good job as Film Curator of the Museum, he also has many other duties there which prevent him from devoting as much time as he might to certain needed projects – e.g., supervising an up-to-date revision of the "Art in Cinema" book (originally edited in 1946 by Stauffacher and published by the Museum); adding to the Museum's rental collection; and helping to establish financial aid for experimental film-making.

The Creative Film Society was formed this year by Robert Pike and includes in its membership Curtis Harrington, Oskar Fischinger, Ettilie Wallace, John and James Whitney, Charles Eames, Elwood Decker, Flora Mock, John Schmitz, Curtis Opliger, William Hale, Helene Sand Turner, Richard Brummer, Wallace Berman, Steve Clensos, Bam Price, and other active film-makers. The purpose of the CFS is three-fold: (1) to show creative films to an art-minded audience,

(2) to provide financial and technical aid to creative film-makers, and (3) to act as a distribution service for its member film-makers. So far, Berman is shooting his experimental film with CFS equipment, Harrington is editing *The Wormwood Star* with CFS equipment, and many of the above-mentioned members are distributing their films through the CFS.

Also in Los Angeles is the Coronet Theatre, which, under the direction of Raymond Rohauer, has shown creative films since 1950, and has one of the most complete collections of experimental films in this country. Many of these films – such as *Plague Summer* by Chester Kessler, *Closed Vision* by Leon Vickman, four abstract films by Don Bevis, and some of Stan Brakhage's latest works – have never or rarely been seen outside this theater but will soon be available for distribution.

Although communication among the film-makers on the West Coast has developed to the point where there is an immediate spread of information on what is happening in Los Angeles, San Francisco, San Diego, and Denver, there is still a pitiful lack of communication between the West Coast and the New York experimental film-makers. At this time, the only active contacts between these two areas are Richard Brummer, who has just returned to New York from Los Angeles, and Helene Sand Turner, who has just come to Los Angeles from New York. Both of these people are familiar with the Creative Film Society in Los Angeles and the Independent Film-makers Association in New York, and perhaps through them the other members of the two organizations will come into closer touch. The biggest problem on the West Coast in the meantime is the fact that many experimental film-makers in New York distribute their own films and in some cases are loathe to send the films out of town. Until there is a good system of film interchange between New York and the West Coast, the growth of the experimental film movement will be stunted. For that matter, there is a need for such a system among all the cities of the United States where experimental films are shown as well as among the various film societies here and their counterparts in Europe and South America.

... But while we're waiting for Utopia, things are happening!

4 Amateur Versus Professional

Maya Deren*

The *major obstacle* for amateur film-makers is their own sense of inferiority vis-à-vis professional productions. The very classification "amateur" has an apologetic ring. But that very word – from the Latin"amateur" – "lover" means one who does something for the love of the thing rather than for economic reasons or necessity. And this is the meaning from which the amateur film-maker should take his clue. Instead of envying the script and dialogue writers, the trained actors, the elaborate staffs and sets, the enormous production budgets of the professional film, the amateur should make use of the one great advantage which all professionals envy him, namely, *freedom* – both artistic and physical.

Artistic freedom means that the amateur film-maker is never forced to sacrifice visual drama and beauty to a stream of words, words, words, words, to the relentless activity and explanations of a plot, or to the display of a star or a sponsor's product; nor is the amateur production expected to return profit on a huge investment by holding the attention of a massive and motley audience for ninety minutes. Like the amateur still-photographer, the amateur film-maker can devote himself to capturing the poetry and beauty of places and events and, since he is using a motion-picture camera, he can explore the vast world of the beauty of movement. (One of the films winning Honorable Mention in the 1958 Creative Film Awards was *Round And Square*, a poetic, rhythmic treatment of the dancing lights of cars as they streamed down highways, under bridges, etc.) Instead of trying to invent a plot that moves, use the movement of wind, or water, children, people, elevators, balls, etc. as a poem might celebrate these. And use your freedom to experiment with visual ideas; your mistakes will not get you fired.

* First published in *Movie Makers Annual*, 1959, reprinted in *Film Culture* 39 (Winter 1965): 45–46.

Physical freedom includes time freedom – a freedom from budget imposed deadlines. But above all, the amateur film-maker, with his small, light-weight equipment, has an inconspicuousness (for candid shooting) and a physical mobility which is well the envy of most professionals, burdened as they are by their many-ton monsters, cables, and crews. Don't forget that no tripod has yet been built which is as miraculously versatile in movement as the complex system of supports, joints, muscles and nerves which is the human body, which, with a bit of practice, makes possible the enormous variety of camera angles and visual action. You have all this, and a brain too, in one neat, compact, mobile package.

Cameras do not make films; film-makers make films. Improve your films not by adding more equipment and personnel but by using what you have to its fullest capacity. The most important part of your equipment is yourself: your mobile body, your imaginative mind, and your freedom to use both. Make sure you do use them.

5 Personal State Meant

John Fles*

The last few weeks of the *Scorpio* trial have made certain things obvious to my mind. Whether we win or not, I have been warned that this theatre will be under constant surveillance; in other words, *de facto* censorship. I went thru this once, at the beginning of my career, at the University of Chicago re: the Bill Burroughs Case. I could not then and will not now accept anything less than what Karl Popper calls "The Open Society". And tho I believe that's coming, as the pressure rises the enemies of the open society gather force, mainly strengthening what in our time we finally have to accept as, at least, part police state. I can not continue to run this program under any kind of censorship nor will I play that other, more dangerous, game and go to jail. Within a period of two to three months Movies 'Round Midnight may (& I emphasize may) cease to exist. Not necessarily, for this is up to those who own the theatre, the Saturday night screenings but, rather, my own somewhat naïve attempt to bring you those films which, without any kind of qualification whatsoever, I thought best or most useful or funniest or most ironical or most pertinent for our time. Now these films will, for the most part, be forced underground and/or be squeezed into some more or less institutional setting, with, again, the politics which imply censorship. To what extent I will ally myself with either or both of these efforts, future strategy will tell. In the meantime there is some hope in the possibility of a newspaper which would tie the entire artistic community, from Pasadena to Venice West, together. Its purpose would be to alert all of us to dangers the society, in the concrete manifestation of police, judges, all the paraphernalia of modern day justice, imposes on the increasingly restless need for total freedom. (This growing need for complete artistic freedom is not unrelated to the best elements within the negro movement.) We must remember, in terms of our own responsibility,

* Previously unpublished; obvious typing and spelling mistakes have been corrected. The expressed need for "a newspaper which would tie the entire artistic community, from Pasadena to Venice West, together", was met a year later with the appearance of the *Los Angeles Free Press*, whose first issue was dominated by the *Scorpio Rising* trial.

that at the moment external law ends, the law, if such it may be called then, must come from inside. And those of us with any sense of history, see the only law coming from inside is love. Let us make no mistake: it is love itself, in all its manifestations, which the police state we find ourselves in, is engaged in destroying.

* * *

Written and read at the Cinema TH. on May 9, 1963, by John Fles

6 A Statement

Curtis Harrington*

The Tenth Muse still awaits its great patron. Until this person comes forth, and it has always been my conviction that such a person will eventually appear, the cinema will continue to be enmeshed in the tyranny of commercial expediency. Let us not fool ourselves: the experimental film, ostensibly free from the aforementioned tyranny, is too trifling, too in love with its petty effects, too introverted, too lazy, and most often ends as a victim, also, for its means by circumstance have been too transcribed. Ironically, the best films have been produced, whatever the consequences to the artist, and they have often been considerable (witness historically the systematic, exteriorly induced decay in the extraordinary talents of Erich von Stroheim, Josef von Sternberg and Orson Welles, as example), within the framework of the commercial cinema.

The world is like a great sea: only the few manage to walk on water. These water-walkers see far and when they manage to communicate their vision to us we receive a marvelous gift. The most marvelous gifts of which the cinema is capable have not yet been given us. Of the ways of communicating vision, surely the cinema offers the greatest challenge, and it is plainly too formidable for most. Yet I am convinced that its appeal should not only be to giants. There will one day be an Emily Dickinson of the cinema.

My own work has suffered in countless ways from circumstance and I won't enter into a detailed accounting. I feel that I must, in any case, assume the major part of the responsibility. I am loathe to accept *all* of it, though perhaps I have little right to take such an attitude. My films bear no name on them other than my own, except, occasionally, for the felicitous one of my composer, Ernest Gold, who does for me what I am truly incapable of doing.

I have recently been making a film called *The Wormwood Star*. It is a film in color, and presents a symbolic portrait of an extraordinary artist, a painter who is named

* First published in *Film Culture* 29 (Summer 1963): 69.

Cameron. The film is an attempt to apotheosize the artist cinematically while she yet lives. She is presented as an alchemist, we observe the Great Work, and out of that mysterious complex of action and magic the ultimate transmutation takes place: the flesh turns to gold.

In the future I shall go farther along the esoteric path that is suggested by *The Wormwood Star*. If I find the means – and I have not done so yet – I shall make a long film in color, which will be called *Voyage Toward The Earth Of Mystery*.

In the meanwhile, inspired by my admiration for those who have, even if only momentarily, crossed with success the commercial chasm, I am attempting to tread gingerly that hovering, swaying tightrope as well.

(1956)

7 Are Movies Junk

John Fles*

To escape reality we go to the Movies. The better the Movie the more complete the escape. Until sometimes we wonder which is more real. Under LSD both realities are equal. Other times we know the sordidness and pain of this life must be replaced. We dream all our senses will be absorbed in the Ultimate Movie. Only then, in reflection, does any idea of Heaven come to us.

From the square hole of the projection booth beams a glimmer of the Post-Atomic Age. Mumblings about montage and acting remain profane. The critics of a Vision are always puerile. To watch men move, even without speaking, is enough.

We know then, transfixed by a ray of sunlight on a Sunday morning on 42nd Street after six days and seven nights of continuous viewing, that we can not end this meaningless existence. Even after the Final Bomb falls, our souls, bathed in light, endure. The Galaxies themselves are distant Movies. The screen exploits Social Reform as it would any other legend. Love's message also is conveyed in its utter two-dimensionality. And the pure darkness of the Universe fades leaving stark Light and Shadow, twins of a sane mind.

We succumb reluctantly to the question posed as it were on the brink of the Abyss: Who is the audience?

* First published in *Film Culture* 29 (Summer 1963): 9.

8 Los Angeles Film Festival

Jack Hirschman*

Something more than a report of the second Los Angeles Film Festival has to be given, for in a very important way the festival did not end in the early morning hours of 13 February with the choice of a winner of the $250 first prize, but it continued for a couple of days more, unofficially.

As for the actual competition, some forty films were entered. Screening began at 7 p.m. on Lincoln's birthday, and nearly nine hours later, less numbed and bloodshot than we thought we'd be, John Fles, Stan Brakhage, and I went off for breakfast to choose the winning film.

The choice we made was a fifty-minute work by Stan Kaye called *Georg*. The decision was a majority one, with Brakhage holding to his preference for a cameo (Jess-like) work by Larry Jordan, while at the same time fully in agreement with the other judges that *Georg* is a work of authority, imagination and prodigy (it is the twenty year-old Kaye's first film).

Made on a shoestring of between three and four thousand dollars (for the most part up in a Topanga Canyon location overlooking the Pacific), *Georg* was written by Kaye as well, who also plays the part of the title-hero's voice. I say *voice*, because there is an intentioned Pirandello device in this film which works marvelously well. The film purports to be a record (in moving pictures, stills, and tapes) of the life of an "unfortunate creature". What happens is that the film opens with Kaye's (Georg's) voice announcing the record to come, but what we subsequently see is that record actually being filmed. Georg in fact is the director of the film, or so the illusion is given. The Georg we see is played by actor Mark Cheka, and

* Originally published in *Film Culture* 32 (Spring 1964): 68–70. An important poet, Jack Hirschman was very active in radical circles in Los Angeles. Dismissed from his teaching position at UCLA for encouraging his students to resist the draft, he eventually left for San Francisco.

Figure 8. *Georg*, frame enlargements.

Georg's wife by Lynn Averil. Microphone and cable punctuate many of the scenes. In one scene Georg-Cheka puts a microphone in front of his wife and says, "Say something". Moreover, as the film develops, the camera and microphone, i.e., the obsession of Director Georg to record his life, become another aspect of the sellout "outside" world intent upon crushing the simple relationship between the couple. When the wife gets sick of the camera, of its directions, the suggestion is that she is sickening of the "visual" Georg. In a memorable stop-action scene, Georg-Cheka attempts to seduce his wife (in the very late months of her pregnancy); and this scene is paralleled with another in which the wife is seen trying desperately to escape from the camera, scurrying behind shack and bush, as though the camera were no less her seducer-husband, which, in fact, by extension it is.

So that it would be dead wrong to read this film as a message film (the "story" is of an ex-Nazi soldier made unfit by the last war to live in or with this civilization, who comes to America, marries, tries making it away from civilization [high above a large American city], only to find his "garden" failing, his wife and infant both dead at childbirth, after the burial of whom he attempts to blow up a nearby missile site which has encroached his mountain, and is shot dead). Kaye is not interested in the kind of message implicit in the story, taken out of context. In fact, quite the opposite. For Georg himself is deeply responsible for the death of his wife, who wanted to "go back" but was refused by her husband, and so Georg's last act has about it no simple pacifist cry but a ludicrous desperate whisper that tells us the most pathetically beautiful thing of all: that we ourselves are as much contributable to the destruction of the bridge between simplicity and complex madness as the civilization we often blame, because of our very frailness, our very unfortunateness, to begin with.

We have seen the kind of play with illusion and reality that Kaye dynamizes, in another film, in Shirley Clarke's *The Connection*. Kaye's treatment is more subtle, more authentic. I was myself most moved by what I would call a staggeringly profound blend of sophistication and innocence. And lest it be thought that Kaye has used his film-within-film device to get round the lack of "polish" of the film, let it be said that the absence of such gloss, the raw almost home-movie quality of the film does not detract one iota from the depth in composition of it and the perspectives this young director is able to achieve. The drama of illusion and reality in fact enhances the despair implicit in the "story" of the film in a way that the absence of such a dimension in a film of a similar order – I am thinking of *Guns of the Trees* – leaves that work – with whatever virtues of naked honesty – touching the ground *too much*, as a poem ought not to, at least overtly. From seeing *Georg*, I think we have seen the birth of an important American film director, a prodigal who brings Welles to mind; and that Kaye is native Los Angeles, and yet of another country of the mind as well, contributes all the more to the sense of a destiny about his future films.

Yet there is another, less public in many ways, side of the story of this second Los Angeles Film Festival. The week in Los Angeles coincided with a series of lectures and showings of the films by Stan Brakhage. For many who had not seen but one or two of Brakhage's films, and for myself, if I may say so, who'd looked forward to seeing more of his vocabulary, the week grew to be a thing of terrible beauty.

Let me start from behind: the purity of this man's vision and the mastery of his medium were things to behold with wonder. In my three years in LA never have I encountered anyone who left himself open for so much and yet was able, perhaps by that very vulnerability, to open up so much in those who were willing to be encountered, either by the man himself (in lecture or in conversation) or by his films. I'm not thinking here merely of reconciling disparate film-makers to friendship by his presence, nor of bringing a sculptor and a poet to certain only half-accomplished ridges in themselves. I'm thinking of the whole Raison d'Etre of Brakhage on display here in three universities, for BREAD, with all that that kind of tour implies. I'm thinking of certain very delicate, very ripping American things this man put himself in the center of.

With him came some hundred copies of his book, *Metaphors on Vision*. I read it through the first night, and later we talked at great length about many of the things in it, a struggle between the "taos" of John Cage and Charles Olson which, it seems, we both had had to encounter somewhere along the way; the aesthetics of film and poem, what Olson had opened, what Creeley, how Zukofsky's work had strengthened his sense of film; and then The Hard Terms, how the lecture tour was absurd/damaging, how the universities, by simply being unconscious… . And yet The Harder Terms, how Olson simply had had to surrender to a university, how Creeley was teaching somewhere in the southwest, Bob Kelly at Bard (and I sitting there with nine years teaching straight back of me, a professor-poet at UCLA, suddenly looking straight at the deeply inset eyes of An Artist and Husband and Father likewise himself – just left his job in South Dakota, left Jane and the kids in Boulder with her folks, no future outside of With Them and The Film – and suddenly Olson's words quoted by Stan in his book: "In the meantime, get to the center, quickly – don't fuck around with small colleges … get to the BIG centers, use them, you CAN, you know …" were no consolation, either to him whom I knew never would make it there, nor to me, who was there but half-sick with what ruthless usage [the only way a poet or filmmaker CAN exist, Olson was right, in a university environment] must pay for at table or splice.) … So it was that Stan, in leather doublet and without any weapon but the can of film in his hand, began very quickly to stand out in my mind like the last of a pack out of Sherwood Forest, understanding where the others had had to go to keep the tables moderately filled, perhaps even himself wishing for the safety of institution (since he's got about as large a family as any poet in America). But there it was: his last job left, the recognition still for the most part existing only among the *makers* and not the receivers of film poems, and nevertheless all the guy wore were open doors.

Premise. Brakhage's favorite word. He used it almost always as verb: *premises, premised.* And it (almost) rhymes with his other favorite word(s): *Bless you*. Those are the two pivots of his being: (1) the Aesthetic Principle, (2) the Love.

I felt the second all over the week. I saw the first whenever he spoke, and particularly in the all-night delicatessen in LA where he and John Fles and I sat down to breakfast after the nine hour marathon. Whatever positions we held before the festival, I think each of us was open enough to have those positions overthrown by a fresh reality, a reality that would leave no question to judgment, especially as all three of us were hopelessly set against the possibility of *really* judging a film after, my God, nine hours of continuous reeling.

The fresh realities were there. But none so staggering as to leave no final question. All three of us agreed that *Georg* was the work of true imagination – Brakhage spoke of its "authenticity" – and all three agreed that of the forty some odd films projected, none was a purely filmic tour de force. Where I, and I believe John Fles also, felt the need to recognize in Stan Kaye a rich and true imagination, not excluding the literary and dramatically theatrical elements which inform that imagination; Brakhage, agreeing, dissented only in so far as, from his point of view, Jordan's *Patricia Giving Birth to a Dream by the Doorway* lay closer to the heart of film.

But there was no argument. It was just that a principle needed to be upheld. One might, too easily I think now, pass over that principle.

It was a principle that certainly could see and accept other modes of filmic expression as genuine, imaginative. And at the same time retain its own integrity of outlook.

Expressed in his book, in conversation, it was expressed again that dawn of the 13th of February.

One might, too easily I think now, pass over that principle, pass over the whole lesson of Brakhage if one did not know his own work.

Two nights later at the same Cinema Theater where the festival was held, the Movies 'Round Midnight series which John Fles originated and out of which the festival grew, continued its showings. Four of Brakhage's films were scheduled, and two weeks earlier the audience had seen a preview of the "feature" film of the night, Isou's *Venom and Eternity*.

Now whether the anti-film quality of the preview setup the audience I don't know; nor do I know whether what happened happened out of the kind of freedom permitted that audience at the Cinema (which gets pretty loose, Saturday night, etc.), or out of a general and inchoate sexual fascism associated with experimental films, and finally, perhaps, I may come to agree with Stan that what happened happened because it happened and that's the way things are and that's what's got to be permitted, finally, only I don't think so at least right now when I think of the laughter and hooting and shitting that accompanied *Daybreak*, the laughter and hooting and shitting out the pain of a million sexual betrayals that accompanied *Wedlock: An Intercourse*, and I feel nothing behind my anger but shame for those harmonicas that went off (like obscenely, man) during the silence of that masterpiece, *Sirius Remembered.*

Which wasn't the first time, I'm sure.
And which won't be the last, I'm sure.

But for the record, which has got to be kept straight and made, if possible, straighter as a few of us return past the rows, past the kiddy section, past the now stilled adolescences:

El Aye, you're a dumbbell at heart, now leave us, there
is *Sirius Remembered* at the end,
there is
by Brakhage re-
membered, alone

9 Seeing is believing

John Fles*

Epistemological slogans

"Calculated confusion of the senses." Rimbaud
"Upsetting the equilibrium." Gurdjieff

Strategy

"The task I'm trying to achieve is above all to make you see." D.W. Griffith

First, the almost purely physical aspect of film, i.e. the optics of images seen on the screen. Moving emotionally with film, say [*The Cabinet of Dr.*] *Caligari*, 1919. The impulse was quickly disordered: the theatricality of Caligari and the painterly perspective of Pabst, Lang, and Murnau's early work led, as Kracauer has said, from Caligari to Hitlerian Cinema (notwithstanding these directors' personal aversion to the Reich). With the Russians, and especially with Eisenstein, came the full intellectual flowering of cinema implied in Griffith's pioneer work; and in particular in the process which Eisenstein called "organic editing" or montage. It was in Paris, tho, that the essential dichotomy of film history began: into photoplay (or the later novelist-journalistic forms of postwar European film-making) and, in Brakhage's words, "film based primarily on vision". From the ferment of surrealism and dada, in the late '20s and early '30s, two films, Cocteau's *Blood of A Poet* and the Buñuel/Dalí *Un chien Andalou*, were the first to unequivocally manifest soul-content, i.e. to take the surrealist's voyage thru the inner self and put it on the screen.

* John Fles was the most important curator and theorist of underground cinema in Los Angeles in the mid 1960s. After screening films from the New York underground at the Unicorn coffeehouse on the Sunset Strip for several years, on Columbus Day 1963, he began midnight screenings at the Cinema Theater at 1122 North Western Avenue, then managed by Mike Getz. Though Fles himself left for New York in 1965 (choosing henceforth to be known as Michael Fles), Getz continued the midnight screenings until the early 1970s. This is a transcription of a pamphlet Fles wrote and self-published in 1964, priced at fifty cents. Its cover was a specially commissioned drawing by George Herms, with another drawing by Naomi Levine as a frontispiece.

So, we have physical discovery, emotional discovery, intellectual discovery, soul discovery. This is film history crammed into a tight schema.

Pound makes these distinctions re: poetry in his basic *ABC of Reading*: innovators, Masters, diluters. I take it that film, visual poetry, displays similar epochs and individuals. The Masters who appear during the first soul-period, e.g. Cocteau, Buñuel, Vigo, Dreyer (*Passion of Joan of Arc*, Paris, 1928) blur into the dilutors of that aesthetic of the early '50s in the U.S.A.: Maya Deren, James Broughton, Kenneth Anger, Curtis Harrington, Sydney Peterson, i.e. The Big Five. Cinema 16 Team took over the classic European faggot sensibility, the sleight-of-hand inherent in the surreal, and applied it successfully to America. But even by that time, say 1956, a new generation of innovators had appeared whose interest was primarily, again, with the physical, i.e. technique. They represented a new era of physical birth in film. (Most interesting "sport" of the period of the dilutors – which began roughly with Deren's work in the early '40s: *Citizen Kane*. Harking back to the aesthetic-emotionalism of German Film, Welles's technical advances, for, e.g. new processes of sound montage which he brought with him from radio, took place just a few years after Lang's initial attempts in the same area. Expressionism led, in Germany, to *M.* and *The Last Will of Dr. Mabuse,* in America to the harder edged container of *Kane*.)

In the ear of the new innovators, as in the ear of the dilutors, the Masters whisper. They grow now to bud later. The Film Masters of our time will discover soul-continents of film; they will portray, and have already portrayed, soul-states without equivocation, without, that is, the craven reference to the literary and painterly models which square the academic critics into whining dogs leaping at one another's balls.

Two films, Gregory Markopoulos's *Twice A Man* and Jack Smith's *Flaming Creatures,* should be especially looked at. In the former, an entirely new sight-sound montage technique has been discovered, but a Grecian mythos informs it – the symbols, thereby are not absolutely pertinent to our time (G.M. tried here to follow in Cocteau's large footsteps); *Flaming Creatures*, on the other hand, presents poetry, i.e. vision, his own flow of mind, erotic images, no bullshit, marred, however, by techniques, tho very funny, which stretch back to von Sternberg and Maria Montez. Both films manifest immaturity: one via what's normally called content, and the other via form. Immaturity defines Innovation.

In theory, Masters will synthesize the work of innovators, but in practice the borderline is imaginary. A potential Master may work in the period of the diluters, as a manifestation of the period (to change roles later), as a "sport" or with facets of both, which Brakhage had circa 1958/59, continuing on to harbinger the age of the new Masters almost singlehandedly. With Brakhage, then, we have reached the beginning of the birth of the new Masters. In Stan's best recent work: *Blue Moses*, *Mothlight*, the *Dog Star Man* cycle (Pt. 4 a letter today said was under way), we see a synthesis of hip film technique and mature spiritual content.

Tactics

> "Two steps forward one step back." V.I. Lenin

The future of film, an art of free men, is undetermined. To some extent, however small, that future depends on Movies 'Round Midnight; on you as an audience, on me, as Film Editor. To a certain extent, in a limited area, I will respond to the collective will of the audience. The fact that that will exists is certain; but the difficulty lies in interpreting, translating, evaluating that will (after all, except by extremely sensitive intuition, the so-called collective will is manifested by discrete individuals). As far as I can see or foresee, I will choose film and entire film-contexts to fulfill that need. That's the extent of my democratic instincts; there's a far greater part of my work which must continue invisibly, i.e. without concrete outward manifestations.

What I would like to suggest is some possible adventurous forms MRM policy could take. First, I believe our original policy of screening creative film-makers, i.e. film-poets, should be continued and strengthened (e.g. the entire month of July 1964 was dedicated to the New American Cinema; three One-Man shows and a recent-works group show). Second, in April, an entirely new policy of programming took shape: *I Am a Fugitive from a Chain Gang* with *Peyote Queen*; *The Last Ten Days* with *Lonely Boy*. This attitude may seem superficial and merely cute, but there's a deeper level of pertinence which the poem the juxtaposed titles make. New superimposed on old. Old question / new answer (answers, by the way, implying future questions ad infinitum). This orientation taken to its most highly expressed (right now) degree would make for the following hypothetical example:

> First stage: *Swing Time* (Stevens, 1936): highest physical ecstasy, song & dance team, sexual love.
>
> 2nd stage: *Monkey Business* (Hawks, 1952): initiation to higher truth, LSD transition, emotional upheaval etc.
>
> 3rd stage: *Ordet* (Dreyer, 1955): the breakthru to truth-value w/in spiritual reality; unveiling the higher man, i.e. first stage on a reintegrated physical/spiritual scale, i.e. the process, once the initial trilogy is set up, is infinity. Each 3rd stage being 1st for a new series etc. etc. (N.B. At MRM the above hypothetical schema would fit into consecutive Saturday midnight screenings, as set up now.)

Besides the commitment to creative contemporary film-makers, which has been met every single week without exception to my knowledge in the close-to-a-year that MRM has been in operation; and the feeble, faltering attempt on my part to make social-psychological-artistic comment via juxtaposition of seemingly diverse film traditions (which, to pay my debts, I learned from the old Charles Theatre on NY's Lower East Side in the early '60s – and which I call "dynamic" programing, i.e. deliberate clash of two strong film elements, say *The Gunfighter* and *Ordet*. N.B. anyone programing film creatively owes a lot not only to the old Charles but also to Dan Talbot's pioneering New Yorker), there is a third way of programing, one which I haven't implemented yet. This is what I call "analytic" programing. This type of programing would, because of MRM's epistemological commitments, deal with subjects usually tabooed – or when dealt with at all, as for instance in the British Film Institute's intelligent series, dealt with a kind of academic-aesthetic paternalism which robs these often wild films of their real content: as blasters of the traditional mores – and I mean of our time, not some, say, mythological Germany of the '20s.

To give a specific, tho thus far unrealized example (N.B. I hope to show a series with this same spirit in October/November 1964): CRIME SERIES: Losey's *Concrete Jungle*; a B sleeper which Ken Anger suggested, *Gun Crazy*; Welles's *Lady From Shanghai*; another sleeper *The Sniper*; Bresson's great *Pickpocket*; Cagney as *Public Enemy*; Nick Ray's *Party Girl*; Susan Hayward in *I Want To Live* &c (each film, not the words of its title, would be a Word in an Infinite Film Sentence ... series implies infinity.)

Other series could revolve, just as loosely, i.e. imaginatively (and legally), around HOMOSEXUALITY, INCEST, MADNESS, THE NEGRO, &c. The point being not that these (say the above) films aren't shown, but that they are never shown together as a conscious attempt to pry loose the accepted (i.e. cancerous) social mores of our time via the lever of rational intensity. Films for these series would be picked with an eye for those which criticize the suppressed societal impulses. Works of men as diverse as Tod Browning (*Freaks*), Michael Powell (*Peeping Tom*), and Erich von Stroheim (*Greed*) – all three shown at MRM during the last year tho not in a shared context – would be combined for one psychological-pedagogical[1] impact. (And, of course, the "dynamic" programing could be combined with "analytic" programing. In the most extreme case: say you have three films which elucidate a theme and which "dynamically" make a progression. The most radical way of dealing with these films, it seems to me now, would be to advertise all three for one night. Then, before the screening, regard *all three as one film, which the very process of montage allows us to do*[2] – and cut the films, at random, into one new film omitting nothing of the original footage, allowing oneself complete freedom otherwise, i.e. sections run backward, upside-down, etc. The possibilities are endless … possibilities always are.)

Three addenda of method, not fitting in any particular place in the logic of this essay, i.e. within the context of the three ways aforementioned.

A. *Theatre in Cinema.* An example will suffice to outline the rich potential in this area. (N.B. mine is a rather formal example: according to Jonas Mekas & others, the New York City area, traditionally the most progressive in the country, has already had happenings involving three or more projectors going on opposite walls simultaneously &/or superimposed, integrated with spontaneous Song, Dance, Poetry etc. etc. Also, I believe, experiments of this type have begun in the Bay Area. As far as I know nothing of this type has occurred in Hollywood. The old dichotomy of Entertainer/Spectator breaks down – everyone is a Participant, relating to the event spontaneously as re-creation.) To get back to a realistic example of what might take place at the Cinema Theater (present H.Q. for MRM): there are a couple of mid-career Hitchcocks which depict a scene wherein a killer escapes into a moviehouse chased by the police. On the screen inside the darkened moviehouse we see a screen version of another killer being shot at by cops. (i.e., a movie-within-a-movie.) Then the first killer begins to get shot at also: Hitchcock's irony is displayed. – Our part in it? We add a third dimension to this already double Illusion/Reality: reality. An actor, sitting in the front row of the Cinema Theater, nervous etc. would jump up, shout etc. etc. – all this should be spontaneous – as two or three "cops" run down the aisle toward him. Gunplay, blanks, could be exchanged & the "killer" runs out of the theatre followed by the "cops". All this, of course, without preparing the audience beforehand, tho with normal pre-cautions for calming them afterwards – just as tho the "real" event had occurred. The exchange need last no longer than twenty seconds (the time the Hitchcock scene lasts on the screen). No explanation need nor should be given. (I am indebted to the Pirandello-minded Fred Engelberg for the above suggestion, tho, of course, its present form and description are on my own.)

B. *Making Movies.* In one sense the extreme example cited above re synthesis of "dynamic" and "analytic" programing – i.e. cutting three films as one – covers this category. I see the trailer for *Children of Paradise* made by Lewis Teague (deriving fairly obviously from avant-garde films shown at MRM) as another example of this category. My refusal to show the last five minutes of *The Invasion of the Body Snatchers* was in a way the creating of a new film, an act of montage. Many people objected to my tampering with another man's work of art. It seems to be a question of how long the cut is, of the context, in determining whether such "tampering" is acceptable or not (e.g. excerpts from *Metropolis* in *Paris Belongs To Us*; from *Passion of Joan of Arc* in *Vivre Sa Vie.*) I regard all footage, raw or developed, as raw footage. It all is. Ultimately, reality can be considered as a Movie we, all of us, Edit. (For the author's further views on the role of the Film Society, of a more metaphysical bent, see "Are Movies Junk", in a recent issue of *Film Culture.*)

Most recently MRM has begun a series of "educational" films and, inspired by Jonas Mekas, *A Film Magazine of The Arts*, Los Angeles Edition. More projects of this kind are in the works and forthcoming.

Obviously the possibilities in the area of Making Movies can only be suggested. But then this entire essay is merely intended as a provocative outline.

C. *One-Man Shows.* The author has a particular bias for this type of programing and it is not accidental that art gallery terminology slips into this discussion. One-Man Shows planned for the near-future include: Andy Warhol; Bruce Baillie; Larry Jordan; James Broughton; Kenneth Anger. The author began this kind of programing (for himself, it has, of course been done many many times in the past) with the Classic avant-garde series at the Westside Jewish Community Center (L.A.) in the summer of 1963 with a One-Man Show of Curtis Harrington's work. The overview and insight proved valuable, therefore my bias for it.

(N.B. as was mentioned above, a recent-works Group Show (NAC) was held at MRM 25 July. Filmmakers are artists and should be treated as such. The full implications of that remark lie outside the scope of this article; but would involve considering The 8mm Revolution, fostered by Stan Brakhage & preached by Jonas Mekas in a famous manifesto in the *Village Voice.*)

Battle summary

To sum up what we have: one, commitment to avant-garde; two, tactical week-by-week programs – "dynamics"; and strategic fully-structured film statements (collages?) (Crime etc.) and all three – Father, Son, Holy Ghost – superimposed, interrelated with ABC addendum.

MRM, a society, depends on mutual empathication between (your) audience – soul and (my) (in the same sense used above) editor-soul.

As we move into the era of new Film-Masters (or Wallace B[erman]'s term: "heavyweights") we simultaneously move into the era of Soul Movies. It is not financial support MRM needs (that we, thanx to you, already have) – but what I might call "soulful support". If the evocation of new forms does not take place within MRM, either you, the audience will cease to attend (or at least that part of you which I love and serve), or more likely, my position being more individually sensitive, I'll lose interest (not a veiled threat, an objectively logical proposition.) Discussing the terms of that equation is what this essay is all about.

– OR, if all life's a movie, what happens when the projector goes off?

John Fles, Hollywood, 4 July 1964

Appendix

Paul Beattie. *L^3*

Talk of proximity to the Orient. Talk of Mountain Men with shaggy beard and quiet pale blue eyes. So this film contains silence. Great spaces like California sunsets, slow against the Pacific; also the joy of running down Fillmore St. with the poets. Visages appear smiling with cosmic wisdom. George Herms draws the bow and becomes The Hunter. White markings on his face I found on mine a thousand years ago. As if here, or in the woods at Healdsburg, one cd accumulate images with quiet dexterity, like a medieval artisan. Yet the work was, to some extent, mocked. It is difficult to withstand such simplicity. Hard for the audience, coming from their lives, living in their skins, not to cry out. Because to descend into Jack Smith's Inferno is easy (the inner wicked smile); but the small stream of Paul's paradise makes for restlessness, makes us see ourselves as we are. Not the epic altering of vision, but working with some force particularly of the West, we're let into a private arcady. Paul's naiveté (from eyes-just-born) is his willingness to share, to extend, this particular universe in the way he does. The water of the unknown lake. The mystic family: the wife in the bower garlanded by her lover-husband: and the children! The final fadeout in the canoe... . This requires a tenacity, a relaxed but muscular laying down, one beside the other, of images actually seen (in dreams, behind grass, in "real" life, in film), without artificial conventions. This is the art of the Country (tho The City appears also; as it does in Murnau's *Sunrise*). This is the art in which the sounds heard are those the artist plays for himself as he works on the film. This is the film in which friends, those whom one loves, appear – to smile, or to clasp something to themselves, or to run down streets. And because Time has been left out of consideration (the spectator operates his own) the film moves into a simple green world that those who love hills know. And the "L" of the title becomes initial of the Word which may not be uttered.

Notes & afterthoughts

1. Having summarily disposed of two of America's most brilliant film-makers,

let me add: I had to sacrifice a richer appreciation of Jack Smith and Gregory Markopoulos for a more inhuman point: bringing film history up to date. I hope thru out I also implied the simple usefulness of the labels I chose: they're too clumsy (& wd be pointless) for precise critical description.

2. The Quantum Theory. "It is though an automobile, moving at an average rate of thirty miles an hour along a road, did not traverse the road continuously; but appeared successively at the successive milestones, remaining for two minutes at each milestone."

Alfred North Whitehead, *Science & The Modern World*, 39

3. Wilhelm Reich's *Cosmic Superimposition.*

4. "Some filmmakers like myself, are working toward "root" hip-mature spiritual content – hold us close – working hard!!

Re. Theater in Cinema.

For Christ sake John don't get caught up in the "show biz" "event" bag – If there isn't *some* ironclad vessel or fort of the opening into the outside world type – for the true *artist* (as opposed to those who shock-twist-smile-and split), then we'll lose the central committee." P.B.

(We'd've liked to rewrite the whole Th. in Cinema section in the light of above comment. I decided maintaining the original breath-rhythm-structure integrity more important than shifting the "meaning" of a single section.)

Notes

1. From the Greek, *pais*, child; and *agein*, to lead. (JF)
2. c.f. Burroughs's Cut-Up *Method in Minutes To Go* & *The Exterminator* passim: "Old Words Keep You In Old Word Slots. Cut Your Way Out". (JF)
3. Paul Beattie had published a collection of Fles's poems. He also made 8 mm films, including one titled *L*.

10 Underground Movies Rise to the Surface

Kevin Thomas*

The presentation of Andy Warhol's *The Chelsea Girls* at the Cinema Theater marks the surfacing of underground films in Los Angeles. For over three years this theater has shown much of this so-called New American Cinema at its Movies 'Round Midnight programs every Saturday, and some of it has been seen at the Cinematheque 16 since it opened on the Sunset Strip last June. But never before has such a film been accessible in a regular art theater run.

Not all of Bergman, Fellini, Antonioni, or even Resnais will prepare audiences for *The Chelsea Girls.* A kind of contemporary Dante's *Inferno*, it consists of eight reels of 16mm film, three of which are in color. Even though two reels are projected simultaneously, the film lasts three hours and twenty minutes.

Each section deals with people who supposedly live in Greenwich Village's venerable Hotel Chelsea, and everyone seems either drug-addicted or sexually deviated or both. They are given parts to act out, but Warhol's busy camera sticks to them until they start revealing themselves in all their self-indulgent misery. Virtually nothing is left to the imagination – visually and especially verbally.

* Thomas's account of underground film's public emergence was first published in the *Los Angeles Times*, 26 March 1967, Calendar section, 7. It contained a sidebar by Jonas Mekas, "A Language All Their Own", describing the even greater popularity of underground films in New York: "Four years ago nobody wanted to show underground movies... . Today, in New York, there are three theaters screening nothing but underground movies. We are an economic reality." Thomas began reviewing for the *Times* in 1962 and was on-staff there for over forty years, consistently publicizing avant-garde film screenings at the Cinematheque 16, the Cinema Theater, the Theatre Vanguard, and other venues. As early as 1964, he gave a very favorable account of two seminal 1963 films, Adolfas Mekas's *Hallelujah the Hills* and Kenneth Anger's *Scorpio Rising* ("*Hallelujah the Hills*: Hilarious, Crazy Film", *Los Angeles Times*, 5 March 1964, C9). He was not always sympathetic, and in a review of what he called "'Phreaky Philms' From Underground" by Storm de Hirsch and others, for example, he argued that "at their pretentious worst, there is nothing so boring as underground movies" (*Los Angeles Times*, 19 July 1968, E 12). But generally his intelligent and discriminating accounts of both US avant-garde and European art films formed an invaluable mainstream counterpoint to Gene Youngblood's more rhapsodic writing in the *Los Angeles Free Press.*

To Mike Getz, the Cinema's departing manager, what is important about *The Chelsea Girls* and any other underground film is not how you react but that you react. He is leaving Los Angeles to introduce Movies 'Round Midnight in theaters in San Diego; Kansas City, Mo.; Champaign, Ill.; Cleveland, and New Orleans. Before taking off, however, he has set up a monthly regular schedule of underground films (and famed screen classics like *The Cabinet of Dr. Caligari*) at the Art Center College of Design, 5353 W. 3rd St., starting Friday at 8:30 p.m. And, of course, Movies 'Round Midnight will continue at the Cinema.

"The underground film-maker's value to society is not yet recognized", says Getz. "He breaks down certain cliché experiences having to do with going to the movies. No matter what your response is, you will find some mystery in it – something completely different from your reaction to a Hollywood movie or even a foreign film. If you're bored you'll find it a different kind of boredom."

Both Getz and Lewis Teague, manager of the Cinematheque 16, report that Los Angeles is not yet a center of underground film-making like New York or San Francisco. Both cite the little-known James Whitney, creator of *Lapis*, as perhaps the outstanding local underground film-maker.

However, those who have the strength and interest to watch movies from 1 a.m. to 3 or 4 a.m. Sunday morning at the Cinema have seen such outstanding films as Stan Brakhage's *Window Water Baby Moving* or Gregory Markopoulos's *Twice a Man*, both beautiful and evocative in their abstractness – the first celebrating the miracle of birth, the second a quest for sexual identity.

Besides Warhol, the best-known underground film-maker is Kenneth Anger. When Getz premiered Anger's *Scorpio Rising* it brought out the law, but it was subsequently declared not obscene in court. Now Teague is currently reviving it along with Anger's uncompleted *Kustom Kar Kommandos, Inauguration of the Pleasure Dome, Fireworks*, and *Eaux d'Artifice*.

Although homosexuality is a major motif in the movies of both Anger and Warhol, their work is thoroughly dissimilar. Anger is a surrealistic stylist in the tradition of Cocteau, while Warhol is simply anti-style.

As campy and pretentious as *Inauguration of the Pleasure Dome* often seems, with its bizarre creatures wandering around in a kind of drugged paradise, it nonetheless has moments of kaleidoscopic beauty and demonstrates Anger's ability to create myriad effects out of almost nothing. A superb colorist, he also counterpoints sound and image for maximum aesthetic and emotional impact in all his films.

His *Scorpio Rising* remains the best of his movies now at the Cinematheque.

Starting from the basic situation of a motorcyclist preparing for a run that will cost him his life, Anger makes this leathered and chained young man the center of a complex homosexual fantasy through a remarkably manipulated montage of Nazi black mass ceremonies, a homosexual orgy and a church film depicting Jesus's progress to the Cross. Far from being either obscene or blasphemous, *Scorpio Rising* indelibly identifies homosexual desires with a wish for death and destruction.

Ultimately, what is important about the emergence of underground movies is their challenge to our conceptions of what we think film art consists of. Whether confusing, pornographic, or just plain boring, they make us aware in new ways of the possibilities of a medium whose potential for art and communication still has scarcely been tapped.

11 Students Reflect Future of Cinema

Gene Youngblood*

Winners of the Third National Student Film Festival were announced last Sunday at UCLA following a two-day orgy of finalists from 152 entries and thirty-seven universities and colleges.

First prizes of $500 were awarded in four categories: dramatic, experimental, animation, documentary. Second prizes and honorable mentions also were designated in each classification.

The University of Southern California (at last) won two well-deserved first prizes. The other two were shared by UCLA and the University of Iowa. Three second prizes went to UCLA; the fourth was claimed by Boston University.

First prize winners were: *THX-1138-4EB* (dramatic, George Lucas, USC); *Cut* (experimental, Chris Parker, University of Iowa); *Marcello, I'm So Bored* (animation, John Milius, USC), and *Keinholz on Exhibit* (documentary, June Steel, UCLA).

Second prize winners were *A Question of Color* (dramatic, Richard Bartlett, Boston University); *Now That the Buffalo's Gone* (experimental, Burton C. Gershfield, UCLA); *An Idea* (animation, Walton White, UCLA), and *The Latter Day* (documentary, Donald MacDonald, UCLA).

Due largely to the influence of the UCLA cinema department, the National

* First published in the *Los Angeles Free Press*, 26 January 1968, 9. Several paragraphs have been omitted. A very similar report on the Festival containing accounts of the same films also appeared a week later in *Time*; see, George W. Black in "Trends: Celluloid Goes To School", 2 February 1968, 50–51. Gene Youngblood began his coverage of experimental film in the *Los Angeles Herald-Examiner* in 1966; moving to the *Free Press* in January 1967, he became one of the counterculture cinema's most utopian voices, as instanced in his proposal here that "viewing student films is like participating in a revolution". Many of his columns were collected in the enormously influential *Expanded Cinema* (New York: Dutton, 1970).

Student Film Festival has become a major factor in the status and growth of American cinema.

Prof. Colin Young, head of the UCLA Theatre Arts Department, noted jestfully in some introductory remarks that, "Since we're honoring 1967 films in 1968, thereby approximating the Academy Awards, we've gone professional".

Those who have followed the progress of student films over the last few years know how professional a so-called "student" movie can be. More often than not, I feel, the alleged "professionals" of Hollywood have much to learn from the students.

Stanley Kramer – who needs to go back to school – once told his UCLA film class that he envied their "freedom to do anything they wanted".

If Mr. Kramer's millions haven't bought him freedom, nothing will, because obviously he doesn't have the desire. And that, more than anything else, is what glows like fire in every frame of student film, no matter how crude or "unprofessional": love of cinema and a healthy irreverence toward archaic traditions.

Student films are living examples of the generation gap that exists between the industry and the public: the films that come out of these young people's minds are not the films they were raised on. And the success – both artistic and commercial – which they constantly demonstrate has had profound effect on the motion picture establishment in this country.

You don't argue, for instance, with the box office cash totals enjoyed by the Los Feliz Theater when the UCLA "Changes" program played two very successful weeks there recently.

I have noted that viewing student films is like participating in a revolution. It is a revolution far more significant than mere progress of an art. It is a revolution in the entire concept and use of the most powerful form of artistic communication in the history of civilization.

For these reasons I would rather see a student film or a so-called "underground" film than a product of the Hollywood-influenced establishment. And for these reasons I thoroughly enjoyed the program of festival winners, though I have several reservations and regrets.

My chief objection is to the selection of Chris Parker's *Cut* over Burt Gershfield's *Now That the Buffalo's Gone* as first prize winner in the experimental category. (My sentiments were echoed by the audience, who hissed when the announcement was made. Gershfield got the biggest hand of the evening.)

I do not understand what "experimental" means. Does it mean unusual? Does it mean confusing? Does it mean non-dramatic? Or does it mean attempting something of which the results are unknown?

And cannot experimental also be dramatic? Doesn't experiment refer exclusively to technique rather than content? In my estimation, *Buffalo* is every bit as dramatic as *THX-1138-4ED*, the first prize winner in the dramatic category. (I'm glad I didn't have to choose between them.)

Indeed, *THX* seemed to me just as experimental as *Buffalo*, if one must use that term at all. Experiment usually connotes an unsure hand, blind groping, but I'm sure Gershfield and Lucas knew exactly what they were doing – more, in fact, than did June Steel, whose documentary *Keinholz on Exhibit* is the kind of film based on chance and improvisation.

Buffalo has been shown so often around Los Angeles that there's no need to go into it deeply now. Briefly, it's a poetic evocation of the death of the American Indian culture through color stroboscopic printing of newsreel footage and western movies. The result is as beautiful and "dramatic" a film as one is likely to see outside traditional literary narrative forms.

Chris Parker's *Cut*, however, is what I call auto-cinema, or self-reflective cinema in the style of *Persona* or Stanton Kaye's *Georg*. A young filmmaker makes a film-within-his-film and muses, all the while, on the meaning of "reality" in the cinema and the various "moral" implications of a cut here, a two-image super there.

There is an extraordinary sequence involving double exposure with delayed simultaneous dialogue: the same man's face is seen in double exposure; one image begins talking, and a few seconds later the other image begins the same speech. The images draw closer together, finally merging, while the two voice tracks become increasingly synchronous ultimately, only one voice.

Outside of that rather extraneous innovation, *Cut* is tedious and overlong, and not half as effective as the earlier *Georg* in the haunting technique of self-reflective cinema.

THX deserves its first prize in the dramatic category. It is a startling evocation of a sterile, computerized future world, in which one man's escape from a maze of subterranean porcelain labyrinths is viewed as through TV monitors.

George Lucas (who now is a production assistant at Warner Brothers-Seven Arts) has created a chilling, poetic and ultimately melancholy future civilization with great economy of style and technique, conjuring up swift visions of terror as did Chris Marker in *La Jetée* (which Lucas tells me he has not seen).

Lucas's use of reflections in glass, endless corridors, and gothic perspectives is as effective as Godard's *Alphaville* or Orson Welles's *The Trial.* And his choice of an organ chorale with the Yardbirds' "Still I'm Sad" is a masterstroke.

...

Marcello, I'm So Bored by USC's John Milius, was a natural winner. It is a devastatingly satirical and highly stylistic collage of the pop scene from the *Vogue* Magazine-Daisy Club set to the Avalon Ballroom and Hell's Angels.

The technique is superimposition with minimal animation. The visual style is out of *Vogue*, yet with the distinctive designs of Richard Poole and the vibrant colors of De Stael. The fragmented dialogue is acutely perfect.

Out of the Beatles' "Taxman", animation becomes live action in a parody of Antonioni's *La Notte*. Shot in color negative, like Gershfield's *Buffalo*, a man and a woman are driving in an open sports car. The car stops, the woman lights a cigarette and announces: "Marcello, I'm so bored". But the audience wasn't.

12 Woman as Ethnographic Film Maker

Chick Strand[*]

I have never really thought of myself as a "woman in film" ... as opposite from "men in film" ... I am a filmmaker (although there certainly seem to be many more men in film than women). I am not so stupid as not to see that there are differences in approach, perceptions, values, motivations, and that these differences stem from the way our culture defines men and women and from the way that we are taught to see ourselves and as men see us. The questions and ways to find answers as to what is womanness underneath all of the cultural definitions are far too complicated and interrelated to have any overt meaning during the act of creativity (at least for me). I do it ... I make the film ... and of course, all the things involved in our concepts of woman and reactions to being a woman come into play in what I do, but I don't stop to analyze my motivations. Neither am I careful to present my films or the women in them in any special light, or with any social significance or in any special manner ... except that it's all special in that it comes from me, a woman. I do it as I feel it. I am well aware that my own perceptions and the presentations of them contain many ambiguities which coincide with the difficulties of understanding what has gone on and is going on between men and women (I am talking about the new awareness) in our society. I am simply not an analytical person and have no real interest in sorting things out for the world at large through my films. But there are women who are good at it and should make coherent statements, define the general problems and suggest solutions through their work.

There is a type of filmmaking in which I think women have an *obligation* to try and present women in a more straightforward manner, and this is in the area of ethnographic film. Information gathering and methodology have already been

* First published in the *Journal of the University Film Association* 26, 1–2 (1974): 16.

Figure 9. Chick Strand.

established in anthropology, and these methods can at least be partially fitted into ethnographic filmmaking. Most anthropologists are male and they consistently manage to make films about males, overemphasizing the male roles and leaving the women as *secondary* role players. Only rarely have women been the "stars" of ethnographic films. I think that this is not only because men don't think about making films about the women but also that men believe that women *do* have a secondary place (after all, what is more important, killing each other off or socializing the children?) and because males have a great problem in relating well to women of the culture. Too often field work about women is left to the anthropologist's wife (who is playing a secondary role to her husband's field work) or to female graduate students. Times are changing. Many gifted women anthropologists are working in the field, writing ethnographics, publishing them and concentrating on the women in the cultures but too few of them are making good films or allowing women filmmakers to come with them to make films.

The first people I make friends with in another culture are the women because I am a woman and because I have had similar experiences. Even working with very remote cultures, women only have to look at each other and nod, or make a small gesture, while admiring a new born child or talking about work or men, to know, without words, about the experience. We feel sisterhood, a feeling of shared experience, shared knowledge, and shared intuition (you cannot use that word in male-oriented anthropology) that males can never feel between themselves. No man can make a film about women in another culture if he wants to make a credible film, simply because the communication that he can never know is beyond a "scientific " approach. What women anthropologists and filmmakers can do is to present the women of the new culture by using the established ways of information gathering and presentation plus a translation of this shared sisterhood.

I made a film about two women of different cultures in an acculturation situation. I knew that no matter how careful I was, there was no way for me to keep myself out of it. If I set up the camera and merely pushed the trigger until I ran out of film, it was still subjective. When, during twenty-four hours, or a week, or a year should one push the trigger? All is arbitrary, all is random, all is culturally defined. So one can be left with very little to go on. There is no way at all for ethnographic films to be objective. There merely are degrees of subjectivity. So I feel that it makes sense for women to offer their special communication in the form of the ethnographic film. There is no way that an ethnographic film can replace or substitute for the written ethnography. The film should be a complement to the written work. It is a means to get into other perspectives of the culture, to meet them, and to identify with them as fellow human beings.

13 *Mouse Enigma: Auto-History of a Film Person*

The Clear Light

777

Peter Mays*

SEEING IS BELEAVING

Chapter One: Vision

The film person was urged into being at the prompting of Jean Cocteau.

Created for him such a compelling experience out of inexpensive ordinary objects that he decided to go into the business himself. He read and discovered to his astonishment that there were *cuts* in films! A person leaping off the top of a building, followed by, say, a shot of a taxi veering and the passenger looking up aghast, followed by a shot of the person's body falling on pavement, looked like he jumped to his death. The nothingness of the cut nonetheless creates an invisible meaning believed but not seen on the screen.

My father was an avid cinematographer of his family, especially his children who were forever growing and disappearing. The record for both my sister and me is extensive, especially in the beginning, in stills and Christmas or Birthday movies made with a rented 8mm camera, processed by Kodachrome and shown on a

* Peter Mays was one of the most active late-sixties underground filmmakers in Los Angeles; his film work may be accessed at http://www.petermaysfilms.com. He wrote *Mouse Enigma* around 1978–79 at the Moonfire Inn in Topanga. This is a very slightly edited transcription of the previously unpublished typescript; it silently omits several footnotes and numerous indications of proposed illustrations.

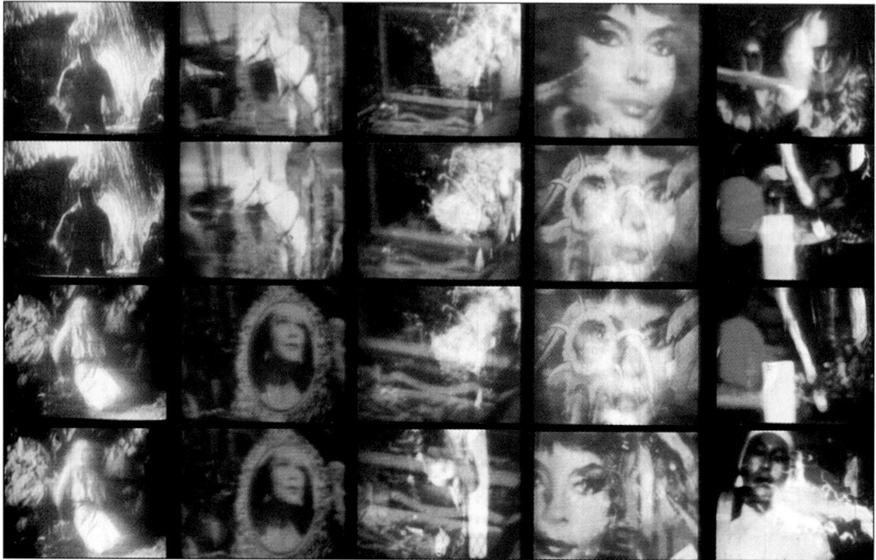

Figure 10. Peter Mays, filmstrip, *Death of the Gorilla.*

rented projector until I was 8 and was given a Kodascope projector with variable speed. I was given several movies as well: a cowboy mob movie called *Rustlers of Dry Gulch*, a Simple Simon fair cartoon, and a Mother Goose and the Old Shoe cartoon.

In the end, my father's home movies were all magic: a family member walking along suddenly changed into another family member, then another, like the four footsteps of Maya in *Meshes of the Afternoon.*

So I recut the cowboy movie to suggest much greater violence and movement.

At UCLA in 1958 I attended a panel discussion about censorship and the arts involving Stanley Fleishman, fresh from a successful defense of the Coronet Theatre on a pornography bust. Raymond Rohauer, owner of the theatre, repeated the deleted and I soon saw: *Fireworks* (Anger), *Plague Summer* (Anderson), *Voices* (Schmidt), and *Closed Vision* (Marc'o). (Anger was seventeen when he made the film, and I was eighteen when I viewed it. It was made in 1947, the year Aleister Crowley died.) For many years I agreed with the prosecutor that the brutality in *Fireworks* was far too horrible and hurt the viewer. (I had to close my eyes.) *Closed Vision* was a really beautiful beach reverie with an adolescent blonde girl with black bathing suit, sand burials, and unrealistically long funeral processions fending off dissonant sandsations: an existential film like *Orpheus*, but more charnel and morbid.

Of course I wanted mystery and shadows, veiling and dimly suggested things such that smoky dancing flicker lights on water became fire in dark flashing sea of disengagement from belief. Dream confusions. Tension and excitement caused by viewing the unknown. Projecting the film on a mirror in a dark summer room, the highlights swam across the distorted ceiling like white leaves or fish. Only black and white left enough to the imagination, eerie and incomplete, vast and suggestive. So I worked for several years on machinery to develop and print 8mm b/w since no lab would. Superior Bulk Film Co. of Chicago supplied the stock. And with my own contact printer, I could do much more than a commercial lab in hand-fading the lamp to create lightning effects, mastering negs on pos and reprinting on other action to create impossible metaphors on vision.

Finally, at the beginning of a long sticky summer lonely vacation I was stuck with plenty of equipment and no ideas. Possibly I should make an exercise film to warm up, on Durer's woodcuts of the Apocalypse? Then I thought to make the Apocalypse itself. A stream of surrealist imagery began to flow thru me, crazed poems of bees and upside down trees and rushes thru grass and door knobs and the phone on wet newspapers, shadow of feet below door, which coalesced into three dream journeys beyond the door. I remember the knob well. By twisting it, I gained entrance to my closet, with its slanting roof and attic door into another much larger floorless attic, and beyond it the void of the garage. I stayed in the first closet for hours, developing cramps and asthma and a white chemical pallor. I could write, shoot, print, edit, and project, all at home where I was fed regularly and slept warmly. (Mouse fantasy.) I was obliged to play many roles, giving the film a narcissistic quality like early Anger, Brakhage, and Deren, suggesting the same restraint as possibly a child would feel and develop into without playmates.

As I'm flashing now I see how *Night* and *Day*[1] conclude the human being, the dream self and the awakened one. I intended the work as a put-down of Christianity by showing what the Bible says, as brutal as bathing in blood. The film is quite linear and unrelieved. A trance state is attempted by flickering or wavering lights and shapes, culminating in a long rising on the plains to the source of light and dark, the cross becomes a sword and brutally ravages the undertaker, myself, and others, by striking light bulbs and breaking off bleeding branches. Blood came from everywhere. (See red bleeding mirror after the white orgasm in *Sister* [*Midnight*]). I was horribly mutilated by Christ, and my spirit passed into his as the shadow hand passed down the flapping leaves of some great book, burying all in a ghostly ordeal I now dimly perceive as an enactment ruse to shuck off the Christian ear and regain entrance to the mould. A vision on acid in 1968 said the *Day* fire and sword cut to water was castration, and the earlier *Night* cycles enacted by myself, mother, and sister (my father wielded the sword in *Day*) had a Freudian interpretation involving the actual family members. I certainly had no knowledge of this at the time.

Vision is unquestionably the book of my life, foretelling as forgiving as re-embered. (The unconscious has many levels.) I loved cutting and hated printing it. Like Griffith, it is structured by faster and faster cuts of parallel actions. Rather than showing something as an element in a story, one projected something into the room to affect the space there. A vague sense of sculpture finally allows the viewer, a mystic in his own right, to come forth unabashed.

Vision had one public screening at UCLA and nearly caused a riot. The audience of seventy-five to a hundred were aroused to a frenzy of howling catcalls, whistling, and stamping of feet by the second reel when they thought the 8mm film had ended with the first reel. Theater Arts students, who were just beginning to accept the innovations of *Citizen Kane* at that time, led in the derision. I felt like I was being crucified since it was I on the screen nearly nude, revealed, etc. *Vision* has never been seen since. It may be the last and most synthetic of the Pacific Coast mystery elemental unreal mirror knife films as beckoned in by Deren and Anger and then banished by them for greater repast. P. Adams Sitney attempts to resurrect and explain the trance film in his tomb *Visionary Film*, but he only reflects the ghost of a trance.

Chapter Two: The One Bedroom ApartmenT

I also abandoned "that" kind of film, and strode with great relief to a second, 16mm film, much simpler and the opposite in every way to my absolutist epic. To *Nuit* I opposed *Hadit.* Instead of a minimal cinema suggesting vastness, I wanted maximal coverage of something very simple. I chose, historically accurate to the smallest detail, allowing, if need be, for microscopic examination, the one bedroom apartment I was living in.

Meanwhile I had built a 16mm drum (motorized) and tank to deliver 400-foot rolls of film, with drying rack above. A 19th century machine for a 20th century medium. I also constructed a 16mm printer centered around the gate and movement of a Cine Kodak magazine, a mistake since the gate is curved, and bipacked films (original and print stock), having slightly different radii, are offset at the gate, moving the frameline beyond the projectable acceptable.

Catapult and his jockey kid brother Fur had left the apartment for the parental home in Anaheim, and I had the museum piece to myself. My camera, then as now, was a Pathé reflex with three lenses, inc. f.95 Angenieux 25mm. Bill Bishop did the lighting. Three friends acted. No sound. Man doing dishes, girl reading sex manual. Something lacking. Black friend interrupts, introducing party space and drunkenness. Man chases girl outside into nearby wooded area, but he can't keep up with her. In the end she sees a vision of him as effeminate and faints. An enormous number of shots covered the simplest bourgeois action in infinitesimal detail cut very quickly, giving the film an omniscient present sense of limitation and social immobility. The film is nonetheless quite vulnerable. Classical music accompanied this short story, which has never been composite printed.

Chapter Three: Stream

So I married the girl and went to the mountains in the summer. I planned to open a 16mm store theater in the fall. Before leaving the city I bought my second issue of *Film Culture*, which seemed to be taking a pro-experimental stance, as compared with the derision that greeted the avant-garde from most film quarterlies. But it was Andrew Sarris's issue on the *auteur* directors, *The American Cinema* (=Hollywood!?!), and in the woods I began to like Sarris's Gnostic stance, and the funny names, like Douglas Sirk or Roland Kirk. We lived in a log cabin in a hot valley in the Sierras, and there was this cool wicked stream nearby, very dark and erotic below, harsher and more violent and clearer above. The amount of changes the stream went thru in the mile or so we knew of it inspired me to a by now insane cutting urge, frantic, supercinema increase in takes, to fulfill myself cheaply by destroying my elitist art sensibility on the rocks and little wild flowers of organic bedlam, discovering shot after shot of terrific compositions and obliterating my narrow aestheticism in the miasmal choking infinity of nature. If I kept the takes under one second, I could get 300–500 per roll. (8mm Kodachrome II, color, the only film available.) I shot about forty rolls, all of which were slightly underexposed, but a lot of the footage was water, incredible and darkly lush and shining.

When wifey-pooh and I got back to big city and could at long last eat ice cream and suck cokes and watch TV, I experienced my first feature from the *auteur* book, which was soon to be many pages long and a vast slippery education for the initiate who can speak without words but in experience itself, and that greater suggestion of depth like the sea, mother lapping among the pinnacles and stubby rock peninsula of the editor's prevision: I speak of darkling *mise-en-scène*, cult mystery movie language of moving camera and light to unfold, uncreased, the meaning in things.

The next issue of *Film Culture* opened my eyes to The New American Cinema: a *politique des artistes* hovering at the edge of a new kind of epic, giant offspring of the film poem of the past, a narrative wedding of mythology and the present. This took two forms: in New York, costume theater pieces, openly phony but much more lavish, colorful, spectacular, and expressive than the '50s death wish libido poems, acting out suggestive Arabian Nights, flowing rivers of stardust, spangles, royalty, gilded mascara fantasies often shot in two, three, or more super-impositions, often randomly achieved in the camera to add to the accidental luxuriousness. The two classics were Jack Smith's *Flaming Creatures* and Ron Rice's *Chumlum.* A group of zen actors developed, and I suppose some kind of prop depot. These films suggested the dawning of a sexual, sensual revolution in America.

The other form was more difficult. The action portrayed was very simple but archetypal: a man climbing a mountain or a man crossing a river. Thru editing creates diversion into metaphor, into time past and future in the river film, into extended physical and analogical parallels from cosmic to microscopic in the mountain film. Strings of association allowed for an emotional, mind-expanding restructuring of reality, flexing new cinematic muscles of association, breaking the time cramp and setting editing loose to range over the visible world. These films were the first mature works of two of the outstanding film poets of the '50s: Stan Brakhage (*Dog Star Man*) and Gregory Markopoulos (*Twice a Man*).

The third major experimentalist of the '50s, Kenneth Anger, also released in 1963 his magnum opus to date: *Scorpio Rising*, which wedded the new editorial power of analogical statement of Brakhage and Markopoulos, not to a simple action, but to the theatricity of Smith and Rice. The third ingredient in Anger's brew was pop culture, the mass appeal of rock and roll, bikers, comics, etc.

Everyone immediately moved on to bigger, more epic efforts: Smith to *Normal Love*, Rice to *Queen of Sheba Meets the Atom Man*, Anger to *Kustom Kar Kommandos*, Markopoulos to *The Illiac Passion*, and Brakhage to *The Art of Vision*. Only the last two were completed, and *The Art of Vision* was achieved in a flash I suppose: the component rolls of *Dog Star Man* seen in extension. This expansion formula is a repetition of Griffith's *Birth of a Nation* → *Intolerance* and is very hard to bring off, but suggests the NAC directors were discovering a new media. Anger's giant soon became *Lucifer* [*Rising*] and Brakhage's [*Scenes from Under*] *Childhood,* both still incomplete and issued forth in chapters.

The store theater fell thru so I sent my wife to work as a clerk-typist at the UCLA bio-med center, and I finished titles, sound, and publicity to enter *The One Bedroom Apartment* in the 1963 Brussels Sprouts Festival run by entertainer Jacques Ledoux.

Chapter Four: Movies 'Round Midnight

As a device to see NAC work, I began a film society at UCLA [the Art Department Film Society, ADFS] in association with Dr. Raymond Brown, whom I had not known before and who turned out to be a dyed-in-the-wool *auteurist*, researching Allan Dwan's fortuity on late night TV. Thus I studied at first hand prints of *Potemkin*, *Sirius Re-membered*, and *Prelude: Dog Star Man*. Brakhage became an overwhelming influence which was to last several years.

I rejected a couple of films on NAC night, including *Blonde Cobra*, a supposedly Baudelarian film I found spotty. The print was picked up the next morning by a stranger at a glance named John Fles. A film *société* he and Freddie Engelberg began at Mother Neptune's was now operating at Midnight at the Cinema on Western near Sunset. John was playing *Cobra* that night in a NAC comedy bill including *Senseless* and *Lemon Hearts.*

It was the end of the Beat era, and something was cutting loose. Saturday Midnight at the Cinema became a scene in Los Angeles. I remember angular women in boots and torn slips for dresses, under low light frayed sweaters and Salvation Army pumps. Sexuality of the very poor. The beat was thin and bleak, dark and off-beat, mild depression against the prevailing Middle Class, almost all of America. Little symbols of criminality kept alive by craving. That fall Kennedy was assassinated and the Beatles appeared on the Ed Sullivan Show. A big change was beginning in pop music: long-haired (!!!) groups like the Animals and the Rolling Stones were moving in from England, the mother country.

Fles was an *outré* and advanced intelligence with a view toward film as junk, continually nourishing and rewarding. Jewels in the dust of galaxies. Movies 'Round Midnight was a dry eclectic night desert space show for heads, sparrow and wet behind the ears, and thin in velvet and black light. Bruce Lane often accompanied my wife and me to these *soirées*. One viewed movies there at least two or three times removed, distance often giving back their original luster.

A voice on the phone said he had some hot footage he couldn't get processed, and John Fles had noticed my equipment and mentioned it to him. He'd pay. So I met Jerry Katz and printed his first film, 16mm b/w, including a lot of night-city jewel lights shot from a moving car, and Jerry, mighty and agile mating his nude wife, a tiny voluptuous dark-haired girl who danced.

Jerry had been in jail, in the navy, and on the road. He was a beat poet moving westerly into the deeply receded pop pornography school of [Wallace] Berman, [George] Herms, and Ben Ségue. Wallace was the fallen angel of the group, and he had incredible connections with Heaven. He was the dark jazz angel who'd had an assemblage/collage show at a major gallery on La Cienega broken up and burned by the police in 1957 and was now underground publishing *Semina*, private editions of photo/poem rearrangement cards, and printing commercial material on a Varifax machine to duplicate things. He became the house artist for MRM.

Jerry wore black at Midnight and got angry for no reason. He was always ready to fight. He became an older brother to me, the Hamlet/Horatio duo, Batman and Robin. We had long intense conversations; I pretended to like his films and he openly disliked mine. Nevertheless there was a heavy interchange of feeling and tone between us, and while I feared him yet he clearly respected me. He was concerned with the relationship of pop and hip, mainstream and marginalia. *The Bead Game*, Ginsburp and McClure, jazz, Dylan, lipstick, light, fashion, culture, and Amerika.

Now the pop visage of modern painting moved forth from its surface and became camp, leaving behind the mold which became the mere remains of format, minimal or conceptual art, continuing to this day as the art of our time, an obvious suicide. Camp was also born one night at MRM, when Fles, spirited by some imp of perversity showed for the first time in such a context, *Flash Gordon Conquers the Universe.* I remember a din of gasping, yahooing, laughing, screaming, gagging, whistling, and overall noise so loud it was pressure, not sound, for at least five minutes.

Incarnating the emergence of camp from pop, that is, the re-emersion of high art into the mass media, after 150 years of increasing involution (ever since the Revolution) was the immobile disheveled fleshy flaccid features of Andy Warhol. Groove *artiste extraordinaire*, Malthusian non-entity, illusionist of art, silkscreen, he began producing celluloid in the groove year 1963, and lo and behold the underground film was in. *Sleep* (eight hours) required such endurance to view that it acquired immediate acceptance. Each film was one shot only, the cinema of Edison, e.g., *Eat* (half hour), a man (Robert Indiana) eating mushrooms very slowly.

Warhol tied together with an invisible silver linkage of endurance/acceptance the previously separate folds of establishment art, underground film, and the mass media, in which arrangement the least known profited the most.

Brussels rejected me and gave *Flaming Creatures* the *Prix Maudit* after Jonas Mekas projected it in his hotel room night after night until arrested by the Royal Police.

At the First Los Angeles Film-makers Festival, Stanton Kaye's film *Georg* won first prize, Kenneth Anger presiding as judge.[2]

Stan Brakhage was announced as judge for Second LAFF.

I begin editing *Stream.*

Chapter Five: The Early German Gorilla

I started working full-time for TRW Systems as an analog programmer in the Control Systems Section, under Will Hindle. Spring 1964 at UCLA was an unusually comprehensive series of German classics of the '20s that I wanted to see for fatalistic reasons. I illegally pocketed over $500, as most of the films were available from MOMA at a reduced rate for schools and I sold a lot of series cards.

At night I spliced 8 mm frames of wildness. The footage naturally fell into an evolutionary pattern. As in *Vision*, and later in *Tantra, Gorilla II,* and *Sister,* there are almost two equal parts. The film was cut under the mantle of SB but came out more violent, harsh, quick, and glistening. I experimented a lot with $A_1B_1A_2B_2A_3B_3A_4B_4$.....or $A_1B_1A_2B_2C_1A_3B_3A_4B_4C_2$ ... trains of single frames resulting in a flashing continuity of two scenes seen at once, one panning left and one moving up, say. The ending would be a cluster $A_1A_2A_3B_1B_2B_3C_1C_2C_3$ repeated three times with two bridges of darker footage moving thru grass, say. Very percussive, twisting, snorting, slowed, calm, then jumping around again, like the strip of film was being brought to life as a snake.

I created two inches to two feet of river serpent at a session, small scales of color inter-dropping life. Played it on my 8mm Kodascope, which did not scratch the slow moving Kodachrome surface. 2nd LAFF came and went, and I entered the 3rd, with Gregory Markopoulos and Jack Smith judging. They were totally incompetent, and rejected me altogether, and gave first prize to a long educational film about a funeral parlor. Dennis Hopper entered a one shot view of the revolving painted lady with buns on Sunset. Kenneth Anger picketed the theater, claiming he'd been beaten up the preceding weekend in a controversy over ownership of a print of *Inauguration.*

As with Brakhage earlier, I had the ADFS pay Smith and Bones to "lecture". They show up late with Dennis Hopper, who'd had them for dinner. Markopoulos showed several rolls of ECO original from his current heart-throb, *The Illiac Passion*, after the briefest precursory inspection of the projectors metallic gate, and Smith spoke as if a rabbit.

Stream was blown up to 16mm for this and subsequent screenings, from 8mm

Kodachrome II to 16mm ECO (to save the contrast) on a printer built for the occasion.

By running the machine very slowly (unlike a lab, I had plenty of time) the result was quite steady. Even though the print stock was camera original, when vacumated and greased it is projectable. As time wore on I cut more and more of the slow late afternoon dark forest, orange petals of light on deep cold veined rocks. I would of course restore it now. Jerry Katz was the only person who ever liked my "leaf" movie; he liked the black between the leaves.

Chapter Six: Ektachrome Dream

This mother womb film, endless and barely begun open shooting, was a coven for all sorts of shorter bewitchments and sad rainbow dream streets, clouded and becoming, seen in minor mist, timeless key shooting and imposing on, capturing light, single frame, painting light in dark camera obscura. I think the first 16mm color camera roll (100') I shot on softly resolute ECO (7255) was sad winter trees in Sullivan Canyon, off Sunset just before Pacific Palisades. In daylight I could close the Pathé's variable shutter to 1/4 or 1/8, and similarly open the lens (thus decreasing depth of field), rapidly pan the camera and produce pixillation (amid softness). On the Moviescope I opened into hidden dream-seeing into dark holes in nature, getting lost in archetypal world, the forest.

I opened up frames around the house as well, usually at night, producing a Peeping Tom effect. The simple photograph of a window pain was exciting. (This voodoo aspect of photography, to capture feeling, creates a sense of power and vital feedback in the endeavorer.) Moving the camera, shutter open, across a running TV separated the syncs into a hole train of gushing media vomit belched into the room, warm, and tingling with human presence.

Or I played with my feet on the wall, interloping the rubber plug.

I could never really get away from the excessive clarity and overall sense of illumination of ECO. I experimented with matted supers thru different colors, each little scene, of course, in motion.

I began photographing the TV thru one color filter, rewind, then thru another color, again up to fifteen times, being aware of the mix of colors I'd used, say all cool purple, greens, and blues, to which I might add one hot gold-gold-yellow with contrast way up, for sense of highlight to dance on darks below. The randomness of the mix, once captured on film, was often unbelievably beautiful. Getting the developed roll back that night kept me going at TRW during the day.

In many ways *mise-en-scène* was developing me. I set up surreal landscapes in the dark room we lived in, involving my naked wife, barefoot on cold linoleum, a mirror surface beclouded with powder of talc; I projected film on it and her, rustle of copra silk on skin, touched a lot, a pure red light bulb near her lips for inner color.

Sometimes she and I ventured into the woods at night, me with camera and she with car headlight and battery-pack, and together we evoked the softest music movement of revealing imaginable. She moved the light thru the thicket looming up everwinding passageways of branches, and I moved the camera in changing depth of focus and size of field (i.e., .95 lens completely open so very narrow depth of field, me moving this plane in counter movement to Judie's.) Rewind and shoot another, again and again, and you don't know where you are in the cordon of wood and corridor of spider web, all dissolving ... .

The sexual energy implicit in this play activity reached sublimated union between Peter and the World in set-ups like my light showgo and a go go TV go go, and most overtly one Sunday laundry afternoon, when, shaking, I photomeshed my erect penis on the bustling city park, and all its girls and bumpers. I had a strong erotic identification with the exterior skin of automobiles (from reading Joyce as a child no doubt) and more darkly with street lamps at night. I was fascinated by the mercury astral white-purple light cast on surrounding living bushy trees, cold green death stare for anyone to see. By long (two sec.) exposure of each frame I could photograph this peculiarly artificial sensation.

With even longer exposures I made night turn into an unreal day no one ever sees.

Every time it rained, my wife and I went out traveling thru glistening rainbow dream streets, and I sputter-splashed light chisel colors into gaping dark camera, resulting in water flashing moving forward fast trips. Extreme close-ups of red tail-lights refracted in drops and dribbles of windshield dancing and splashing disrobed me. I love it. (Wet dreams.)

Katz was very critical of my delusory sublimation powers, and openly said I should get out on the street if I was going in that direction. Be physical. Jerry's films were even more sublimated than mine, except when photographing his tough beatnik friends making love. Jerry's second film was abstract: long rose and soft reds brightened irregularly by a passing sharp light-shade of crimson yellow and occasionally a cluster of single or triple frames, snatched photographs of trench-coat girl or naked night manikin.

Bruce Lane made a film called *Orange* in super-8 at UCLA about this time, on objects and people colored orange.

Pat O'Neill made his worst film, his second expressing his displeasure with the advertising media, quote a big step for the former design student, called *Dump*, and Bob Abel took a more traditional route, producing a documentary on beer and racing moved into a commercial career with Wolper.

Jerry and his wife move to Topanga, following Berman's move there.

Chapter Seven: The Ape

I have a bingo bongo nature in that I don't want to receive nurture only, but also like putting it back. My defense and vengeance against the machine tit and all the junk crap we've had to sit thru, like commercials and quiz shows, is my boob tube film *Death of the Gorilla*. It's a mow down of the filter trips I trapped late nights, patiently filming and coloring in different scenes, often involving thousands of extras and expensive action, impossible to recreate today for less than $1,000,000, which I did not have and didn't know how to raise. A Japanese scifier on afternoon TV was over half special effects (whoopee!), outer space zen ray space shit battles. A deadly cold French scifier screamer. John Hall and Maria Montez in *Arabia*. Pascale Petite in an Egyptian period piece, being delivered to the Pharaoh in a rug. Mothra, King Kong, the Vikings, corpses rising from the grave, Tarzan and Jane, the river Nile, cities exploding, etc. everything the low budget film-maker needed, delivered to the home nightly. I could set up my camera very carefully (mouse fantasy), and scan the screen even as the screen scanned, so I didn't know where I was moving ('till I got to the edge and dropped off), and just judged by what I saw thru the viewer, the secret of good movie-making, along with equally thoughtless cutting. I colored each movie according to some palette, and learned to be very particular about what I shot, lest I ruin twenty intricate Moorish brothel nets with one super of a flat blue siding. I soon fell into filming exotica, the primitive and the futurist, with the contrast up, at f.95 thru a selection of twenty to twenty-five stage gels, on ECO (7255), at 12 fps or less to get reds.

After eight months of TV schedules, I climaxed, achieving a superimposition passage in Arabian horse rose and tans that even in utter randomness was perfect. I would not change a frame or grain. After that the magic stopped, and things got blurry and muddy.

I cut weird little dramas out of the confused lustful composites, like a blue woman in a sinking ship looking into a porthole and seeing red Egyptians having a doll orgy. Horse pentagram woman and falling boulder frightens and disperses Kong audience exploding three people up four thousand mile volcanic tube from Atlantis into magic rings on mirror table, and Yvette Mimieux kissing a statue's toe as space men burst thru flowers. Cut to red Mars flying saucers cutting up DC. About forty sequences emerged with often very shaky bridges or inserts of priestess speaking as if in a dream. Cut with no sense of direction, but moving thru modern man's mind like a train bursting at the seems, to an Apocalyptic destruction of earth by meteorites from above and volcanoes from below, leaving you in a long Astral void war followed by a cold moon landing death. Last dim glimpse of purple veiled Marlene ambiguously fingering and examining tones on a necklace as if the sequence of the film.

To give it substance and as an experiment in upping media inflo, I constructed a different sound barrier for each tiny shot, usually one to five seconds, though some passageways were long and blue and murky and called for slow whale-like whooshing rumbles. I learned how sound can carve out the meaning of a shot, and determine what you see. Place 1/2 second later a different content gelled out of the same viscera churning between six levels on the screen.

Then I issued the movie as a spectacle, *The Death of the Gorilla*. By cutting across so many jungles, the archetype of adventure came out crazed and beating his chest. I barely understand him.

Unfortunately the emotions are cancelled or backtracked so often that *Gorilla* okays piss poor. Thom Andersen got it seen in NYC on LA bill. It was intended as a media overload piece, and in writing now I wish I could slow it down. *Gorilla* obtains a hypnotic grip on me every time I peer back into favorite frames, like Tarzan tied to the tree of life and being butted by the blue helmet woman. I recut it in 1970 by snapping a sound print back into the title sequences, and, stoned on mescaline, reassembled the deck along holier lines. Crowley was a heavy influence. In this second, road version, Kong reappears in the second half, alive and well, unemasculated, and I left you alive and panting with the most romantic fire Arabia sequence (the perfect one), formerly a dream within Egypt. This second version is *The Ape of Thoth* Edition.

Gorilla II dissatisfied me at Jan Wolf's twenty-first birthday party, and in the hot theater ambience of the Fox Venice in 1975 I cut a much shorter version subbed *Gorilla Major*, rationalizing to make the rejects into *Gorilla Minor* and possibly a third, baby gorilla or a monkey. I may re-issue it sometime as a multiple screen being, and play all the slabs simultaneously. I expect to recut the film again and again until I can solve it, because I know the material is hot. The sound is much too synchronous, leading me in my next work to experiment with separate rhythms and even different content in sight and sound, which is a wonderful spacious discovery space I claim to be an initial explorer of. Dialectic ultimately solved the congealed soundfilm problem.

Jerry Katz also made a TV superimposition film, without filters but often from a solar TV at his parents'. He focused on contemporary life except for *Hercules in Atlantis* fire footage. Jerry was a realist whereas I was a fantasist. We both liked Godard. All his films were silent, and were all later destroyed.

Chapter Eight: The Star Curtain

The Star Curtain is a bewitchment. I dare not speak of it long. It blows toward us from outer space. In it the phallus seizes its wand, and its rites scream believe it alone says I, creator of the void. The stars are my pimpled adolescent in sense. *Tantra* remakes it as an origination myth. That is the only time it will be recut.

I entered the Curtain again, a deep blue one, stoned out of my mind at Cresthill, stumbling and falling backwards, hitting the floor with my back and automatically pushing my head under chair with feeling of pushing thru blue/black curtain and into black space with stars like outer space, where I was for several seconds before I pulled back.

The Star Curtain is a statemyth about the curtain and the screen and the illusion between them, namely the curtain parts or pulls up. It is a stasis film, an archetypal, mock-up, equivalent of a movie and the act of seeing one. The curtain gives the show class.

The curtain going up means the show will begin. This is often the most exciting and mysterious moment for the filmgoer. Instead of progressive motion, I then show a series of slabs featuring parts of a young woman's body.

I projected a painting-on-film on the face and open lips, buttocks, thighs, and belly of a young woman. This forms the first two rolls, the second darker, painted on, with sound of water and occasional passage of a light.

Thru a dim wit magazine I bought a sex tease strip, ten short shots of pantied but topless breasts. I especially liked *Fanny Makes Good*, a ten second eclipse of a reclining girl crawling away from the camera, centered on her behind which seemed to be winking like kids.

Looped, I shot her off the silver screen, blasting the roll with white painted frames and overall white frame, a soft focus rim supered over that entire roll, and sound of ocean waves slowly faded up.

None of the rolls were edited. The third one featured a mildewed white cunt close up, with painting footage projected on it. This is the famous butterfly jewel sequence, framed with black bras pulled off deep purple breasts, even as the curtain was pulled off the stage. Orange frames this roll.

The fourth roll (White Fanny was the fifth in original *Curtain*, later cut to make way for *Tantra*, which indeed, as I think about it now, replaces the more mental and severe quality of White Fanny with a severe mental trip.) The fourth features four little marionette/moviescope shows. By hand movie the girlie footage back and forth irregularly, it looks like they are rubbing their bodies on things. Dark blue moon fades up twice, and five times naked red woman raises arms in slow victory. Small turquois stills in center, of Fay Wray running thru the blue jungle like a heartbeat, being whipped by leaves.

Piercing thru all, pin-hole stars gleam, brighten, and fade. This roll, if you allowed yourself to be hypnotized by the preceding low key slowed music and the flickering deceiving imagery (projected on vasolined raincoat, etc.), this sequence can easily seem three dimensional.

In the original *Curtain* I then played twenty seconds of the painting-on-film itself, then White Fanny, very sandy and slowly fading in *Ocean*, then brief dim shot of flames over my genitals as signature, then *The End* card.

This version played for several years as proto-light-show, especially at the Cinemateque-16, a store theatre on the Strip in 1965–67.

Notes

1. *Day* and *Night* were the two parts of Mays's film *Vision* mentioned below.
2. In fact *Georg* won first prize at the second Los Angeles Film Festival in 1963, the judges being John Fles, Stan Brakhage, and Jack Hirschman. See above Jack Hirschman, "Los Angeles Film Festival".

PART II
SCHOLARSHIP

Introduction

David E. James

With the exception of two written specifically for this volume, these historical and critical essays have been developed from papers presented on the panels at the *Alternative Projections: Experimental Film in Los Angeles 1945–1980* conference held at the School of Cinematic Arts, USC, 12–14 November 2010.

14 Scarlet Woman on Film

Inauguration of the Pleasure Dome and *The Wormwood Star:* Kenneth Anger, Curtis Harrington, Marjorie Cameron, and Los Angeles Alternative Film and Culture in the Early 1950s

Alice L. Hutchison*

In Xanadu did Kubla Khan
A stately pleasure-dome decree ...

A savage place! as holy and enchanted
As e'er beneath a waning moon was haunted
By woman wailing for her demon-lover! ...

For he on honey-dew hath fed
And drunk the milk of Paradise[1]

– Samuel Taylor Coleridge

The last years of the 1940s and early 1950s was one of the most socially repressive times in American history. Nevertheless, it was a time when the visual and literary arts were more closely aligned and intertwined than ever, and avant-garde developments in Europe, especially Surrealism, were drawn upon by the two anomalous independent young filmmakers in Los Angeles, Kenneth Anger and Curtis Harrington. Both started making films as young as nine years old and fourteen, respectively, and both were admirers of Maya Deren, who came to Los Angeles in 1941 from New York, the same year the US entered World War II.

The psychological manifestations of grappling with the horrors of war in the 1940s and '50s became embodied in creative developments that have resonated

* The author wishes to acknowledge Kenneth Anger and the Cameron-Parsons Foundation, Los Angeles, CA, in the preparation of this research.

Figure 11. *The Wormwood Star*, frame enlargement.

since. Fleeing the German occupation of France and other parts of Europe, a number of illustrious European artists, writers, composers, architects, and filmmakers arrived in Los Angeles, including Man Ray and Jean Renoir. Important collectors of modern European art likewise arrived in Los Angeles with significant master works of European modern painting, such as those of the major patron of Surrealism, Edward James. Conversely, just a few years later, a number of Americans soon fled the McCarthy-era Red Scare, leaving an inhospitable post-war restrictive paranoid culture behind.

Both Anger and Harrington left for Europe by 1950, where Anger remained until the end of 1953, while Harrington returned to Los Angeles earlier that year. They soon cultivated colleagues, a vibrant group of avant-garde artists, writers, and personalities, who often gathered at the private soirées held by flamboyant aesthete Samson de Brier in Hollywood. Alternative culture was driven underground and into private residences, providing the social and artistic interminglings which gave birth to the creative synergies of the time. This scene was embodied in two proto-psychedelic, pre-LSD, avant-garde films, *Inauguration of the Pleasure Dome* (1954) and *The Wormwood Star* (1956). Reflecting altered states of consciousness, both were precursors to the psychedelic trance films to come over a decade later, and both manifested poetic realism drawn from uncensored images from the unconscious energized with the supernatural and imagery from private, decadent hermetic realms, microcosms infused with beauty in proximity to the macabre.

Curtis Harrington's nine earliest experimental films from 1942 to 1956 are very rarely screened (or now lost)[2] but should take their place beside Anger's early work in any film history, particularly an American one, despite the inconsistent commercial work he produced after *The Wormwood Star*. Harrington's collaboration with Marjorie Cameron in *The Wormwood Star* was his last personal, poetic, experimental film before he shifted into the commercial realm with *Night Tide* in 1959 (released in 1961), in which Cameron also appears.

Curtis Harrington has discussed a fairly lively international cinematic scene in Los Angeles in the late '30s-'40s. The Linda Lee theaters downtown showed Japanese films, giving him his first un-subtitled exposure to Kurosawa,[3] and Clara Grossman, a left-wing gallerist from New York, had opened a contemporary art gallery in Hollywood. There she showed the early programs available from the Museum of Modern Art film library with extensive screenings of European films, including Soviet films, in particular Eisenstein, and silent cinema. She sought out figures who were still living, but ignored by Hollywood, including D.W. Griffith. Anger and Harrington first met at Clara Grossman's gallery at one of her screenings. In a letter from teenage Anger to Harrington in October 1945 discussing the brutality of the Zoot suit riots, Anger laid out a premise that would entwine them as lifelong friends, competitors, and sparring partners, but most of all as kindred spirits: "May we labour together on this thing, be it concoction, confection, or conception: may we enrich our understanding in multifold by the collaboration".[4]

After an evening of insults following a screening of their films *Fireworks* and *Fragment of Seeking* at the Schindler House in 1948, and upon receiving Jean Cocteau's luring fan letter after *Fireworks*'s sensational reception in Paris, Anger left Los Angeles for Europe for over a decade. He was living in Rome when he decided to come back to LA following the death of his mother, and he filmed *Inauguration* in December 1953. Harrington also made his way to Paris and London, making the short black and white film *Dangerous Houses* in London in 1951, and *The Assignation*, in color, in Venice, Italy, in 1952. But he was also back in Los Angeles by 1953, a return that Anger deplored, saying: "I'm somewhat sorry to hear that you've walked back into that Maw of Mammon – Hollywood. I can't imagine a less conducive place to be ..." "... our creative position remains as anomalous today as it was when we brought out that manifesto of 'Creative Film Associates' six years ago [in 1946]".[5]

Upon his return to Hollywood, Harrington complained that it was a "cultural sink-pot ... easily the most demoralizing spot in the world".[6] At the same time in Rome, Anger was reading flamboyantly decadent, scandalous fin-de-siècle Italian poet Gabriele D'Annunzio's *Il Fuoco* (1900). The Vatican had reacted to D'Annunzio by placing all of his works in the Index of Forbidden Books. Its characters burning with feverish enthusiasms seem to have influenced Anger's wildly romantic vision for *Inauguration of the Pleasure Dome,* which he described in a letter to Harrington as "such garlanded excesses of feeling...how wonderful to have lived in an epoch when personalities could be so richly colored!" In the same letter, Anger said he had "no intention ever of returning to the U.S."[7]

And yet, within a couple of months, Anger was back in Hollywood attending his mother's funeral, and the proceeds of her will immediately went into his new film. Attending Renate Druks's Halloween masquerade party "Come As Your Madness", all the attendees concocted fabulous costumes around their own obsessions, Gods and Goddesses. These costumes were augmented in Anger's film, shot at the Barton Avenue Hollywood house of Samson de Brier. It was here that Anger and Harrington fortuitously met for the first time Marjorie Cameron, the artist and widow of Jack Parsons. She had been brought onto the set by mutual friends Renate Druks and Paul Mathison, whom she had met in San Miguel de Allende, the artists' colony in Mexico. A few months earlier, Harrington was spending most of his time with Mathison and Druks, and he had described them in his diary as being involved with "a local Aleister Crowley group, known as the Thelemites". Mathison had described Cameron to Harrington as "Crowley's spiritual wife (though she never actually met Crowley; he died the day she set foot in England), the true 'Scarlet Woman' ... They are, it appears, fanatical and dangerous".[8]

Anger used artistic colleagues as his actors – visionary artist Cameron, author Anaïs Nin, filmmaker Harrington, designer Mathison, Samson de Brier, Dior model Joan Whitney, sculptor Katy Kadell, and painter Druks. Cameron described Anger at work as "like the animal trainer in a circus...He has a way of making everybody do what he wants them to".[9] Cameron described the experience of filming as a chance for all of them to "express our repression. We were what I call the Freudian generation... I think we became interested in psychology first. And psychology sort of released us, allowed us to talk about these things that had formerly been veiled in a literary context. We were able to be shocking."[10]

A filmic improvisation inspired by the Coleridge poem "Kubla Khan", and

Figure 12. *The Wormwood Star*, frame enlargement.

following a Dionysian interpretation of one of Aleister Crowley's rituals, Druks's party inspired many of the costumes in Anger's film, with Anaïs Nin as the Moon Goddess Astarte with her head enclosed in a birdcage, and blond designer Paul Mathison as a Nordic-looking Pan. When Cameron introduced herself on the set for the first time as "The Scarlet Woman", Anger famously replied, "That's obvious ... I've been waiting to meet you for a thousand years!" Cameron as "herself", The Scarlet Woman, Whore of Babylon from the Apocalyptic Book of Revelations, soon found her counterpart in Samson de Brier's "Great Beast", wriggling long cardboard fingernails, and soon eclipsed the Moon Goddess, Nin. Harrington's reaction after his experience in the film: "It will be an extravaganza that has not been seen since the Golden Age of the German cinema. For those able to appreciate it, the film will also be quite humorous."[11]

In 1956 Curtis Harrington created the short film *The Wormwood Star,* a poetic evocation of Cameron and her work. At the time, it was one of the first films to be made on a contemporary artist. *The Wormwood Star* happens to be the only remnant of Cameron's paintings featured in the film in which the artworks are not merely portrayed but inhabit the screen space. It is the only documentary evidence of the existence of these paintings, which were later destroyed as part of

Figure 13. *The Wormwood Star*, frame enlargement.

Cameron's self-abnegating creative process, one of metamorphosis, transformation, and regeneration. Her imaginative drive to physically manifest her subconscious and altered states of consciousness embodied fantastic and mythological creatures, protean growth, in figurative and abstract delicately rendered ink drawings and gouache paintings, most of which have never been seen publicly. With hand-drawn titles by Paul Mathison, the films' opening sequences feature a close-up of the Seal of Solomon, with the titles, "Concerning the Knowledge and Conversation of the Holy Guardian Angel as revealed to: Cameron". A sequence of "still-lives", close-ups of the artist's symbolic talismans, the poet's emblems: red rose and book, objects and reflections of her face as she mirror-gazes in divination, intentionally create screen space and a looking glass through which a viewer enters into another realm. With cutting, the camera literally enters through the mirror into the magickal world of her imagery. The mirror device, also used throughout *Inauguration* to imply entry into another world, was perhaps also in homage to Cocteau's *Blood of a Poet* and Maya Deren's *Meshes of the Afternoon*. Harrington's camera is filled with Cameron's paintings that graphically illustrate a hallucinatory desert procession of angels, ethereal children, biblical and pan-cultural personages.

Mystical Cameron recites the lyric words from her Magickal Diaries, her own poetry, revealing deepest yearnings and a journey into deep realms of the imagination and into cosmic planes of consciousness. Her penetrating gaze, which burnt through the screen in Anger's *Inauguration of the Pleasure Dome*, sears the screen again with her characteristic Sphinx-like cool, embodying wisdom in this microcosm of her own realm. A red rose, placed upon an open book, a close-up of her closely cropped blazing red hair, the flash of color of a red stocking, and the talismanic drawings and writings as she recites her poetry. Harrington was also presciently aware of Cameron's currency as an artist, seeing the parallels and affinities between the lyricism in her work and that of her Surrealist contemporaries Leonora Carrington, whom Cameron had met during her time in the San Miguel de Allende artist's colony, and artist Leonor Fini, whom Harrington had met in Paris in the early '50s.[12]

Harrington has described his conception of the film as "a symbolic portrait of an extraordinary artist, a painter who is named Cameron ... an attempt to apotheosize the artist cinematically while she yet lives".[13] Shot on 16mm Kodachrome Commercial,[14] the color of the film stock is particularly rich.

Cameron was one of the driving forces in the development of 1950s Beat culture, assemblage, and underground film in Southern California. As a magnetic figure in the Los Angeles avant-garde community, Cameron attracted a younger generation of artists who saw her as mentor, colleague, inspiration, and friend; they were admirers of her commanding work in painting and poetry. This group also included preeminent American assemblage artist George Herms and filmmaker Bruce Conner. She was married to rocket-scientist and occultist Jack Parsons, one of the co-founders of Jet Propulsion Laboratory in Pasadena, who tragically died at the age of thirty-seven in a chemical explosion at their Pasadena home in 1952. He introduced her to the writings of Aleister Crowley, which are embodied through her magickal diary and the poetry she recites in Curtis Harrington's short film; and his influence upon her lifelong esoteric researches is visually manifested throughout her imaginative work.

Cameron was one of very few women artists on the West Coast of the United States who committed herself to the pursuit of a career as a serious artist during the 1950s and '60s (and through to the end of her life), during this period of intense social conservatism. With unusually gifted dexterity and sensitivity, she was as brilliant a painter and draftsperson as she was a poet. While contemporaries in New York included Lee Krasner, Helen Frankenthaler, and Joan Mitchell, or the expatriate Surrealists in Mexico such as Leonora Carrington, each of whom struggled with the bondage of social constraints to be taken seriously as artists who happened to be women, Cameron was an anomaly on the West Coast. She strongly identified with (and felt she personified) the spirit of Joan of Arc, persecuted and burnt at the stake. According to Anger, Cameron's paintings were "magical talismans and had to be destroyed lest they turn and destroy the creator", stating "she was doing art for the sake of the magick and her soul. She never sold her paintings."[15]

Harrington described Cameron as an intensely personal artist who lived in her own imaginings, reflected in her poetry and diaries, and he had very much admired her. *The Wormwood Star* was his personal homage to her work and persona.

Soon thereafter, Cameron befriended Wallace Berman, who also much admired her work, and who put her on the cover of the first issue of his publication *Semina*. This issue contained an erotically charged, peyote-inspired drawing by Cameron that precipitated the closing of Berman's 1957 exhibition at the Ferus Gallery by the Los Angeles Vice Squad when the drawing appeared within his sculptural-installation, *Temple* [c 1952–57]. Her *Peyote Vision* drawing, waved in front of the police officers by the artist Ed Keinholz, caused the Vice Squad to shut down the show for putative obscenity and to arrest Berman. Berman was so upset by the whole saga, he moved his family to the more liberal San Francisco, and Cameron decided she would never exhibit again in a commercial gallery.

Cameron's creative outpourings manifested in various media with interrelated and interconnecting themes. Around seven hundred artworks, manuscripts of poetry and journals that she created remain in existence to this day, most of which have only ever been seen by her closest friends, including artist George Herms. An untold part of West Coast art history, she played a significant role in the birth of the "goddess movement" (celebrating female energy and emergence from millennia of patriarchal bondage and exclusion), and for the rest of her life sought spiritual growth and mystical enlightenment. In consideration of the difficulties faced by a woman artist in the mid twentieth century (an anomaly at that), there were often times when she spent many years in poverty, and in isolation in the desert, was unable to obtain access to art materials, but she kept a typewriter, and drew, and composed poetry in her diaries and journals, drawing upon deeply personal imagery, plumbing the depths of the unconscious.

Cameron has been overlooked by art historians for possibly three main reasons: she destroyed much of her own work as part of her creative process; the trends of Modernism left an artist such as Cameron on the sidelines as her work was often figurative at a time when abstraction became synonymous with Modernism; and her often esoteric subject matter may have further alienated her from potential support within the art world.

In 2011, Cameron was included with George Herms and Wallace Berman as a key figure in the California Assemblage group, with her work on view at the J. Paul Getty Museum's *Pacific Standard Time: Art in Los Angeles 1945–80* exhibition. Finally, we may soon have the opportunity to view more of her work in its full glory.

Notes

1. Excerpted from "Kubla Khan – Or A Vision In A Dream" (1797).
2. Prior to *The Wormwood Star*, Harrington had previously made eight pioneering experimental 8mm and 16mm short films; his first at fourteen years old, *Fall of the House of Usher* (1942, 8mm); *Crescendo* (1942, 8mm); *Renascence* (1944/5, 8mm); *Fragment of Seeking*, (1946, 16mm); *Picnic*, (1948); *On the Edge*, (1949); these three making an early triptych; *Dangerous Houses* (1951) filmed in the bombed out ruins of St Johns' Wood, London, a mythologically inspired short black and white film based on an incident in Homer's *Odyssey*, which Harrington later rejected, removing it from distribution; and *The Assignation*, his first in color, filmed in 1952 in Venice, Italy.
3. Ed Crouse, ed., "Curtis Harrington Interviewed", in *Curtis Harrington: Cinema on the Edge*, ed. Amy Greenfield (New York: Anthology Film Archives, 2005), 27.
4. Unpublished letter from Kenneth Anglemeyer to Curtis Harrington, 12 October 1945. Curtis Harrington papers, Margaret Herrick Library, Academy of Motion Picture Arts and Sciences, Beverly Hills, CA. Retrieved 10 November 2010; referred to henceforth as Harrington papers.
5. Kenneth Anger unpublished letter to Curtis Harrington, Rome, 3 August 1953. "Manifesto of Creative Film Associates", 1946, addendum to this essay; both, Harrington papers.
6. Curtis Harrington diary, 29 June 1953, The Montecito, Hollywood, CA, 5, Harrington papers.
7. Unpublished letter from Anger to Harrington, Rome, 3 August 1953, Harrington papers, op. cit.
8. Curtis Harrington diary entry, 29 June 1953, The Montecito, Hollywood, CA, 5, Harrington papers.
9. Cameron (1922–1995). Sandra L. Starr interview with Cameron, *Lost and Found in California: Four Decades of Assemblage Art* (Los Angeles: James Corcoran Gallery, Shoshana Wayne Gallery, Pence Gallery, 1988), 77.
10. Ibid. Part of Cameron's stoic intensity on screen was not only a reflection of the death of her husband the year before, but also the harrowing effects of her experiences witnessing the horrors of war first-hand, while working in the Navy; the deaths having a profound impact upon her psyche: "We were totally disillusioned. The public in general was not as sophisticated about the Second World War as most people who had been in it, and coming back we didn't find much sympathy or interest. So we kind of hung together as a group." Sandra L. Starr interview with Cameron, *Lost and Found in California*, 63.
11. Curtis Harrington diary, 11, Harrington papers.
12. Surrealism in film perhaps reached its apotheosis in 1945 with Salvador Dalí's collaborations in Hollywood, namely his dream sequences for Hitchcock's *Spellbound*, anticipating altered states of consciousness manifest later in Anger's *Inauguration*.
13. Curtis Harrington, "A Statement by Curtis Harrington", 1956, first published in *Film Culture* 29 (Summer 1963), reproduced in *Curtis Harrington: Cinema on the Edge*, 22–23.
14. "a relatively new film stock ... which is the reason the film has not faded after all this time... that held its color, in a way that ordinary Kodachrome did not". – Curtis Harrington, quoted in interview with Douglas Bell, 2000, *Curtis Harrington Oral History*, 146, Margaret Herrick Library, Academy of Motion Picture Arts and Sciences, CA.
15. Brian Butler, "The Wormwood Star", in *Book of Lies*, ed. Richard Metzger (New York: The Disinformation Company Ltd., 2003), 210.

15 Against Transparency

Jonas Mekas, Vernon Zimmerman, and the West Coast Contribution to the New American Cinema

Josh Guilford

In an early, 1960 survey of the then-nascent New American Cinema (NAC) movement, Jonas Mekas warned independent filmmakers of a regionally specific danger faced by artists working on the West Coast: "the shadow-killing and all leveling California sun".[1] While celebrating the flashes of stylistic modernity shown by the low-budget Hollywood melodrama *Private Property* (Leslie Stevens, 1960), which Mekas considered "a very typical example of what the West Coast contribution to the New American Cinema will be", Mekas nevertheless criticized this cinematic equivalent of "newsstand literature" for its superficiality.[2] Attempting to understand the disparity between independent film productions shot in New York City and in Los Angeles, Mekas ventured that the sun in California must simply "[affect] one differently", explaining: "basically, the West Coast film makers seem to take life as a plain, one-level phenomenon, without any shadows or nooks and corners. In this shadow-less sun all the proportions of life seem to have been bleached out. Death, Birth, Sickness, Sex – everything acquires the color of a wax-museum."[3] Mekas then extended this curious bit of meteorological essentialism into a critique of the Los Angeles-based docu-fiction *The Savage Eye* (Ben Maddow, Sidney Meyers, and Joseph Strick, 1960), arguing that its cynical representation of the human condition could "be explained only by the fact that it was shot in Los Angeles", even adding that, had the same scenes been shot in New York, they "would have acquired a certain sadness, a certain humaneness".[4]

Coming in the midst of a broader argument about how a fervently anti-Hollywood generation of independent filmmakers was being fostered by a specifically

"East Coast cinematic climate", Mekas's attack on West Coast cinema in this passage stands as a reminder that the NAC's opposition to Hollywood was initially conceived not only in aesthetic, financial, and ideological terms, but in geographical terms as well.[5] While the West Coast – or more specifically, the city of Los Angeles – is positioned in his essay as a hostile terrain whose depthlessness and transparency were having a dehumanizing effect on its inhabitants, New York figures as a variegated space replete with recesses and shadows, as a more "humane" environment conducive to the serious ethical endeavors pursued by members of the new generation. In the moment of the NAC's emergence, then – when this movement was "Still weak, still often frail"; when Mekas assumed his self-appointed position as "midwife" of the new cinema – Mekas's ability to distance the NAC conceptually from then-dominant configurations of the cinematic seems to have benefited from an actual physical distance from Hollywood, a material separation from the locus of the American culture industry that allowed him to imagine the NAC as inhabiting an *other* space outside the reach of dominant culture, one whose shadowy "nooks and corners" could provide the vital shelter required by this movement in its most vulnerable, natal period.[6]

This early critique of Los Angeles cinema elucidates a distinctly *heliophobic* tendency structuring Mekas's film criticism from this period: a fear of the violent and transformative impact of illumination, and particularly that suffered within the overexposed expanses of Los Angeles. While this fear is not exactly antithetical to the condition of cinéphilia, it is nevertheless surprising to find a professional movie critic suffering from it, especially one better known for celebrating cinema's status as a mystical "art of light".[7] How should we understand the concern Mekas's early criticism exhibits over the debilitating brilliance of California culture? Moreover, how do we account for the rather rapid dissipation of this initial regionalist emphasis? As early as 1962, the year that witnessed the publication of his most influential survey of the NAC's films, "Notes on the New American Cinema", Mekas reframed this movement as a distinctly national phenomenon, abandoning his statements about regional specificity in favor of more general remarks about the new American artist and even embracing a set of films produced in California by Ron Rice and Vernon Zimmerman.[8] While Rice's work is by now well known within experimental film circles, Zimmerman's films have been forgotten by film history despite the significant critical and institutional recognition his work enjoyed in the early '60s. In 1962, his first completed work, *Lemon Hearts* (1960), was awarded a $1,000 Rosenthal Award for the most original production directed by an American under the age of twenty-five by the Museum of Modern Art. That same year, Mekas pronounced Zimmerman to be "[perhaps] the most talented newcomer to the American

Figure 14. Ingrid Lothigius in *To L.A. … With Lust.*

cinema in a long time", and celebrated his second film, *To L.A. … With Lust* (1962), as "the best satire on Hollywood made by anybody".[9] Clearly the West Coast had something to contribute to the NAC after all. But how did these distinctly Californian productions gain affiliation with the NAC?

The following essay approaches these questions by situating Mekas's early criticism of West Coast cinema as an expression of late-modern anxieties about the breakdown of privacy. More specifically, I consider how Mekas's concern over the condition of exposure suffered and perpetuated by filmmakers working in Los Angeles constitutes a regionally inflected iteration of what Deborah Nelson has recently identified as a much broader "privacy crisis" that took shape in American society at the end of the 1950s.[10] By tracking how Mekas's particular phrasing of this crisis turned on a claim regarding the deprivatizing effects of cinematic narrativization, I also consider how his simultaneous embrace of a "plotless cinema" pursued by artists of the NAC stems from an investment in the intimate potential of cinematic excess, or the nonsignifying components of the filmic image that exceed all narrative function and all efforts toward systematization. I end by discussing the excessive logic of Zimmerman's early experimental comedies, primarily *To L.A. … With Lust*, considering how such works ask us to rethink existing conceptions of the NAC, as they seem to have done for Mekas as well.

–

Mekas's comparisons of *Private Property* and *The Savage Eye* to degraded forms of popular entertainment like wax museums and newsstand literature reveal a familiar strain of East Coast elitism subtending his early criticisms of Los Angeles cinema. However, such remarks must be differentiated from arguments put forward contemporaneously by late-modernist critics working to preserve the borders of high culture from the parasitic advances of the popular. Mekas did not only believe that the aesthetic values governing high artistic practices of the postwar era were as restrictive as the conventions structuring mass cultural production. He also believed that the import contemporary critics were attributing to the blurring of high/low distinctions was outweighed by a more urgent crisis of destabilized borders facing the postwar avant-garde: namely, the breakdown of previously operative divisions between public and private spheres; or – more exactly – the progressive eradication of all stable realms of private experience by modernity's hostility to interiority. In Mekas's critical schema, the excessively rational products of mass culture, and particularly the Hollywood "Product Film", are seen to erode the private on the level of both production and reception, preventing the artist from exploring inner experience by imposing rigid conventions that inhibit personal expression, and subsequently restricting the viewer's ability to encounter truly intimate cultural products.[11] This elision of intimacy from the cultural sphere was said to be impeding the modern individual's capacity to cultivate interiority at all, thereby threatening the very existence of "man's soul".[12]

While this concern may seem foreign to readers immersed in a contemporary media economy increasingly driven by personal expression, Mekas's anxieties about the loss of interiority were not uncommon within Cold War American society. As Deborah Nelson has detailed in *Pursuing Privacy in Cold War America*, at the end of the 1950s, pronouncements regarding the "loss" or "death" of privacy suddenly erupted in nearly every level of American social, political, and cultural discourse, fundamentally disturbing traditional notions of the private as a stable domain of protective enclosure.[13] As a distinctly American iteration of what Nelson perceives as a far more general "topological crisis" in late modernity, wherein "bounded spaces of all kinds seemed to exhibit a frightening permeability", privacy's emergence as a "lost thing" in American culture at the end of the 1950s motivated highly disparate efforts to preserve traditional configurations of the private, as well as attempts to "[invent] new privacies" more compatible with the increasing porosity and instability of late-modern life.[14]

In one strand of this privacy crisis, the mass media's role in maintaining a dangerously conformist brand of "public opinion" came under intense scrutiny from artists, cultural critics, sociologists, and political theorists who increasingly faulted mass culture for rendering previously-operative forms of interiority obsolete. Aspects of this position can be seen, perhaps most famously, in David Riesman's *The Lonely Crowd* and Herbert Marcuse's *One-Dimensional Man*, but it was also a central component of writings on the NAC.[15] In a particularly extreme iteration of this critique, for instance, Allen Ginsberg identified the American mass media as the primary instrument of a "vast conspiracy to impose one level of mechanical consciousness on mankind and exterminate all manifestations of ... contemplative individuality".[16] As a regionally inflected articulation of such anxieties, Mekas's critique of West Coast cinema's superficiality was thus less motivated by Los Angeles's reputation as "the mecca of popular culture" than by its status as the home of what he derogatorily referred to as the "public arts", or those forms of publicity where, in Ginsberg's words, "the deepest and most personal sensitivities and confessions of reality are most prohibited, mocked, suppressed".[17]

We can better understand how Mekas's statements about the "shadow-killing and all leveling California sun" intersect with his concerns about private experience by briefly turning to Hannah Arendt's contemporaneous analysis of "The Public and Private Realm" in *The Human Condition*. Drawing on classical thought, Arendt traces a long history of affiliation between the private realm and notions of depth and darkness, while also formulating a conception of the public sphere as a shallow realm of pure appearance and visibility. Rather than referring to an illusory façade masking some hidden truth, in Arendt's writing, "appearance" is the very condition of what we understand as reality, designating aspects of experience that are commonly perceived and, unlike solely private or subjective sensations, can be confirmed in their reality by others. In this sense, her association of publicity with visibility and illumination stems – in part – from the public sphere's status as a space of recognition, whereby "public" denotes a state of being recognized by others. While this condition of recognition is attributed a supreme import by Arendt, she also warns against the destructive effects that publicity can have on private experiences, describing the light cast by the former as a distinctly "[harsh]" one and even asserting that certain dimensions of intimate life "cannot withstand the implacable, bright light of ... the public scene".[18] Though somewhat vague, this warning reflects Arendt's belief that any effort to transpose private experiences into public contexts entails a basic transformation of those experiences, whereby the most personal passions, thoughts, and sensations comprising our intimate lives are "deprivatized and deindividualized, as it were, into a shape to fit them for public appearance".[19] The process of making things public thus entails more than a simple "expression" of intimate feelings. It involves a fundamental transmutation through which the opaque and irrational movements of inner experience are fashioned into an impersonal, common form that can be recognized by others – a process of deprivatization that Arendt associates with artistic practices such as storytelling.

Though it is unclear if Mekas was familiar with Arendt's writings, his film criticism from the early '60s harbors distinct affinities for her observations about the potentially destructive effects of illumination. Take, for instance, the worry he exhibits in an earlier critique of *The Savage Eye*, where he attacks this film for making the intimate activities it depicts – such as a striptease, a drag ball, and a "religious gathering, where the believers go through their open-hearted confessions, mystical passions, and trances" – appear "cruelly funny, as most private passions [become] when they are blown up out of their proper context and dragged into the blazing sunlight to entertain the outsider".[20] Mirroring Arendt, Mekas here characterizes the act of exhibiting documentary footage of "private passions" to a public audience as an unnatural displacement of such passions from their original, intimate context to a hostile realm of mass entertainment. And he also isolates a violent distortion or magnification attained in this process, whereby intimate activities are "blown up" to abnormally grand proportions or made to assume a distended form more appropriate to the scale of public spectacle. This condemnation of *The Savage Eye*'s distorting effects is no doubt partly a response to its highly stylized cinematography, which frequently employs unconventional angles and disorienting close-ups to make the persons it "documents" appear grotesque. Yet Mekas's criticisms actually have more to do with issues of narrative, and specifically with the film's subordination of documentary footage to a homogeneous dramatic structure.

Organized around the life of a fictional divorcée named Judith who moves to Los Angeles to escape her failed marriage, *The Savage Eye* turns continuously from staged scenes depicting Judith's loneliness to candid documentary shots of mostly poor, elderly, and recently-injured Angelenos caught in various unflattering poses as a way of providing some broader, allegorical significance to her story. Though this representational strategy is not exactly conventional, the film progresses in accordance with a traditional narrative structure that begins with Judith's arrival at Los Angeles Airport, tracks her slow decline into spiritual oblivion, accelerates into a climactic car race/accident, and concludes with Judith contemplating a rose-colored love on the beach. For Mekas, this attempt to inject some vitality into a familiar storyline through the use of documentary footage constituted an unnatural distension of the persons and activities it depicted for two basic reasons.

First, in making this footage signify a simplistic idea (spiritual decline), it had to ignore the particular motivations that drove its individual subjects to perform these activities, thereby negating their concrete singularity for the sake of elaborating a "bigger", abstract claim about Humanity in general. Second, by imposing a traditional dramatic structure on this footage, it elided all the "little" contingencies saturating the material reality it documented – those insignificant details, fleeting gestures, and chance occurrences that film is uniquely equipped to register but which have no place in a classical narrative economy. Despite its *verité* pretensions, then, *The Savage Eye* remained firmly within the regions of "plot", demonstrating an adherence to an essentially theatrical mode of organization employed by dominant commercial cinema as a way of taming the potential senselessness of the filmic image. In Mekas's view, plot-based modes of film practice were not only uncinematic – denying film's capacity to register the contingency of material existence – they were also immoral, stemming from a "false" effort to transcend the messiness of human experience by forcibly ordering it in accordance with a grand aesthetic structure.[21]

Although they are articulated in a series of unsystematic writings published throughout the 1960s, Mekas's statements about the distorting effects of plot represent a prescient prefiguration of Stephen Heath's subsequent critique of cinematic narrativization in "Narrative Space". In Heath's terminology, "narrativization" designates the specific discursive process through which cinema endeavors to create a legible and unified narrative world.[22] This process turns on a crucial "conversion of seen into scene" or "holding of signifier onto signified" whereby the continual and potentially excessive "wealth of movements and details" registered by the filmic image are ceaselessly contained within a coherent signifying system, or attributed a specific meaning and position within an organic narrative economy.[23] For Heath, the development of a system capable of containing these excessive movements and details – namely, continuity editing – was central to cinema's historical elaboration of a coherent "narrative space" ordered in accordance with the idealized "image of vision" invented by renaissance perspective: a stable, mastering vision that implies a whole worldview, a utopian projection of the world as rational, harmonious, and transparent.[24]

The primary danger of this development, according to Heath, came in its ideological support of an illusory, transcendental subject position. For Mekas, narrativization appeared more urgently as an injunction on interiority, where the latter was conceived as an irrational realm of "spontaneous" psychical, emotional, and spiritual impulses, rather than the permanent reserve of a centered, unified self. This conception of the inner grounded Mekas's belief that any effort to represent private experiences through the use of a traditional narrative framework necessarily entailed an eradication of their very privateness – which is to say, their inherent disorder and opacity, their inability to adhere to the logic of appearance. And it was this belief that motivated his aforementioned characterization of *The Savage Eye*'s reversion to narrative as the equivalent of dragging the "private passions" depicted in its documentary material "into the blazing sunlight". Instead of some conservative reaction to a display of taboo content, he deemed the film immoral because it employed a mode of representation that was incompatible with – even harmful to – its subject matter. In characterizing *The Savage Eye*'s acquiescence to the representational logic of the "public arts" as a cruel act of exposure, this critique reveals the "shadow-killing and all leveling California sun" about which Mekas warned members of the new generation to be Hollywood film itself, or more exactly, the specific form of narration perfected by classical Hollywood cinema.

The NAC's pursuit of an alternative film practice – a rough, unpolished, blood-colored cinema – came largely through a wide scale effort to loosen the boney grip of narrativization, as artists such as Robert Frank and Alfred Leslie, Lionel Rogosin, and Mekas himself began pursuing a "plotless cinema". In Mekas's writings, the sudden emergence of this new cinema in the US amounted to a wholesale rejection of classical aesthetic strictures and a turn toward a more ethical mode of film practice rooted in a radical openness to the world, or an attempt to utilize film's indexical properties to "capture life in its most free and spontaneous flight" rather than forcibly molding it into the shape of a totality.[25] In other words, this was a film practice that reveled in excess. It was an aesthetic of "desublimation" that sought to immerse itself in the heterogeneity of material existence, or in the wealth of opaque, nonsignifying "noise" that structures modernity's everyday lifeworld.[26]

In keeping with the correspondences he perceived between the unstructured contingency of material existence and the chaotic impulses comprising inner experience, Mekas invested this excessive film practice with a distinctly intimate value. He believed encounters with the concreteness of material reality were capable of "cut[ting] into one's consciousness with the sharpness of a lash" in a manner that could "burn [man] out, purify, him, change him", effectively piercing through the outer shell of one's rational ego to impact a deeper level of consciousness.[27] Film's special facility for registering and distributing contingency to a public audience thus rendered it highly useful to an avant-garde formation seeking to counter the abstract, impersonal tendencies of late-modern American society. The unsystematized detail; the chance occurrence; the amateur imperfection: all of these generated a certain affective intensity, an existential *thisness* that translated into an experiential immediacy. By embracing such markers of cinematic excess, it was Mekas's belief that artists of the NAC could bring the individual back in touch with a dwindling interiority, revitalizing that "area in the human mind (or heart) that can be reached only through cinema ...".[28] While Mekas frequently characterized this redemptive project as a turn toward a more "personal" cinema, it might better be conceived as an effort to transform an industrially-organized, mass entertainment form into a technology of *intimate publicity*, or into a medium of public address that, in direct contrast to the logic of transparency governing traditional manifestations of public discourse, retained the opacity of its subject matter, emitting a sort of "dark incandescence" capable of generating new sites of intimate encounter.[29]

It seems fitting that Mekas initially conceived the NAC as a phenomenon specific to the shadowy recesses of New York City. Indeed, his interest in cinematic excess developed contemporaneously with diverse avant-garde movements in New York that sought to establish new relations with chance, materiality, and the everyday, from Abstract Expressionism to experiments with aleatory music, Fluxus, Judson, and the Living Theater. Of course, similar experiments were being conducted outside New York as well, and from his first writings on the NAC, Mekas established parallels between East Coast filmmakers and artists working in other regions of the US. Yet the binary Mekas imagined existing between East and West Coast film cultures was only fully destabilized with the emergence of the early, California-based productions of Rice and Zimmerman, whose improvisational films drew from the sub-cultural energies swirling through San Francisco and Venice in the late '50s and early '60s.

Rice's and Zimmerman's first films – *The Flower Thief* (1960) and *Lemon Hearts* respectively, both of which star Taylor Mead – were conceived and shot in San Francisco in 1960, where the artists first met. Upon screening in New York City in 1962, both films were immediately assimilated within Mekas's redemptive rubric, championed as exemplary instances of a "post-*Pull My Daisy*" approach to filmmaking he called the Poetry of the Absurd – a mode of practice that was deliberately out of harmony with reason, abandoning all artistic and moral conventions to gain access to a region of "poetry and wisdom" existing "beyond all intelligence ...".[30] Later that year, Mekas extended the contours of this subgenre to include Zimmerman's second film, *To L.A. ... With Lust*, which Zimmerman shot in Venice and Los Angeles.[31] Rice's second film, *Senseless* (1962), gained inclusion within the rubric of the NAC as well, perhaps due in part to Rice's own conception of the film's deliberately incoherent formal structure – which combines footage shot in Mexico and Venice that was originally intended for two separate productions into a single twenty-eight-minute film – as a fulfillment of the plotless cinema then being promoted by Mekas.[32] Merely two years after Mekas posited New York City as the true "center" of the NAC's rebellion, this movement was swiftly decentralized, shown to be dependent not on geography, but on a capacity to disarticulate the transparent vision of reality elaborated by dominant cinema.

Upon a viewer's return to Zimmerman's catalog, Mekas's description of *Lemon Hearts* and *To L.A. … With Lust* as anarchic, poetic forays into plotless cinema may seem misguided. Indeed, Zimmerman's particular brand of experimental comedy adheres much closer to narrative conventions than the work of his more subversive contemporaries. The films frequently employ traditional narrative cues and standard framing, and cultivate a more distanced mode of address than that found in such a flagrantly exhibitionist film as *Flaming Creatures* (Jack Smith, 1963). Yet on closer inspection, Zimmerman's rather haphazard storylines, which string together improvised scenes, expressive imagery, and isolated gags in a loose parody of classical plot structures, bear an only superficial resemblance to Hollywood's tightly contained narratives. Moreover, his work also exhibits a marked filthiness that resonates with some of the messier avant-garde experiments of the period, luxuriating in what Allan Kaprow once referred to as the "dirty" aspects of material reality that are traditionally whitewashed from artistic practice.[33]

Zimmerman's interest in dirt and excess comes through in numerous aspects of *Lemon Hearts*, a comedic protest against modern progress. The backdrop is San Francisco's Western Division, a decaying, Victorian era neighborhood that prompted the film's production upon being slated for urban renewal. Drifting through this liminal area in his characteristic, casual slumpiness like a bit of urban flotsam, Mead is seen rummaging through trash in an alleyway, picking his nose while dressed unconvincingly as a woman, playacting in crumbling houses, spitting, and assuming possession of a discarded suitcase filled with refuse while wearing what one critic described as "the world's tiredest fatigues".[34] The sense of material entropy conveyed by Mead's surroundings, attire, and general posture is echoed by the soundtrack, wherein he drones out a poem about loose socks, dirty fingernails, and smelly underwear in a groany delivery that emphasizes the grain of his voice. Zimmerman's shaky, handheld cinematography and imperfect exposures give the image track a comparably rough, strewn-together quality. Amplifying the imagery are the glaring disjunctions between audio and visual edits that resulted from an imprecise addition of a dubbed soundtrack to originally silent footage – a disjunction that reminds us that film is material, too.

Figure 15. Ingrid Lothigius in *To L.A. … With Lust.*

The disorder of the quotidian is also emphasized in his third film, *Scarface and Aphrodite* (1963), an experimental documentary of Claes Oldenburg's Happening, *Gayety*, which was produced in Chicago in February of 1963. Like other Happenings, *Gayety* took the form of controlled randomness, combining a series of loosely orchestrated, alogical activities involving defamiliarizing engagements with quotidian objects and materials played out in an expansive performance environment.[35] Tracing a disorienting trajectory through this environment, Zimmerman's camera roams about, refusing to impose coherence on the various isolated objects and nonsensical activities it discovers, such as a man wearing scuba flippers who drops, then picks up a pile of firewood, or another man shoveling sand out of a bed. The film's disjunctiveness is further amplified by Zimmerman's use of rapid montage, non-synch sound, and – in the film's most thrillingly inharmonious sequence – recorded audio from a moment of the performance when a pop song by The Exciters, "Tell Him", could be heard playing asynchronously on two sources.

If the unclean aesthetic of these films suggests Zimmerman's aversion to the coherent totalities demanded by classicism, his predilection for aesthetic incoherence is made most explicit in *To L.A. … With Lust.* A delightfully schlocky ode to the City of Angels, *To L.A. … With Lust* mercilessly mocks and debases the idealized vision of reality projected by classical Hollywood cinema. The film opens in the disheveled apartment of its protagonist, an aspiring actress played

Figure 16. Ingrid Lothigius v. Camille Roulin in *To L.A. … With Lust.*

by the Swedish poet Ingrid Lothigius. In a voiceover, Lothigius speaks of the paradisal life she leads as a movie star, describing details of her appearance and daily routine that contrast with the scenes depicted on screen: instead of a night gown, she wears frumpy pajamas; instead of beginning the day with some juice and exercise, she munches on breath mints, strikes a match on the dirt-blackened base of her foot, and lights a cigarette; instead of a beautiful garden with a private swimming pool, her window looks onto a field of oil rigs; etc. Ridiculing numerous fantasies about the California lifestyle being promoted at the time – natural beauty, the cult of the body, the promise of luxury, fame, and leisure – this sequence also revels in its own filth, attributing a certain base glamour to Lothigius's incongruity with the Hollywood ideal.

As this scene progresses, a few additional sequences further tarnish abstract images of beauty. In the first of these, Lothigius is framed in a grotesque close-up, which juxtaposes her dumb smile, oily skin, and matted hair with the Utopian vision offered by a poster of Van Gogh's *Portrait of Camille Roulin* hanging on the wall behind her. Unlike similar close-ups in *The Savage Eye*, here, Zimmerman's camera demonstrates its allegiances with Lothigius: twice in this brief shot it goes out of focus, blurring foreground and background equally in some failed attempt at a rack focus that equates Zimmerman's imperfect technique with Lothigius's blemished appearance. In the second sequence, Lothigius is found in her bathroom before the mirror, describing the happiness she gains from gazing at her reflection as we watch her abjectly blowing her nose, gargling, and brushing her teeth with an excessive amount of toothpaste, her lips covered in foam. In the third, she sits on her toilet, flipping through an issue of *Vogue Beauty* that depicts typically flawless ideals of femininity. Upon realizing she is out of toilet paper, she tears out a page from the magazine featuring a classically beautiful woman in a backless dress, crumples it up, and puts it to more practical use as the screen goes black.

Though numerous other moments in *To L.A. … With Lust* are worthy of discussion, one final sequence reveals how Zimmerman's investment in "dirty" content further inflects this work's formal composition. Toward the middle of the film, we see Lothigius performing a rather macabre dance in what she imagines to be a nightclub, but is actually an abandoned pier on the beach. The footage is shown in negative, making Lothigius look ghostly, draped in a black gown, mouth and eyes glowing with some spectral energy as her figure blends into the dark void of the horizon, the loud drone of an unseen freighter drowning out her voice. Freed up by the film's excessive logic, this jarring, opaque, senseless image – the uncanny double of Hollywood's transparent fantasies – would have no place in a traditional narrative economy. Disorienting and irrational, yet also unexpectedly touching, this sequence reveals a point where the ridiculousness of Zimmerman's films slips from the realm of the absurd into that of the *obtuse.* Taking the latter – in Roland Barthes's sense of the term – to designate a purely visual phenomenon that exceeds the rational operations of narrative and information, this sequence carries a disturbingly affective intensity capable of more radically "subverting… the entire practice of meaning".[36] To Mekas, such obtuse phenomena were not only opaque in themselves. Upon being projected, they were also able to generate intimate "shadows" or "secret places" wherein the viewer could "cultivate forbidden virtues and forbidden beauties", such as the anarchical "confusion of emotions" being denied expression by the repressive rationalism of modern mass society.[37] Always conceiving the value of cinema relationally, from the position of spectatorship, Mekas thereby invested such absurd, obtuse images with an *abstruseness* as well, an imperfect – but vital – ability to "guarantee the darkness of what needs to be hidden against the light of publicity".[38]

Notes

1. Mekas, "Cinema of the New Generation", *Film Culture* 21 (Summer 1960): 17.
2. Ibid., 17, 18.
3. Ibid., 17–18.

4. Ibid., 18.
5. Ibid., 8.
6. Ibid., 7; Mekas, *Movie Journal: The Rise of the New American Cinema, 1959–1971* (New York: Macmillan, 1972), ix.
7. Mekas, "Where Are We – the Underground?" in *The New American Cinema: A Critical Anthology*, ed. Gregory Battcock (New York: Dutton, 1967), 21.
8. Mekas, "Notes on the New American Cinema", in *Film Culture Reader*, ed. P. Adams Sitney (New York: Cooper Square Press, 2000), 103.
9. Pauline Kael et al., "Films of the Quarter", *Film Quarterly* 15:4 (Summer 1962): 40; Mekas, "Movie Journal", *Village Voice*, 7 June 1962, 10.
10. Deborah Nelson, *Pursuing Privacy in Cold War America* (New York: Columbia University Press, 2002), xii.
11. "The First Statement of the New American Cinema Group", in *Film Culture Reader*, 80.
12. Mekas, "Notes on the New American Cinema", 103.
13. See Nelson, introduction and ch. 1.
14. Ibid., 26, xiii.
15. David Riesman, *The Lonely Crowd: A Study of the Changing American Character* (New Haven, CT: Yale University Press, 2001); Herbert Marcuse, *One-Dimensional Man: Studies in the Ideology of Advanced Industrial Society* (Boston: Beacon Press, 2001). For related analyses of the NAC, see especially Stan Vanderbeek, "The Cinema Delimina: Films from the Underground", *Film Quarterly* 14.4 (Summer 1961); and Ken Kelman, "Anticipations of the Light", in *The New American Cinema*.
16. Allen Ginsberg, "America's Nervous Breakdown: Poetry, Violence, and the Trembling Lambs", *Village Voice*, 26 August 1959, 1.
17. Cécile Whiting, *Pop L.A.: Art and the City in the 1960s* (Berkeley, CA: University of California Press, 2006), 3; Mekas, "New York Letter: Towards a Spontaneous Cinema", *Sight and Sound* 28:3–4 (Summer–Autumn 1959): 121; Ginsberg, "Nervous Breakdown", 1.
18. Hannah Arendt, *The Human Condition* (Chicago: University of Chicago Press, 1958), 51.
19. Ibid., 50.
20. Mekas, *Movie Journal*, 16.
21. Ibid., 49.
22. Stephen Heath, "Narrative Space", in *Questions of Cinema* (Bloomington, IN: Indiana University Press, 1981), 43.
23. Ibid., 37, 39.
24. Ibid., 31.
25. Mekas, "New York Letter", 119.
26. On "desublimation", see Naomi Schor, "Desublimation: Roland Barthes's Aesthetics", in *Reading in Detail: Aesthetics and the Feminine* (New York: Methuen, 1987). On "noise" in cinema and modernity, see especially Juan A. Suárez, *Pop Modernism: Noise and the Reinvention of the Everyday* (Urbana, IL: University of Illinois Press, 2007).
27. Mekas, "Movie Journal", *Village Voice*, 1 July 1959, 6, 11.
28. Mekas, "Notes on the New American Cinema", 105.
29. Georges Bataille, *Inner Experience* (Albany, NY: State University of New York Press, 1988), 47.
30. Mekas, "Notes on the New American Cinema", 101.
31. Mekas et al., "Films of the Quarter", 40.
32. Rice's interest in "plotless cinema" is related in P. Adams Sitney, "Ron Rice: *Senseless*; *Chumlum*", program notes, The Avantgarde Film Tuesday Series at the Jewish Museum, 10 December 1968, np.
33. Allan Kaprow, "Happenings in the New York Scene", in *Essays on the Blurring of Art and Life*, ed. Jeff Kelley (Berkeley, CA: University of California Press, 2003), 18.
34. Barbara Ullman, "Far-Out & Foreign", *Better Home Movie Making* (September/October 1965), np.
35. For a detailed discussion of Happenings and a documentation of Oldenburg's *Gayety*, see Michael Kirby, *Happenings: An Illustrated Anthology* (New York: Dutton, 1966), esp. 241–261.
36. Roland Barthes, "The Third Meaning: Notes on Some of Eisenstein's Stills", trans. Richard Howard, *Artforum* 11.5 (January 1973): 49.
37. Mekas, *Movie Journal*, 75.
38. Arendt, *Human Condition*, 71.

16 Vicarious Vicario: Restocking John Vicario's Forgotten *Shoppers Market* (1963)

Ken Eisenstein

We live with things. We perch upon them, claw and cradle them, raise them, and they raise us, grow us, throw us. One special site for such circular and confused interaction is, as Allen Ginsberg has memorialized it, the supermarket:

> What thoughts I have of you tonight, Walt Whitman, for I walked down the sidestreets under the trees with a headache self-conscious looking at the full moon.
> In my hungry fatigue, and shopping for images, I went into the neon fruit supermarket, dreaming of your enumerations!
> What peaches and what penumbras? Whole families shopping at night! Aisles full of husbands! Wives in the avocados, babies in the tomatoes![1]

Ginsberg's shopping list suggests that visual artists should be equally struck by the grocery store's "brilliant stacks of cans", its glowing and darkening produce, and the people who place and purchase all this and more. And they have been. To register just two examples here, first take William Eggleston and his earliest successful effort in color. After staying up one night, the photographer decided to:

> go to Montesi's, the big supermarket on Madison Avenue in Memphis. It seemed a good place to try things out. I had this new exposure system in mind, of overexposing the film so all the colors would be there. And by God, it all worked. Just overnight. The first frame, I remember, was a guy pushing grocery carts. Some kind of pimply, freckle-faced guy in the late sunlight. Pretty fine picture, actually.[2]

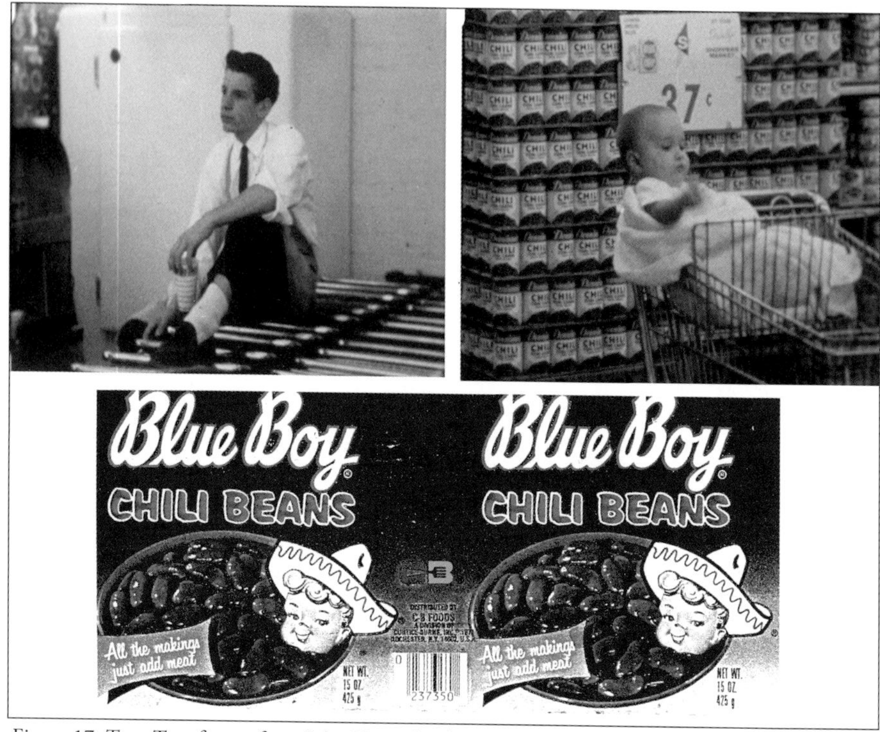

Figure 17. Top: Two frames from John Vicario's *Shoppers Market* (1963). Bottom: Hollis Frampton's *Chili Bean Brand Blue Boys* from his *By Any Other Name* – Series 1

The image to which Eggleston refers, whose shadow play (visible on the wall) introduces the artist, opens the seventy-five-picture portfolio *Los Alamos* (1965–1974).[3] While none of the series's other entries appear to come from inside Montesi's, this "first frame" was likely followed, on the day of its making, by others that did. Presumably, part of what made the supermarket "a good place to try things out" would have been the cornucopian color that it held in store.

Second, consider a different series, one that withholds the human component that both Ginsberg and Eggleston depend on: Hollis Frampton's *By Any Other Name* – Series 1 (1979). Made up of twelve color xerographs of food labels, the images themselves remain unaltered save for any imprecision in the Xerox 6500's capacity for color reproduction, plus one conceptual kink: the edibles depicted on each of the wrappings are subjected to a criss-crossing of brand name and product name via Frampton's titles. By simply playing with this systematic procedure, unheard of flavors are evoked in a game that enriches the task of errands (what would the sad male children of *Chili Bean Brand Blue Boys* [formerly Blue Boy Brand Chili Beans] taste like?). The action produces parallel phantom packaging for hard-to-swallow stingers like *Tuna Brand Chunk Light*

Bumblebees and too-big-for-one-bite *Sweet Pea Brand Green Giants*. Frampton believed these imaginary inversions improved upon the underlying situation of the supermarket, which he feared was an "artless place":

> an ocean of modularized substance where everything in sight is meant only to be consumed, destroyed, wasted, returned as quickly as possible to the domains of amorphy or thermodynamic affinity. Where everything goes down the drain, anything goes. A certain appetite of mind can, then, find more nourishment in the label on the can than in its contents: a poetic, if wayward, feast.[4]

The mental morphing of Frampton's peculiar addendum to retail preserves sustenance; his food for thought is indigestible in the best sense.

I corral these examples alongside John Vicario and his 1963 film *Shoppers Market* in order to begin to pen loosely a range of aesthetic responses to the eponymous site, to start drawing the outer rings of a target whose bull's eye we will now approach. If Eggleston's Memphis and the east coaster Frampton's "appetite of mind" offer two handles that seem at some distance from the larger effort at hand – engagement with David James's *The Most Typical Avant-Garde: History and Geography of Minor Cinemas in Los Angeles* (2005) (at least Ginsberg was in the right state) – then let me explain something of the curiosity that struck me when I first learned of the existence of *Shoppers Market*. Inspired by the ways that James's geographical approach reshapes our understanding of given historical terrain, I took up a search in The Film-Makers' Cooperative's online catalog for the terms "Los Angeles" and "L.A." in the "Description" field, and turned up the following:

> John M. Vicario
>
> **Shoppers Market** (1963) 16mm, color, sound, 22 min
>
> Genre: Experimental
>
> "a documentary film of marked lyrical and experimental tendency which was photographed and recorded in a L.A. supermarket. It consists of five sequences: 1) description of people 2) Comedy 3) choreographing natural movements 4) transformation fo [sic] visual reality 5) empathy"
>
> Rental: $20.00[5]

The film's date, combined with its shooting location, had me wondering whether or not Vicario might have been responding to specific goings-on in the early 1960s Los Angeles art scene, which had seen, in the summer and fall of 1962, two major events in the history of American Pop Art: Andy Warhol's first one-man show (held at the Ferus Gallery) and Walter Hopps's exhibition *New Painting of Common Objects* (held at the Pasadena Art Museum and considered the first show dedicated to Pop as a movement in the United States). Images of supermarket products could be found at both venues, with Ed Ruscha exhibiting

Actual Size (1962) and *Box Smashed Flat* (1960–61) in Pasadena (these paintings feature a can of Spam and Sun Maid Raisins, respectively), and the Warhol debut comprising itself of thirty-two *Campbell's Soup Cans*.[6] Irving Blum, director of the Ferus, installed Warhol's paintings along a shelf as a "pretty obvious joke on the supermarket-commodity subject", and a review of the show, "Soup Can Painter Uses His Noodle", reported that the nearby Primus-Stuart Gallery had set up a window display of real soup cans as a spoof.[7] Could Vicario's film have been another related response?

The only pieces of information that I could initially find about the filmmaker or *Shoppers Market* were that it had been produced by University of California, Los Angeles's (UCLA's) Theatre Arts department; that Vicario's one other screen credit was as camera operator on Francis Coppola's *Dementia 13* (1963); and that during that shoot, Vicario had been accompanied by the woman he was then dating: Eleanor Neil (now Eleanor Coppola), who had studied art at UCLA.[8] These details all amplified my hypothesis, since Vicario's connection to the college established Los Angeles residency, and his connection to Neil increased the chances of contact with the art world.[9] The catalog description of *Shoppers Market*, with its inclusion of "lyrical", "transformation", and "empathy", started to sound more and more like it could be a reaction to the ethos that was about to be christened "The Cool School".[10]

A visit to The Film-Makers' Cooperative and a flatbed viewing of *Shoppers Market* altered the course of such thinking. Instead of the direct engagement with Spam and Campbell's imagery that I had dreamed up for the film's "comedy" section, or a full blown analog to post painterly abstraction in the "transformation" section, the film centered itself much more on the human presence at its location, and paid a marked attention to the world of sound.[11] I will discuss the film – which has now been preserved and transferred to video for online reference thanks to Adam Hyman (Los Angeles Filmforum) and Mark Toscano (Academy Film Archive) – in detail below, but first I want to fill in a little of what I learned about it and its maker.[12] In the files that the Coop keeps on each of its members, there were two documents that helped shed some needed extra light. A clipping from one of the Coop's paper catalogs gave a fuller entry than the one online. It identified Vicario himself as the author of the above description and included additional blurbs from Colin Young (Head of UCLA's Motion Picture Division) and Pauline Kael.[13] The UCLA connection was confirmed in the production info, festival screenings were listed ("Brussels, Venice, Los Angeles Festivals and Flaherty Film Seminar"), and soundtrack credits given (important data since these last are not included in the film's end titles). A separate Coop inspection card suggested what already seemed evident considering the scarcity of available information on the film and its maker, namely that even after exhibiting at the likes of Venice and Knokke-le-Zoute (where *Shoppers Market* screened in the festival's opening program with films by Bruce Conner, Arthur Lipsett, Donald Richie, and Ann Arbor Film Festival founder George Manupelli), many films just fall by the wayside.[14] Any interest in Vicario's film appears to have tapered off by the late 1960s when the Coop inspected it on five occasions, presumably after rentals. Since 1971 it has been handled three times, last in 1983.

Imagine Vicario's surprise at hearing from someone interested in *Shoppers Market* after all these years.[15] Having chalked up its early international festival success to a European fascination with American supermarkets, he had come to feel that the film was not particularly good, nor quite finished; he imagined partial remedy could be had by correcting the misstep of a young filmmaker's over-excitement about his footage (which had led to the inclusion of almost all of it in the final cut). Conceived either as an undergraduate class project, or as a side project supported by the 16mm Bell & Howell non-sync cameras in UCLA's equipment pool, Vicario put together a crew of three friends (Dennis Jakob, Jack Carlson, and Sharon Compton) to accompany him on shoots at his neighborhood supermarket at the intersection of Lincoln Boulevard and Ocean Park Boulevard in Santa Monica. Over the course of a two-week period in what was probably the fall of 1961 (pre-dating Los Angeles's summer of soup cans), each collaborator shot a single hundred-foot roll of film to supplement the footage and sound that Vicario was taking himself.[16] Compton was an art student who had never used a motion picture camera before, but she was enlisted because Vicario admired her sensibility (she ended up filming the soft focus material, close-ups of cans, the flower, and the masks that provide the film's climax [discussed below]). Vicario recalls a conversation with Compton about the humor involved in the product name for Miracle Whip; on this occasion, the young director, with his loose and dispersive approach, appears to have been wielding a most gentle one.

Vicario spent a few months editing the groups' footage, struggling at the beginning to find a shape for it. He held preview screenings for friends, and part of the completed film was shown at a student showcase in UCLA's Royce Hall, most likely in 1962. (The Coop catalog's date of 1963 seems to be the more official release date, marking when the film hit the international festival circuit). *Shoppers Market* was considered for the Los Angeles Film-Makers Festival, but Vicario has a dim recollection of John Fles making changes to the program at the last minute, which resulted in the film not being screened.[17] In addition to the presentations in Venice and Brussels, a private showing was arranged for Pauline Kael at her home in Berkeley.[18] Kael's ex-husband, the 1950s Berkeley area repertory theatre owner Ed Landberg, was attending UCLA in the early 1960s, and he helped Vicario, who was making a trip up to the Bay Area for a family visit, set up the screening. It was there that Vicario secured his oral (rather than printed) endorsement, which he admits he may have exaggerated for publicity purposes (in fact, the way Vicario puts it now is that Kael damned the film with faint praise). While with a friend in New York (c. early 1964), Vicario met the Mekas brothers (who were friends of his friend), and he decided to leave a print with the Coop.[19] Although he began another observational film at the Santa Monica pier, where he filmed the skating rink and merry-go-round (the latter with Eleanor Neil), and despite completing a feature length screenplay (which, as he recalls, neither Carroll Ballard nor Colin Young, both associates from UCLA, thought much of), Vicario slowly drifted out of the film industry after also dropping out of school.[20] He found the feature filmmaking process a tedious one; the last film he worked on was *The Glory Stompers* (Anthony Lanza, 1967).

Born in New York City in 1934, Vicario developed an early passion for the two tendencies that produced the stylistic emphases of *Shoppers Market*: documentary photography and musicality. At the age of ten, he received a still camera from his father, making special use of it on a trip to Guatemala in 1948 where he investigated effects with infrared film. Enrolled at St. Mark's School in Massachusetts in the late 1940s and early 1950s, Vicario's interest in music was fostered by both his roommate and his music teacher, with whom he took extra classes. His passion for contemporary composers came through George Sackett, a pianist friend back in New York. At the age of sixteen, Vicario's stepmother arranged a month long apprenticeship with her friend Ralph Steiner, whose film *The City* (co-directed with Willard Van Dyke, 1939), then unknown to Vicario, would become a major source of inspiration.[21] After high school, a year spent with his sister in Boulder, Colorado, was followed by another back east near Pittsfield, Massachusetts. It was filled with movie going, including screenings at The Berkshire Museum's Little Cinema where Vicario saw Bresson and Fellini, as well as shorts by Curtis Harrington and Charles and Ray Eames (e.g. *Blacktop: A Story of the Washing of a School Play Yard* [1952]). In 1955, Vicario moved to Berkeley for school and to be closer to his father, who had moved out west. After about a year and a half of studying philosophy and attending screenings at Landberg's theaters, Vicario decided to head south for UCLA, enrolling in their undergraduate film program.

Once at UCLA, Vicario's planned pursuit of fiction filmmaking took a turn toward documentary.[22] His first project was a three-minute short about his new neighbor's children; the family had moved from Oklahoma, and Vicario was drawn to what was for him their unique look. His next two course-based films veered toward the surreal and symbolic qualities of Harrington, and of Cocteau's 1946 *Beauty and the Beast* (another film he admired). Both centered on encounters between a male and female character. The second, made in Dorothy Arzner's directing class, was based on an afternoon that Vicario had recently had at the Museum of Modern Art (MoMA) in New York. The film starred the dancer Kate Hughes Rinzler (who was about to help her husband Ed Pearl launch the Ash Grove folk music club), and took place in a simulated gallery hung with prints by Cézanne, van Gogh, and Henri Rousseau's *The Sleeping Gypsy*. The Rousseau was Vicario's favorite painting, remembered from childhood trips to MoMA with his biological mother. It now overlooked a fictionalized amorous exchange set to music from Ravel's *Daphnis et Chloé* (1912).

Vicario's points of reference also contained another significant strain besides the lush one surfacing above. For his twenty-first birthday he had received another photography related gift: the then brand new catalog for Edward Steichen's exhibition *The Family of Man* (1955). This primed him for a number of key encounters that he would have with the documentary tradition at UCLA. While the crew work that Vicario did on other student productions was mainly fiction based (e.g. Mark McCarty's *Cross Country Runner* [1962] and Abe Martin Zweiback's *August Heat* [1961]), his exposure to films such as Basil Wright's *Night Mail* (co-directed with Harry Watt, 1936) and *The Song of Ceylon* (1934) in Colin Young's courses was formative.[23] Wright himself was a visiting professor at UCLA toward the end of Vicario's time there (c. 1962), and the student filmmaker assisted the veteran in documenting a local performance of Puccini's *Madama Butterfly*, during which Vicario became fascinated by the non-deliberate gestures of the singers during rehearsals.[24] This concern with mundane human movement grew into a dominant one via other exposures. Vicario, after all of these years, can still picture the close-ups of hands in *The City* (another film that he was introduced to by Young). He also had a strong response to the early photographic work of Ralph Gibson, whom Vicario met through fellow classmate Don Heitzer while Gibson was still studying at the San Francisco Art Institute. Gibson's portraits of life on that city's streets were testaments to the richness of dailiness, and they fired Vicario's one completed filmmaking effort, *Shoppers Market*, to which we will now turn.[25]

Taking off from the basic documentary value inherent in the footage in *Shoppers Market* (styles of dress, individual comportment and ambulation, signage, etc.), Vicario's skill as an editor, especially in terms of his use of sound, produces an intriguing meditation on the supermarket as site of social and psychic interaction. The film's first two shots form a prologue that distinguishes itself as such via its vantage point and introductory verbal statement. These are two of only three shots in the entire film that are taken from a second story level within the supermarket (the third comes at a key juncture three-quarters of the way through the film).[26] The notions of overview, survey, and observation are established here from afar, though the rest of the film will play out on the ground floor in close proximity to its subjects. Emphasis is laid at the beginning upon a special feature of the market. When the first shot tilts up from a clerk building a product display, a banner above him reads "7 Days A Week For Your Shopping Convenience", as a sound insert has an employee vocalize that "it's a big operation you know / it's twenty-four hours". In the middle of this line Vicario cuts to his second shot: a pan left which eventually reveals the complementary and completing banner, "Open 24 Hours". The totality of time at play here is stated as an objective fact characterizing an aspect of modern urbanized shopkeeping, but as the film progresses, especially through its stranger moments, a puncturing psychological clock, a different awl of time, is also brought to bear.

The first section, "description of people", presents customers and co-workers alike conversing, inspecting goods, and taking breaks, all under a slightly crowded mix of the spatialized sound of the store's occupants, its background music, and the interruptive public address system announcing phone calls and other pages. Vicario plays with the environment's elongation of synchronous sound in that just as the public address covers enough space to create simultaneous "syncs" (not just sync), Vicario rubs different sounds against images and each other. One line uttered from an individual cashier to her customer ("your change is in the slot sir") floats "asynchronously" over a customer whose lips remain closed as she chews gum. Whether or not she is really in earshot is anyone's guess. This disembodied yet personal interaction follows two versions of the same thing from the loudspeaker. Over a shot of the most elderly shopper presented thus far, we hear the first of what will be three important heckling laughs. A number of recorded conversations that may or may not originate with whomever we are looking at continue along this distending path. Pushing beyond the simple slippage of a non-sync camera unit, the track is highly fabricated, and it takes a further cue from the market's Muzak as Vicario pipes in non-location sound. All of these challenges to the simple title of "description" erupt in the first implementation of this when ambient sound is overcome by the mysterious ethereal textures of Vladimir Ussachevsky, hardly a staple. The second cackle, which penetrates the Ussachevsky, and is again inserted over an elderly woman (more disoriented than the previous one), adds a sinister quality that is eventually diffused after a shot of a baby is followed by a grouping of young children and teenagers. Within its first six minutes, the film's opening section sketches out the poles of space, time, and personhood along the axes of age, public/private, the always open/inward personal closure, and creature comforts.

A number of static moments, customers waiting on line or frozen in contemplation of product, slow the film down to a near halt, preparing the launch of Vicario's "comedy" section with a minor commotion stirred up by a one-dollar sale on muumuus (set to Duane Eddy's twangy guitar). This gives way to the most extended and humorous conversation in the film. The discussion, about man's "innate" need for love and the difference between "present day society" and Eskimo culture's varying successes at keeping this need centered, is laid in over people poking through the refrigerated section, a man inspecting eggs, and a pair of women studying a package of EverSweet baking chocolate. "Love" is concretized in dairy and cacao and cooled in a wry comparison between market culture and Eskimo. When it is stated that Eskimos have "no neurosis as far as real severe cases", the film's third and final ghoulish chuckle is heard, unleashing both a challenge to the romanticization of Eskimo life and further evidence of the neurotic. Importantly, this new pairing alters the link set up in the earlier laughs on/at older patrons, setting up a demonic entity that preys on the infirm and the frail as manifested in the elderly (Vicario thought of the aged customers as the film's treasures), but also on the longing for a different way of life. The section ends most rambunctiously with kids goofing around, indecisive purchasers, and parents exerting discipline to the jittery sound of the "Stereophonism" movement from Carlos Surinach's *Hollywood Carnival* (1956).

"Choreographing natural movements" (section 3) groups similar actions together based on activity (bagging, gliding, pushing, scanning), and once handling enters the equation, the intensity of the section begins to pick up. Products are fondled and squeezed by customers as the crunching sound of the cash register begins to be introduced. Ussachevsky returns here momentarily to interrupt the flow, redirecting people's touches to their own bodies, before a stuttered reacceleration brings a rotisserie, a spinning "Glass wax" sign, a price marking gun, and the manually dexterous operator of the now visible cash register to frenzy. The circuitry of the products' arrival, announcement, and anticipated annihilation (to recall Frampton) comes full circle as the register spits out its white-tongued receipt. The clicking and clacking drops out as the third shot from the mezzanine level appears, serving as a reset button that triggers reminders of the film's opening along with a shot recalling the muumuu section. As the film enters new territory in its "transformation of visual reality" section, a sign reading "Everlasting

Figure 18. Left: Two frames from John Vicario's *Shoppers Market* (1963). Right: The penultimate cut from John Vicario's *Shoppers Market* (1963).

Flowers" enchants or decants a lollipop display and the Christmas light bulbs that move along a conveyor belt as a rack focus dematerializes them. Bartok's eerie and terrifying *Music for Strings, Percussion, and Celesta* (1936) scores the scene as little fuzzy figurines haunt the soft spirals of fruits and flowers being clutched by human hands. A repeated alternation between loose carrots and a pair of canned items comes into focus (abalone and peaches side-by-side echo Frampton's twisted "ocean of modularized substance") and then shakes giant squids, dragons, and Dolores Canning Company's mascot free from other labels. However, rather than emancipatory, the sequence's inclusion of desiccated corn and a bowl of fake fruit set up a sense of contagious possession; the shoppers don grotesque Halloween masks.

But Vicario doesn't leave us stranded in this netherworld. As a shot of someone's buttocks tilts up and is cut to a single rose being wheeled around in a cart catching the light of the sun, the Bartok switches to what Vicario identified as "Vivaldi-Bach" for the film's short final section: "Empathy".[27] As the fertilized flower (everlasting or not) stitches together the film's final honorific portraits of customers of all ages (one woman wears a flower brooch, a young woman with an Occidental College sweatshirt is juxtaposed with a toddler and his ice cream cone

Figure 19. John Vicario (left) at the screening of *Shoppers Market* at the Cinefamily, 21 January 2012. With him (right) is Baylis Glascock, whose *Film Exercise No. 2* screened on the same program.

[West/Eskimo]), it rounds the market's visitors into a circle of life, of raising and raised, of producing and clothing, in an attempt to bind a more humane loop: closing time. Of the film's final human figure, seen before an epilogue offers the only two exterior shots of the market, we might ask, along with Ginsberg:

> Ah, dear father, graybeard, lonely old courage-teacher, what America did you have when Charon quit poling his ferry and you got out on a smoking bank and stood watching the boat disappear on the black waters of Lethe?[28]

Now, the same question must be put to John Vicario, who died at age seventy-nine on 28 August, 2013.

Notes

1. Allen Ginsberg, "A Supermarket in California", in *Allen Ginsburg, Collected Poems, 1947–1980* (New York: Harper & Row, 1984), 136. The phrase quoted in the next sentence is from same. The poem was written in 1955.
2. Cited in "Chronology", in Elisabeth Sussman and Thomas Weski, *William Eggleston: Democratic Camera, Photographs and Video, 1961–2008* (New York: Whitney Museum of American Art, 2008), 271. The passage comes from Stanley Booth, "William Eggleston", *Salon.com*, 7 September 1999. Accessed 10 March 2014. http://www.salon.com/people/bc/1999/09/07/eggleston. The "fine picture" can be seen at Art Blart. Accessed 10 March 2014, http://artblart.files.wordpress.com/2010/05/william-eggleston-untitled-n-d-boy-with-trolleys.jpg.
3. The entire series can be viewed as a thumbnail at Christie's (Sale 2036, Lot 144), accessed 10 March 2014, http://www.christies.com/LotFinder/lot_details.aspx?intObjectID=5119471.

4. Hollis Frampton, "Notes: *By Any Other Name*", in *On the Camera Arts and Consecutive Matters: The Writings of Hollis Frampton*, ed. Bruce Jenkins (Cambridge: The MIT Press, 2009), 298. The notes were written late in 1980 for a 1981 exhibit entitled *Animated Images/Still Life* held at Macalester College in Minnesota (Jenkins, *On the Camera Arts*, 297). For more on *By Any Other Name*, see Bruce Jenkins and Susan Krane, *Hollis Frampton: Recollections/Recreations* (Cambridge: MIT Press, 1984).
5. The price has since been raised to align with a $3 per minute rental fee (accessed 10 March 2014, http://film-makerscoop.com).
6. Related soup can paintings by Warhol were also part of Hopps's show.
7. Kirk Varnedoe, "*Campbell's Soup Cans*, 1962", in *Ferus*, 2nd Edition (New York: Rizzoli International Publications, Inc., 2009), 45. "Ferus-Type Soup Cans", in *The Andy Warhol Catalogue Raisonne 01: Paintings and Sculpture 1961–1963*, ed. Georg Frei and Neil Printz (New York: Phaidon Press Inc., 2002), 70.
8. See the British Film Institute's Film & TV Database (http://ftvdb.bfi.org.uk/sift/title/346227, accessed 10 March 2014), and Gene D. Phillips, *Godfather: The Intimate Francis Ford Coppola* (Lexington: University Press of Kentucky, 2004), 23.
9. Neil's work, as I later discovered, was of a different temperament than that of the artists associated with Ferus. She was represented by the funkier, more expressive, Ceeje gallery. Two examples of Neil's tapestry hangings are depicted in *Los Angeles Times* articles which describe their content as "a study in textures and colors of violet, olive green and gold" and "joyous and colorful birds in a fanciful cage". ("Humble Yarn Speaks in an Artful Voice", *Los Angeles Times*, 25 March 1962, 18; and Virginia McIntire, "For Top Impact", *Los Angeles Times*, 17 June 1962, D6).
10. Alexandra Schwartz discusses the early 1960s Los Angeles relationship to Pop and this particular appellation (Philip Leider's) in her *Ed Ruscha's Los Angeles* (Cambridge: The MIT Press, 2010), 35–47.
11. Clement Greenberg's *Post Painterly Abstraction* exhibit opened at the Los Angeles County Museum of Art in April of 1964. It was conceived of as the "objectless" companion to yet another important Pop show, Lawrence Alloway's *Six Painters and the Object*, which had been at the same museum the year before.
12. http://vimeo.com/81296583, accessed 10 March 2014.
13. Young's reads, "… one of the most interesting films ever produced at the Motion Picture Division;" Kael's: "… reveals that John Vicario is a talented and promising young film-maker".
14. In conjunction with P. Adams Sitney's 1968 "Report on the Fourth International Experimental Film Exposition at Knokke-le-Zoute", *Film Culture* published a "List of Films Shown" from that year's festival and the earlier 1958 and 1963 events (*Film Culture* 46 [1967 [sic]]: 11). James Broughton, one of the jurors for the 1963 festival, makes no mention of Vicario's film in his review "Knokke-le Zoute" [sic] (*Film Quarterly* 17:3 [Spring 1964]: 13–15) and concludes: "nothing at Knokke had as much poetic mystery as the murals by Magritte and the paintings by Delvaux that grace the walls of the Casino. Yet one must not expect to encounter a new genius every five years." Vicario's film did receive brief mention in Raymond Borde's review of the festival in *Positif* (60 [Avril–Mai 1964]: 61) where it was grouped with a set of American films that touched on "les labyrinthes de la métaphysique sociale". Vicario takes on "les Supermarchés et leur décor crétinisant [moronic]", as Kenneth Anger tackles fascism, Stan VanDerBeek the atomic bomb, and Bertram Brown racism (*Scorpio Rising*, *Summit* and *Breathdeath*, *The Winner*). The Venice Film Festival database confirms that the film showed there in 1963 (http://asac.labiennale.org/it/ricerca/, accessed 11 March 2014).
15. All biographical information below was obtained during half a dozen phone conversations that I had with Vicario in October and November of 2010. I was able to track his phone number down using the Internet.
16. A session with a sync rig was begun but got cut short when Vicario's satirical friend Bill Stein's questions insulted the store manager that they planned to interview.
17. For more on John Fles see David James, *The Most Typical Avant-Garde: History and Geography of Minor Cinemas in Los Angeles* (Los Angeles: University of California Press, 2005), 221–227; and selections in the "Historical Materials" section of this volume.
18. The Flaherty listing in the Coop catalog remains a mystery to Vicario; the film is not part of their database of films screened (http://flahertyseminar.org/the-flaherty-seminar/films-screened/, accessed 11 March 2014).
19. The film is listed in the "Film-Makers' Cooperative Catalog" as published in *Film Culture* 37 (1965): 63.
20. Vicario did begin editing the carousel footage with Henk Badings music in mind; he was also drawn to the percussive bells that were part of the ride's acoustic (see Vicario's attention to sound and music in the discussion of *Shoppers Market* below).
21. After eventually seeing the film at UCLA, Vicario would later have the chance to express his admiration for it directly to Steiner at his stepmother's dinner table.
22. Registrar records still need to be consulted, but this was probably the first term of 1957.
23. The student films mentioned here are listed as recent standouts from the UCLA program in Colin Young, "University

Film Teaching in the United States: A Survey", *Film Quarterly* 16.3 (Spring 1963): 47. The Melbourne International Film Festival database lists their dates (http://miff.com.au/festival-archive, accessed 11 March 2014).

24. In a second article, "Teaching Film at UCLA", Young states that:

> the most important of the new influences have been – the documentary forms of Robert Flaherty and of cinema-vérité, and the work of the National Film Board of Canada; the experiments in the European cinema – especially those of Antonioni, Fellini, Rouch, Resnais and Godard; and the technological advances which sometimes go hand in hand with the stylistic changes. Until a couple of years ago the students rarely took their camera off the tripod…now the light reflex cameras and the light recorders and microphones are at a premium. (*Journal of the University Film Producers Association* 16.4 [1964]: 21)

Relatedly, see David James on the role of film schools in non-industrial film culture (James, *The Most Typical Avant-Garde*, 205).

25. For a glimpse of Gibson's photography, see *Ralph Gibson: Early Work* in the University of Arizona's Center for Creative Photography's series *The Archive* 24 (1987). This booklet also includes some images from Gibson's and Roger Kennedy's *The Strip: A Graphic Portrait of Sunset Boulevard* (1966).
26. This second story was probably a landing outside of offices. A different Shoppers Market, at Wilshire Boulevard and Berkeley Street, was outfitted with a mezzanine in 1960, but its specific purpose is left unclear in "Remodeling of Santa Monica Market Reported Complete", *Los Angeles Times*, 12 June 1960, 19.
27. I have not yet identified the BWV number for the Bach.
28. Ginsberg, "A Supermarket in California", 136.

17 Raymond Rohauer and the Society of Cinema Arts (1948–1962)

Giving the Devil His Due

Tim Lanza

In a letter dated "Late December, 1969", and prompted by a reading of Parker Tyler's book *Underground Film: A Critical History*[1] Stan Brakhage wrote the following:

> Dear Raymond,
>
> I certainly *never* thought I'd ever be writing you any kind of fan letter; but I guess that's what this writ intends, in a way, to be … I decided to write to you this morning, while listening to Straus's "A Hero's Life", which had the effect of reminding me of many events in my own early living; and I remembered, amidst the music, one Los Angeles night, many years ago, when you drove me from The Coronet Theatre to my residence of the time: during the rather long drive, I remember I told you something about the kind of film I intend to be making many years hence – (amazing!, that I knew then so much about what I would be doing that the conversation was, in fact, accurate prophecy: you, of course, cannot be expected to remember it at all: but I did tell you, then, that I would eventually make a very long film about childhood: and I am, now, several years in midst of a prospective 8 hour film called "*Scenes From Under Childhood,*" and have for many years been making a number of films drawing their inspiration – as I then predicted in that conversation – from the daily activities of domestic living.)
>
> I suppose the Strauss reminded me of all this because his "Hero" is a hero of domestic living – that particular piece followed, in his life, by a "Domestic Symphony" in fact ... these sources being, in these days, of great historic comfort to me as I pursue these aesthetically almost UN-chartered areas of my present work – all this rather unimportant to you, I imagine: (I remember, at the time, your asking "Why would you want to do that?" ... to which I'm sure, I then had no answer – and perhaps haven't an answer now either): but the point of this letter IS that these memories served to remind me that WE were, then, that close in friendship as to permit me to confide some of my most distant dreams, that night.[2]

The "Raymond" Brakhage addresses in his letter was Raymond Rohauer, who, if known at all today, is likely to be remembered for two things: first, his relationship with Buster Keaton, with whom he became a business partner in the mid 1950's in order to re-release Keaton's silent comedies; and second, his reputation for questionable, if not unethical, business practices. Some of those practices, such as tenaciously asserting ownership on films that were either in the public domain, or to which he had only a tenuous chain of title, are likely true;[3] others, such as the claim that in advertisements for his film programs he consistently misspelled the name of French poet and screenwriter Jacques Prevert as Jacques "Pervert" to sensationalize his screenings, are demonstrably false.[4] Rohauer's involvement in film exhibition and distribution in Los Angeles beginning in the late 1940's, in particular his involvement in the access to and exhibition of experimental film, is not well known. But it is undeniable that the activities of his Society of Cinema Arts, particularly through the exhibition of film at the Coronet Theatre (where Brakhage would briefly work and later refer to as the best public theatre for the regular presentation of film in the country), had a profound impact on a generation of filmmakers and scholars living in the Los Angeles area during the 1950's.

Born in Buffalo on 17 March 1924, Rohauer moved to Los Angeles with his mother as a teenager, and graduated from Hollywood High in 1945. While in high school, he had a small non-speaking part in the MGM short feature *Main Street After Dark* (Edward Cahn, 1945). From existing typed and handwritten treatments and radio and film scripts, it is clear that he was also pursuing producing works of his own. These scripts display an interest in the macabre, with titles such as "The Man and the Snake", a handwritten treatment dated 24 February 1945, and "Bats of Death", a typed radio script which is undated.[5] In 1947, he wrote, produced, directed, shot, and acted in a seventy-five minute long amateur film with non-synchronized sound entitled *Whirlpool*. It is best described as a gothic psychological drama about a piano player who is driven mad by his landlady, and who attempts to kill her by placing a snake in her room. Rohauer's character is a young mute whom the composer had befriended. While primarily a supporting role, he also acts as the point of view of the film through narration in Rohauer's voice that supplies the only spoken component of the soundtrack. The film received generally favorable reviews in the weekly trade journal *Hollywood Revue*[6] and in the amateur movie makers periodical *Home Movie*, which called it "the surprise amateur film of the year".[7] At times, the camerawork is used expressively to suggest a psychological and emotional state through the use of extreme close-ups and shots through beveled glass, as well as chiaroscuro lighting that creates an ominous and claustrophobic effect. Unfortunately, the film is weighed down by a ponderous and pretentious narration, which was described in the non-theatrical 16mm film magazine *Film World* review as "stilted and verbose".[8] The original version included several color inserts, though these were removed when Rohauer trimmed the film down to five reels, which is how it appears today in the sole surviving 16mm black and white print. The color inserts, which are mostly comprised of landscape shots, were retained as outtakes. While the *Home Movie* article mentions that Rohauer had already begun work on a second film entitled *Riptide*, there is no evidence to suggest that this or any other film was ever made, though a script for a film entitled "The Ghoul" does survive, indicating a planned shooting to begin in September of 1947.

It was also at this time that Rohauer formed the Society of Cinema Arts, a film society self-described as "a non-profit organization entirely philanthropic in its purpose, devoted to preserving and presenting fine motion pictures of the past".[9] The earliest documented public program is for a series of lectures and films sponsored by the Society in conjunction with Robert Wade Chatterton's Memorable Film Society that took place on Monday evenings from 1 March – 26 April 1948, and was held at the International Recorder's Auditorium on Sunset Boulevard. The program consisted of the presentation of now classic Hollywood and European films with guest speakers, including Jean Renoir, who attended a screening of his film *The Southerner* (1945), and Fritz Lang, who was present for a screening of *Hangmen Also Die* (1943). While this program focused primarily on studio films from America and abroad, it is worth noting the appearance of Rohauer's film *Whirlpool*, which is described in the series' notes as an experimental sound feature. Rohauer's follow up to this program in late June of 1948 was billed as a "Salute To Yesterday: a tribute to the many artists who contributed to the history of the movies", and was solely devoted to Hollywood film.[10] Guest speakers included producer and Vitagraph co-founder Albert E. Smith, and actor Jackie Coogan. Among the films screened were D.W. Griffith's *Judith of Bethulia* (1913), and Griffith himself is listed as a Special Invited Guest; however, unlike the photographic documentation of the participation of Renoir, Lang, Smith, and Coogan, there is no real evidence to show that Griffith, who would die a month later, was in attendance. No documentation of the Society of Cinema Arts's activities after this program and for the entire year of 1949 was found, but the following year saw Rohauer and the Society move to an important new venue and with greatly expanded programming.

In 1950, the twenty-five year old Rohauer began presenting occasional programs at the Coronet Theatre at 366 North La Cienega, which became for the next twelve years the Society of Cinema Arts's primary venue. The earliest an-

Figure 20. Photograph of the Coronet Theatre by Danny Rouzer.

nouncement found for one of these programs was for a six day series co-sponsored by Kenneth Anger and Curtis Harrington's Creative Film Associates, entitled "Illuminations". The program was billed as the West Coast premiere of ten new avant-garde films, though the veracity of that claim is in doubt. The films screened nightly from 20–26 January 1950, and included Anger's *Escape Episode* (1944), *Fireworks* (1947), and *Puce Moment* (1949); Harrington's *Fragment of Seeking* (1946) and *Picnic* (1948); James Broughton's *Mother's Day* (1948); and Sidney Peterson's *The Lead Shoes* (1949).

On 8 August 1950, the Society premiered what it called the 1st Annual International Film Festival, which offered over the course of the month nightly screenings organized into seven separate programs. While featuring important silent and sound films, such as Paul Leni's silent horror film *Waxworks* (1924) and Sergei Eisenstein's *Ten Days That Shook The World* (1928) and *Thunder Over Mexico* (1932/34), half of the Festival's programming days were devoted to experimental film. It included a four-day program of selections from the collection of the San Francisco Museum of Art, such as Frank Stauffacher's *Zigzag* (1948) and *Sausalito* (1948). It also included a five-day program of American and

French works, such as Gregory Markopoulos's *Xmas-USA* (1949) and three films by Man Ray. There was also a five-day program entitled "The Abstract Film As Entertainment", which included eight films by Norman McLaren. A preview of upcoming Society screenings at the Coronet, printed on the back of the festival announcement, lists a variety of American and European silent and sound studio pictures, short films about artists, and dance films. When taken with the experimental films from the festival, these other films provide a clear view of the programming direction that the Society would take.

Similar to already existing film societies, such as that of Paul Ballard's in Los Angeles and Amos Vogel's Cinema 16 in New York, the Society of Cinema Arts offered a variety of experimental, Hollywood, European, Soviet, Asian, educational, documentary, animation, dance, and medical films. What is most impressive is the sheer volume of work presented during each calendar period, and Rohauer's ability to sustain consistent screenings every day of the year for more than a decade. He ran multiple films each evening, as well as matinees on the weekends. In a letter to Vogel, Frank Stauffacher described Rohauer and his programming as follows:

> He is young, and really does not know very much about the subject of experimental films. He is a promoter, and he deals in strange sources of films, but nevertheless he is square, and can be trusted … . He presents films quite indiscriminately, that is, without much selection. I've never been to any of his showings, so don't know what his attendance is. But he has been quite helpful to me in finding certain films, and in showing my own. He is shrewd, and no doubt makes a fair financial go of his showings.[11]

It would be an understatement to suggest that this opinion regarding Rohauer's trustworthiness was not universally shared. In a 1954 letter to Amos Vogel from Kenneth Anger, Anger responded to Vogel's wrongful perception that a screening of *Fireworks* at the Coronet was an intentional violation by Rohauer of Cinema 16's distribution rights in the film. Anger informed Vogel that he had sold the rights to Rohauer when he needed money to complete the rescoring of *Inauguration of the Pleasure Dome* (1954) but had done this "… advisably, since not only by my own experience but in the experience of Curtis [Harrington] and others, Rohauer is not a completely trustworthy person".[12]

Larry Jordan, who was hoping to establish a new theatre with partners in San Francisco, wrote a letter to Rohauer dated 27 January 1957, regarding Rohauer's participation as sole supplier and co-programmer of films for the theatre (which became The Movie on Kearney Street). The letter hints at Rohauer's reputation:

> With an eye for setting up a strong theatre operation, let us get to some fair agreement when we see you next, that will be almost as good as your being here, actively participating. I know what people say about your dealings, Raymond, and that doesn't matter – precisely for this

> reason: I have no interest in doing anyone in, and so no one can ever do me in. You can use me, sure. I am willing to be used, but remember that I know I am being used. And being willing to be used, there is no reason to be sly or cunning about using me.[13]

More bluntly, in an e-mail to me from Jane Wodening, who had been married to Stan Brakhage from 1957 to 1986, Wodening recalls Rohauer this way:

> The one visit I remember, in San Francisco, sitting around the kitchen table with him, carefully parrying his attempts to get us to offer him something. And when he left, I wanted to wash the walls.[14]

However, in order to assess Rohauer's impact objectively, we must consider the actual programming that he was responsible for by taking a look at the available program calendars. As with the majority of primary source material used for this paper, most of these calendars were found in the files held by the Rohauer Collection in Columbus, Ohio. Additional calendars and related documents and information were provided by the ONE National Gay and Lesbian Archives in Los Angeles, the Stan Brakhage Collection at the University of Colorado at Boulder Library Archives, and the Alternative Projections website sponsored by Los Angeles Filmforum. While a complete set of calendars was not available for the entire twelve years that the Society of Cinema Arts was active on a daily basis, we do have documentation that represents about twenty-five percent of the programming. Sometime between 1950 and the beginning of 1951, daily programming began in earnest at the Coronet, which Rohauer specifically stated was not a theatre; he instead dubbed it "The Coronet- Louvre Museum of Arts and Sciences", bringing "genuine art and experimental film to the discriminating film devotee".[15]

The available calendars for the Coronet and for the Riviera-Capri, a two screen theatre on Hollywood Boulevard that was used by the Society of Cinema Arts from 1960 to 1962, reveal programming that was built around a variety of recurring themes. The programs ran from one night only to between two and eight consecutive nights.[16] Extrapolating programming trends from the available data, we can form a reasonably accurate picture of the most commonly scheduled programs, and the frequency at which they were offered. About twenty-three to forty-six percent of the time, the Society offered a series of dance shorts, a French comedy or drama, a festival of UPA cartoons, a German silent or early sound feature, or short documentaries about art or artists. Fifty to sixty-two percent of the time, a viewer would have had the opportunity to see an evening of films based on Shakespeare plays, a collection of science education, mental health and medical films, a program of Soviet features, or a wartime Nazi propaganda film. The three most frequently scheduled programs, each appearing on more than

Figure 21. Society of Cinema Arts calendar covers. Left to right, the dates are: 12 April – 13 May 1951; 1 February – 7 March 1952; 20 June – 7 August 1959; 17 April – 18 July 1962.

eighty percent of the calendars available, were: first, collections of silent and early sound American comedies, with the works of Chaplin being screened most often; second, and bearing witness to the importance Rohauer placed on the avant-garde, were programs of old and new American and European experimental films; and third, English language features by established directors, such as Alfred Hitchcock, John Huston, John Ford, and Orson Welles.

Of all the experimental films screened, the works of Stan Brakhage were shown most frequently, appearing on forty percent of the available calendars. The films shown include *The Way To Shadow Garden* (1954), *Interim* (1952), *Reflections In Black* (1955), *Loving* (1957), *Window Water Baby Moving* (1959), and *Wedlock House* (1959). Other frequently repeated experimental films included Jean Cocteau's *Blood of a Poet* (1930), Luis Buñuel's *Un Chien Andalou* (1929), Hans Richter's *Dreams That Money Can Buy* (1947), James Broughton's *Pleasure Garden* (1953), Bruce Conner's *A MOVIE* (1958), and works by Curtis Harrington, Sydney Peterson, Gregory Markopoulos, and Robert Pike. Films by members of the Gryphon Productions group, including Willard Maas's *Geography of the Body* (1943) and *Image In The Snow* (1952), Maas and Ben Moore's *Mechanics of Love* (1955), and Marie Menken's *Visual Variations On Noguchi* (1945), *Hurry! Hurry!* (1957) and *Glimpse of the Garden* (1957), accounted for thirty percent of the experimental programs scheduled, as did Kenneth Anger's *Inauguration of the Pleasure Dome* and *Fireworks*. *Fireworks* alone appeared in six of the thirty-one available calendars, and it was a screening of this film that led to a raid on the Coronet by the Los Angeles Vice Squad. On 11 October 1957, The Coronet screened the experimental films *Plague Summer* (1951) by Chester Kessler, *Closed Vision* (1954) by Marc'o, John Schmitz's *Voices* (1953), and Kenneth Anger's *Fireworks*. Rohauer was found guilty on the charge of exhibiting obscene material, a charge that was later overturned by a ruling of the Appellate Department of the Superior Court of Los Angeles in 1959.[17] With the inclusion of special pleas to his patrons, the calendar for The Coronet was used by Rohauer before and after his conviction and successful appeal to wage a publicity war against the censorship of his programming, though it also served as an effective promotional tool for the theatre.

The Society also presented special events, such as a four-day series of works by Oskar Fischinger beginning 2 January 1951, the highlight of which was Fischinger himself giving what was, according to Elfriede Fischinger, the first public demonstration of his Visual Color Symphonies.[18] The Coronet Theatre program notes described the event as follows:

> Oskar Fischinger in person, with a startling public demonstration of his invention. Visual

> Color Symphonies. This new visual instrument can make it possible for anybody to produce and create fantastic color plays without the use of a camera, other photographic equipment or machinery. Rich and beautiful colors are obtained responding to the desires of the player. The movements are spontaneous, expressive according to mood, temperament, and feeling of the performer. Extremely easy to play, it can be used as standard equipment for television and entertainment in homes and hospitals.[19]

In addition, the Society played host to a program of films by Maya Deren presented by the filmmaker, the premiere of Willard Maas and Ben Moore's *Narcissus* (1956), the West Coast premieres of Brakhage's *Anticipation of the Night* (1958) and Robert Frank and Alfred Leslie's *Pull My Daisy* (1959), and the Los Angeles premieres of Hans Richter's omnibus film *8X8* (1957) and Ron Rice's *The Flower Thief* (1960). Through these events and the regular screenings offered, The Coronet became one of the most important film venues in LA. In an interview with Adam Hyman, filmmaker Peter Mays stated that he received his education in film history through screenings at the Coronet, in particular recalling screenings of *Geography Of The Body*, *Fireworks*, the early works of Stan Brakhage, the Buñuel films *Un Chien Andalou* and *L'Age d'Or* (1930), and the early Soviet films.[20] Also in an interview with Hyman, Pat O'Neill recalls the impact of repeated screenings of Bruce Conner's *A Movie* there.[21] When asked if the Society of Cinema Arts's programs were at all influential to his growth as a scholar or his knowledge of film history and aesthetics, Raymond Fielding, then a film school student at UCLA, now Dean Emeritus for the Florida State University Film School, replied:

> Absolutely so. They were part of my film education. The Coronet showed classic titles that were rarely screened in the United States in those days. Even when I became a professor of film at UCLA I was unable to get for my classes some of the titles that were featured at the Coronet. I think that film students and devotees considered the Coronet an important educational and cultural asset.[22]

Filmmaker Larry Jordan described the influence of the Coronet as "substantial", saying that he and Brakhage went there because it was really the only place they knew of on the West Coast that showed the films they were interested in seeing.[23]

Rohauer's public screenings, especially of the experimental films, was in part made possible through the life of print contracts that he negotiated beginning in 1951 with several filmmakers, including Brakhage, Anger, Harrington, Markopoulos, Peterson, Maas, and Man Ray. By the end of the decade, Rohauer had expanded the Society's reach beyond Los Angeles by establishing a distribution arm in conjunction with the Audio Film Center and the Cinema Guild. He offered many of the films programmed at the Coronet to film societies, universities, film clubs, and other venues around the country, and published a catalogue in 1958.[24] In addition to the license fees for screening or distribution rights paid to these artists for works already made, Rohauer contributed funds and film stock for the creation of new films. He advanced money to Willard Maas for the completion of *Narcissus*, and would remain in touch with Maas well into the late 1960's, when Rohauer became the film curator for the Huntington Hartford Gallery of Modern Art in New York. Rohauer also provided color stock for Gregory Markopoulos's *Eldora* (1956), and had more than a decade-long relationship with the filmmaker, beginning with correspondences dating back as early as 1950 when the filmmaker was living in Toledo, Ohio. He also commissioned Brakhage's *Flesh of Morning* (1956), though the ownership of the film would cause a rift between the two. This despite a Letter Agreement from Brakhage to Rohauer dated 23 April 1956, that begins:

This is to specify that the 16MM film *Flesh of Morning* is your property with all world rights for distribution, rental, print sale, theatrical and television showing.[25]

Brakhage quickly came to feel betrayed by Rohauer's claim of co-ownership of the film, and a new Agreement was drawn up just one month later to stipulate that the two each owned fifty percent of the film until a formal settlement could be reached. It was not until 1962, by which time Rohauer had given up the Society of Cinema Arts and had left California, that they reached a formal agreement, in which Rohauer relinquished his claim to ownership in exchange for a fifty per cent royalty on future earnings. While the two continued to correspond on a friendly basis, with Brakhage detailing aspects of his life and the work that he was doing, as well as frequently chiding Rohauer for writing only about business, it was really not until Brakhage's letter of late December 1969 that the filmmaker seemed to be ready to put the past behind them and acknowledge Rohauer's importance. And so, it seems fitting to conclude by returning to the closing paragraphs of Brakhage's letter:

> I think you were the first person, in my adult living, whom I'd felt really betrayed me (over the "Flesh of Morning" matter): and you did, thus, encourage a too-heavy enmity from a, then, rather too-sure-of-himSELF young man: in the meantime, I've been "betrayed" by many people, naturally enough, and have grown old enough to realize that MY sense of what happened is not, perhaps, the *only* rightful viewpoint ... have come to see that you probably *thought* you had an economic right to part ownership of "Flesh of Morning" – (which is to say, I *still* think you were in-the-wrong but have lived long enough now, experienced enough living, to realize that YOU probably didn't then think-so ... thus possibly weren't *consciously* "cheating" me: that realization has made a tremendous difference in my feelings about you – has much tempered whatever anger I've, in the meantime, maintained toward you ... the passions of Youth being so strong that they can cast a shadow over a man's whole life unless he grow-up enough to throw some light upon them): anyway, I am, this morning, suddenly no longer angry with you; and I just felt like writing and telling you – to whom this may not matter at all – about that conversion of feeling.
>
> The "fan" part of this letter is, then now, simple: you have, in your life, done a great deal for

Figure 22. Stan Brakhage (left) and Raymond Rohauer (right) on balcony of Rohauer's apartment in New York, NY.

film, and for the particular area of film that is my whole life's concern: you deserve much praise for this – praise which I have reserved, all these years, because I felt that much hurt by what I took to be your betrayal of me. You are a controversial figure, naturally ... drawing much public condemnation in the petty conversations of the "film world": and, while I have not talked much *against* you, I certainly haven't taken opportunities to speak much in your favor (harboring this youthfully righteous "grudge" as I have been doing): I am now, suddenly, ashamed about that (that I let my personal feelings interfere with any possible public defense of your good work – tho', in fairness to myself, I *have*, on a number of occasions, defended you at least within the framework of "give The Devil his due" and praised The Coronet Theatre for what it was certainly worth, thus ... : "the best public theatre for regular presentation of filmic works-of-art ever created, yet, in this country": still and all – I've been too cautious in recognition of your efforts...

Ah, well! – I won't go on-and-on ... (it occurs to me that YOU may take this letter as a sign that I WANT something from you – that I'm flattering you, or some-such, to accomplish something ... only Time would show, I suppose, that that's not the case).

I'll send this letter, then (rather as if putting a note into a bottle – a note that simply says "hello" or some-such ... *not* one asking for anything ... and cast it sea-wise – for the fun-of-it), and wish you, simply, a Happy New Year ...

Blessings,

Stan[26]

Notes

1. Parker Tyler, *Underground Film: A Critical History* (New York, NY: Grove Press, 1969).
2. Stan Brakhage, letter to Raymond Rohauer, late December, 1969. Personal files of Raymond Rohauer, Rohauer Collection Archives, Columbus, Ohio. In order to remain faithful to Brakhage's idiosyncratic orthography, grammar in all passages from his letters have been left unchanged.

3. One of the most often cited of which was the lengthy lawsuit initiated by Rohauer acting on behalf of Epoch Producing Corporation against the Museum of Modern Art and distributor Paul Killiam over the rights to the Griffith film *Birth of a Nation* (1915). For a concise overview, see Anthony Slide, *Nitrate Won't Wait: a history of film preservation in the United States* (Jefferson, N.C.: McFarland & Company, Inc., 1992), 48–49.
4. Cited in John Baxter, "The Silent Empire of Raymond Rohauer: The Ever Expanding Power of the Cinema's Strangest Mogul", *The Sunday Times Magazine* (London), 19 January 1975, 32–33, 38–39; and in William K Everson, "Raymond Rohauer: King of the Film Freebooters", *Grand Street* 49 (Summer 1994): 188–196. Of the thirty-one calendars available in the Rohauer archives, eight list films that include a credit to Prevert. None are misspelled.
5. An intriguing photo of a young Rohauer and two other men at an apparently on-air microphone of Los Angeles radio station KFWB suggests that Rohauer also tried his hand as a radio personality. The photograph, marked on the back in Rohauer's hand as being from 1947, identifies his companions as writer Leo Guild and "Criswell", who would later be known as "The Amazing Criswell", a radio personality and psychic who was known for his wildly inaccurate predictions and who would go on to appear in three films by Ed Wood, Jr. There is no indication as to the content of the scripts they hold in their hands.
6. Reed Porter, "Ray Rohauer Creates Imaginative Flight In 16MM 'Whirlpool'", *Hollywood Review*, 25 February 1947, 6.
7. J.H. Schoen, "Hollywood Genius" *Home Movie,* April 1947, 216–217, 240–242.
8. *Film World* Vol. III, No. 6, June 1947.
9. "1st Annual International Film Festival" pamphlet, Society of Cinema Arts, 8 August to 17 September 1950.
10. "Salute to Yesterday" program handbill, Rohauer Collection Archives.
11. Frank Stauffacher, letter to Amos Vogel, 4 May 1951, as cited in *Cinema 16: Documents Toward a History of the Film Society*, ed. Scott MacDonald (Philadelphia: Temple University Press, 2002), 162.
12. Kenneth Anger, letter to Amos Vogel, 28 August 1954, as cited in *Cinema 16*, 237.
13. Larry Jordan, letter to Raymond Rohauer, 27 January 1957. Personal files of Raymond Rohauer, Rohauer Collection Archives, Columbus, Ohio.
14. Jane Wodening, e-mail message to author, 5 October 2010.
15. Coronet-Louvre Museum of Arts and Sciences, pamphlet, 2 January to 9 March 1951.
16. A Coronet calendar from September of 1956 also shows that the Society of Cinema Arts was sponsoring screenings at the Theatre Now at 716 N. La Cienega Blvd. in what had been the Turnabout Theatre. It is unclear how long this theatre was being used by the Society, but in a letter from Rohauer to Brakhage dated 10 February 1957, Rohauer informs Brakhage that the Los Angeles Building Department closed the theatre on 30 November of the previous year, claiming that the building was unsafe.
17. Whitney Strub, in his book *Perversion for Profit: The Politics of Pornography and the Rise of the New Rights* (New York: Columbia University Press, 2011), 38–39, lays out a convincing argument that the Los Angeles Police Department was targeting Rohauer, whom Strub mistakenly refers to as "Richard Rohauer", and the Coronet due to its reputation as being a gathering place for gay men.
18. "Writing Light", Center For Visual Music, accessed 30 October 2011, http://www.centerforvisualmusic.org/WritingLight.htm
19. Coronet-Louvre Museum of Arts and Sciences, pamphlet, 2 January 2 to 9 March 1951.
20. Peter Mays, in interview with Adam Hyman, 4 December 2009.
21. Pat O'Neill, in interview with Adam Hyman, 6 June 2010.
22. Raymond Fielding, e-mail message to author, 3 October 2010.
23. Larry Jordan, in telephone interview with author, 8 October 2010.
24. The sixteen-page catalogue, registered for copyright by Society of Cinema Arts, is representative of the programming at the Coronet itself. Silent shorts and features by D.W. Griffith, Charlie Chaplin, Jean Renoir, Abel Gance and others were offered, as were sound features by Fritz Lang, Carl Theodor Dreyer, Alfred Hitchcock and Frank Capra. In addition to Brakhage's *Flesh of the Morning*, *Daybreak* (1957) and *White Eye* (1957), the last two presented in the catalogue as two separate films, a number of experimental films were made available, including those by James Sibley Watson and Melville Webber, Gregory Markopoulos, and Larry Jordan. Rounding out the catalogue were various documentaries, animation, propaganda, and mental health films.
25. Stan Brakhage letter to Raymond Rohauer, 23 April 1956. Personal files of Raymond Rohauer, Rohauer Collection Archives, Columbus, Ohio.
26. Brakhage letter to Rohauer, late December, 1969.

18 For Love and/or Money: Exhibiting Avant-Garde Film in Los Angeles 1960–1980

Alison Kozberg

Between 1960 and 1980, avant-garde film exhibition in Los Angeles enjoyed a period of unprecedented growth and collaboration.[1] This brief history takes these exhibitors as its primary objects of study, and identifies curatorship as a critical juncture where the entanglement of capital and cultural values is visible. During the 1960s and 1970s, public exhibitions were the primary mediator between experimental film and the public, and consequently taught viewers how to engage with and appreciate non-narrative, abstract, and artisanal cinema. However, many of these exhibitors were also businesses, and their curatorial strategies reflected the objectives of audience cultivation and financial sustainability. Accordingly, this history traces how cultural values, capital, and institutional resources shaped curatorial practices and public perception. By revealing notions of value and quality as constructed rather than innate, this deliberately anti-nostalgic project advocates for the ongoing revision of artistic paradigms, and seeks to work through avant-garde film's past in order to encourage a challenging and heterogeneous future.

Going Underground: Subversion in the 1960s

The 1960s were an intensely vibrant and financially successful period for experimental film in Los Angeles, when the stated rejection of mainstream conservatism attracted audiences and linked cinema to the developing counterculture.[2] Alienated from commercial resources and institutions, theaters developed independent strategies for marketing and audience cultivation in order to establish a small, semi-commercial film infrastructure that functioned separate from, but alongside, those of Hollywood. The production and presentation of subversive content using resources abandoned or neglected by the commercial film industry contributed to the widespread use of the term "underground", a cultural descriptive lifted from a 1961 article by computer film innovator Stan VanDerBeek.[3] While lightly suggesting tawdry content, "underground" also aptly described the blending of formal and social radicalism, and the subordination of individual films to innovative, interactive presentations and experiences.[4]

The primary innovator of cross-genre, extra-filmic programming in Los Angeles was a radical poet and paperback bookseller named John Fles. Fles believed in the power of context to inform and shape an artwork, and was curious about how an eclectic array of images and experiences might impact the mind and body. Beginning in the late 1950s, he was an important participant in Chicago and New York's underground literary communities, and counted beat poetry, particularly the work of LeRoi Jones, the Living Theater, and early efforts by Jonas Mekas at the Charles Theater on Ave B, amongst his most significant influences.[5] While exposing Fles to experimental form, these artists and venues also modeled ways to disrupt artworks' boundaries and to challenge their audience.

Fles's early editorial and curatorial efforts extended his peers' commitment to abstract form and forceful content, while revealing a pronounced interest in popular culture. Beginning with his 1959 publication *The Trembling Lamb,* a slender volume of writings by Antonin Artaud, Carl Solomon, and LeRoi Jones, paired with a cover photo of Jean Harlow, Fles explored how the avant-garde's abstraction and brutality might highlight narratives lurking beneath the surface of popular culture.[6] The volume demonstrated Fles's willingness to combine art with commercial imagery, a tactic he used to pressure artworks' boundaries and augment their meanings.

In 1963, Fles returned to Los Angeles, borrowed a projector from *Holy Barbarians* author Larry Lipton, and founded the Trak Film Group, a small and itinerant film series. The series was intimate, informal, and included a combination of Expressionist films such as *Blood of a Poet* (Cocteau, 1930), *Metropolis* (Lang, 1927), *The Cabinet of Dr. Caligari* (Wiene, 1920), and lesser-known experimental works by Bruce Baillie, Christopher Maclaine, and Stan Brakhage. This programming strategy proposed contemporary experimental works as the progeny of the European avant-garde, subtly linking their shared concern for consciousness and loose narrative causality. Fles also developed cross-genre pairings including an

April double feature of Bruce Conner's *A MOVIE* (1958) and the "Early American Dada" film *Duck Soup* (McCarey, 1933), which united the films in a common anarchism.[7] By christening *Duck Soup* as Dada, Fles simultaneously proposed that counter-cultural impulses existed within the commercial cinema, and that such impulses could be made visible to savvy viewers. The program was crucial to Fles's curatorial development, and presaged his ongoing effort to clarify and create cinematic meaning through programming.

Fles further supplemented his programming efforts by cultivating the tone and setting of the series. The screenings took place in non-theatrical spaces including Mother Neptune's, a coffee shop in East Hollywood where guests could pay a \$1.50 donation to casually watch from pillows on the floor. He also extended and promoted the series' underground and communal sensibility by advertising shows with bold, hand addressed, printed postcards designed by local artists including Bob Alexander and Wallace Berman.[8]

In autumn of 1963, outfitted with a substantial mailing list, Fles approached Mike Getz, the young manager of the Cinema Theater on Western Avenue in Hollywood, about establishing an ongoing series. The theater was a large, single screen art house owned by Getz's uncle Louis K. Sher, the entrepreneur behind the Art Theatre Guild chain.[9] In 1963, the art cinema movement was at its peak, and the Cinema Theater regularly had its pick of international masterworks by Ingmar Bergman, Jean Renoir, and Satyajit Ray.[10] Sher was hospitable to the collaboration, and Getz and Fles set out to establish a weekly, experimental, midnight movie program.

Fles and Getz established the aptly titled Movies 'Round Midnight as a society with a nominal subscription fee, since members-only organizations were subject to less legal oversight. Inspired by Jonas Mekas's efforts in New York, Fles inaugurated the series on Columbus Day, 1963, with an ambitious triple feature of *Dog Star Man Part I* (Brakhage, 1962), *Flaming Creatures* (Smith, 1963), and *Twice A Man* (Markopoulos, 1963).[11] The event's flyer encouraged viewers to discover "the New American Cinema", a term used by Mekas in *Film Culture* to describe spirited, personal films made outside of commercial institutions. Though concerned with introducing Los Angeles to the New York avant-garde, and committed to continuing Mekas's practice of curating single artist shows, Fles was equally invested in developing a local community bonded by shared, immersive theatrical experiences.

In 1964, Fles authored his manifesto *Seeing is Believing*, a short, passionate text that positioned the curator as the primary force in guiding the audience's perspective and shaping cinematic meaning. Under the subject heading "Strat-

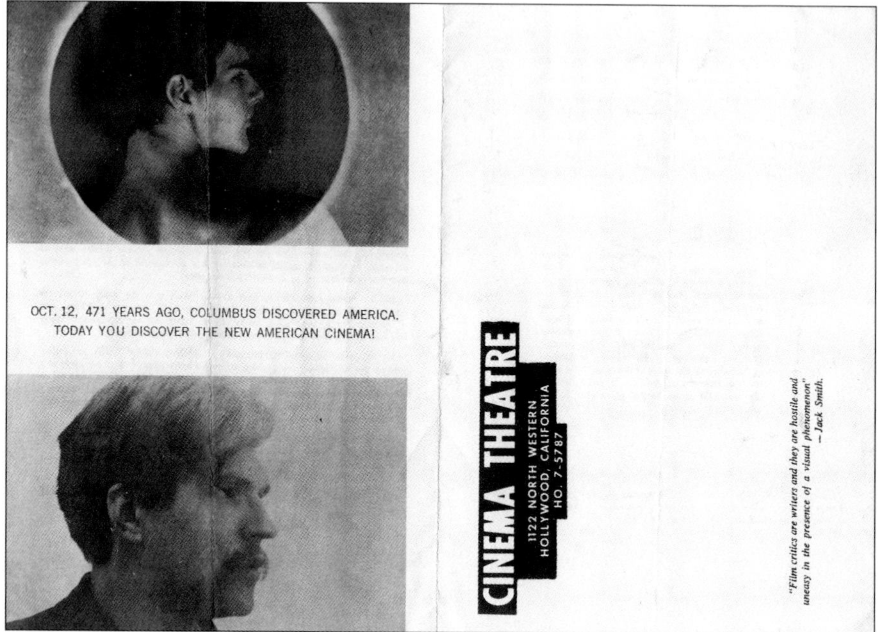

Figure 23. Inaugural Movies 'Round Midnight Program from 12 October 1963. The program featured caption reads, "Oct. 12 471 Years Ago Columbus Discovered America. Today You Discover the New American Cinema!"

egy", Fles printed the D.W. Griffith quote: "The task I'm trying to achieve above all is to make you see". Though he was not explicitly interested in pedagogy, the quote reveals his persistent concern with nurturing viewers' insights and alerting them to popular culture's suppressed and subversive content. Influenced by Eisenstein's theories of montage, Fles argued that the curator was an editor with the power to create meaning through juxtaposition, to respond to the audience's will, and to expose social taboos.[12] He experimented extensively with these ideas throughout 1964 and 1965, and regularly paired experimental works such as *The End* (1953) and *The Man Who Invented Gold* (1957) by San Francisco filmmaker Christopher Maclaine, and *Breathdeath* (1963) by Stan VanDerBeek, with genre fantasies including *Tarzan of the Apes* (Sidney, 1918), *Sudan* (Rawlins, 1945), and *Mars Attacks the World* (Beebe and Hill, 1938).[13]

By the mid-1960s, the appropriation and critique of popular culture artifacts were widely acknowledged as central to contemporary arts production. Already tremendously influential in New York, pop art, synthetic materials, and Hollywood refuse had particular resonance in Los Angeles, a city long known and occasionally reviled as a bastion of commercialism. Writing for *The Partisan Review* in 1964, literary critic Susan Sontag linked the contemporary preoccupation with low culture to "camp", a newfound taste for extravagance and irreverence.[14] Her essay provided an apt description of New York trio Jack Smith, Ken Jacobs, and Ron Rice's practice of perverting Hollywood by appropriating its ephemera and aesthetics. These filmmakers' works influenced Fles, who developed programs intended to provoke viewers and to puncture commercial cinema's presumed propriety. Using double features such as the West Coast premiere of Rice's decadently shabby *Chumlum* (1964), paired with the Flash Gordon serial "Rocket Ship", starring a well-muscled Buster Crabbe, Fles exposed queer eroticism as central to mainstream narratives.[15] According to Fles's somewhat utopian vision, cultural appropriation was capable of transforming society and upending its "accepted (i.e.) cancerous social mores".[16]

Despite Fles's radical aspirations, his efforts primarily attracted an audience sympathetic to his sensibilities.[17] While able to effectively skewer Hollywood at Movies 'Round Midnight, Fles never introduced his tactics into purely commercial, high profile spaces or deliberately confronted unsuspecting spectators. The persistence of stringent obscenity laws notwithstanding, Fles's members-only, midnight series generally played to curious, sympathetic parties, and consequently avoided government oversight and legal restriction. However, the Cinema Theater's regular evening programs had no membership policy, and attracted a more eclectic audience, leaving manager Mike Getz far more vulnerable to legal action. In March of 1964, Getz decided to screen a double feature of Kenneth Anger's gay biker fantasy *Scorpio Rising* with Aldofas Mekas's *Hallelujah the Hills* during the theater's regular program.[18] On 7 March a Hollywood vice squad raided the double feature and confiscated Anger's film, declaring it lewd and obscene.[19] The arresting officers primarily objected to its overt depictions of homosexuality, particularly documentary-style footage of a raucous stag party. In the subsequent court proceedings one of the arresting officers testified that the film "showed contempt for, pardon the expression, for the square", and the prosecution entered a few of the film's blurry stills, believed to depict erect penises, into evidence.[20] Though the trial's all-women jury initially found Getz guilty, his lawyer, the famed first amendment advocate Stanley Fleishman, succeeded at having the charges dismissed on appeal.[21]

The trial, which coincided with similar proceedings against Jonas Mekas in New York, garnered considerable media attention, and galvanized the underground film community.[22] Getz's arrest occurred mere weeks before Anger was awarded a sizable Ford Foundation Grant based on *Scorpio Rising*'s artistic merit, a coincidence that diminished the charges as provincial and reactionary. By 1964, the original Production Code's extensive list of prohibitions was largely out of synch with prevailing social mores, and the MPAA's enforcement of them was dwindling.[23] Consequently, the trial, which drew attention to Anger and the Cinema Theater, distinguished the venue from its pedestrian Hollywood counterparts, legitimized its underground status, and alerted audiences to the availability of racy content. Restrictions relaxed even further that June after the Supreme Court ruled that the First Amendment protected all creative expression, except hard-core pornography, in *Jacobellis v. Ohio* (1964). Empowered by legal protection, independent theaters proceeded to capitalize on the trial's publicized sensationalism and advertise their programs' eroticism.[24]

In 1965, Fles decided to leave the Cinema Theater, believing that the underground film movement had reached its peak.[25] Fles was correct in observing that underground cinema was attaining decidedly above-ground visibility and commercial viability. Fles's successor Getz was also attuned to these opportunities, and designed Movies 'Round Midnight's subsequent marketing to highlight the series' subversive content and youthful exuberance. Later that year while discussing Movies 'Round Midnight's ongoing success with *Los Angeles Times* film critic Kevin Thomas, Getz appreciatively observed: "our audience is beautiful, young – a beautiful segment of our society".[26] In sentiment and tone, Getz's statement echoed the rhetoric regularly espoused by Andy Warhol, the artist whose work would transform the underground. Already a well-known cultural icon, Warhol began 1965 by designing a candy-colored cover for the *Time Magazine* story "Today's Teenagers".[27] The cover preceded a flurry of media coverage and the ascent of Warhol's factory girls as fashion icons, which signaled the dissemination of "underground" as a stylistic instead of political categorization.[28] Warhol's studio, "the factory", was a decidedly hierarchical celebrity showcase, as demonstrated by 1965's star-studded "50 Most Beautiful Party", and ultimately more equipped to train good consumers than political radicals.

In 1966, Cinematheque 16, a small storefront exhibitor located on the Sunset Strip, joined the Cinema Theater in regularly screening underground film. Flanked by the Strip's music venues, Cinematheque 16 was well positioned to attract young consumers disenchanted with Hollywood output. Exploitation film producer Robert Lippard owned the venue and, though open to experimental cinema, he was primarily concerned with generating a profit. Lippard hired Lewis Teague, a former NYU student familiar with underground cinema, to program the theater. After a few poorly attended single-artist shows and documentary screenings, Teague began to successfully promote eclectic shorts programs as "Psychedelic Film Trips". Though primarily consisting of abstract, non-narrative

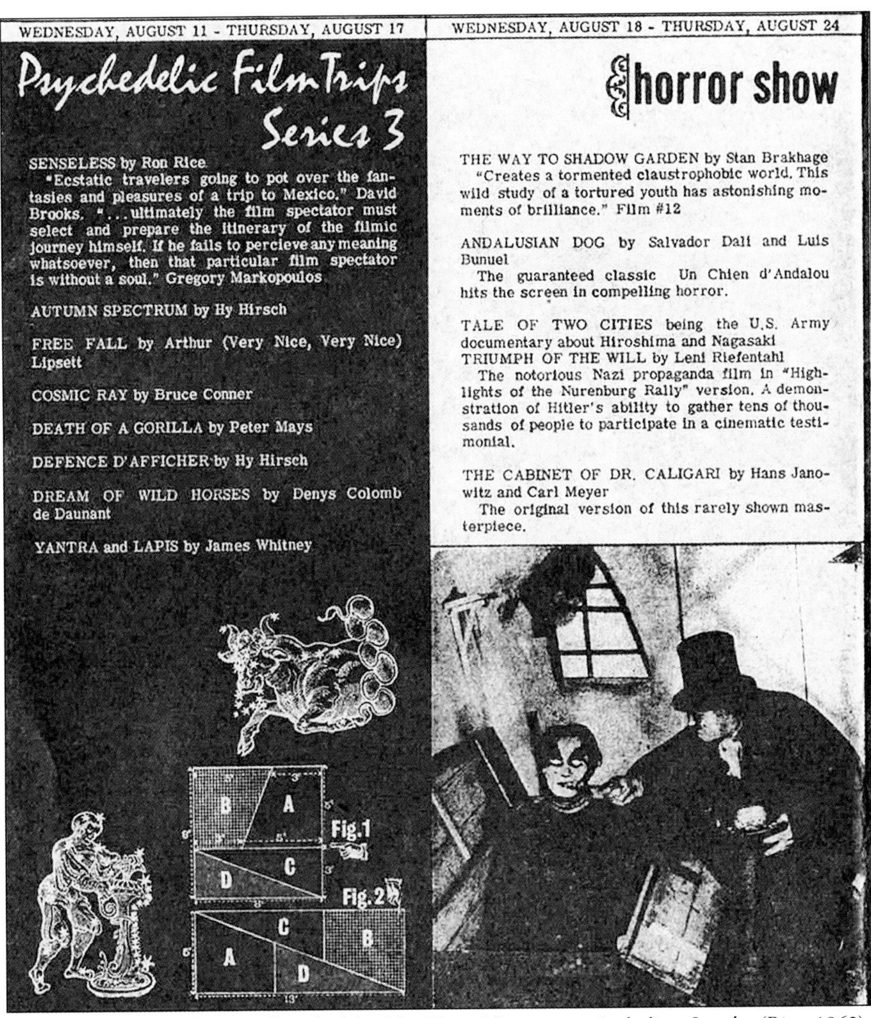

WEDNESDAY, AUGUST 11 - THURSDAY, AUGUST 17

Psychedelic Film Trips Series 3

SENSELESS by Ron Rice
"Ecstatic travelers going to pot over the fantasies and pleasures of a trip to Mexico." David Brooks. "...ultimately the film spectator must select and prepare the itinerary of the filmic journey himself. If he fails to percieve any meaning whatsoever, then that particular film spectator is without a soul." Gregory Markopoulos

AUTUMN SPECTRUM by Hy Hirsch

FREE FALL by Arthur (Very Nice, Very Nice) Lipsett

COSMIC RAY by Bruce Conner

DEATH OF A GORILLA by Peter Mays

DEFENCE D'AFFICHER by Hy Hirsch

DREAM OF WILD HORSES by Denys Colomb de Daunant

YANTRA and LAPIS by James Whitney

WEDNESDAY, AUGUST 18 - THURSDAY, AUGUST 24

horror show

THE WAY TO SHADOW GARDEN by Stan Brakhage
"Creates a tormented claustrophobic world. This wild study of a tortured youth has astonishing moments of brilliance." Film #12

ANDALUSIAN DOG by Salvador Dali and Luis Bunuel
The guaranteed classic Un Chien d'Andalou hits the screen in compelling horror.

TALE OF TWO CITIES being the U.S. Army documentary about Hiroshima and Nagasaki
TRIUMPH OF THE WILL by Leni Riefentahl
The notorious Nazi propaganda film in "Highlights of the Nurenburg Rally" version. A demonstration of Hitler's ability to gather tens of thousands of people to participate in a cinematic testimonial.

THE CABINET OF DR. CALIGARI by Hans Janowitz and Carl Meyer
The original version of this rarely shown masterpiece.

Figure 24. Calendar featuring "Psychedelic Film Trips 3," a program including *Senseless* (Rice, 1962), *Free Fall* (Lipsett, 1964), *Cosmic Ray* (Conner, 1962), *Death of a Gorilla* (Mays, 1965), *Défense d'Afficher* (Hirsch, 1959), *Dream of Wild Horses* (de Daunant, 1960), *Yantra* (Whitney, 1957), and *Lapis* (Whitney, 1966). Cinémathèque 16 Calendar, August–September 1966.

films, the programs benefited from Teague's savvy marketing, which promised consciousness-expanding experiences analogous to an acid trip.[29]

The effective marketing and exhibition of underground cinema peaked in December 1966 with the New York release of Warhol's dual-projection, superstar showcase *Chelsea Girls*. The film later premiered in Los Angeles at the Cinema Theater in March of 1967, the same month that Verve Records released *The Velvet Underground and Nico*, the band's debut album. The sprawling film combined informal documentation, gregarious posturing, intimate portraits, and underground music in an unwieldy performance, executed by projectionists nationwide according to Warhol's instructions. The film ran for over six months, making its way from underground to mainstream theaters. Its vignettes included lingering footage of chanteuse Nico trimming her bangs, Mary Woronov disciplining International Velvet and Ingrid Superstar, and a grim climax in which a drug-addled Ondine attacks Ronna Page. Widely acknowledged as underground cinema's breakthrough into mainstream distribution, the film's alternately chic and sadistic sequences also demonstrated an unsettling affinity for narcissism, consumerism, and misogyny.

Subsequent programming at the Cinema Theater and Cinematheque 16 developed upon *Chelsea Girls*'s expanded mode of presentation, and echoed its themes, emphasizing self-discovery, liberated sexuality, and drug use. Though the Cinema Theater had been experimenting with psychedelic programs since 1965 when Fles hosted a somewhat stilted recreation of a drug trip by Ken Kesey's Merry Pranksters, it was not until 1967 that the two venues fully embraced psychedelic culture.[30] That year, Cinematheque 16 projectionist Jeffery Perkins hosted a multiple projector light show to accompany a screening of *Now That The Buffalo's Gone* (Gershfield, 1967), a hallucinogenic tribute to American Indians. The show, which laid the groundwork for the formation of Single Wing Turquoise Bird in 1968, opened the cinematic experience beyond the projector and screen to encompass a stimulating, immersive environment.[31] The program coincided with the rise of psychedelic rock, a music genre that fused utopianism's technological and pastoral impulses in a sound that blended folk sensibilities with aggressive electronic enhancement. This new sound spurred the use of analogously dizzying graphics on concert posters and album covers. By 1967, Movies 'Round Midnight's brochures clearly reflected this trend, and regularly featured undulating illustrations of nude women, biomorphic shapes, and starbursts.

The concurrent liberation of mind and body was central to the underground's utopian fantasies, which conflated freedom with the easy availability of female bodies.

Writing for his 1970 anthology *Expanded Cinema*, *Los Angeles Free Press* critic and techno-utopianist Gene Youngblood proposed a bill of rights for the year 2000 that "would defend human liberty, not civil liberty", and ensure the rights of "health, truth, reality, sexual fulfillment, study, travel, peace, intimacy, leisure, the right to be unique".[32] Youngblood's formulation of essential rights was consistent with the widespread identification of individualism and sexual gratification as fundamental to escaping the repression and conformity of "square"

Figure 25. 11 November 1967, "Woman What in God's Name is Inside of You?" featuring *Womancock* (Linder, 1965) and *The Passion of Joan of Arc* (Dreyer, 1928). The description of *Womancock* includes Linder's statement that: "The film captures her ruthless and sinister capacities. It celebrates her complexity, her bizarre mating rites, her beauty and her dark compulsions." Movies 'Round Midnight Calendar November–December 1967.

living and Hollywood cinema. This sentiment, as well as awareness of its popular appeal, was immediately evident in underground film programming. In its Winter 1967 calendar, Movies 'Round Midnight announced an upcoming double feature of *The Passion of Joan of Arc* (Dreyer, 1928) and Carl Linder's orgiastic *Womancock* (1965) with a long, sinuous drawing of a nude woman arching her back. Linder's explicit film was advertised with a quote that read: "it celebrates her complexity, her bizarre mating rites, her beauty and her dark compulsions". The same season featured the programs: "Movies for the Aggressive Man and His Woman! (It's time you showed her where it's at)", and "I'd Love To Turn You On", a shorts package that included the film *The Psychedelics*, advertised as "abstractions of reality using psychedelic patterns projected onto nude female bodies".[33] Though seemingly light-hearted, these programs and nostalgic recollections of Cinematheque 16 attendees in "minis" and "hot pants" reflected the counterculture's persistent objectification of women, behavior that feminist Robin Morgan described as "reinstituted oppression by another name".[34]

With the exception of "The West Coast Black Cinema Festival", a program featuring *Prelude to a Revolution: Huey Newton in Jail* (Evans, 1966) at Cinematheque 16's Pasadena venue, representations of topical political issues were largely absent from Los Angeles's underground film programs.[35] While consistently pursuing social resistance through self-discovery, experimentation, and sexual liberation, underground venues remained detached from direct political action and overtly political filmmaking. Writing for *Playboy*'s "Sex in Cinema" series in 1967, film critic Arthur Knight argued that the underground's primary selling point was its "concentration on forbidden topics" including "perversion, homosexuality, sadism, drugs". However, Knight dismissed the depiction of such topics as filmmakers merely "thumbing their noses at convention" before critiquing audiences for believing they were "thumbing right along with them simply by attending the screenings".[36] Though critical, Knight's *Playboy* article signaled mainstream curiosity about underground cinema.

Instead of upending the social order, Cinematheque 16, Movies 'Round Midnight and its 1968 successor Underground Cinema 12's taunting of conservative mores effectively exploited both Hollywood's stagnancy and the informal pornography industry. Though sexploitation films still enjoyed hearty theatrical circulation, a vibrant market had also developed for 16mm loops and beaver films, many of which screened in the same storefronts and venues as experimental works.[37] Though initially successful, exhibitors' blend of sex, humor, and abstraction depended on gaps in the commercial marketplace. Consequently, the viability of underground cinema was irreparably damaged by the emergence of the New Hollywood with *Bonnie and Clyde* (Penn, 1967) and the Warhol-inspired *Midnight Cowboy* (Schlesinger, 1969), and development of a 35mm commercial pornography industry following the Supreme Court's decision in *Stanley v. Georgia* (1969). The availability of sex, drugs, and rock n' roll in pristine, linear features diminished underground cinema's audience, and by 1972, the Cinema Theater was primarily exhibiting sexploitation films, and Cinematheque 16 was screening pornography. However, interest in film art and theatrical engagement persisted and laid the foundation for the rise of non-profits and midnight movies during the following decade.[38]

Philanthropy and Funding in the 1970s

Following the collapse of underground cinema's semi-commercial infrastructure, newly formed non-profit exhibitors abandoned crowd-pleasing, transgressive revelry in favor of encouraging intellectual engagement. These efforts benefited from increased Federal arts funding, the ascent of film in the American university, and a rise in arts philanthropy. Underpinning both Federal funding and philanthropy was the shared objective of social betterment, articulated in the National Endowment for the Arts's authorizing legislation as a commitment to "high standards and increased opportunities ... in the best interest of the nation's cultural progress".[39] Though broadly stated, this objective, and its privately funded equivalents, tended to favor arts initiatives that demonstrated American cultural excellence, served a pedagogical function such as providing historical knowledge or nurturing arts appreciation, and engaged with predetermined standards for determining artistic quality. By the 1970s, all of Los Angeles's regular experimental film exhibitors were non-profits, and many were staffed by former students or teachers from local art and film schools. Consequently, many of the decade's programmers were highly aware of curatorship's pedagogical functions, and concerned about equitable exhibition and scholarly responsibility. Supported by external funding, and inspired by museum display and the methods of discourse analysis, Los Angeles's film curators developed methods to clarify film history and eventually to interrogate value, precedent, and homogeneity.

One of the earliest pedagogically informed exhibitions in Los Angeles was the Yankee Underground Film Festival at Occidental College in April of 1968, mere weeks before the internationally resonant May uprisings in France. The daylong festival was a direct response to the contentious political climate, and demonstrated an acute awareness of the role students might play in revolutionary activity. Inspired by contemporary international and experimental cinema's formal achievements and political impulses, English professors Marsha Kinder and Bill Moritz designed the festival to introduce their students to difficult works. The ambitious chronological survey opened with Porter's trance film *Dream of a Rarebit Fiend* (1906), and culminated in an explosive program of contemporary films that included Pat O'Neill's *7362* (1967), Bruce Conner's found footage *Cosmic Ray* (1962), and Robert Nelson's irreverent *Oh Dem Watermelons* (1965).

In contrast to the previous decade's provocations, the festival emphasized experimental cinema's history and helpful methods for analysis. The program's clear, linear structure arranged the films into a narrative, allowing viewers to observe reoccurring tropes and trace historical progress. Since most of the films exhibited were non-narrative, abstract, and deliberately distinct from Hollywood product, a substantial amount of context was provided in the event's bound program notes. The volume featured contributions from Kinder, Moritz, and Robert Pike, the founder of the Creative Film Society, and included studies on local filmmakers, an explanation of the meaning of experimental film, and suggestions for frustrated viewers.[40] Clearly written, and academically informed, the notes anticipated curators' growing investment in providing clear explanations and supplementary materials.

Though he maintained a commitment to pedagogy throughout his career, Moritz soon became wary of retrospective programs' potentially exclusionary effects. Following the 1969 establishment of Anthology Film Archives, and the 1972 publication of P. Adams Sitney's hugely influential "historical morphology" *Visionary Film*, Moritz became concerned that surveys were irresponsible, lacked perspective, and prematurely summarized the history of experimental film.[41] Having previously worked at the Creative Film Society and established his own film distribution agency, the Los Angeles Film-Maker's Cooperative, Moritz was keenly aware of the scope of experimental film production in California, and resented its meager treatment in Sitney's work. Moritz subsequently embraced single-artist shows as a suitable corrective to these sweeping master narratives. While maintaining retrospectives' qualitative assurances, single-artist shows encouraged deeper engagement with fewer works, and contributed to a canon that could grow continuously.

In 1973, a job offer from the Theatre Vanguard, an avant-garde performance arts non-profit in West Hollywood, provided Moritz with the resources to expand his curatorial efforts. The organization's president was Judith Stark, a former dancer and emerging philanthropist committed to funding local artists.[42] Stark was a committed modernist with a taste for the aesthetics, if not the political implications, of early avant-gardes, and she supported exhibitions of modern dance and experimental and electronic music. Her faith in the value of these works was absolute, and she hoped to use the Theatre Vanguard to compensate worthy artists and edify the public. Though Stark primarily envisioned the Theatre Vanguard as a performance venue, Moritz's practice of inviting filmmakers to appear in person effectively imbued screenings with a comparable singularity.

Empowered by Stark's financial support, Moritz developed an ambitious curatorial agenda, and in two years exhibited over twenty-five single artist shows. These programs, which included works by Chick Strand, Pat O'Neill, John Whitney, and Jules Engel, and featured computer films, animations, and ethnography, articulated an extremely eclectic and contemporary vision of experimental cinema.[43] Program notes frequently included excerpts from interviews with filmmakers, distribution catalogues, and recent articles in *The Village Voice* and *Film Culture*, alerting audiences to the methods and language regularly used to analyze experimental film. In accordance with Moritz's ethical commitment to authoring minor instead of master histories, the series offered weekly revisions to the experimental film canon and highlighted the achievements of individual filmmakers.

Despite Moritz and Stark's shared loyalty to local artists, Moritz's malleable conceptions of artistic quality and excellence ultimately proved irreconcilable with Stark's rigid commitment to the formal attributes of historic avant-gardes. Tensions between them erupted in 1975, when Stark vetoed a scheduled presentation by gay artist John Jack Baylin, occasionally referred to by the stage name "Count Fanzini". Largely known for producing "bum bank" an extensive collection of derriere photographs, Baylin was a zine innovator and performer whose mass-produced fan magazine *Fanzini* combined gay pornography, advertisements, film stills, and cartoons. Given Moritz's belief that extreme formalism privileged the educational background and tastes of an elite few, Baylin's deliberately accessible presentations were undoubtedly an exciting affront to prevailing notions of artistic quality.[44] Outraged by Stark's decision and finally cognizant of their incompatible values, Moritz promptly resigned from the theatre. In response to Moritz's departure, board vice-president Robert Houston justified Stark's decision to the *Los Angeles Times*, stating: "it was not a question of subject matter. It was a question of quality."[45] Houston's statement, like Stark's recollection that the theater established "high standards", assumed that some artworks were objectively superior and that this superiority was visible to cultural arbiters with sufficient taste and training. Though disinterested in gritty presentations, and upset by her conflict with Moritz, Stark continued to support experimental film, and after a brief hiatus reopened the theater's film program with Douglas Edwards as Moritz's replacement.

Edwards was the young film programmer at a local arts and crafts gallery The Egg and the Eye.[46] An ambitious and consummate professional, Edwards rejected experimental film's historic marginalization, and attempted to build inroads into Los Angeles's film and art communities. In contrast to Fles, Teague, and Getz's shared emphasis on cultural subversion, Edwards treated experimental film as essential to art history, film studies, and commercial film production. He believed that techniques honed in experimental films drove innovation in features and commercials, and that media works by Stan Brakhage, John Whitney, and Louis Hock were masterpieces, worthy of recognition by the arts establishment.[47] Well prepared, gracious, and often in a suit, Edwards had an innate skill for arts administration, and expertly gained Stark's confidence while asserting his own creative control. He mastered the National Endowment for the Arts's grant distribution system, and after heightening the theatre's commitment to media pedagogy, he successfully secured funding for its film programs.[48] The series underwritten by the NEA included: "Cineprobe: An Ongoing Study in American and International Non-Commercial Filmmaking", and the twelve-part retrospective "The History of American Avant-Garde and Experimental Cinema".

Inspired by museum curatorship and recent film scholarship, Edward's programs offered viewers legible explanations of the historic relevance and artistic merits of experimental film. "The History of American Avant-Garde and Experimental Cinema" began in January of 1976 with a program of European films, including *Le Retour á la Raison* (Ray, 1923) and *Le Ballet Mécanique* (Leger, 1924), before proceeding to American shorts, including *The Fall of the House of Usher* (Harrington, 1942), *The Life and Death of 9413: A Hollywood Extra* (Florey, 1928) and *Manhatta* (Strand, 1921) in March.[49] In accordance with the Theatre Vanguard's overarching preference for modernism, this retrospective defined experimental film based on similarities to the European avant-garde, and showcased films featuring representations of the subconscious, mechanical experimentation, and formal abstraction. While relating experimental film to the Theatre Vanguard's other curatorial efforts, the retrospective also constructed a coherent, self-contained historical narrative that was easily understood by a broad audience. Clarity was an extremely important tool in Edwards's ongoing effort to make experimental film widely accessible and appealing, goals he tirelessly pursued through outreach to the *Los Angeles Times*, coordination with other venues, and participation in film events like The Los Angeles International Film Exposition (FilmEx).[50] Edward's promotional efforts were effective, and by 1977, Theatre Vanguard was the hub of a vibrant, collaborative experimental film community.[51]

Over the course of the 1970s, the diversification of the National Endowment for the Arts's grant programs, under the leadership of Nancy Hanks, subsidized a combination of large and grassroots arts organizations. Though small community organizations did not boast artistic exhibitions of the same scale as museums or ballet companies, their targeted community outreach appealed to Hanks's vision of bringing the arts to all Americans, and promised cultural and economic

Figure 26. Terry Cannon circa 1980, photographed by Judith Gordon.

development in rural and economically depressed areas.[52] In her annual reports for 1975 and 1976, Hanks cited the arts' economic and educational contributions as one of the agency's long-term benefits, portraying arts funding as patriotic and economically sustainable.[53] This vision of artists as workers and exhibitors as businesses received its most substantial endorsement in 1973, when Richard Nixon signed the Comprehensive Employment and Training Act (CETA). Intended to fund job training and combat unemployment, CETA paid workers at non-profit arts organizations following the passage of the 1974 Emergency Jobs and Unemployment Assistance Act. These federal efforts nurtured both large, modernist institutions like Theatre Vanguard, and smaller outfits sensitive to regional, politicized and craft-inspired artworks.

In Los Angeles between 1975 and 1978, CETA directly benefited Pasadena Filmforum, The Los Angeles Independent Film Oasis, and the Brockman Gallery Film Festival.[54] Though geographically and ideologically distinct, these three organizations all built upon Edwards's practice of presenting clear, organized programs, and used curatorship to interrogate dominant values and historical narratives. For Pasadena Filmforum and the Los Angeles Independent Filmmaker's Oasis, two organizations deeply influenced by the legacy of the underground film movement, exhibition presented an opportunity to increase the visibility of unknown filmmakers, and contest the avant-garde film canon.

Prior to the contemporary microcinema movement, the decidedly community-oriented and informal Pasadena Filmforum was the most eclectic, open independent film exhibitor in Los Angeles. Founded in 1975 by Terry Cannon, a fresh-faced San Francisco State graduate, with seed money from Pasadena's

Community Spirit Organization, Pasadena Filmforum was an inviting community organization intended to accommodate both amateurs and professionals and to facilitate lively conversation.[55] In contrast to Edwards, who trained Cannon on how to author a successful grant application, Cannon deliberately maintained his organization's small scale and low operating costs, both of which allowed him to host unconventional and financially risky programs.[56] Beginning in 1976, he screened jazz films, ethnography, animation, and a steady stream of thematic shorts packages and single artist shows. The organization was decidedly intimate and homey, more akin to a living room than a theater, particularly after relocating to a large sofa-filled backroom at the Aarnun Gallery on East Colorado Blvd.[57]

Despite the organization's low overhead and Cannon's commitment to an anti-qualitative curatorial project, Filmforum gradually began to adhere to established methods for exhibiting experimental cinema. By 1978, the organization was primarily screening experimental film in a combination of single artist shows and programs of abstract works. This shift coincided with the nationwide standardization of experimental film culture and programming. The establishment of film courses, an increase in scholarly publication, and the widespread use of a small group of distributors furnished exhibitors throughout the country with text for program notes, contact information for filmmakers, information about travel schedules, and access to prints. These resources also taught programmers about history and contemporary discourse, and directed them towards filmmakers considered interesting and creatively significant. Despite its practical appeal, the professionalization and consolidation of experimental film's infrastructure also homogenized exhibition, and provoked anxiety about insularity.

The fear of exclusion from a rapidly circulating and increasingly influential version of experimental film history was particularly potent amongst filmmakers working in Los Angeles. Looking back on the 1970s, Los Angeles-based filmmaker Morgan Fisher recalled the overwhelming sense that Jonas Mekas, P. Adams Sitney, and their cohort determined "who was going to have a career and who wasn't".[58] Despite Sitney's interest in "structural film", a categorization given to films based on the subordination of content to form, his surveys of the period largely ignored the rigorously structured works made by Fisher and his peers Grahame Weinbren and Roberta Friedman in Los Angeles. Already marginalized by the commercial film industry, these filmmakers were troubled by their absence from scholarship allegedly intended to promote filmmakers with aesthetic concerns and production methods similar to their own.

In 1976, Fisher, Freidman, and Weinbren joined Beverly O'Neill, Pat O'Neill, Amy Halpern, David Wilson, Diana Wilson, and Susan Rosenfeld to form the

Los Angeles Independent Film Oasis, an itinerant, non-profit exhibitor committed to screening works by living artists.[59] Modeled on cooperatives in New York and San Francisco, Oasis was the first democratically-programmed, artist-run experimental film exhibitor in Los Angeles and the first in which women enjoyed parity with their male colleagues.

Formally trained in film and art, Oasis's founders were highly attuned to contemporary academic discourse, and curated programs to augment and challenge prevailing values. Despite the programmers' various formal and thematic interests, they shared an overarching commitment to local artists, disregard for the dominant canon, and an interest in how curatorship created meaning. Due to its democratic approach to curatorship, Oasis regularly alternated the basis for its programs, and during its five operational years presented shows based on tonal, geographic, institutional, and formal continuities, constructing a radically dispersed vision of experimental cinema that opened films to multiple modes of analysis. This curatorial eclecticism was particularly groundbreaking in its inclusion of female filmmakers in formal, thematic, and contemporary programs, a direct affront to the dominant tendency to either exclude female filmmakers or to present their work in programs with a gendered premise.[60] Though innovative, Oasis's sensitivity to the formal content of female filmmakers' works reflected their overarching preference for abstraction and detachment from contemporary didactic and documentary filmmaking.

During the late 1960s, the third cinema movement and the dispersal of its films and theories to American universities renewed scholars and filmmakers' interest in the political potency of documentary, polemical, and realist filmmaking techniques. In Los Angeles, the primary outlet for these works was Ethno-Communications, a film production and theory program founded at UCLA in 1970 in the wake of affirmative action protests. In addition to screening contemporary political cinema, Ethno-Communications trained students in low-cost, mobile filmmaking techniques. The program was extremely effective, and taught its graduates how to produce independent films using readily available resources, and encouraged them to pursue political objectives. By 1977, many of its graduates, including Larry Clark and Haile Gerima, had completed independent feature films shot on location, exploring Black experiences in Los Angeles. Though stylistically diverse, these works shared a commitment to unflinching realism and an interest in poetic structuring and improvisation informed by the legacy of jazz. However, despite critical success and the circulation of their films to international festivals, graduates from Ethno-Communications faced systematic exclusion from Hollywood, and were generally overlooked by experimental film venues preoccupied with formalism.

Though frustration about inequitable exhibition opportunities was widely felt, filmmakers maintained differing opinions about whether inclusion in either Hollywood or in the experimental film communities was a worthwhile venture. For many, including Clark and fellow Ethno-Communications graduate Sylvia Morales, highly-abstracted filmmaking was a luxury enjoyed by filmmakers working without a sense of immediate political urgency.[61] However, for Clark's colleague Ben Caldwell, whose landmark 1979 film *I&I: An African Allegory* featured elliptical editing, lyrical sequences, and a dreamy realism, contemporary avant-garde filmmaking depended on the innovations of African-American artists, and was formally and thematically indebted to jazz and vernacular craft.[62]

In 1980, following the completion of *I&I*, Caldwell began conversations with Alonzo and Dale Davis, the proprietors of the Brockman Gallery (a commercial fine-arts space in Leimert Park) about programming their annual film festival. The resulting program, "Los Angeles: The Ethnic Experience", took place during three weekends in October at the Barnsdall Park Auditorium in Hollywood.[63] For the 1980 program Caldwell built upon the preceding years' international festivals: "Films from Africa and the Caribbean" and "South America and the Surrounding Islands", to consider how minority populations in Los Angeles resisted the brutality of imperialism. Drawing on the theories of UCLA professor Teshome Gabriel, Caldwell's program visualized third cinema as defined by its political sensibilities and capable of exceeding geographic, racial and formal boundaries.[64] Consequently, Caldwell's extremely heterogeneous program, which included works by Julie Dash, Haile Gerima, Visual Communications, Billy Woodberry, Chick Strand, the Victor Jara Collective, and Sylvia Morales, sharply contrasted with the formal and historical curatorial efforts of other organizations. In a groundbreaking departure from precedent, Caldwell subordinated form to social function and revealed how cine-poems, animation, and documentaries might collaboratively contest the aesthetics, industrial underpinnings, and capitalist values of commercial cinema.

The festival, which contested dominant methods for categorizing art, marked a turning point for independent film exhibition in Los Angeles. While benefiting from the resources afforded by CETA and public funding, the festival also anticipated the crucial roles that historiographic inquiry and discourse analysis would play in future curatorship. However, the tremendous curatorial successes of the late 1970s immediately preceded two major blows to arts funding. The first occurred in 1978, when California voters passed Proposition 13, a dramatic reduction to property taxes that gutted the state's funding and ultimately eviscerated its contributions to the arts. The second occurred in 1980, when the extremely conservative Ronald Reagan was elected to the office of president. During his presidency, Reagan dramatically reduced the NEA's budget, which siphoned funds away from many small arts organizations. By 1982, the Los Angeles Independent Film Oasis and Theatre Vanguard had closed, though Edwards continued to program film for a series at UCLA. Despite cuts to funding, Brockman Gallery Productions continued sponsoring public performances and exhibitions throughout the 1980s, though with a reduced emphasis on film. Only small Pasadena Filmforum, which was renamed Los Angeles Filmforum in accordance with its relocation, maintained regular film programming, though without a permanent space.

However, despite financial challenges and the shuttering of specific organizations, the bonds forged during the 1970s between curatorship and historiographic inquiry proved indelible and laid the foundation for future programming and scholarship. The contours of the experimental film canon would continue to be heavily contested throughout the following decades by exhibitions including "El Ojo Apasianado" (Los Angeles Filmforum, 1983), a showcase of works by Mexican and Mexican-American artists, and "Scratching the Belly of the Beast" (Los Angeles Filmforum, 1994), a survey of experimental media in Los Angeles that examined contributions by African-American, Latino, female, and video artists. However, the most dramatic reconfigurations of hierarchy and reimagining of the relationships between artists, curators, and audiences would take place in community art centers including the KAOS Network, founded by Ben Caldwell in 1984, and the Echo Park Film Center, founded by Paolo Davanzo in 2002. Through tireless community outreach and creative, occasionally informal and deliberately anti-canonical programming, these organizations have demonstrated that the methods for producing and exhibiting experimental media can and must undergo constant revision to remain insightful, transformative and truly avant-garde.

Notes

1. This essay addresses the curatorial histories of cinemas variously described as avant-garde, underground, experimental, and minority. Though these terms have distinct and historically specific applications, they also collectively laid the foundation for the cinematic history, style, and canon that this volume addresses. Consequently, I have attempted to apply each term in accordance with its historically specific usage while simultaneously acknowledging the ways these terms intersect in the contemporary discourse of avant-garde cinema.
2. The evidence of hearty underground film attendance during this period is largely anecdotal, since no surviving attendance records or box-office paperwork have been located. However, Movies 'Round Midnight programmers John Fles and Mike Getz's recollections of regularly filling the five hundred seat theater are substantiated by the stories of other theater attendees, and by Thom Andersen's description of the theater's controversial and crowded screening of Andy Warhol's *Sleep*. See Michael Fles interviewed by Adam Hyman, Alternative Projections: Art in

LA 1945–1980, http://alternativeprojections.com/oral-histories/michael-fles, 27 June 2009, Tape 3:11; Mike Getz interviewed by Alison Kozberg. Alternative Projections: Art in LA 1945–1980, http://alternativeprojections.com/oral-histories/mike-getz, 12 June 2010, Tape 1:4 and Thom Andersen, "The '60s Without Compromise: Watching Warhol's Films", *Rouge* No.8 (2006). Retrieved from http://www.rouge.com.au/8/warhol.html, accessed 1 March 2014.

3. Stan Vanderbeek, "The Cinema Delimina: Films From the Underground", *Film Quarterly* 14. 4 (Summer 1961): 5–15.
4. For an in-depth investigation of the multiple ways that underground films represented and integrated countercultural activity during the 1960s see David E. James, *Allegories of Cinema: American Film in the Sixties* (Princeton, New Jersey: Princeton University Press, 1989).
5. Fles, 2009, Tape 1:13–14.
6. John Fles, *The Trembling Lamb* (New York: Phoenix Bookshop, 1959).
7. Trak Film Group Postcards, April, May, and June 1963, Courtesy of Thom Andersen.
8. Fles, 2009, Tape 1:17.
9. Sher is likely best known as the owner of the Heights Art Theatre in Cleveland Heights, Ohio, the venue where manager Nico Jacobellis's famous refusal to post signage required by local censorship restrictions led to the landmark supreme course case *Jacobellis v. Ohio* (1964). Largely remembered for Justice Potter Stewart famous description of pornography ("I know it when I see it"), *Jacobellis v. Ohio* afforded first amendment protections to all films except for hard-core pornography. See John Lewis, *Hollywood v. Hardcore: How the Struggle Over Censorship Saved the Modern Film Industry* (New York and London: New York University Press, 2000, 2002), 131–132.
10. 1963 is often identified as a peak for art cinema in the United States, both because the number of art house theaters increased to a record 450, and because Richard Round and former Cinema 16 director Amos Vogel started The New York Film Festival. See Tino Balio, *The Foreign Film Renaissance on American Screens 1946–1973* (Madison: University of Wisconsin Press, 2010), and Barbara Willinsky, *Sure Seaters: The Emergence of Art House Cinema* (Minneapolis: University of Minnesota Press, 2001).
11. Movies 'Round Midnight Calendar, October 1963, Courtesy of Thom Andersen.
12. John Fles, *Seeing is Believing* (1964). In his manifesto, Fles described his goal of screening a combination of single-artist, dynamic, and analytic programs. However, Movies 'Round Midnight's remaining program notes suggest that Fles ultimately screened the cross-genre juxtapositions necessary for his dynamic and analytic programs more frequently than single-artist shows.
13. During February of 1964, Movies 'Round Midnight featured the following programs: *Vampyr* (Dreyer, 1932) with *Scotch Hop* (Maclaine, 1959) and the Bela Lugosi serial *The Creeping Shadow Chapter 3* on 1–2 February; *Sudan* (Rawlins, 1945) with *The Man Who Invented Gold* (Maclaine, 1957) and *The Creeping Shadow Chapter 4* on 8–9 February; *Venom and Eternity* (Isou, 1953) with a surprise film by Stan Brakahge and *The Creeping Shadow Chapter 5* on 15–16 February; *The End* (Maclaine, 1953) with *Tarzan of the Apes* (Sidney, 1918) on 22–23 February. Movies 'Round Midnight Calendar, February 1964, Courtesy of Thom Andersen.
14. Susan Sontag, "Notes on Camp", *Against Interpretation and Other Essays* (New York: Picador, Straus and Giroux, 1966).
15. Movies 'Round Midnight Calendar, January 1964, Courtesy of Thom Andersen.
16. John Fles, *Seeing is Believing* (1964), 18.
17. The most notable exception to Fles and Getz's harmonious relationship with their audience was a 1964 screening of Andy Warhol's *Sleep* in which frustrated viewers flooded the theater's lobby and demanded a refund. Andersen, "The '60s Without Compromise", 2006.
18. "New Comedy Opens Today", *Los Angeles Times*, 4 March 1964, C13.
19. "Film Labeled Lewd to be Seen in Court", *Los Angeles Times*, 30 April 1964, A2 and "Exhibitor of Scorpio Film Found Guilty", *Los Angeles Times*, 14 May 1964, A2
20. The People of the State of California Plaintiff vs. Michael Aaron Getz Case no. 207224 Section 311. 2 Vol. 1. Box 250. Stanley Fleishman Papers. UCLA Special Collections.
21. Fleishman was a prominent First Amendment attorney who for decades defended the right of free speech in causes ranging from Henry Miller's *Tropic of Cancer* to the adult film *Deep Throat*. He argued several obscenity cases before the US Supreme Court, including *Smith v. California* and *Alberts v. California*.
22. During March 1964, Jonas Mekas was arrested twice on obscenity charges, the first time for screening Jack Smith's *Flaming Creatures* and the second time, one week later, for screening Jean Genet's *Chant d'Amour*. See "Cops Raid Homo Films Again", *Variety*, 18 March 1964, 5.
23. Philip K. Scheuer, "If It's Good Box Office It's Decent – The New Hollywood", *Los Angeles Times*, 21 March 1964, J2.

24. The Cinema Theater revived *Scorpio Rising* in January of 1965 as a double feature with Tod Browning's controversial *Freaks* (1932). The film showed frequently throughout 1965 and 1966, including screenings in Toronto, Paris, at the Bleeker St. Theater in New York, Janus Films in Washington D.C., and the Hull House Film Festival in Chicago.
25. Fles, 2009, Tape 3: 26.
26. Kevin Thomas, "L.A. Lags in Art Film Appreciation", *Los Angeles Times*, 19 December 1965, M17.
27. "Today's Teenagers", *Time Magazine*, 29 January 1965, cover.
28. See Eugenia Sheppard, "Pop Art, Poetry and Fashion", *New York Herald Tribune*, 3 January 1965, 10–12; Andy Warhol, "Superpop or a Night at the Factory", interviewed by Robert Vaughan, *New York Herald Tribune*, 8 August 1965, 7–9; *Esquire*, August 1966.
29. Lewis Teague interviewed by Alison Kozberg, Alternative Projections: Art in LA 1945–1980, http://alternativeprojections.com/oral-histories/lewis-teague, June 19, 2010, 5, accessed 1 March 2014.
30. Kevin Thomas, "Midnight Show Proves Ghastly", *The Los Angeles Times*, 13 January 1965, D6.
31. Jeffery Perkins interviewed by Adam Hyman, Alternative Projections: Art in LA 1945–1980, http://alternativeprojections.com/oral-histories/jeffrey-perkins, 5 June 2010, 37, accessed 1 March 2014.
32. Gene Youngblood, *Expanded Cinema* (New York: E.P Dutton & Co, 1970), 180.
33. Movies 'Round Midnight Calendar, November–December 1967, Courtesy of Thom Andersen.
34. Robin Morgan, "Goodbye to All That" in *The Sixties Papers: Documents of a Rebellious Decade*, eds. Judith Claviar Albert and Stewart Edward Albert (New York: Praeger, 1984), 511.
35. Kevin Thomas, "Three Blacks View the Racial Situation", *The Los Angeles Times,* 30 October 1968, I9.
36. Knight, Arthur and Hollis Alpert, "The History of Sex in Cinema, Part XV: Experimental Films", *Playboy*, April 1967, 196.
37. Eric Schafer, "Gauging a Revolution: 16mm and the Rise of the Pornographic Feature", *Cinema Journal* 41. 3 (Spring 2002): 3–26.
38. Beginning with the establishment of Underground Cinema 12 in 1968, Mike Getz became increasingly committed to developing comedic and subversive late night screenings. In the early 1970s, he substantially expanded the scale of his programming efforts, renamed his series "Midnight Movies", and began hosting screenings at the World Theatre in Columbus, Ohio, the Art Valley Theatre in Tempe, Arizona, and the Towne Theatre in Sacramento, California. Informed by Getz's interest in interactivity, humor and audience cultivation, these screenings laid for the groundwork for the interactive cult movie screenings of the 1970s and 1980s. For an in depth study of midnight and cult movie screenings see J. Hoberman and Jonathan Rosenbaum, *Midnight Movies* (New York: De Capo Press, 1983).
39. Donna M Binkiewicz, *Federalizing the Muse: United States Arts Policy & The National Endowment for the Arts 1965–1980* (Chapel Hill and London: University of North Carolina Press, 2004), 9.
40. *Yankee Underground Film Festival* Program Notes, April 1968. Courtesy of Marsha Kinder.
41. William Moritz, "Three Books on Experimental Film", *Film Quarterly* 25.4 (Summer 1972): 31–34; William Moritz, "Beyond 'Abstract' Criticism", *Film Quarterly* 31.3 (Spring 1978): 29–39.
42. Stark was a consummate philanthropist and would later sit on the boards of the Bella Lewitzky Dance Foundation, the Arnold Schoenberg Institute, the Craft and Folk Art Museum, and CalArts. See Myrna Oliver, "Judith Stark, 96; Former Dancer Began Arts Foundation, Experimental Theater", *Los Angeles Times*, 2 January 2006, http://articles.latimes.com/2006/jan/02/local/me-stark2, accessed 27 October 2012.
43. Of the forty-five programs that survive from the 1973 and 1974 seasons, twenty-five were single-artist shows with additional shows pairing two artists including John with James Whitney and Ken Feingold with Chris Langdon. See Programs 1973, 8-f.53, Vanguard News 1973–1975, 9-f.63, Programs 1974, 8-f.54, Programs 1975, 8-f.55, Collection of the Margaret Herrick Library, Theatre Vanguard Collection.
44. Though Moritz appreciated and celebrated abstract and non-objective works, he was wary of positioning them as the inevitable result of artistic accomplishment or progress. Instead he advocated for careful, rigorous analysis that clarified its parameters and avoided generalizations. In one particularly scathing critique of Malcolm Le Grice's *Abstract Film and Beyond,* he observed, "Le Grice never comes to terms with the fact that his formal cinema is a parasitical pastime of an intellectual elite in a capitalist country". See Moritz, "Abstract' Criticism", 31.
45. See Gregg Kilday, "Vanguard Fuss Cuts Out Films," *Los Angeles Times,* 15 February 1975, B5; "Correspondence between Kevin Thomas and Judith Stark March 5, 1975", Correspondence- General 1975, 2-f.8, Collection of the Margaret Herrick Library, Theatre Vanguard Collection.
46. "Newsletter 4:3, May 1972", Publications, The Egg and the Eye Gallery, Folder 6:13, Box 1, UCLA Library Special Collections, Craft and Folk Art Museum Records.

47. See Mitch Tuchman "Douglas Edwards: Guardian of the Avant-Garde Film", *The Los Angeles Times*, 2 October 1979, F12; Carol Tucker "Lobbyist for Film and Video as Art", *The Los Angeles Times* 17 September 1982, H10.

48. "1976 Annual Report", National Endowment of the Arts, http://arts.gov/sites/default/files/NEA-Annual-Report–1976.pdf, accessed February 2014; "Theatre Vanguard Project Grant Application June 17 1975", Grant Applications 1975–1979, 6-f.39, Collection of the Margaret Herrick Library, Theatre Vanguard Collection.

49. Programs 1976, 8-f.56, History of the American Avant-Garde Series, 7-f.40, Collection of the Margaret Herrick Library, Theatre Vanguard Collection.

50. Amongst Edwards's efforts were the creation of a mailing list for a "Film Art Exhibitors Educators Federation" to coordinate filmmakers' travel and exhibition plans, and collaboration with the American Federation of the Arts to create travelling series and facilitate collaboration. See "Correspondence between Douglas Edwards and Steven Aronson", Correspondence General –1976, 2-f.12; "Correspondence Film Art Exhibitors/ Educators Federation Nov 1 1976", Film Art Exhibitors/ Educators Federation 1976, 4-f.24, Collection of the Margaret Herrick Library, Theatre Vanguard Collection; For discussion of the relationship to *Los Angeles Times* see Kevin Thomas interviewed by Adam Hyman, Alternative Projections: Art in LA 1945–1980, http://alternativeprojections.com/oral-histories/kevin-thomas, 21October 2010, accessed 1 March 2014.

51. For a description of experimental film exhibition in the late 1970s, see Robert Sklar "Experimental Film Showcase in Hollywood?" *American Film 3* (1978): 41–42.

52. *National Endowment for the Arts: A History 1965–2008*, ed. Mark Bauerlein with Ellen Grantham (Washington DC: National Endowment for the Arts, 2008).

53. "1975 Annual Report", National Endowment for the Arts, http://arts.gov/sites/default/files/NEA-Annual-Report–1975.pdf, accessed February 2014; "1976 Annual Report", National Endowment for the Arts, http://arts.gov/sites/default/files/NEA-Annual-Report–1976.pdf accessed February 2014.

54. While Brockman Gallery Productions received CETA funding directly, both Pasadena Filmforum and The Los Angeles Independent Film Oasis hosted screenings at organizations receiving CETA funding, the Pasadena Community Art Center, and the Los and LAICA, respectively.

55. Terry Cannon "Filmforum: The Pasadena Years, 1975–1983", *Scratching the Belly of the Beast*, (Los Angeles: Filmforum, 1994), 6.

56. Terry Cannon interviewed by Adam Hyman, Alternative Projections: Art in LA 1945–1980, http://alternativeprojections.com/oral-histories/terry-cannon, 14 November 2009, 23, accessed 1 March 2014.

57. Cannon, 14 November 2009, 24–25.

58. Morgan Fisher, "Missing the Boat", *Scratching the Belly of the Beast*, 12.

59. The first Oasis screening took place in 1976 at the Haymarket bookstore in Westlake, and over the course of the next five years the organization would also host screenings at Founder's Hall at the University of Southern California in West Adams and at LAICA's locations on Robertson and Downtown Los Angeles. See "Los Angeles Independent Film Oasis Panel Discussion", Alternative Projections: Art in LA 1945–1980, http://alternativeprojections.com/symposium/los-angeles-independent-film-oasis-panel, accessed 19 February 2010, 11; Grahame Weinbren interviewed by Mark Toscano, Alternative Projections: Art in LA 1945–1980, http://alternativeprojections.com/oral-histories/grahame-weinbren, accessed 19 February 2010, 34.

60. Though works by women including Shirley Clarke, Chick Strand, Maya Deren, Freude Bartlett, and Yvonne Rainer screened in Los Angeles prior to the formation of Oasis, the series undeniably included female filmmakers in an unprecedentedly heterogeneous array of programs including "Funny Business" (30/5/1976), "Films with Few Images" (29/5/1977) and "A Group Show: Some Interesting New Films" (13/8/1978).

61. Recalling her experiences at Ethno-Communications, former student Sylvia Morales observed: "The non-color students were involved with films concerning relationships, personal films. But for us there was a sense of urgency, so we set aside our desire to make personal films in order to make ones which reflected our communities." See Renee Tajima "Ethno-Communications; The Film School Program that Changed the Color of Independent Filmmaking", *The Anthology of Asian American Film and Video* (New York: Third World Newsreel, 1985), 38; Larry Clark Interviewed by Alison Kozberg, 12 April 2011.

62. Ben Caldwell interviewed by Alison Kozberg, 29 April 2011.

63. "LA's Bicentennial Film Festival Set", *Los Angeles Sentinel*, 16 October 1980, B5.

64. In his landmark 1979 dissertation, authored as a doctoral candidate at UCLA, Gabriel articulated a transnational, highly politicized formulation of third cinema. Gabriel writes: "The principal characteristic of Third Cinema is really not so much where it is made, or even who makes it, but rather, the ideology it espouses and the consciousness it displays. The Third Cinema, therefore, is that cinema of the Third World, which stands opposed to imperialism and class oppression in all their ramifications and manifestations." See Teshome Gabriel, *Third Cinema in the Third World: The Dynamics of Style and Ideology*. Diss. (University of California Los Angeles, 1979), Print. 42.

19 Kent Mackenzie's *The Exiles*: Reinventing the Real of Cinema

Ross Lipman*

A study of *The Exiles* is a study in parallel histories. *The Exiles* is in many ways a "missing link" or stray evolutionary chain in the development of cinematic language. Its unique production methodology, which arose from an effort to attain a location veracity that would only truly become attainable with technological innovations arising a few short years later, led directly to the formulation of a unique aesthetic, perfectly suited to the film's theme.

The Exiles was originally produced by several graduates of the University of Southern California (USC) film school led by director Kent Mackenzie in collaboration with cinematographers Erik Daarstad, Robert Kaufman, and John Morrill. It was later followed by an amazingly detailed USC thesis by Mackenzie documenting the production history.[1] Reading Mackenzie's thesis, one quickly realizes that he and his colleagues were trying to reinvent the language of cinema from scratch. This revolution included both production techniques and aesthetic form – creating a work that at once echoed and broke down existing film strategies. Wrote Mackenzie, "We felt that we had to reject all the old methods and structures and study our subjects so intensely that we could develop new methods and structures of our own".[2] Or as one viewer noted at an early test screening, "You have succeeded in finding the form of formlessness".[3]

Mackenzie's revolution was achieved through a wonderful mix of improvisation

* "Reinventing the Real of Cinema" is adapted from a longer essay called "The Savage Ear of Kent Mackenzie". Excerpts from Kent Mackenzie's thesis and photos of *The Exiles*'s production are reproduced courtesy of Milestone Film & Video and ©1961 Kent Mackenzie.

Figure 27. Right to left: Kent Mackenzie, Robert Kaufman, Erik Daarstad, unknown cast member.

and consideration, touching on a multiplicity of themes both specific and general. The initial reviews of the 2008 Milestone re-release, for example, invoked a remarkably disparate breadth of topics,[4] ranging from the film's portrayal of Native American[5] life,[6] to its documentation of the downtown Bunker Hill neighborhood and a lost moment in Los Angeles history,[7] to its placement as a non-Hollywood cinema focused on human interaction (in parallel to Cassavetes and the French New Wave),[8] to its music – by the Revels, and including Native American chants.[9]

Ultimately these diverse strands are united in the theme of Exile. Like the Native Americans starring in the film, who lived as a distinct community in the heart of downtown Los Angeles, Mackenzie and his colleagues created their own unique cinema in the heart of America's cinema production capital, a cinema that was at once distinct from both Hollywood and Mackenzie's own independent contemporaries.[10]

A Cinema of Exile

Mackenzie's initial inspiration came from a story in *Harper's* in March 1956 by Dorothy Van de Mark, "The Raid on the Reservations", which Mackenzie described as "a discussion of the continuing shenanigans on the part of the white man to obtain Indian land". He goes on, "I was shocked and immediately wanted to go to war via the film medium".[11] On the encouragement of his employer, Charles Palmer, president of Parthenon Pictures, he made a research trip to the San Carlos reservation near Gobe, Arizona. He soon discovered, however, that his interests lay more in the plight of the young Native Americans who were moving away from the reservations to larger cities. He ultimately wound up focusing his interests on a group living in Bunker Hill in downtown Los Angeles, an area he had previously documented in another short film, *Bunker Hill – 1956*. More specifically, he focused on the bars near Third and Main Streets.

Yet this is ultimately just one part of his material. At the core of his art is an in-depth investigation of the complex relationship of truth and fiction in cinema. Cinematographer John Morrill stated that he originally viewed the film not as narrative but as a "documentary".[12] This may in part have been based on notions of what the word "documentary" meant at time of the film's production.[13] Mackenzie's thesis suggests that the director viewed it someplace in between document and story.

From today's vantage the film is indeed better seen as a hybrid. It's not so much the documentation of a tangibly manifest reality, but rather the *creation* of a unique "cinematic" reality that speaks directly back to the world of physical truth – while remaining distinct from it. It is the cinema of Exile.

The film's concept of Exile begins with Mackenzie himself. The director spent years integrating with the Native community he depicted, gaining their trust over time and involving them in both the film's production and content creation in an almost unprecedented way. Yet despite his success in this regard, by sheer definition he could never truly be the *same* as his subjects, and his camera provided a further sense of distance. He ultimately noted, "I made the early mistake of trying to be 'one of the gang.'... I think I could have preserved my own outlook and identity much more clearly had I understood that you can seldom really become part of an unfamiliar group".[14]

While Mackenzie was arguably as much of an "insider" as a white man with a camera could be, he was simultaneously an "outsider", and his uniquely *in-between* position as architect of this extremely close-up vision can be viewed precisely as the personal experience of Exile. It infuses his understanding of the documentary aspects of the film in what might be described as an authentic depiction of "subjective reality".

This concept, however, goes beyond Mackenzie's own involvement to the formal aspects of the film, and even the technical aspects of its production. For example, the cinematography – despite certain myths – was not an exact, clear recording of life's events, but rather a recreation of its experience. The film's lighting provides a useful analogue. The cinematographers did not exclusively use existing light, but rather supplemented it with their own sources, and in some cases simply re-created its effects. Mackenzie notes:

> In most circumstances what could be photographed with natural light did not simulate what the eye perceived ... All the bar sequences and other night interiors had to be lit from scratch, and even the night street exteriors were usually augmented.... In the shot where Homer and Rico walk away from Rico's apartment, for instance, there were lights set all the way down the alley.[15] Our approach to the lighting was always the same, however, not to introduce unnatural effects but to light the location to photograph the way the eye perceived it.[16]

As detailed in Mackenzie's thesis, *The Exiles*'s purportedly realistic cinematography was actually carefully crafted – and is ultimately an interaction between incidental light and the skill, ingeniousness, and sometimes sheer desperation of its brilliant young crew.

In reading through the thesis, one realizes that Mackenzie was in fact developing and in turn applying a rigorous aesthetic and philosophical agenda at every level of production, from abstract concept to physical detail.[17] A tension results that fires the film, a tension between immersion and distance, between literal truth and its cinematic recreation. In this way, Mackenzie arguably parallels the photographer Edward Curtis, whose photographs he uses to frame the film at the beginning, by showing the gap between past and present, between myth and truth. Curtis famously "staged" his photographs to help ennoble the image of the Native American. They're beautiful, romantic works, but they represented a reality that no longer existed, or was at least fading, at the time the images were taken. Mackenzie, in contrast, sought to avoid the painterly and the Romantic, and pursued instead the dark underbelly of reality, the dirt under the fingernails. In this aspect he evokes not so much Curtis, but his own contemporary, Robert Frank, whose *The Americans* was published in 1958, as *The Exiles* was shooting.

Diegetics in Exile

While the concept of Exile is in fact evident at almost every stage of development, it is perhaps nowhere more cogent than in the creation of the film's soundtrack. The soundtrack's successes, and in some respects even its failures, help illuminate the nature of the work's "subjective truth".

A key to understanding this is recognition of the precise moment of *The Exiles*'s production: 1957–1961. Shooting of the film began in January 1958, and one hence needs to recognize its fantastic location cinematography not as a contemporary, but as a pre-cursor to the US portion of the Direct Cinema movement

Figure 28. *The Exiles,* Hill X at night.

and the French *Cinema Vérité.*[18] *Primary,* by Robert Drew (along with Ricky Leacock, Albert Maysles, and D.A. Pennebaker), was considered by many to be the first American "Direct Cinema" film, and the first to "successfully" use lightweight portable equipment for synchronizing sound and image. It was made in 1960, but the production sync (which involved several technical innovations by Leacock) drifted terribly, and the film was extensively post-synchronized. Although the Nagra III sound recorder (with an electric motor) was developed in 1957, there were still problems preventing its effective use for many years. It wasn't until 1962 that the Nagra III and its accompanying technology were developed sufficiently to allow reliable sync.

One therefore needs to understand that despite its groundbreaking use of location shooting, and the outer form of sync sound, the sound one hears in ninety-nine percent of *The Exiles* was not recorded at the time of production. The film's creation dates mark it as an overlooked moment in cinema history, between the largely asynchronous social documentaries of the '40's, and the vérité '60's.[19]

The foremost factor in a consideration of its soundtrack is therefore its post-dubbing, or "looping".[20] *The Exiles* was shot on location in downtown Los Angeles, primarily with a 35mm Arriflex camera. Significantly, sound was usually recorded simultaneously, if not truly synchronously. Given the film's low budget, Mack-

Figure 29. *The Exiles*, Sam Farnsworth on Hill X set with Magnerecorder.

enzie could not afford a blimp to reduce the camera noise, or a synchronous motor.[21] Although they did record rudimentary live sound for many scenes, the attendant camera noise prevented its actual usage in the film. Mackenzie was thus forced into re-recording the soundtrack later, exiling the images from the sounds with which they were originally embodied.

This estrangement has an eerie effect, creating a sensation of alienation in the viewer, even as it depicts alienation in it characters. Conversely, the film's voice-over narration – which one would normally think might have a near-Brechtian distancing effect – draws the listener precisely *into* the minds of the characters.

Diegetics In Exile: Dialogue

In the case of the spoken dialogue, there was no written script, and Mackenzie used the original location recordings as a guide track as much as possible. Every effort was made to get the studio recordings to match the guide tracks. Mackenzie always brought several Indians to the studio, and they drank beer and kidded each other throughout the session to stay relaxed, even as they recorded. He wrote, "We would make use of all the stutterings, overlaps, and other normal elements of the Indians' speech patterns, and we would treat this dialog [sic], not as the most important element of communication in the film, but merely as another sound effect in the environment".[22]

In one of his most radical gestures as a realist, he ultimately utilized the spoken word not so much for the signifying code of its language, but treated it, rather, as pure sound. To this end, "We purposely intended to obscure dialog at times with music or other background noises. The dialog as Homer and Rico walk through the Third Street Tunnel, for instance, was intentionally swallowed in the sounds and echoes of the cars rushing through the tunnel."[23]

Not surprisingly, this methodology led to trouble. Mackenzie continues, "When we dubbed the picture this was difficult to explain to the professional and more orthodox mixers, because they were used to clarity of speech above most other considerations".[24] One sees herein Mackenzie's inventing a personal language of sound cinema.

He nonetheless noted that the re-recorded lines "…did not carry the excitement of the original production tracks".[25] This is apparent in the way the dialogue is spoken, which on occasion sounds slightly unnatural – even as one appreciates what a good job has been done. An excellent example of this would be the scene in which Tommy enters the Ritz café. This extended tracking shot's complexity would have made the recording of good location sound virtually impossible, being filmed as it was prior to the availability of more portable equipment. Its most awkward moment occurs midway through the shot, when the actor walking behind Tommy speaks. At a quick glance it appears that *Tommy's* lines are poorly done, resulting in a slippage in the "suspension of disbelief". Only upon close viewing does it become apparent that the line is actually well dubbed – but for the actor standing behind Tommy. Even without that confusion, the scene's original spontaneity would be nearly impossible to emulate perfectly in a studio post-dub, under any conditions.

The sense of unease in the film goes beyond the spoken lines to the actual quality of the sound – or precisely what Mackenzie considered his true material. He notes, for example, that "we could never achieve an outdoor presence no matter how many background tracks we added, and we could not effectively vary the perspective on the [sound] stage".[26]

This is no doubt linked to the conceptual contradiction of aiming to emulate reality via a method that, by unfortunate technical necessity, prevented its effective original capture. The split filming and looping ensure something that's neither fact nor fiction, but something in between.

However, one can use the film's "failures" in verisimilitude to pinpoint what it has in fact *succeeded* in creating. Mackenzie observed amongst his many challenges that "one odd problem which surprised everybody ... was the tremendous rapidity of the Main Street patter on the original dialog tracks. Sometimes six or eight words would have been said in the space of ten frames. The Indians tried to duplicate this in the looping, but it was very difficult for them to talk that fast when they thought about it, although they did it all day without thinking about it."[27]

The operative phrase here is "without thinking about it". The process of post-dubbing the dialogue by definition forced the actors not into an act of spontaneous creation, but conscious *re*-creation. This consciousness, or self-awareness, represents a fall from a state of grace, a banishment from self and home that is precisely tantamount to Exile. The film's new reality, or subjective reality, is in fact Exile itself. This tension between reality and its alienated representation underlies the film and drives the unique sensation of cold fire that infuses it.

Diegetics In Exile: Narration

The tendency of the looped *dialogue* to create an experience of alienation in the viewer is inversely mirrored in its counterpart, the non-synchronous narration. The narrated sequences in fact draw the viewer directly into the minds of the film's subjects.

While this was precisely Mackenzie's aim, its success is nonetheless tied up in the means by which it was recorded. In this case, perhaps ironically, Mackenzie had to take his subjects *away* from a place of comfort to achieve the effect. He at first tried to record the narration in the Indians' homes, but he noted that the background noise from the streets was overpowering, and, more critically, "The Indians were embarrassed to reveal their feelings because there was always someone dropping around. They would grandstand for their buddies, giving us self-conscious jokes about their life. They were seldom alone on Main Street and only reflected or revealed their inner thoughts on rare occasions." [28] The studio, which one might think would be clinical and off-putting, was a better alternative in that it offered an anonymity the Indians needed to open up.

However, there were still problems to solve. Mackenzie observed that "once they were at all removed from Main Street they felt ill at ease".[29] To remedy this, Mackenzie tried a number of techniques, which in fact varied with each subject. He wrote, "I often spent several hours talking with Yvonne before she would be ready to record. Tommy usually took some drinks, and he was quite high when he gave the narration which comes over the drunk scene in the gas station. Homer was often left alone on the stage to think about his past for as much as an hour before recording."[30]

And yet there's another key to the narration's success. While the recordings give the impression of being spontaneous speech, they're in fact highly edited. Mackenzie described some of his strategies, writing: "Breaths and mumbles and phrases such as 'man' and 'you know' were eliminated whenever they interfered with intelligibility. However, [in some sequences], breaths and mumbles were retained or even inserted to build the drunken mood. In a few cases we had ... to actually construct words out of consonants and sounds drawn from other words ... to clarify words which were badly slurred or mumbled. There were whole sections of narration track which consisted of one to four frame cuts."[31]

This would at first seem to contradict his earlier statement about the vagaries of daily speech, and speech as pure sound; yet a contradiction is not so straightforward. Whereas obscuring on-screen dialogue, or masking it with other diegetically motivated noises makes fundamental sense from a realist perspective, obscuring voice-over narration does not.

Even here Mackenzie carefully re-envisions his task. He states that in contrast with conventional film narration of the era, he was "... not after information, but an emotional quality and general attitudes and feelings".[32] Mackenzie's editing of actual speech to create, rather, the likeness of it, cuts to the heart of his methodology. In instance after instance, he needed to alter content-as-recorded to create the *semblance* of a more literal truth.[33]

Reality Lost and Regained

Towards the end of the thesis, Mackenzie asks, "Is there any such thing as 'objective reality'?"[34] Acknowledging that one had to select and emphasize certain aspects of the world, he went further: "We began to see that control and manipulation of elements were... far more important than we had ever imagined".[35] As justification for this viewpoint, he proceeded to delineate the impact the camera can have on the events it records, in essence changing the flow of reality's fabric. This is well understood today, but Mackenzie, critically, arrived at his conclusion not through theoretical exercises, but rather through careful observation of his own working process.

He then pinpoints another fundamental justification for artistic control: that the technical means of recording image and sound have their own inherent physical limitations, and do not actually replicate what the human eye perceives. Different photographic films, lenses, recording devices, etc., each "alter" physical reality even as they capture it, according to their distinct mechanical properties.[36]

From these two factors – the camera's effect on what it records, and its technologically limited means of recording – Mackenzie arrived at a radical conclusion: artistic intervention is in fact *required* as a fundamental corrective for the act of filming's own inherent limits. He wrote, "It seems to me that to minimize the intrusion of the crew and to adjust the technical means of reproduction so that they will represent with accuracy,... control is required on the part of the filmmaker. He has to use every method and trick at his disposal to reconstruct what was there before he came or to construct completely anew the elements he needs to express what he perceives."[37] Thus we see cinematic reality as an interaction between the world and the filmmaker. The filmmakers' interventions in this view act as counterbalance to the mitigating effects of filmmaking's own impact on "external" reality.

Herein, Mackenzie unknowingly arrives at a conclusion not dissimilar to the more classical cinema he sought to reinvent. In 1960 – concurrent to *The Exiles*'s post-production – Siegfried Kracauer published his *Theory of Film*, the seminal work on the nature of photographic reality. In it, Kracauer traces the twin impulses of realism and formalism in cinema to the Lumière brothers and Méliès; citing them as dialectical, and announcing room for the true art of cinema in the interplay of their polar tendencies. He saw cinema as the tool by which modern man, through this interaction, might redeem a lost sense of the physical world. In Los Angeles, Mackenzie was at that same moment developing through direct practice his own unique variant of this equation, concluding that the essence of the filmmaker's art was in fact nothing less than the careful shaping of a *subjective* reality.

In the case of both Mackenzie and his Native American subjects, it is the cinema of Exile. At the heart of the film is a split consciousness, embodied in its split creation process of filming and sound recording. It points to the issue of self-awareness, the existential crisis depicted in the film. In the difficulties the Indians faced in their studio sessions trying to re-create the speed of their original ad-libbed dialogue, and in their parallel difficulties creating more intimate narration in the presence of their friends, one sees problems by no means unique to Native Americans, but rather common to the modern condition. They speak to the pain of being self-aware, the severing of a wholed self from a state of unconscious being. They speak to modern man's displacement from himself.

Notes

1. Kent Robert Mackenzie, *A Description and Examination of the Production of The Exiles: A Film of the Actual Lives of Young American Indians*, A Thesis Presented to the Faculty of the Graduate School, University of Southern California, 1964, 1, in *The Mackenzie Papers,* included in *The Exiles* DVD, Milestone Film & Video, 2009.
2. Ibid., 13.
3. Ibid., 84.
4. Excerpts from a sampling of these reviews can be found on the Milestone website for the film at: http://www.exilesfilm.com/reviews.html, accessed 25 January 2014.
5. At the time of this essay's revision in 2014, the term "Native American" remains in common usage but has moved from a recent historical position of preference. Some suggest that the decline in acceptance is due to a bureaucratic quality associated with census–taking (in which tribe differentiation is ignored), yet acknowledge that the term is still widely used. Borgna Brunner, "American Indian versus Native American", http://www.infoplease.com/spot/aihmterms.html, accessed 25 January 2014. A number of contemporary artists and activists indeed seem to veer away from it, but not in one particular direction. Photographer Pamela J. Peters, who has created a series of contemporary images inspired by *The Exiles*, prefers "American Indians" and, context-dependent, "Indigenous". "Pamela J. Peters Photography", http://www.tachiiniiphotography.com/about-me.html, accessed 25 January 2014. Contrarily, the writer and filmmaker Sherman Alexie said he prefers the term "Indian" because he views both "Native American" and "American Indian" as oxymorons. Phone conversation between Sherman Alexie and Dennis Doros, Fall 2007. The term "First Nations" has its advantages, but as its reference context is Canadian it has limitations as well. In essence, a diversity of terms can be noted in contemporary speech. Acknowledging the multiple forms in play, this essay primarily utilizes the "Native American" formulation. However, it retains Mackenzie's original "Indians" when quoted, and also within the text body, context-dependent, to denote the specific individuals who participated in the film's production.
6. As an example, see Wesley Morris, "A Study of Outcasts in Their Own Land", *Boston Globe*, 26 September 2008. http://www.boston.com/ae/movies/articles/2008/09/26/a_study_of_outcasts_in_their_own_land/, accessed 25 January 2014.
7. As an example, see Andrew O' Hehir, "All-night Party in a Lost City", *Salon.com*, 10 July 2008, http://www.salon.com/2008/07/10/exiles/, accessed 25 January 2014.
8. As an example, see Jonathan Rosenbaum, "The Exiles" capsule review, *Chicago Reader*, http://www.chicagoreader.com/chicago/the-exiles/Film?oid=1150997, accessed 25 January 2014.
9. As an example, see Quintin, "The Exiles", *Cinemascope* on-line, http://cinema-scope.com/currency/currency-the-exiles, accessed 25 January 2014.
10. In the early pages of his thesis, Mackenzie denounces mainstream American / Hollywood cinema, and freely admits finding inspiration within works from the international art cinema canon, as well as from documentary traditions. However, he states that "… even the best of (these works) often made use of theatrical conventions and methods", and otherwise distinguishes his work from theirs. Mackenzie, 13. Independent auteur John Cassavetes is included in a short list appearing in the final pages of the manuscript, marking filmmakers "… who were completely unknown, or just verbal rumors, when we began in 1958" (Mackenzie, 128). No mention is made of forbears Helen Levitt, Sidney Meyers, and Morris Engel, or other East Coast filmmakers such as Lionel Rogosin, who were concurrently developing a cinema that bears relevance to Mackenzie's interests. This may suggest that he was unfamiliar with their work or did not consider it immediately connected.
11. Mackenzie, 21.
12. John Morrill, at the Los Angeles premiere screening of *The Exiles*'s restoration, in the Billy Wilder Theater of the UCLA Film & Television Archive on 15 August 2009. Morrill's comments were made in a panel with Erik Daarstad, Merle Edelman, Lawrence Silberman, and Norm Knowles, moderated by Jan-Christopher Horak. Audio recording included in *The Exiles* DVD.
13. I did not press Morrill for clarification on his comment, but took his use of the word "documentary" to refer to films such as Leo Hurwitz's *Native Land* or any number of works by Robert Flaherty, which intermingle forms of acted scenarios with documentary footage and/or commentary.
14. Mackenzie, 26.
15. In describing the methods used to shoot this scene, cinematographer Erik Daarstad recounts, "For the exteriors the bare 40 watt bulbs on the porches were replaced with brighter bulbs and then used both as part of the scene and as the motivating source". In contemporary cinematographic language, motivated on-set light sources are called "practicals", but the *Exiles* camera team's interventions went well beyond that. Daarstad continues, "Masterlites and clip lights were hidden behind stairways and poles, etc. or placed just out of camera range". Erik Daarstad, letter to Kent Mackenzie, February 1964, excerpted in Mackenzie, 64.
16. Mackenzie, 62. John Morrill states further, "In order to photograph natural light as it appears to the eye, it is usually

necessary to expand or contract the brightness range". John Morrill, letter to Kent Mackenzie, December 1963, excerpted in Mackenzie, 63.

17. This is immediately evident in a mere glance at the chapter names of Mackenzie's account, which include, "Attitudes Leading to *The Exiles*, Research and Scripting, Directing and Acting, Photography, Voice Recording, Editing, Music and Sound Effects". Mackenzie, Table of Contents.
18. The celebration of this aspect of *The Exiles* has gone well beyond favorable. Richard Brody notes that "... the night photography alone would make the film immortal. Few directors in the history of cinema have so skillfully and deeply joined a sense of place with the subtle flux of inner life." Richard Brody, *The Exiles*, *The New Yorker* Film File, 7 July 2008, http://www.newyorker.com/arts/reviews/film/the_exiles_mackenzie, accessed 25 January 2014.Perhaps most famously, director Thom Andersen celebrates it as one of the best documentations of Los Angeles in cinematic history in his classic film essay, *Los Angeles Plays Itself* (2003).
19. Though of paramount importance, the Nagra was in fact just one technical innovation amongst many that resulted in a true shift in cinema's production landscape between the time of *The Exiles*'s shooting and the writing of Mackenzie's thesis; a shift that allowed greater opportunity for both location shooting and informal production methodologies unbound by studio limitations. Mackenzie was well aware of these changes, and personally details developments in everything from cameras to microphones to lights to film stock, which would have dramatically impacted the techniques he developed to address their absence. See Mackenzie, 129–130.
20. Looping refers to the technical process whereby a film's dialogue is post-dubbed. Mackenzie had his production soundtrack transferred from its original quarter-inch audiotape to 16mm magnetic film, and cut into a circular loop. This could be played continuously for the actors to listen to through headphones as they attempted to replicate the lines. For an account of his process see Mackenzie, 76. The only dialogue in the film which was not post-dubbed occurred in the opening supper scene, the reservation scene, and the Hill X sequence.
21. In addition to the Arriflex, the crew sometimes used an NC Mitchell and an Eclair Camerette. Mackenzie notes that a synchronous motor was occasionally used with the Arriflex to avoid speed variations and flicker, but the camera remained unblimped. Mackenzie, 60.
22. Ibid., 74.
23. Ibid., 75.
24. Ibid., 75.
25. Ibid., 76.
26. Ibid., 76.
27. Ibid., 78.
28. Ibid., 79.
29. Ibid., 80.
30. Ibid., 80.
31. Ibid., 91–92. One presumes he is discussing the narration in the gas station sequence, as the text clearly distinguishes narration from dialogue, however this is not certain.
32. Ibid., 78.
33. Mackenzie provides excerpts of the full narration transcripts and their subsequent editing in Appendix E of his thesis, 152–155.
34. Ibid., 115.
35. Ibid., 121.
36. Ibid., 122.
37. Ibid., 122.

20 Taylor Mead, a Faggot in Venice Beach in 1961

Marc Siegel

In the fall of 1963, while in Los Angeles with Andy Warhol for the artist's show of Elvis Presley portraits at the Ferus Gallery, actor, poet, and filmmaker Taylor Mead joined Warhol for a radio interview with Ruth Hirschman of KPFK at Pacifica's North Hollywood studios. During this seminal and much discussed Los Angeles trip, Warhol of course made his early experimental narrative *Tarzan and Jane Regained ... sort of* (1963) in which Mead embodied the "Lord of the Jungle" as a scrawny sissy. Throughout the radio interview, Warhol remains typically circumspect and primarily leaves it to Mead to provide in-depth answers to Hirschman's questions about pop art and the artist's newfound interest in filmmaking. Following a brief discussion of *Tarzan and Jane*, Hirschman asks Mead if he thinks the films of the New American Cinema are "social comments".[1] He replies, "Oh, definitely. They're brutal. Brutally satirical and completely thumbing their nose at Hollywood and TV and everything that's present." Mead explains that the films of the New American Cinema are aligned with the way "Hollywood used to work, in which there were idea men and you'd reel off a film in a day and you had a ball doing it". He opposes this more spontaneous, amateur style of early filmmaking to what he sees as the deadening professionalism of contemporary Hollywood. As he puts it:

> Like nowadays, if a workman three studios over hammers in a nail while an actor is doing a great scene even though that's barely picked up they'll reshoot the whole scene without any regard to whether the actor was functioning on screen...all they care about is a cold, technical thing with no sounds and the décor is all perfect–no dust on the floor.[2]

Hirschman pushes further and asks about the relevance of the term "underground" as a descriptive for the New American Cinema. In response, Mead criticizes

Figure 30. Taylor Mead in *Passion in a Seaside Slum.*

> any appellation like even avant-garde or even New American Cinema, anything that isolates a movement is unfortunate, I think, because all kinds of people like the movie I made in Venice, California, *Passion of the Seaside Slum* [sic] that was shown to every type of audience ... the impact was tremendous and yet it was put together spontaneously and according to the semi-rules of this new cinema.[3]

Passion in a Seaside Slum was one of two 8mm color films that Mead made with Robert Wade Chatterton in 1961. The other film is called *The Hobo and the Circus.* Neither film has received any attention in scholarship on Mead or the New American Cinema. Moreover, *Passion,* which depicts gay male cruising, drag, and police harassment in an astoundingly frank and light-hearted manner–perhaps as good an example as any of the new cinema "thumbing its nose" at present values – does not surface in accounts of queer underground cinema either. This lack of attention to the films is in itself not remarkable given the problems of categorization invoked by Mead. Indeed, both films exist at the nexus of queer, Beat, amateur and avant-garde film subcultures. In an interview in November 2008, Mead singled out *Passion* as a film that should be screened more frequently, particularly because of its potential relevance to contemporary gay audiences.[4] A closer look at the Mead literature indicates that he had been regularly singling out *Passion* as an exemplary film since at least the 1963 Hirschman interview.[5] Following his lead, then, I would argue that by incorporating Mead's collaborations with Robert Wade Chatterton, particularly *Passion,* into our scholarship on the avant-garde, we can better account for both the range of work by this seminal underground performer and the diversity of representations of homosexuality within the underground. Moreover, Mead's 1961 depiction of a self-assured *faggot*, as his character is described in the credits of *Passion*, stands as a surprisingly early cinematic example of an uninhibited representation of queer desire and queer culture. The very appropriation of the derogatory term "faggot" to label Mead's decisively swishy characterization anchors the film to queer culture's long tradition of managing and even redirecting the shaming effects of homophobia. With this essay, then, I am interested in acknowledging the breadth of Mead's work, while focusing on these little-known 8mm collaborations with Chatterton in Venice, California.

Until his death at the age of eighty-eight in 2013, Taylor Mead appeared in well over a hundred underground films. His nelly, irreverent performances in around thirty films throughout the 1960s alone – most famously, Ron Rice's *The Flower Thief* (1960) and *The Queen of Sheba Meets the Atom Man* (1963), Andy Warhol's *The Nude Restaurant* (1967) and *Lonesome Cowboys* (1967–68), as well as numerous other Warhol films and films by Robert Downey, José Rodriguez Soltero, Gregory Markopoulos, Rudy Burckhardt, Vernon Zimmerman, Adolfas Mekas, and John Chamberlain – have already secured his place in scholarly accounts of the period.[6] Additionally, Mead appeared on stage in plays by Leroi Jones, Charles Ludlam, Michael McClure, and Frank O'Hara, among others, and in a happening by French artist Jean-Jacques Lebel.[7] He is truly, as Callie Angell put it, "the doyen of underground performance".[8] Between 1961 and 1968, Mead also made a series of dazzling single and multiple frame 16mm "Home Movies".[9] He claims to have begun filmmaking out of boredom when he decided to purchase a 16mm film camera during a stay in Mexico City.[10] Due to the high costs of film stock, he chose mainly to film in single frame, so as to get as many different individual images for the money as possible. These cinematic travel diaries documenting Mead's impressions in Mexico, the United States, and Europe condense social and political events, landscape and architectural views, and interpersonal interactions into a stream of single images that pass by in seeming equivalence and at breakneck speed. The films thus offer a visual parallel to the aphoristic style of the five volumes of Mead's written poetry.[11]

Mead was in fact a doyen of Beat poetry readings as well. Like many disaffected kids of the North American middle-class, Mead was inspired by Jack Kerouac's *On the Road* (1957) and Allen Ginsberg's "Howl" (1956) to leave his hometown (Detroit, in this case) and travel across country to San Francisco in the mid-'50s. He began actively participating in the Beat scene as it was slowly dissipating in the late '50s, publicly reading his "scatological and defiant poems"–as he described them–in North Beach coffee houses and jazz clubs.[12] Although homosexuality and homosexual themes were not uncommon in the scene, Mead's combination of explicitness, self-deprecating humor, and radical sexual libertarianism gained him a degree of notoriety.[13] For example, his 1961 poem *Autobiography (after a poem by Ferlinghetti)* begins with the lines: "I have blown/and been blown/I have never had a woman".[14] After detailing various disappointments with his family, run-ins with the law, and violent, witty or erotic encounters with strangers and celebrities, the poem concludes thusly: "And I went into the Times Square Duffy Square/subterranean toilet with one of the movies' Tarzans/and he showed me his big peter/and I showed him my small one/because it was cold and/I didn't want to get it excited unless I was sure/something great was about to take place/And it didn't".

In 1959 and 1960, Mead made two films in San Francisco that catapulted him to the center of the burgeoning New American Cinema, and earned him the moniker "the first underground superstar": *The Flower Thief* (Ron Rice) and *Lemon Hearts* (Vernon Zimmerman).[15] Since the scene in San Francisco was on the wane, and the weather too cold, Mead headed south to Venice in 1961 and discovered not only a warmer location, but also a place with a still lively Beat scene, centered around the Gas House (an important cultural institution) and the Venice West Café.[16] There was in fact quite a bit of exchange between the North Beach and Venice Beat scenes. For instance, Eric Nord, who founded the hungry i nightclub and worked at the Co-Existence Bagel shop in North Beach (central Beat hangouts for many years), appeared with Mead in *Flower Thief* and was also the official greeter at the Gas House in Venice.[17] About his move to Venice, Mead notes, "I slept on the beach or in the back stairwell of the Gas House or on the floor of the Venice West coffee house. I soon became involved in another fun film project...and nobody got up before noon".[18]

Chatterton's *Passion in a Seaside Slum* was Mead's "fun film project". Mead doesn't mention a second film he made with Chatterton called *The Hobo and The Circus*, a film that is much simpler in structure, yet nevertheless quite interesting in terms of his development as an actor, particularly with regards to his debt to silent film comedians. Mead's sense of ridiculous and devious play, his knack for physical comedy and – given his meager appearance – his astounding athleticism have led critics to link his acting to that of the great silent movie comedians, particularly Charlie Chaplin and Harry Langdon. Susan Sontag, for example, in a review of Mead's 1964 performances in O'Hara's and Jones's one-act plays, describes him as "a sort of consumptive, faggot Harry Langdon".[19] In his own assessment, his acting "had a lot to do with the books [he] read and the mood of the times – the prevailing attitudes of the disenfranchised and the fun of being able to say and do almost anything – the more ironic and 'strange' the better".[20]

We might therefore characterize Mead's acting style as a kind of contemporary commentary on the silent movie comedian, one that appropriated the anarchic and effeminate aspects of, say, a Chaplin or Langdon performance for their relevance to the oppositional and antinormative Beat or queer subcultures. This quality of Mead's acting would certainly have interested Chatterton, who was himself a great enthusiast and collector of silent film comedies, a distributor of Laurel and Hardy films, and Stan Laurel's long-time friend.

The Hobo and the Circus, described in its credits as a "musical pantomime duet", is really two comedy shorts edited together. In *The Hobo*, Mead, dressed in baggy pants, a black vest, t-shirt and a boater (silent film comedian Harold Lloyd's typical hat), emerges from a public bathroom in a Venice park, moving around awkwardly and twirling a cane, as if half-heartedly citing the gait of Chaplin's "Little Tramp". He clowns with some children on the grass, surreptitiously picks flowers, lies down on a park bench, and goes through some hilarious antics eating a banana and munching on its skin, before he exits the park, awkwardly twirling his cane once again. *The Circus* is a more straightforward affair with Mead clowning around with various toys and objects in front of a multi-colored garage door for an audience of about ten children and a yapping dog. For comic effect, Chatterton employs Méliès-like stop tricks to make Mead disappear and reappear, much to the children's amusement.

Passion in a Seaside Slum is slightly more advanced technically, although eyeline matches, continuity, and all the trademarks of professionalism are still less of a concern than the production of an entertaining film with all "the dust on the floor", to recall Mead's words above. The twenty-eight minute short opens with almost two full minutes of beautiful establishing shots of Venice (the streets, street signs, houses, canals, and oil derricks), before a cut returns us to the Venice city sign. A pan down the sign post reveals the colorful credits written on pieces of white paper and tacked onto the wood. The film then picks up Mead in a white t-shirt and jeans sitting near a sidewalk fanning himself with a large dried out palm frond. He soon becomes enamored by a well-built masculine stud with a fishing rod in hand, apparently on his way to go fishing in one of the canals. Mead follows him, hilariously attempting to stay out of sight by holding the single palm frond in front of his face. The stud, clad in a denim jacket and blue jeans, comes across as a kind of amiable hustler or rough trade type; he can't help but notice Mead, but chooses to regard him throughout with friendly disinterest.

When the man gets to a bridge and feigns fishing, Mead takes the antenna from a small portable radio and uses it as a magic wand to transform himself into various, ever more implausible drag guises to alternately seduce, tease, taunt, and

Figure 31. The Faggot (Taylor Mead) and the Stud (Bob Dufour), *Passion in a Seaside Slum.*

chastise the man.[21] Chatterton employs Méliès stop tricks in order to produce Mead's split-second transformations. For his part, the affable – and now bare-chested – muscular stud seems bemused and amused, though not aroused by Mead's antics. In a spectacular climactic scene, Mead uses the wand to make himself disappear, only to resurface in the distance descending the steps of an oil storage tank in thrift store, Ziegfeld girl attire. (The end credits attribute Mead's gowns to "Balenciaga, Christian Dior and the Salvation Army". But they're obviously more the latter.) Mead's striking appearance does secure a moment of joking interaction with the man, but fails to attract his sustained interest. Finally, a tall, corpulent man approaches, sizes up the stud, ridicules Mead, and walks off embracing the masculine hunk. ("The Slob", as the man is pejoratively described in the credits, is played by Chatterton himself.) The film concludes when a policeman arrives to harrass Mead, only to succumb to his charms and walk with him, arm in arm, into the distance. A cut to an indoor location reveals what appears to be a torn photo or illustration tacked to a wall and depicting a fairy tale castle on a hill. The image is marked in black ink with the following text: "… and so like in all good *normal* fairy tales, *they too* lived happily ever after!" The underlining of the words "normal" and "they too" in this final text would seem to make explicit the film's self-consciousness about its queer critique of the standard heterosexual couple formation that concludes a typical fairy tale romance. Additionally, the end credits articulate what Mead's peformance obviously implied throughout the film, namely that he appeared in the role of "the faggot".

About *Passion in a Seaside Slum*, Mead writes:

> I played eight or more roles in this film–all bizarre, outrageous, non-pornographic but upsetting to many mores. In the last scene I descend a winding staircase on a huge oil storage tank in a Rockettes costume and go off into the sunset with a policeman. Everything about the film was illegal at the time, including our use of private property. Our audiences found it hilarious. However, one person I admired enormously was shocked–Stan Laurel. Bob Chatterton was a very good friend of Laurel's so we took the film to his apartment in Santa Monica to show him and his wife. Mrs. Laurel loved it, but Stan was shocked. Sometime later though, he admitted to being amused.[22]

Much of the pleasure in watching *Passion* derives of course from Mead's wacky and overly exuberant performance as an effeminate man – a faggot, indeed – so thrown into ecstasy by the sight of a muscular, bare-chested fisherman that he tries anything to get his attention. With spastic energy, Mead manages to perform both being interested in the fisherman and mocking himself for this interest, and thus allows us to laugh with him at the awkwardness of gay desire. In a 1964 review of Warhol's *Tarzan and Jane Regained…Sort of*, critic James Stoller beautifully describes the effects of this aspect of Mead's acting style: "The evocations of joy, wonder and sheer playfulness that Taylor Mead provides…are so convincing and remarkably moving it scarcely matters that he is also mocking nearly everything he does; it is enough that he begins by doing it".[23] In the same review, Stoller also praises Warhol's film in terms appropriate to Chatterton's, namely as "one in which homosexuality has genuinely been accepted to the point where it can be kidded; despite the apologetic lyrical aura which usually surrounds the subject, there are other valid ways of portraying it un-ominously".[24] Stoller then proceeds to distinguish Warhol's Mead from Ron Rice's use of the actor in *The Flower Thief*, with, in his words, "its portentous culmination in a pick-up on the beach".[25] *Passion*, made two years earlier than Warhol's film and shortly after Rice's, may perhaps be an even more apt choice to prove Stoller's point, for *Passion*'s playful flirtation scenes between "the faggot" and "the stud" offer the complete opposite of the solemnity hovering over the cruising scene in *The Flower Thief*.

I would like to extend this argument about the significance of *Passion* not only to Mead's faggotry – and Mead was a relatively public and acknowledged faggot throughout the 1960s[26] – but also to the broader history of queer underground cinema as well. Suffice it to say that incorporating *Passion* into accounts of the queer underground compels us to acknowledge a pre-Warhol, pre-*Flaming Creatures* (Jack Smith), pre-*Scorpio Rising* (Kenneth Anger) – hence a pre-1963 – example of unapologetic, playful, witty, and explicit queerness in the underground. *Passion*, therefore, falls chronologically between the earlier homoerotic psychodramas of Gregory Markopoulos, James Broughton, and Anger, and the later lush-exotic and minimal-realist depictions of queer subcultures we find in Smith and Warhol. Before concluding this essay with some remarks about *Passion*'s distribution and reception history, I would like to provide some background information on Chatterton himself.

As David James notes, Robert Chatterton founded a film society in Los Angeles in the mid to late 1940s in the aftermath of earlier projects by Anger, Harrington, and Paul Ballard, among others.[27] Chatterton, who was a second cousin of early film star Ruth Chatterton, was himself an extra in Hollywood in the 1940s. He appeared, for example, in a scene with Jennifer Jones in *Duel in the Sun* (King Vidor, 1946) and danced for a moment with Vera-Ellen in the Danny Kaye vehicle *The Kid from Brooklyn* (Norman Z. McLeod, 1946). In 1947, he conceived an elaborate plan for Stage Door 16mm Productions or the "Little Theatre of the Screen". He intended to work with a regular company of producers, writers, and performers on the production of numerous narrative features and short subjects, which he would then present on programs in a kind of touring roadshow at various theaters throughout the country. The Stage Door 16m productions would be supplemented by what he called "old time features", 35mm silent Hollywood films. A brochure he produced and sent on 8 June 1947, to Raymond Rohauer, who was meant to be a producer-director for the new production company, lists the production of about nine feature films and twice as many shorts over a two year period. Unfortunately, I have not been able to confirm whether any of these films were made.[28]

Chatterton, however, definitely made more films than the two Mead comedies discussed here. He premiered his film *Echoes of Venice West* in the context of a protest against the closing of the Venice West Café in 1965.[29] He also owned a store front on Ocean Front Walk in Venice in the '50s, and in 1959 he formed the Venice Citizens and Property Owners Committee for Cultural Advancement to support the Gas House when it was being pressured to close by the police and a conservative community group.[30] Chatterton even recruited Stan Laurel and Igor Stravinsky as signees on his petition. More research is needed to reveal exactly how Chatterton met Laurel, but he does seem to have been a trusted friend (as letters from Laurel indicate) and a primary distributor of Laurel and Hardy films thoughout the '50s and early '60s.[31]

A flyer for a series of events sponsored by the Creative Arts Film Society in San Francisco in the late 1960s indicates that Chatterton was an experienced and popular lecturer on and presenter of silent films and early comedies. For that particular series, he presented four programs, including one featuring his own films, and one each on Laurel and Hardy, Rudolph Valentino, and *The Phantom*

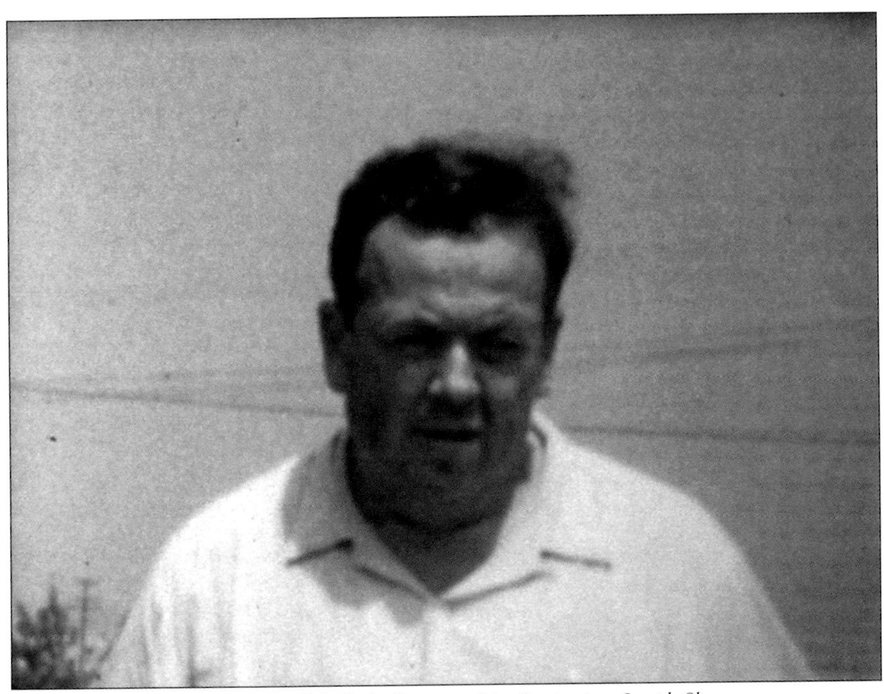

Figure 32. The Slob (Bob Chatterton) in *Passion in a Seaside Slum.*

of the Opera (Rupert Julian, 1925). The program notes emphasize the "shocking", "private", and "behind the scenes" nature of the information that Chatterton was expected to reveal about Hollywood and gay life on each evening. A photo of Laurel and Hardy, for instance, is captioned wth the following quote, "Hey Stan, I hear Bob Chatterton is telling all the funny things about our private life … they say, he even tells all about the hilarious skeletons in your family closet, what do you think about that???". The Valentino program includes a bonus, silent comedy short, *Mr. Bride* (James Parrott, 1932), starring Charlie Chase, which is described as "one of the 'Gayest' [sic] films of all times…*and we do mean GAY!*" (emphasis in original) The program of Chatterton's own films includes *The Underground Express* (undated), *Passion*, and a film referred to as "two swinging satires on TV cigarette commercials".[32] Chatterton describes *The Underground Express* as a color documentary that "speeds relentlessly from scene to scene, Greenwich Village, N. Beach, Venice West, and Haight Ashbury … The Fuzz, The Civic Bigots, and the Square Society – Versus – the Hippies, The Beatniks and the Homos. A film that will shock, amaze, and quite possibly scorch your eyeballs."[33] The description of *Passion* continues in this vein of promising – and almost hawking – a taboo experience, as it is proclaimed to be:

> delightfully GAY, delectably CAMPY and deliriously HYSTERICAL!!! A handsome rugged

> weight lifter decides to spend his day fishing, he is joined by a flirtatious homosexual. A fishing rod turns into the QUEEN FAIRY's magic wand…and from then on, it's an absolute gas! You'll flip over the ZIEGFELD GIRL sequence. A film that could not be shown until recent years, who knows, perhaps you are still not ready for this one.[34]

In the late 1960s and early '70s, Chatterton ran the Parlour Cinema, a small screening series in the living room of his two-bedroom apartment in North Hollywood. It was invitation only, and as regular attendee Richard Lamparski notes, the rules included "no talking once the projector begins to roll and no comments that could be considered criticism or ridicule no matter what was on the screen".[35] Chatterton remained a well-known film lecturer, enthusiast and presenter in Los Angeles until his death in 1985.[36]

By way of conclusion, I would like to quote from a letter that Mead wrote to friends in Santa Monica, presumably in the mid-1960s, criticizing the amateur circuit in which Chatterton presented *Passion*. In an entry in the third volume of his *Excerpts from the Anonymous Diary of an New York Youth*, he implores his friends to:

> find out what Chatterton is doing with *Passion in a Seaside Slum* – we can show it here in New York at several theatres and I have a right to see it or know what's what. I can't understand why he is being evil with me over this. But after 3 *years, 4 years* of nothing one begins to wonder a little. What a royal goof off.
>
> I'm afraid he is showing it sort of sub rosa and to undercover snickering groups which is the last thing I ever hoped would ever happen to any of my works. Also it is badly scratched – he didn't bother to have a 16mm print made when it was more suitable. – Even so I'm sure there are labs in New York that could do a good job – If only he would correspond with Jonas Mekas (at Filmmakers Coop. 414 Park Ave. South).[37]

It seems that Chatterton may have heeded Mead's request and contacted the Film-maker's Cooperative. Both *Passion* and *The Hobo and the Circus* are listed in distribution by the Coop in their 1965 catalogue. The following quote by Chatterton accompanies the rental information for *Passion*:

> A fantasy on the third sex relationships. For those who wish to delve further into the psyche of Taylor Mead. Actually one day I loaded Taylor, another friend, a box of costumes, and myself (armed with an 8mm camera) into my station wagon and we went out to (strictly for kicks) "shoot some movies". We had absolutely nothing in mind, just the urge. We started to shoot…with never a thought of public showing. Suddenly, three days later, we found we had not only a barrel of fun, but that we had a movie of sorts on our hands … . Taylor, I believe is more fond of *Passion* than even *Lemon Hearts* or *The Flower Thief*.[38]

Despite this listing, the Coop strangely has no rental information on the films whatsoever, which would seem to indicate that they were never actually in distribution in the first place. The Coop's 4th Catalogue from 1967 still includes the films, but notes: "no prints on deposit at this time". Indeed, Mead would have to wait about forty-five years to see a 16mm print of *Passion in a Seaside*

Slum when, thanks to a grant from the National Film Preservation Foundation to Los Angeles Filmforum, this early contribution to queer underground film was preserved in 2011 and made available in new prints.

Based on the example of Chatterton and Mead's collaborations on the delightfully, delectably and deliriously queer 8mm films *Passion in a Seaside Slum* and *The Hobo and the Circus*, I would suggest that scholars interested in charting innovations in queer cinematic representation might need to look not simply beyond the New York underground of Anger, Smith, and Warhol, but beyond the avant-garde itself to the diverse, yet elusive world of amateur filmmaking.[39]

Notes

1. Ruth Hirschman, "Pop Goes the Artist", in *I'll Be Your Mirror: The Selected Andy Warhol Interviews*, ed. Kenneth Goldsmith (New York: Carrol & Graf, 2004), 39.
2. Ibid., 39.
3. Ibid., 39.
4. Interview with the author, 17 November 2008.
5. See Taylor Mead, "Acting: 1958–1965", in *The American New Wave 1958–1967*, ed. Bruce Jenkins and Melinda Ward (Minneapolis: Walker Art Center, 1982), 15–16; and Mead, *On Amphetamine and In Europe: Excerpts from the Anonymous Diary of a New York Youth Vol. 3* (New York: Boss Books, 1968).
6. See, for example, Callie Angell, *Andy Warhol Screen Tests The Films of Andy Warhol Catalogue Raisonné Volume 1* (New York: Abrams/Whitney Museum of Art, 2006), 126; Jack Sargeant, *The Naked Lens: An Illustrated History of Beat Cinema* (London: Creation Books, 1997), 69–90; David James, *Allegories of Cinema: American Film in the Sixties* (Princeton: Princeton University Press, 1989), 120–124; and my article, "Taylor Mead (1924–2013)", *Art Forum* (October 2013): 71–72.
7. For more on Mead's collaboration with Lebel, see Lebel, "Happening et cinema. Le laboratoire vivant", *Jeune, dure, et pure! Une histoire du cinema d'avant-garde et expérimental en France*, ed. Nicole Brenez and Christian Lebrat (Paris: Cinémathèque Française and Milan: Edizioni Mazzotta, 2001), 236.
8. Angell, *Andy Warhol*, 126.
9. Thanks to a National Film Preservation grant, Anthology Film Archives was able to restore the three extant installments of Mead's home movies, which are catalogued under the following titles: *My Home Movies* (1964); *Home Movies–Rome/Florence/Venice/Greece* (1965); and *Home Movies/NYC to San Diego* (1968).
10. See Mead, "Acting", 16, and Bartlett Naylor, "Grand Tour Hardly Emaciated", (undated), Taylor Mead file, New York Film-makers Cooperative.
11. Taylor Mead, *Excerpts from the Anonymous Diary of a New York Youth* (Venice, CA, 1961); *Second: Excerpts from the Anonymous Diary of a New York Youth* (New York: Self Published, 1962); *On Amphetamine and in Europe*; *Son of Andy Warhol: Excerpts from the Anonymous Diary of a New York Youth Volume 4* (New York: Hanuman Books, 1986); and *A Simple Country Girl* (New York: YBK, 2005).
12. Mead, "Acting", 14.
13. To this effect, see Daniel Kane, *All Poets Welcome: The Lower East Side Poetry Scene in the 1960s* (Berkeley: University of California Press, 2003).
14. Mead, *Excerpts*, 1961. Reprinted in John Giorno, "Taylor Mead: An Interview", *Gay Sunshine* (Summer 1975): 2.
15. Mead may be, for better or worse, most famous today for his association with Warhol, but we should not forget that he was already a recognized underground film personality before he began working with the pop artist in 1963. Mead was "B.A.", as he liked reminding interviewers and audiences, "Before Andy".
16. This was not Mead's first trip to Southern California, since he not only attended acting courses at the Pasadena Playhouse in the late 1940s, but also hitchhiked across country many times over in the 1940s and '50s.
17. Mead and Nord also appeared together in another film by Bob Chatterton, *Echoes of Venice West*, made sometime between 1959 and 1962, and described on a 1977 program of the Pasadena Filmforum (later Los Angeles Filmforum) as "the story of the Gas House and its heroes, with poetry by Lawrence Lipton and featuring Taylor Mead, Eric 'Big Daddy' Nord, and Iris Tree". I thank Adam Hyman for locating and drawing my attention to this document and

Terry Cannon (via David James) for providing the date. For more on Nord and the Venice Beat scene in general, see John Arthur Maynard, *Venice West: The Beat Generation in Southern California* (Rutgers University Press, 1993).

18. Mead, "Acting", 15. Marcy Rodenborn, whose father was a close friend of Chatterton's, confirmed this account of Mead's vagabond lifestyle: "I guess my Dad also lived in a storefront, squatted really, with Taylor Mead and 5 other guys. He said all the other guys kept saying Taylor was from money and wouldn't last the winter, but every night he would wash out his socks and hang them up and Taylor ended up being one of the few who could stand it." Email message to author, 3 May 2013.

19. Susan Sontag, "Going to theatre, etc." in *Against Interpretation and Other Essays* (New York: Farrar, Straus, Giroux, 1966), 157. Ray Carney and Jack Sargeant link Mead to Chaplin and Langdon respectively. See Sargeant's discussion in *Naked Lens*, 72. For his part, Mead claimed, "I'm much better than Charlie Chaplin ... [who] to me was mechanical, repetitious". See "An Interview with Taylor Mead", in Sargeant, *Naked Lens*, 83.

20. Mead, "Acting", 15.

21. The portable radio (and later portable cassette or CD player) was long a common Mead prop, one he employed, for example, to generate musical accompaniment for his poetry readings. Apparently, in 1961, he "used to wander the streets of Venice Beach all through the night with the portable radio blasting classical music". Marcy Rodenborn, email message to author, 3 May 2013.

22. Mead, "Acting", 16.

23. James Stoller, "New American Cinema (Sort of)", *Moviegoer* (1964): 67.

24. Ibid., 67.

25. Ibid., 67. Viewed from today's perspective, the pick-up scene in Rice's film – which is depicted through close-ups as a face-to-face, consensual interaction – doesn't come across as ominous and portentous as it seems to have appeared to Stoller in the early '60s. Mead and the other boy even end up together on an amusement park ride! If there's an "apologetic lyrical aura" to the scene, it derives mainly – I believe – from the solemn classical music on the soundtrack.

26. See Sally Kempton, "The Homosexual Clown as Underground Star", *The Village Voice*, 30 November 1967, 19 & 49; Parker Tyler, *Underground Film: A Critical History* (New York: Da Capo Press, 1969), 227; and Parker Tyler, *Screening the Sexes: Homosexuality in the Movies* (New York: Holt, Rinehart and Winston, 1972), 337–338.

27. David James, *The Most Typical Avant-Garde: History and Geography of Minor Cinemas in Los Angeles* (Berkeley: University of California Press, 2005), 217.

28. Tim Lanza generously shared the documentation about this project that he discovered in the course of his research on Rohauer. See his essay in this volume.

29. Maynard, *Echoes of Venice West*, 122.

30. Ibid., 166.

31. See Charles Barr, *Laurel and Hardy* (London: Movie Magazine, 1968), 141; and Peter Underwood, *Death in Hollywood* (London: Warner Books, 1992), 86. Chatterton also made a "home movie" of D.W. Griffith's 1948 funeral. See *The Griffith Project Volume 11*, ed. Paolo Cherchi Usai (London: BFI, 2007), 218–221. Chatterton is described here as a Los Angeles "film enthusiast" who "had for many years compiled special theme programs of 16mm film and presented 'film talks' at local venues. Chatterton was well-known and respected in the Los Angeles film circle from the 1940s until his death in the 1980s."

32. This unnamed short is likely *The Next Sixty Seconds*, a film Chatterton presented at Pasadena Filmforum in 1977. For Filmforum, it is described as "a satire on television commercials which you'll never see on the tube". The Filmforum program also refers to a further Chatterton film, a work in progress entitled *Today I Died*, which "documents the life of Fowad Magdalani, 'a Venice artist better known as 'Mad Mike,' who committed suicide over the death of Venice West as he had known it". See "Program Notes", Pasadena Filmforum, 28 October 1977.

33. Creative Arts Film Society Program, n.d.

34. Ibid.

35. Richard Lamparski, *Hollywood Diary* (Boalsburg, PA: Bear Manor Media, 2006), 147–151.

36. According to Marcy Rodenborn, Steve Martin consulted with Chatterton for advice while making *Pennies from Heaven* (Herbert Ross, 1981). Email message to author, 3 May 2013.

37. Mead, *On Amphetamine and in Europe*, 206.

38. *The Film-Maker's Cooperative Catalogue No. 3* (New York: The New American Cinema Group, Inc., 1965), 20.

39. The work of photographer and amateur filmmaker Avery Willard certainly offers a good starting point. Willard began making physique and drag films in the mid-1950s under the name of "Ava-Graph Productions". For more information, see his book *Female Impersonation* (New York: Regiment, 1971). See also Cary Kehayan's documentary short, *In Search of Avery Willard* (2012).

21 Ed Ruscha's Moving Pictures

Matt Reynolds*

Ed Ruscha uses the language of film when he talks about making art in Los Angeles. He uses terms like "editing" and "montage" and often says that what he likes about the city "has to do with the movies" because in L.A. everything seems "so cinematic".[1] Ruscha's oeuvre explores the close connections between the Hollywood movie industry and avant-garde art practices in Los Angeles during the 1960s and 1970s. *Every Building on the Sunset Strip* (1966) is an excellent example. Bound accordion-style and unfolding to a length of twenty-seven feet, the book is a continuous panorama of Sunset Boulevard between Laurel Canyon and Cory Street. The north side of the street appears at the top of the page and the south side is displayed upside down at the bottom.

Taken with a motorized Nikon camera mounted on a tripod in the back of a truck, Ruscha meticulously pasted the individual photographs together to approximate the illusion of a single uninterrupted image. The top and bottom strips resemble an unspooled movie reel, the width of the printed image being approximately 35mm, or commercial cinema's standard gauge. Art historian Cecile Whiting foregrounds other cinematic properties of the book: "The layout of the photographs…mimics a filmstrip yet delineates no visual, spatial or narrative development".[2] These two features – the foregrounding of materiality and the conscious rejection of narrative – are, of course, among the defining features of experimental cinema.

Ruscha's paintings, drawings, and books have been the subject of rigorous formal

* My thanks to Ed Ruscha Studios and Gagosian Gallery, specifically Mary Dean, Susan Haller, Paul Ruscha, Gary Regester, and Gregory Heine for their unfailing generosity, time and assistance. Research for this project was supported with a Perry Grant from Whitman College. I am grateful to Olivia Mitchell for her invaluable assistance and insight, and to Stefanie Barrera who photographed the Ruscha books in the Whitman College archives.

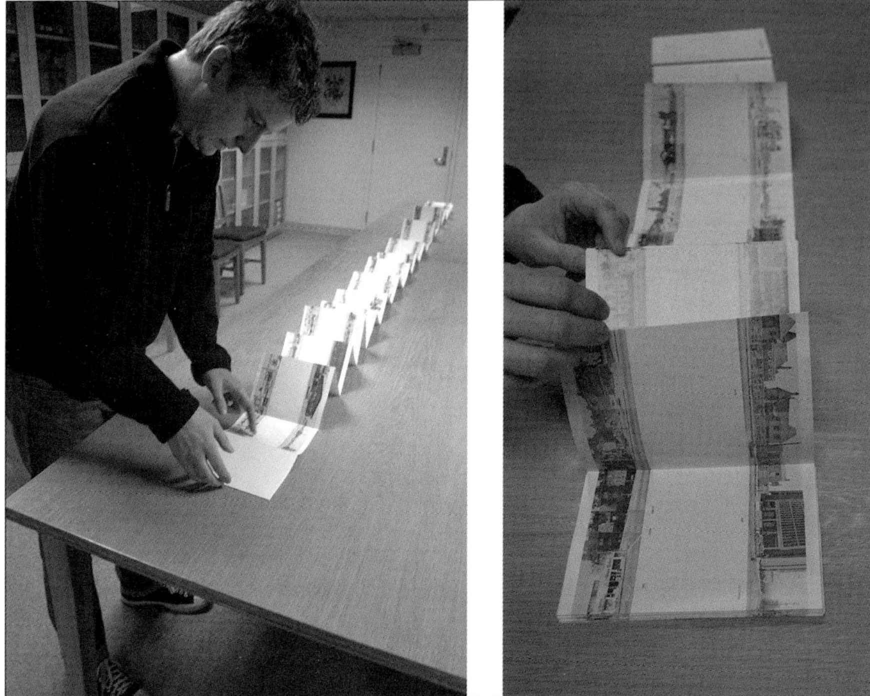

Figure 33. *Every Building on the Sunset Strip* (accordion fold).

analyses that are used to illustrate spatial layout and urban design, and that are identified as pioneering examples of Pop art, conceptualism, and documentary photography. How does our understanding of the artist's output change if examined through the lens of film criticism? This essay will approach Ruscha's work, particularly the street photography books *Every Building on the Sunset Strip* and the more recent *Then & Now: Hollywood Boulevard 1973–2004* (2005), as "paracinematic" texts. Paracinema "identifies an array of phenomena that are considered 'cinematic' but that are not embodied in the materials of film as traditionally defined", writes Jonathan Walley.[3] The paracinematic label, here applied to Ruscha's photo books, unsettles the rigid boundaries between artistic practices and the illusion of media specificity all too frequently policed by art historical discourse. Instead of separating these artistic practices, we might instead emphasize the productive cross-disciplinary dialogues between movements like Minimalism, conceptualism, and the structural film movements of the 1960s and 1970s. This essay will read what I am calling Ruscha's "Boulevard" books alongside key experimental films and other artworks that explore the tension between stasis and movement. Understanding these books cinematically disrupts the familiar symbolic economy that situates the museum and gallery in opposition to the commercial, profit-driven sphere of the movie theater. Ruscha's paracinematic texts prompt us to rethink the cultural hierarchies and biases that separate art production from filmmaking and thus elevate one practice at the expense of the other.

Additionally, exploring the cinematographic qualities of Ruscha's books provides a unique perspective on the Getty Research Institute's initiative *Pacific Standard Time: Art in L.A. 1945–1980.* Ruscha's output is consistently and directly informed by popular culture and mass media in Southern California, but his work has been reified within a high culture/high art discourse that reaffirms cultural hierarchies and disavows the productive dialogues and "crosscurrents" between diverse media practitioners operating outside of accepted strata of artistic production and reception. While the "more than sixty" exhibitions staged as part of *Pacific Standard Time* (*PST*) initiative uncovered new, important points of contact between artists working outside of accepted practices, or between marginal communities isolated from established gallery and museum environments, "movies" were again relegated to second-tier status because of their semantic association with Hollywood and the film industry.

* * *

During the 1960s, Ed Ruscha, along with David Hockney, was the most famous artist working on the West Coast.[4] He was affiliated with the Ferus gallery on La Cienega, and included in the Pasadena Art Museum's groundbreaking exhibition of American Pop art "New Painting of Common Objects" alongside Andy Warhol and Roy Lichtenstein. In 1970, he represented the United States in the Venice Biennale. Shortly after, Ruscha joined Leo Castelli's New York gallery, which represented many of the most prominent Pop, Minimal, and conceptual artists of the period.

Ruscha's iconography fetishizes movement. Motion is both theme and subject matter of virtually all his work. Whether he is depicting streets, gas stations, words, or consumer products like a can of spam, Ruscha consistently disturbs the static properties of painting and photography, instead giving his images directionality, destination, and motion. Motion in his paintings takes multiple forms, particularly in those works where the artist depicts words (*Damage*, 1964), objects, or buildings (Norm's Coffee Shop or the Los Angeles County Museum of Art) engulfed in flames. Fire for Ruscha connotes instability, destruction, and urgent transformation.

The tension between stasis and movement is present in his photo books as well. The first of these, *Twentysix Gasoline Stations* (1963), features black and white photographs of service stations taken by Ruscha along Route 66 on separate trips from Oklahoma to L.A. and back. In other books like *Royal Road Test* (1967), *Every Building on the Sunset Strip*, *Thirtyfour Parking Lots* (1967), *Real Estate Opportunities* (1970), and *A Few Palm Trees* (1971), the road figures prominently as a motif, acknowledged directly in the title or figuratively through the evocations of storefronts and vacant lots one might encounter through the window of a moving car. More recently, Ruscha did a series of collages and image plates for a limited edition reprint of Jack Kerouac's *On the Road* (2011).

Ruscha's work is also deeply imbricated with Los Angeles as a space of cultural production tied to the movies, the entertainment industry, and Hollywood.[5] Hollywood as signifier is a recurrent motif in Ruscha's work, and his physical presence in the neighborhood consistently informs the subject matter of his work. He maintained a studio there at different periods of his career: an apartment with a darkroom he shared with fellow Oklahoman Joe Goode in East Hollywood and a studio on Western Avenue less than a mile from both Sunset and Hollywood Boulevards, where he stayed for nearly two decades.[6] Ruscha obsessively depicts the street, in particular the streets of Hollywood, most famously in *Every Building on the Sunset Strip*. Many of his iconic paintings, including 1962's *Large Trademark with Eight Spotlights*, *The Back of Hollywood*, one of numerous studies he made of the Hollywood sign, and *Hollywood is a Verb* (1983) are just a few examples of how the neighborhood occupies its own chunk of the artist's psychic real estate.

Like the work of other Pop artists, Ruscha used mass culture (Googie coffee shops, cans of spam, parking lots) to transform a broader understanding of the avant-garde. Alexandra Schwartz has written extensively about Ruscha's close alliance with figures associated with New Hollywood, particularly Dennis Hopper. "L.A. visual artists and New Hollywood directors were both reflecting – and initiating – profound cultural shifts, and were greatly influencing one another".[7] Ruscha's own films serve as important reminders of his attempt to merge classical Hollywood's cinematic conventions with experimental strategies. Both *Premium* (1971) and *Miracle* (1975) utilize a linear narrative structure, employ professional craftspeople, crews, and actors, and are characterized by standard continuity editing that emphasizes identification with the protagonists. *Premium*, for example, tells the intentionally odd story of a man (played by Larry Bell) making a very large salad on top of a mattress in a cheap motel room. When he finishes, he leaves to pick up a date, brings her back to the room, and demands that she lie down on the bed. After dousing her with vinaigrette, he abandons the woman to buy some crackers (Premium brand saltines) and eats them without returning.

Premium, it should be noted, is a filmed version of *Crackers* (1969), one of Ruscha's earlier books, a work often described as a collection of photographs resembling film stills.

Miracle is more self-consciously surreal. An auto mechanic becomes obsessed with rebuilding a carburetor. Like the protagonist of *Premium*, he too sabotages a date with a beautiful woman (in this case Michelle Phillips, actress and former pop star, with whom Ruscha had been romantically involved) when he becomes engrossed in his work. Over the course of the thirty-minute film, both mechanic and garage are subtly transformed. By the end, the man's grubby overalls become a pristine lab coat and the garage once filled with nude pinups and greasy auto parts becomes a sanitized work environment. These movies can be said to mimic the star system of classical Hollywood cinema. "Indeed, his filmmaking style seems more akin to the escapist spirit of old Hollywood tales than to 1960s-era avant-garde filmmaking practices", Schwartz observes.[8] But if his movies reflect a more "conservative" approach to avant-garde filmmaking, as Schwartz implies, his photo books provide examples of using fine arts practices to create a more radical rethinking of the cinematic medium.

* * *

Beginning in the early 1960s, Ruscha began using the photo book to explore the relationship between movement and static imagery, most famously in *Every Building on the Sunset Strip* and subsequently with *Then & Now: Hollywood Boulevard, 1973–2004*. He frequently acknowledges his indebtedness to the photo books of Robert Frank and Walker Evans, among others.[9] Over a sixteen-year period, he produced sixteen books culminating with *Hard Light*, a collaborative project with conceptual artist Lawrence Wiener in 1978. The photographs that make up *Then & Now* were taken in 1973, seven years after the publication of *Every Building on the Sunset Strip*. Throughout this period Ruscha was also photographing the major boulevards and avenues of Los Angeles using equipment and methods similar to those he employed on Sunset Boulevard.[10]

Twentysix Gasoline Stations provided a template for the Boulevard books in several ways: a title that refers to the content in matter-of-fact way, a snapshot aesthetic, limited press runs, very few words (if any) on the page, and layouts characterized by differently sized images whose subjects were captured from varying perspectives and distances. Stations are identified by a caption stating the name and location of each business. The layout of the photographs and the text varies from page to page. Some photographs are spread across the fold with the label underneath, while other photos face each other from opposite pages or are stacked on top of one another with the caption on the verso.

Figure 34. *Then & Now: Hollywood Boulevard 1973–2004.*

While the Boulevard books are conceptually similar, they are visually distinct from the other photo books. *Every Building on the Sunset Strip* is a "leporello" – a term used in German publishing for tourist souvenirs featuring urban panoramas printed on a long sheet of paper and folded accordion-style.[11] Because of this format, the book is impossible to "read" in any traditional way; it is simply too cumbersome to leaf through casually and, once unfolded, it defies linear progression. To look at the book is to handle it, walk around it, focus in on specific images or locations, search for identifiable landmarks, to constantly adjust and re-adjust your proximity to, and perspective of, the text. For Ruscha, this embodied engagement also has an explicitly cinematic dimension. It promotes "the act of editing [the photographs] in your own mind as you move through the pages".[12] Other critical assessments focus on the white strip in the middle of the

Gramercy Place

- 5600 -

page as a "stand in" for the street. The book's layout mirrors the experience of driving; traveling east, the hills appear on your left and the flatlands extend beyond the facades on your right.

An analysis of *Then & Now* reveals how his concern with motion is informed by cinematic convention. *Then & Now*, like *Every Building on the Sunset Strip*, is a continuous photographic panorama of the streetscape along Hollywood Boulevard. Ruscha worked with a similar set of self-imposed directions. He and a crew drove a Datsun pickup truck equipped with a motorized Nikon camera mounted in the bed and fitted with a perspective control lens and 250-exposure cassettes. They drove the six-mile stretch of Hollywood Boulevard from the curvy residential hillsides of the west to the flatlands of the east, turning around at Hillhurst, and shooting the opposite side of the street on their way back to the point of origin. Along the way, they took one photograph approximately every ten to fifteen feet.

Ruscha planned to use these images in a book similar in form to the Sunset Boulevard publication, but because the two-and-a-half mile Strip produced nearly thirty feet of pasted together pages, a Hollywood Boulevard book was more logistically and financially prohibitive. As a result, the photographs and contact sheets stayed in storage for decades, until 2004, when the artist re-photographed the Boulevard using the same model Nikon camera but this time shooting in color film. The negatives from both periods were then scanned, and image composites were "sewn" together using digital software. The process of digitization erased the seams between individual photos so prominent in *Every Building on the Sunset Strip*, enhancing the panoramic effect and creating a greater sense of visual continuity.

The photographic panorama is, of course, an antecedent of the cinema, and was frequently used to capture the bourgeoning urban centers of the late 19th century. That Ruscha chose this format to photograph and display the streets of Hollywood, a space synonymous with the film industry, is in itself an important link between the books and the medium of the movies. But the photographs might also be compared to the pre-cinematic motion capture experiments of Eadweard Muybridge, whose serialized pictures of human figures or animals also demonstrate how the cinematic apparatus is ultimately a product of the still photograph. Muybridge's zoopraxiscope, which he used to project the images, was itself a precursor to Edison's kinetoscope and the "flip book" technology of Herman Casler's mutoscope. All of these devices were dependent on the rapid exhibition of minutely detailed, frozen moments to create the illusion of sustained movement, also known as the "persistence of vision". When the Lumière Bros. showed their first films in 1895, the presentation would often begin with the animation of a still frame by means of the hand-cranked projector, and the short strips would often be shown forward and backward.[13]

It is crucial to recall that "before the advent of the Lumière cinematograph, paper had been the privileged medium for cinematic movement".[14] Paper negatives, spools, strips, and rolls formed the material component of motion pictures. Thus, the book and the movie are intimately connected from the earliest stages of cinema's development. "Yet even after 1895, during the hundred years that saw film dominate the production of moving images, the film image kept returning to paper."[15] In the 1920s and '30s, artists like El Lissitzky, Alexandre Rodchenko, Varvara Stepanova, and Hans Richter "looked for an equivalence to the succession of images in the simultaneity of page organization" and viewed the film book "as a substitute of sorts for the projector".[16] Richter used photographic montage to create an illusion of movement on the printed page, while Rodchenko and Stepanova thought of the book as a "machine". Their collaborative book *Soviet Cinema* (1936) was an examination of the apparatus of filmmaking and exhibition that used flaps and foldouts to create a dynamic experience for the reader. "Turning the pages, the reader gets to unfold them, make choices, to go back, to establish relationships, to compare, etc."[17]

The material production of Ruscha's books was similarly dependent on cinematic conventions. Pages from the artist's notebooks from 1973 illustrate how Ruscha and his crew shot Sunset and Hollywood Boulevards. The camera mounted in the truck bed and the film-reel-like appearance of the images effectively mark both books as among the longest tracking shots in the history of cinema. The flatness of the photographs is another crucial reference point. Sitting behind the passenger-side seat in the pickup bed, the photographs were taken from across the street. As the truck traveled east, the viewfinder was trained on the north side of the street shooting across three lanes of traffic so that a uniform consistency between the curb and the top of the frame could be achieved, allowing the rooftops of all but the high-rise buildings or tall trees to be seen in the final prints. This framing technique deemphasized the human presence along the streets. Much is made of the frontal "deadpan" effect and the depopulated feel of the images as an indication of Los Angeles as a new model of postwar urban living, in which the car is the preeminent mode of transport at the expense of pedestrian travel.[18]

Here I want to offer another way of reading these visual motifs. Most buildings and cross streets are viewed head-on, but the editing occasionally reveals a sidewall jutting out into the frame at an odd angle. Viewed in tandem with the eerily empty streets, this defiance of the laws of perspective enhances the feeling that the viewer is looking at a film set on a studio lot, as if peering around the corner or poking one's head inside a window would reveal the support beams, planks, and plaster supporting the illusion of fully formed architecture.

Over the years since these early series of images were produced, Ruscha and his crew have continued to adapt and incorporate the equipment of commercial cinema in their ongoing photography of the city's major thoroughfares. Early proofs of the updated Hollywood Boulevard series commissioned by Steidl for *Then & Now* were shot with a high-end digital movie camera. Ultimately, Ruscha decided against using this footage because the quality of the image did not match the original 1973 series. Beginning in the 1980s, Ruscha's crew began renting vans from nearby film studios because they were easily adapted to the needs of shooting while driving. Windows could be popped out, more equipment and crewmembers could be near at hand, special odometers were dropped through a hole in the back to more accurately gauge the time and space between each photograph, and the activity itself didn't stand out to passersby or to police who were often attracted by the activity of a film crew in an open truck-bed driving slow and taking pictures.[19]

While the similarities between *Then & Now* and *Every Building on the Sunset Strip* are apparent, it is important to note the differences. The images taken in 1973 are arranged along the top of the page and juxtaposed with their 2004 counterparts so that the panoramas face each other and are aligned. Instead of two strips facing one another, *Then & Now* contains four strips that juxtapose two sides of the street taken over thirty years apart so that the similarities and differences of the landscape, storefronts, houses, and facades along Hollywood Boulevard become the subject matter of the work. With the turn of every page, *Then & Now* foregrounds movement through time and space, forcing the reader to confront the changing built environment of the city, while reflexively questioning the medium-specific properties of the book itself. Whereas the earlier book featured the accordion fold, *Then & Now* is hardcover and sewn through the fold to create a more traditional binding. The book is 148 pages, and, because of the binding, when read from left to right could be said to "begin" at Sunset Plaza Drive and "end" at Hillhurst Avenue. If, however, the book is flipped, beginning and ending points become more ambiguous. Most importantly, the juxtaposition of the two time periods marks a distinct break from the format of his other books. Whereas previous books presented synchronized snapshots of streets or other urban forms isolated in a single moment, *Then & Now* is both synchronic and diachronic. This structural approach to the city creates an even more dynamic experience for the eye. There is no detail that grabs and holds our attention for any length of time. Our relationship to the book is defined by a series of restless glances that telescope in and out, constantly taking in parts within the whole and zooming back out again to assess the page itself.

* * *

The tension between static and moving images in Ruscha's work, and the use of the technological apparatuses associated with commercial cinema in Ruscha's work problematize the boundaries between different artistic media. Kevin Hatch argues that "a Ruscha photo book constitutes more than a conceptualist gesture but less than a formalist statement, more than a documentary but less than a critical negation of art photography. Rather, it quite happily exacerbates the various gaps in between."[20] Recent work on Ruscha by Whiting, Schwartz, and

Allan notes the concurrence between Ruscha's books on urban form and critical reassessments of urban space by writers like Henri Lefebvre, Reyner Banham, Kevin Lynch, and Denise Scott Brown and Robert Venturi. Banham, Lynch, Brown and Venturi, it should be noted, wrote extensively on Los Angeles, often using Ruscha's photographs to illustrate their points about spatial form, vernacular architecture, and urban design. Banham interviewed the artist for the BBC produced documentary *Reyner Banham Loves Los Angeles* (1972) while Lynch, Brown and Venturi all used street photographs taken by Ruscha to illustrate their ideas about the centrifugal development of the postwar American metropolis.

If Ruscha's book can be categorized as works of conceptual art, or be used as a typology of buildings and streets, or viewed as a documentation of urban morphology, can they also be looked at as films? The most obvious point of connection between Ruscha's books and cinema would be through the structural film movement. Structural films share numerous characteristics with Ruscha's work.[21] There is, however, surprisingly little critical discourse devoted to the interstices between the two movements. Nevertheless, a brief outline of some of the shared concerns might open up new ways of interpreting Ruscha's work.

The heyday of conceptualism is generally agreed to have taken place from 1966–1972, although conceptual practice continues to be a feature of much contemporary art. Sol LeWitt's famous essay for *Artforum* "Paragraphs on Conceptual Art" (written a year after publication of *Every Building on the Sunset Strip*) provides a blueprint *ex post facto* for Ruscha's approach to the photo books. Most important for LeWitt is the formation of a plan. "When an artist uses a conceptual form of art, it means that all the planning and decisions are made beforehand and the execution is a perfunctory affair ... the plan would design the work."[22] The plan in Ruscha's case to shoot *Every Building on the Sunset Strip* or the spaces and buildings along Hollywood Boulevard amounts to an organizing principle that is, I would argue, as important as the end result. It is a structural dimension that foregrounds the process of its own construction and upon which the final product is predetermined. P. Adams Sitney defines structural film in just this way: "... the shape of the whole film is predetermined and simplified, and it is that shape which is the primal impression of the film".[23] A.L. Rees states that structural film "sought to explore visual and cognitive ideas of structure, process and chance then appearing in the other arts...In structural film, form became content".[24]

By emphasizing process, the Boulevard books play out the tension between movement and stasis in interesting ways. The photographs are frozen, crystallized moments in time. But the form of the texts demand that those photographs move through the turning of pages, the rotation of the book, the folding over of the flaps, etc. In order to best appreciate the books, they must be *in motion*; they must be moving pictures.

The photo in motion was the explicit subject of numerous experimental films and videos from the 1960s and 1970s. Hollis Frampton's *(nostalgia)* (1971) is ostensibly "about" the artist's shift from photography to cinema as his preferred medium of artistic expression. In it, twelve individual photographs are placed on an electric burner, slowly heated, and burned to a crisp. It shares with Ruscha a fascination with the still image ablaze. Frampton's *Zorns Lemma* (1970) has been described as "more or less … a succession of one-second still shots of words inscribed around the city". Its production coincided with the artist's essay on Muybridge's *Animal Locomotion* series (1887) in *Artforum*.[25] A renewed interest in Muybridge's chronophotography, inspired in part by Frampton's essay, informed the work of numerous conceptual artists during this same period. Sol LeWitt, Douglas Huebler, and Hans Haacke all used serial photography as a device to situate individual experience within larger institutional frameworks: cities, museums, corporations, etc.

Artists working on the West Coast, like Eleanor Antin, Allan Sekula, and Robert Flick also used serial photography as a form of institutional critique or as a means to represent the industrial landscape. Antin's *Carving: A Traditional Sculpture* (1972) features 148 black-and-white sequentially arranged pictures of the artist standing nude before the camera and in profile that document her weight loss over a thirty-seven day period. Sekula described his *Untitled Slide Sequence* (1972) as a "motion study" of workers leaving a San Diego aerospace factory, and once referred to his photographs as "disassembled movies".[26] Both artists self-consciously reference early or proto-cinematic animations of the still frame, like Muybridge or the Lumière Bros.' *Workers Leaving the Lumière Factory* (1895). Likewise, Sekula's use of the slide projector to convey sequential activity emphasizes the discipline of art history's own reliance on (and repression of) the carousel's literal role in moving pictures across a field of vision. Flick's large-scale prints are composites of hundreds of smaller, successive frames of streetscapes taken from the window of a moving car.

In Southern California, because of the proximity to the commercial film industry, and because of institutional initiatives like the Long Beach Museum of Art's pioneering video production and exhibition program, artists during this same period were also fascinated by the interdependence of static and moving imagery. Morgan Fisher, John Baldessari, and Gary Beydler all used still photographs as a basis for their experimental films and videos. Fisher's *Production Stills* (1970) displays a succession of seven Polaroid photographs, placed by hand before the camera lens. An off-screen narrator describes the contents of each picture, simultaneously describing the production of the film the still photographs serve to document. In *Walking Forward, Running Past* (1970), Baldessari videotapes sequential photographs of himself walking towards the camera, then running past it. As the video progresses, Baldessari's pace accelerates in an attempt to create the impression of animating the still photographs.[27]

In its technical precision and seamlessness, Beydler's *Pasadena Freeway Stills* (1975) is perhaps the most deliberate exposition of the artificial boundaries that define and demarcate cinema and photography. Sequential photographs are replaced at an increasingly rapid pace before the viewer's eyes so that the still images take on the illusion of movement. The photos depict a point-of-view perspective of a car driving along the Arroyo Seco Parkway that separates downtown Los Angeles from the San Gabriel Valley. The film appeared almost a decade after *Every Building on the Sunset Strip*. Nevertheless, the two works occupy similar artistic terrain. They are both road movies that document specific, localized, and historically important areas of the city. They are both preoccupied with the stillness that lies at the core of the moving image. And they emphasize the simultaneity of different temporal and spatial dimensions. Beydler contrasts an interior frame in which action speeds up then slows down with an exterior frame in which the action slows down and then speeds back up. Folding the pages of photographs of Sunset Boulevard juxtaposes non-contiguous parts of the street. This activity makes the "beginning", "middle", and "end" of the books ambiguous and relative. In a more direct manner, the alignment of different eras of Hollywood Boulevard in *Then & Now* makes it impossible to ignore the changes to the street that have taken place over time. The editing in our minds Ruscha asks us to perform always situates the photographs in relation to what comes before and what comes after, what was then and what is now. But before and after, then and now are indeterminate.

Beydler once equated his hands with the "projector mechanism", and was quoted as saying that he "wanted to be a human projector".[28] Beydler, Baldessari, and Fisher were exploring ways to make movies outside the traditional (commercial) uses of the medium. *Pasadena Freeway Stills* thus evokes the paracinematic properties of Ruscha's Boulevard books. In paracinematic works, "the medium of film was not necessary to produce the 'effect of film'".[29] According to Walley, "Studying paracinema ... forces us to reconsider the role of the film medium, and mediums in general, during a key moment in the history of the avant-garde".[30]

Implicit in Walley's argument is the notion that the avant-garde is not exclusive to the "fine arts" but to multiple practices and mediums. The striking similarities between the work of structural filmmakers and conceptual artists active during this period expose the false dichotomy that pits different media against each other through their "essentialist" qualities.

Now that *Pacific Standard Time* (PST) has completed its second phase, we might ask to what extent the sixty-plus exhibitions that took place around Southern California from 2011–13 acknowledged cinema's role in "the story of the birth of the Los Angeles art scene and how it became a major new force in the art world"?[31] Two shows were devoted exclusively to film: Los Angeles Filmforum's *Alternative Projections: Experimental Film in Los Angeles 1945–1980*, and UCLA Film and Television Archive's *L.A. Rebellion: Creating a New Black Cinema*. At first glance this seems to be a paltry number, but a quantitative analysis alone can't provide a complete picture. Experimental films and videos were shown in theaters or on monitors at numerous other exhibitions. Moving imagery was used as a didactic supplement to the display of art and architecture. And installations devoted to individual artists frequently featured clips or montages used to demonstrate innovative multimedia practices. Nevertheless, it is worth speculating whether *PST* complicated the cultural hierarchies and canons that privilege one form of artistic practice (painting and sculpture) over another (cinema), or whether it ultimately further entrenched those same hierarchies? The history is obviously still being (re)-written but the title of the Getty Center's *Pacific Standard Time: Crosscurrents in L.A. Painting and Sculpture, 1950–1970*, widely regarded as the initiative's "flagship" exhibition, speaks volumes.[32]

I have argued here that one way to address the value of moving pictures to the history of Los Angeles art is by looking at the fertile connections between Ruscha's photo books, conceptual art, and structural cinema. By way of concluding, I want to point to a fascinating detail contained within *Every Building on the Sunset Strip* that might further demonstrate the rich interdependencies between a broader range of artistic practices during this era. At the 8816 address located on the south side of Sunset Boulevard, Ruscha photographed the marquee of the now-defunct Cinematheque 16 advertising "Vivian by Bruce Conner".[33]

Conner was himself a multimedia artist well known for his assemblage sculptures and the landmark found footage film simply titled *A MOVIE* (1958). Cinematheque 16 specialized in the exhibition of avant-garde, art house, and experimental movies, and was located less than a mile from Ferus's at the northern end of La Cienega. *Vivian* (1965) is a three-minute document of Conner's exhibition at the Batman Gallery in San Francisco the previous year. He used a hand-held camera and a jerky stop-motion style to track his then-girlfriend Vivian Kurz

Figure 35. *Every Building on the Sunset Strip* (detail): Cinematheque 16 advertising "Vivian by Bruce Conner."

around the gallery, ending with the actress entombed in a display case surrounded by signs that say "Do Not Touch This". Conner used Conway Twitty's rockabilly version of the Ray Evans and Jay Livingstone hit *Mona Lisa* (1950) as the soundtrack. Karen Beckman and Jean Ma argue that art history has had to contend with the increasing ubiquity of the projected image in contemporary art. They call for "fruitful intellectual exchange between art history and cinema studies". Such exchange might allow these fields "mutually to energize and strengthen, rather than undermine each other, and to assert the continued primacy of creating spaces for historical, aesthetic, and theoretical reflection in both".[34] Ultimately, this document of a lost moment of the city's film history within Ruscha's paracinematic work might provide a road map to discovering new intersections between art and film.

Notes

1. Ed Ruscha, "Ed Ruscha", *Artforum*, October 2011, 297.
2. Cecile Whiting, *Pop L.A.: Art and the City in the 1960s* (Berkeley: University of California Press, 2006), 95.
3. Jonathan Walley, "The Material of Film and the Idea of Cinema: Contrasting Practices in Sixties and Seventies Avant-Garde Film", *October* 103 (Winter 2003): 18. Walley differentiates paracinema as a category associated with avant-garde film with the "paracinema" label often applied to cult or "trash" films.
4. Whiting.
5. Ibid., 68–69.
6. Alexandra Schwartz, *Ed Ruscha's Los Angeles* (Cambridge: MIT Press, 2010), 106.
7. Ibid., 69.
8. Ibid., 96.
9. Schwartz, 122.

10. Since 1973, Ruscha or a crew directed by him has been re-photographing major city streets using the same or similar technology, and approximating the style and format of previous panoramas. These streets include Sunset Boulevard and Hollywood Boulevard as well as Normandie, Vermont, and Pico, to name a few. The Getty Research Institute recently announced the purchase of these negatives and prints for their archives. Stephanie Cash, "Getty Acquires Important Ruscha Photo Trove", *Art in America*, 7 October 2011.
11. Walter Benjamin notes the form and style of the leporello in his famous essay "Dream Kitsch". Benjamin, *The Work of Art in the Age of Technological Reproduction and Other Writings on Media*, eds. Michael Jennings, Brigid Doherty, and Thomas Levin (Cambridge: Harvard University Press, 2008), 236.
12. Schwartz, 274. And Ken D. Allan, Ed Ruscha, "Pop Art and Spectatorship in 1960s Los Angeles", *The Art Bulletin*, XCII.3 (2010): 246. Ruscha also released an even more limited edition of the book that featured unbound 2' x 3' C-print pages that could be pulled out and arranged in an unlimited number of ways, like a deck of playing cards that can be shuffled, ordered, and re-ordered. This Ed Ruscha multiple is a set of 142 photographic prints, housed in a handmade wooden crate signed and numbered in an edition of ten.
13. François Albera, "From the Cinematic Book to the Film-Book", in *Between Still and Moving Images*, eds. Laurent Guido and Oliver Lugon (New Barnet, UK: John Libbey Publishing Ltd., 2012), 213.
14. Olivier Lugon, "Cinema Flipped Through: Film in the Press and in Illustrated Books", in *Between Still and Moving Images*, eds. Laurent Guido and Oliver Lugon (New Barnet, UK: John Libbey Publishing Ltd., 2012), 138.
15. Ibid.
16. Lugon, 144.
17. Albera, 205.
18. Ed Ruscha, *Leave Any Information at the Signal: Writings, Interviews, Bits, Pages*, Alexandra Schwartz, ed. (Cambridge: MIT Press, 2002), 71. For a broader discussion of the "deadpan" label as it is applied to Ruscha's photography, as well as an inventive reading of the artist's work in relation to the films of Buster Keaton, see Aron Vinegar, "Ed Ruscha, Heidegger, and Deadpan Photography", *Art History* 32:5 (2005).
19. I am grateful to Susan Haller, Paul Ruscha, and Gary Regester at Ed Ruscha Studios for their assistance in explaining the shooting process and adaptation of equipment for the street photography project.
20. Kevin Hatch, "'Something Else: Ed Ruscha's Photographic Books", *October* 111, (Winter 2005): 126.
21. Benjamin Buchloh, "Conceptual Art 1962–1969: From the Aesthetic of Administration to the Critique of Institutions", *October* 55 (Winter 1990). Buchloh actually refers to *Twentysix Gasoline Stations* as "proto-conceptual" since it predates the work of those New York artists to whom the term was most often applied.
22. Sol LeWitt, "Paragraphs on Conceptual Art", in *Conceptual Art: A Critical Anthology*, eds. Alexander Alberro and Blake Stimson (Cambridge: MIT Press, 1999), 12–13.
23. P. Adams Sitney, *Visionary Film: The American Avant-Garde, 1943–2000*, Third edn (Oxford: Oxford University Press, 2002), 348.
24. A.L. Rees, *A History of Experimental Film and Video* (London: BFI, 2008), 72.
25. Guillaume Le Gall, "The Suspended Time of Movement: Muybridge, a Model for Conceptual Art", in *Between Still and Moving Images*, eds. Laurent Guido and Oliver Lugon (New Barnet, UK: John Libbey Publishing Ltd., 2012), 343.
26. Marie Muracciole and Ali Akay, *Allan Sekula: Disassembled Movies 1972–2012*, e-flux announcement, http://www.e-flux.com/announcements/allan-sekula-disassembled-movies, accessed 25 February 2014.
27. All three works were shown at an Alternative Projections screening on 12 May 2002, with the title "Moving Pictures: Painting, Photography, Film". My thanks to Adam Hyman for sharing information about this event.
28. Benjamin Lord, "Gary Beydler (1944–2010)", x-tra online, http://www.x-traonline.org/past_articles.php?articleID=416, accessed 5 October 2011.
29. Walley, 16.
30. Walley, 30.
31. Getty Research Institute, "Pacific Standard Time Fact Sheet" press release, 9 February 2011.
32. Numerous reviews accurately situate the Getty show as the hub around which other, ancillary shows revolved. See for example Roberta Smith, "A New Pin on the Art Map", *The New York Times*, 10 November 2011, or Christopher Knight, "Review: 'Crosscurrents in L.A. Painting and Sculpture, 1950–1970'", L.A. Times, 29 September 2011.
33. My thanks to Adam Hyman for pointing out this detail.
34. Karen Beckman and Jean Ma, "Introduction", *Still Moving: Between Cinema and Photography* (Durham: Duke University Press, 2008), 5.

22 Asco's Super-8 Cinema and the Specter of Muralism

Jesse Lerner

Throughout the 1970s, the Chicano arts group Asco created a series of very short Super-8 films, most of which are documentation of their performances and political street theater.[1] These small-gauge shorts – fragments, really – offer fleeting glimpses of the group's radical blend of activism, performance, and conceptual art making in public spaces, though there is also at least one attempt at creating a brief surreal narrative, *Sr. Tereshkova* (1974). Today, only traces bear witness to Asco's filmmaking. The scarcity of primary documents is not just the result of the lack of adequate preservation efforts; it is also the inevitable consequence of the sometimes intentional practice of destroying unique materials, including their Super-8 reversal films. One founding member tells of periodically burning film reels, photographs, and negatives of work from his Asco years in his mother's backyard, while other materials have fallen victim to improper storage, careless handling during moves, and further misfortunes.[2] However, despite this and other obstacles, it is possible to engage Asco as filmmakers by reading their Super-8 films through the practice and promise of mural painting.

Their interviews, scripts, statements, and writings, as well as the surviving fragments of their Super-8 films make clear that the specter of muralism haunted the group in its early years. Even before their christening as Asco, they created *Walking Mural*. In this Christmas Eve 1972 work, the artists processed down Whittier Boulevard, a main thoroughfare of East Los Angeles, as characters such as the *Vírgen de Guadalupe* with a mantle of aluminum foil and painted cardboard, an adorned *calavera* on the back of her head, and as an inverted Christmas tree in crepe. When Gronk taped Patssi Valdez and Humberto Sandoval to an exterior wall, an action whose documentation in both photographs and Super-8 film survives, the performance was called *Instant Mural* (1974). When the groups protested against the Los Angeles County Museum of Art's exclusion of Mexican-American artists, the critique took the form of paint on an exterior wall: *Spray Paint LACMA* (1972). Gronk's statement in *Murals of Aztlán: The Street Painters of East Los Angeles* (James Tartan, 1981) suggests murals and ephemeral actions were, for him at least, overlapping categories: "most of my murals or a lot of the times they're just instant murals, they just happen and sometimes they only last for about five minutes, a half an hour, and then they're gone".

Muralism emerges not so much as a recurring theme or point of reference as an obsession, so much so that we might think of their Super-8 films not simply as the documentation of otherwise ephemeral performances but as a filmic response to and activation of muralism. In contrast to 16mm and 35mm film, the Super-8 image is as likely to wind up on a wall – like a mural – as on a screen. In an interview from 1976, for example, we find the following exchange:

> NEWORLD: What type of work will you be doing soon?
>
> GRONK: To do a mural in semen.
>
> HERRÓN: I think I'm going to paint a mural in the rain, in tempera paints to see how long it will last. Start petitioning to remove the ugly murals that make East L.A. a disgrace. We all know which ones they are.[3]

But beyond the merits of those "ugly murals", what is the bone that Asco has to pick with muralism as an art form? I will argue that Asco's critique of muralism is three-fold, hinging on questions of ethnicity, politics, and public space, and speculate as to how moving images offered the group a powerful alternative.

Several of Willie Herrón's quips in the above-cited interview make it clear that the muralism that Asco rejects has its origins in Mexico. "I'd like to see Siqueiros come back to life in City Terrace", he says, referring to his own neighborhood in the East Los Angeles district overlooking downtown.[4] How would David Alfaro Siqueiros, *el coronelazo* – whose efforts to bring his school of revolutionary Communist muralism to Southern California ended in censorship and acrimony – engage the dynamics of the Chicano metropolis?[5] "I'd like to receive Orozco's left arm in the mail."[6] Again, the reference is to muralism's shortcomings – Orozco's left hand was crippled, mutilated in a childhood accident involving gunpowder.[7] It is not Ambrogio Lorenzetti and Thomas Hart Benton who are singled out for this lighthearted ridicule, but rather the protagonists of the Mexican cultural renaissance, two of the *tres grandes* (José Clemente Orozco,

Figure 36. Harry Gamboa, Jr., "Willie F. Herrón III and Gronk in front of the *Black and White Mural*, Estrada Courts housing project, Boyle Heights", 1979.

Diego Rivera, and David Alfaro Siqueiros) of the Mexican mural movement, and more specifically, the two that worked in Southern California.

Muralism is at the center of Asco's origins. Herrón and Gronk had worked collaboratively on murals, most notably *Moratorium: The Black and White Mural* (1973) at the Estrada Courts housing project. In fact, they began their professional lives as artists working within state-supported mural painting workshops. In 1973, Los Angeles County had received federal funds through the Comprehensive Employment and Training Act (CETA), a job training and employment program aimed at low-income workers and the unemployed. Ten artists were hired to paint murals in collaboration with El Monte city high school students. The municipal response was negative, perhaps because of an inability or unwillingness to distinguish between graffiti and murals, and exacerbated by ethnic tensions in a suburb whose Anglo population was losing its status as the majority group. A mural of an *Adelita* by Robert Gil de Montes and Gronk was whitewashed over, and another proposed project by Joe Janusz and Ron Reeder depicting Godzilla menacing the local mall proved controversial. In response to these perceived threats to public interest, the city council passed an ordinance banning murals. In this anxious climate, images of a giant Japanese monster and what was by then a cliché of *PRI-ista* public art – Casasola re-imagined by Jesus Helguera re-imagined by two young Chicano painters – were seen to be menacing and unwelcome. C. Ondine Chavoya, Karen Moss, and others have documented how El Monte city's ban on murals led to the establishment of a storefront gallery at the El Monte Community Service Center, where local artists could show indoors, and then subsequently to the 1977 move to the less inhospitable environment above a bridal shop at Second and Broadway, in downtown Los Angeles, where the gallery became known as LACE (Los Angeles Contemporary Exhibitions).[8] CETA funding was once again crucial, now funneled though a Latino/a veterans' group, The Friends of the American G. I. Forum. Over thirty years later, and after numerous transformations and relocations, LACE remains a mainstay of the contemporary art scene in Los Angeles. By the time of the move to downtown Los Angeles, the core membership of the group had grown to thirteen, and included Asco members Harry Gamboa, Jr. and Gronk. What this background suggests is that muralism is not simply a straw man for the founders of Asco. Rather, it figures large in the immediate creative histories of at least three (Gronk, Gamboa, and Herrón) of the original four artists. Muralism inhabits a contradictory position for these artists, a practice that the state was prepared both to finance and to outlaw, a tradition of public art that they were prepared both to reject and, by calling their performances "murals", to situate themselves within.

The members of Asco were not the first to reject the legacy of the *tres grandes.* More than once does their critique recall certain Mexican artists' rejection of muralism two decades earlier. When José Luis Cuevas decried the *cortina de nopal* in 1957, in an article against the Mexican mural movement first published in the *México en la Cultura* (the weekly arts supplement to the daily newspaper *Novedades*), his attack was directed at an insularity that he claimed pervaded the national school. This "cactus curtain" effectively cut Mexican artists off from outside influences, promoted mediocrity, and dictated orthodoxies of style and content. His voice was not alone. Juan Soriano offered a critique that focused on muralism's ideological role, rather than its stultifying effect on art production:

> Those murals are only tourist bait. They're the same kind of thing as those giant posters of the travel agencies: *Visit Mexico*. Furthermore, those murals reveal nothing ... Diego Rivera created a completely bureaucratic art. He made himself a propagandist of the victorious revolution.[9]

One senses that the members of Asco would have agreed with both these criticisms, though as artists they chose a path very different from those of Soriano or Cuevas. Two decades later, Chicano artists were still struggling with the expectation that muralism be adopted as the appropriate or even obligatory artistic form used to reach "the community". Part of Asco's rebellion was directed at the assumption that Chicano artists should paint on walls and on public buildings, by virtue of their ethnicity or national heritage, and that they inevitably draw on a limited set of national and cultural icons. "The *Vírgen de Guadalupe,*

Emiliano Zapata, Che Guevara, all of these symbols that we may or may not have wanted to use at one point or another, we avoided them", Herrón stated. "And we avoided them because they just seemed too common and too stereotypical in terms of our representations."[10] These expectations are restrictive and overly limiting, like the masking tape used to bind Valdez to the wall in *Instant Mural.*

The adaptation of muralism by artists of the Chicano movement of the 1970s follows much the same logic as Mexican muralism did a half century earlier: to make an appeal through art to an audience that does not frequent art museums or galleries, one must bring the art to the audience and couch it in a legible, explicit, figurative style. Asco went elsewhere. As one contemporary, Carlos Almaraz, said of Asco: "They were not into plastic art. They were really into other ideas."[11] Both the muralism that Asco rejected and the street actions that they turned to are engagements of public space – the street, rather than the museum or gallery. The promise of muralism is its accessibility (from the street) and legibility, the usurpation of the exceptionally successful strategies of capitalist advertising for other ends, or as Siqueiros wrote:

> *vamos a impulsar el aprendizaje de la pintura mural exterior, pública, en la calle y bajo el sol, en los costados libres de los altos edificios, donde ahora se colocan afiches comerciales, estratégicamente ubicadas frente a las masas, mecanicamente producida y materialmente adaptada a las realidades de la construcción moderna.*
>
> [We will promote the study of exterior mural painting, in the street and in plain daylight, on the sides of tall buildings, where today mechanically produced commercial posters adapted to the realities of modern construction are displayed strategically in front of the masses.][12]

Seemingly following Siqueiros's exhortation, Asco did in fact work in the street and in plain daylight, though the strategies they chose were very different.

Contemporaneous with the experiments of Asco, any number of Mexican arts collectives similarly challenged assumptions and expectations. These collectives, known in Mexico as the *grupos*, include the *Proceso Pentágono*, *Grupo Suma*, *Taller de Arte e Ideología*, *No Grupo* and others. They share with Asco a turn to performance and ephemeral actions, the dissolution of individual authorship in favor of a collective identity, the preference for non-traditional spaces for art exhibition, and an engagement with the era's turbulent politics. *Grupo Mira*'s mass-reproduced graphics for radical political causes echo Asco's early work for the periodical *Regeneración*. In the spirit of Asco's ersatz-Oscars, the "No Movie Awards", *No Grupo*'s Melquiades Herrera awarded himself a Nobel Prize for art.

Maris Bustamante is author of an insightful essay in which she compares Asco with Mexico's *No Grupo,* the collective in which she participated from its start in 1977 to its dissolution in 1983.[13] The parallels are striking: like Asco, they came into maturity in the context of the radical upheavals of 1968, and their

Figure 37. Harry Gamboa, Jr., "Instant Mural," 1974.

works reflect both the international upheaval of student and civil rights movements that questioned fundamental assumptions of the status quo, and the radical questioning of art's commodity status. Wary of art's unstated assumptions, and skeptical of its ideological role, these collaborations sought to undermine art's traditional social functions. The use of humor is another common trait; or as Bustamante writes: they shared "a discourse full of private jokes that eventually became concrete positions".[14] She and others suggest that these parallels were less the result of direct contacts or reciprocal influences as it was of a more general, shared zeitgeist, though significant contacts and exchanges between the Mexican and Chicano photographers did take place starting in the early 1980s under the auspices of the *Consejo Mexicano de Fotografía*, through their international colloquiums, events in which Gamboa also participated.

As telling as the parallels are the divergences between Asco and the Mexican *grupos*. Unlike Asco, the *grupos* exhibited in the nation's most prestigious spaces, not at the margins of the dominant cultural institutions. In 1978, for example, *No Grupo* showed at the National Palace of Fine Arts, and in 1979, 1980, and 1982, they performed at the *Museo de Arte Moderno* (MAM). Four of the other *grupos* – *Próceso Pentágano*, *Suma*, *Tetraerdo*, and *Taller de Arte e Ideología* – represented Mexico in the X Paris Biennale of 1977.[15] In contrast, Asco's access was largely limited, during its active years, at least, to Chicano-run spaces such as the then newly-created *Galería de la Raza*, the streets and public spaces of the city, for which there were no gate keepers, or artist-run spaces, such as LACE, which they had a hand in creating.[16] The equivalents in the USA of *No Grupo*'s exhibition venues – Washington's National Gallery or New York's MoMA – were off limits for Asco and most of their contemporary rebellious cohorts. In challenging arts institutions' politics of exclusion, Asco's gestures are closer in spirit to the pressure put on MoMA and other museums by the Arts Workers' Coalition. Far from official exhibitions, these were unauthorized protests staged on the (and questioning the entrance criteria of) arts institutions' drawbridge.

Beyond the question of access to mainstream spaces, the relationship to muralism is the most striking divergence between the Asco and the *grupos*. When members of the *grupos* painted on a wall, this would take the form of *Suma*'s stenciled silhouettes or slogans in spray-paint, not murals. For *No Grupo*, the national tradition of muralism (which the muralists had self-consciously articulated, linking their own practice to Pre-Columbian murals) was, in Bustamante's words, "never an option".[17] Instead of the *tres grandes*, *No Grupo*'s extended play on the patricidal impulse instead took on figures such as Gunter Gerszo, the Hungarian-born Mexican painter of lush geometrical abstractions, and José Luis Cuevas. It is their engagement with the latter that is most revealing here; theirs is a playful critique not of muralism, but of muralism's critic. Returning to Mexico after three years of self-imposed Parisian exile, Cuevas presented the solo exhibition called *El hijo pródigo* at Mexico City's *Museo de Arte Moderno*. *No Grupo* engaged the returning artist in a number of ambivalent collaborations, with which Cuevas sportingly played along. Bustamante packaged "authentic" drops of the artist's sweat, which was proof of his creative labors.[18] Another member of *No Grupo*, Rubén Valencia, offered collectors to replicate Cuevas's signature on any unauthenticated or forged artworks by the master.[19] But there is one of the *No Grupo*'s short, Super-8 films inspired by the Cuevas exhibition that best embodies the essence of their critique. It shows a Cuevas drawing climbing down from its frame in the *Museo de Arte Moderno*'s gallery space and exiting into that institution's parking area, just off the busy *Avenida Reforma*. Before making it to the avenue, the drawn figure is run over by a Volkswagen Bug exiting the parking lot. In the ever-shifting balance of art and life, Cuevas's masterly draftsmanship has no chance at survival. Like Asco's fake news releases, designed to disseminate through the mass media (e.g. *Decoy Gang War Victim*, 1974), and their actions in the city's streets, much of the work of the *grupos* aimed to enter the spaces of daily life, not simply those of the art world.

Fifteen years earlier, when the *Museo de Arte Moderno* had just opened, Cuevas's attack on the nationalist school was a controversial matter, and the Museum itself was very much a contested site. It was at MAM in 1965 that an outraged muralist disrupted the *Primer Salon de Artistas Jóvenes* [The First Salon of Young Artists] that featured Cuevas's coterie. "Abstract painters", Benito Messeguer interjected, "go against the thesis in painting which we inherited from the Mexican Revolution". A melee ensued – the popular press dubbed it "*la bronca*" ["the brouhaha"].[20] But by 1979, the date of the *Hijo pródigo* exhibition and *No Grupo*'s engagement with Cuevas, the debate was settled, and as his solo show at MAM would suggest, Cuevas and his group had emerged triumphant. For the *grupos*, to go after muralism would be to attack a cause that had been already defeated.

In Agnes Varda's 1981 documentary on public art on the streets of Los Angeles, *Mur murs*, muralism makes its final returns as Asco's troubling, haunting presence. This playful film records murals and muralists, roaming from the awkward Tai-chi exercises executed in front of Margaret Garcia's *Two Blue Whales* mural on the Westside's Venice Boulevard to anonymous *rotulos*, roller disco on Venice Beach, and an infinite unending accumulation of tags, from the Mechicano Art Center (1969–78) to the public interventions of Judy Baca and Kent Twitchell. Baca's talking head reverberates with Asco's tagging of LACMA and efforts to create alternative venues: "I started painting murals because I realized that when I was 23 that I'd never seen a Chicana in a museum. And there was probably very little chance that I would take my work and put it into the art establishment." Rather than using the film to document one of their murals, Asco contributes a sort of *tableau vivant*, that literally crashes and burns on of the back wall of East Los Angeles's artist-run exhibition space, Self-Help Graphics. Gamboa describes the scene:

> The idea was we were going to create all of Chicano history and burn it all, and we were just going to start brand new because it's been all messed up already. It's all fucked up. We're going to fix it by eliminating everything, just scorch it and then start brand new. And during this period of time Willie and Gronk were making paper people and paper objects ... just butcher paper they would staple and paint and so they made a big giant high heel and people ... . We had convinced the people at Self-Help that we were just going to paint the wall with tempered paint, and afterwards we would wash it clean. As it turns out it was a hundred degrees that day and it baked in and stayed on for about ten years ... . The two eyes were the two windows and Willie and Gronk were going to be teardrops falling out of the eyes on ropes. Herrón tied a rope that was longer than the drop and when he jumped he got injured and Gronk didn't jump and I was setting fire to everything and Willie had the idea to use gasoline. And there's one scene where I'm dumping gasoline and I light it and I'm engulfed in this flame and I didn't catch on fire because I had ripped some black tar paper off a wall, formed it into a hat that looked kind of like an inverted Napoleon hat and at the same time almost like a marionette ... . I painted my face white, almost like Marcel Marceau, and the idea was that I would do all these destructive acts and destroy things while everybody was dancing and hula hooping and doing all kinds of weird things.[21]

The final edited sequence, punctuated by rapid-fire jump cuts not unlike those

Figure 38. Harry Gamboa, Jr., "Death of Fashion," Asco performance for Agnes Varda's *Mur murs*, 1981.

that fracture the group's own Super-8s, bears out much of this. Once again, we see Asco's practice at an intersection of performance, muralism, and film. The setting of the action documented is an exterior wall, the sort of canvas favored by contemporaneous Chicano muralists. Unlike *Walking Mural*, *Instant Mural*, and other earlier performances, this action was staged specifically for the camera. It was to be Asco's last performance as a group.

Though brief, the sequence from Varda's film provides an audiovisual record of this action that is far more evocative than the silent Super-8 fragments (much of which are now destroyed or simply lost) that typifies their own documentation. While Asco was not formed until later, some of the original members had worked together since the late 1960s. Gronk, Patssi Valdez, and Robert Legorreta (a.k.a. Cyclona) performed together in *Caca-Roaches Have No Friends* and *Piglick*, both from 1969.[22] These were ephemeral actions and street performances that survive only in the accounts, a couple of fliers, and a few photographs, the latter now archived and exhibited for the first time in *Asco: Elite of the Obscure*, the group's 2011–12 retrospective at the Los Angeles County Museum of Art and the Williams College Museum of Art. The exhibition raises the question of what to exhibit when the artists featured resist the notion that their role is to make objects for exhibition. Other Asco performances, like *Cruel Profit* (1974–75), can still be witnessed in fragmentary bits of film that last only a few seconds, in addition to photographic documentation, such as the latent images on the emulsion of the exposed film after the action. These traces raise the question: what is the relationship between painting and the performance, and between the performance and the photographic processes (still or moving) that record it?

In his defining text on the New York School of "action painters", Harold Rosenberg had famously stated two decades earlier that, "at a certain moment the canvas began to appear to one American painter after another as an arena in which to act … . What was to go on the canvas was not a picture but an event."[23] If this statement immediately evokes the image of that celebrated student of Benton and Siqueiros, Jackson Pollock, it is not so much his paintings that come to mind as it is Hans Namuth's film footage and photographs of the "event": the artist at work (1950). More so than contemporaneous artists exploring performance in Southern California (Chris Burden, Barbara Smith), the artists of Asco remained engaged with painting, both through their artistic practice and through their use of the "mural" designation. Addressing the complexities of Asco's parallel engagements with film and muralism does not embellish the dominant art history narrative about the emergence of performance out of late modernism's endgame with the addition of a handful of previously neglected Latino/a artists. Nor is it enough to simply complicate the origin stories of Chicano cinema with an avant-garde counterweight to the essentialist epics of *I am Joaquín* (Luis Valdez and *El Teatro Campesino*, 1969) and *Yo soy Chicano!* (Jesús Salvador Treviño, 1972). Rather, these Super-8 fragments perhaps help break away from any number of restrictive binaries that stultify our understanding of the most exciting recent experiments in both film and the visual arts.

Notes

1. The original group was composed of Patssi Valdez, Gronk [Glugio Nicandro], Willie Herrón, and Harry Gamboa, Jr, occasionally abetted by Humberto Sandoval. In the 1980s the membership of the group expanded and became more flexible.
2. Harry Gamboa, Jr., oral history interview with Jesse Lerner, 9 May 2010, part of the Los Angeles Filmforum's "Alternative Projections", a Pacific Standard Time initiative.
3. Harry Gamboa, Jr., "Gronk and Herrón: Muralists", in *Urban Exile: Collected Writings of Harry Gamboa, Jr.*, ed. Chon A. Noriega (Minneapolis: University of Minnesota Press, 1998), 34. Originally published in *Neworld* 2.3 (Spring 1976): 28–30.
4. Harry Gamboa, Jr., oral history interview with Jesse Lerner, 9 May 2010.
5. *America Tropicál*, Siqueiros's mural on Olvera Street, was whitewashed shortly after completion, and *Street Meeting* similarly disappeared from view quickly. The only Southern California mural of his that escaped this fate was *Portrait of Mexico Today/Retrato actual de México*, which was commissioned for the garden of the home of filmmaker Dudley Murphy, where it remained until its recent relocation and restoration by the Santa Barbara Museum of Art. See *Mexican Muralism in the United States* (Albuquerque: University of New Mexico Press, 1989).
6. Gamboa, "Gronk and Herrón: Muralists", 33.
7. MacKinley Helm, *Man of Fire: J. C. Orozco* (New York: Harcourt, Brace, and Co., 1953), 10.
8. Karen Moss, "LACE's First 10 Years: From El Monte to Industrial Street", *LACE: 10 Years Documented* (Los Angeles: Los Angeles Contemporary Exhibitions, 1988), 6. See also C. Ondine Chavoya, "Tactics of Ephemerality: Interventionist Public Art in Los Angeles" (paper presented as part of the symposium "Phantom Sites: Rethinking Identity and Place in Contemporary Art", Los Angeles County Museum of Art, 5 April 2009).

9. Juan Soriano, "Interview with Elena Poniatowska", *Evergreen Review* 7 (1959): 146.
10. Willie Herrón, transcript of oral history interview, 5 February–17 March 2000, Archives of American Art (Washington, DC Smithsonian Institution), accessed 1 October 2010, http://www.aaa.si.edu/collections/oralhistories/transcripts/herron00.htm.
11. Carlos Almaraz, transcript of oral history interview, 6 February 1986–29 January 1987, Archives of American Art (Washington, DC Smithsonian Institution), accessed 1 December 2010, http://www.aaa.si.edu/collections/oralhistories/transcripts/almara86.htm.
12. David Alfaro Siqueiros, "*Hacia la transformación de las artes plásticas* (*Proyecto de manifesto*)", *Textos de David Alfaro Siqueiros*, ed. Raquel Tibol (México, D.F.: Fondo de Cultural Económica, 1974), 37.
13. Maris Bustamante, "Synchronies between Asco and No Grupo", in *Asco: Elite of the Obscure*, eds. C. Ondine Chavoya and Rita Gonzalez (Ostfildern: Hatje Cantz, 2011), 308–317.
14. Bustamante, "Synchronies", 311.
15. *Presencia de México en la X Bienal de Paris, 1977: Representacion enviada por el Instituto Nacional de Bellas Artes y exhibida simultáneamente en el Museo universitario de ciencias y arte*, UNAM, México (México: UNAM: 1977).
16. The exception would be the exhibition "Chicanismo en el Arte", shown at LACMA 6–26 May 1975, in which Asco members participated both under their own names and the pseudonym Jetter Letter.
17. Bustamante, "Synchronies", 314.
18. Sol Henaro, *No Grupo: Un zangoloteo al corsé artistico* (México, D.F: Museo de Arte Moderno, 2011), 68.
19. Henaro, *No Grupo*, 72.
20. In Diana C. DuPont, "Gerzso: Pioneering the Abstract in Mexico", *Risking the Abstract: Mexican Modernism and the Art of Gunther Gerzso* (Madrid: Turner/Santa Barbara Museum of Art, 2003), 153–155.
21. Harry Gamboa, Jr., oral history interview with Jesse Lerner, 9 May 2010.
22. Jennifer Sternad Flores, "Cyclona and Early Chicano Performance Art: An Interview with Robert Legorreta", *GLQ: A Journal of Lesbian and Gay Studies*, 12, no. 3 (2006): 475–490.
23. Harold Rosenberg, "The American Action Painters", *The Tradition of the New* (New York: Horizon Press, 1959), 25. This text was originally published in *Art News* in 1952.

23 Inner-city Symphony: *Water Ritual #1: An Urban Rite of Purification*

Veena Hariharan

Barbara McCullough and the L.A. Rebellion

Barbara McCullough belongs to the second wave of filmmakers of the L.A. Rebellion that emerged following the establishment of the Ethno-Communications program at UCLA in 1970.[1] Theirs was a radical politics inspired by the tidal wave of color – anti-colonial struggles abroad and the war against internal white colonialism at home. They also attempted to challenge the racial implications of American capitalism through their efforts to regain the institutions that marketed and distributed black culture so that the profits from this could be ploughed back into the black community.[2] Rebelling against representations of African Americans in mainstream media, they connected with Africanicity through their creative links with Third Cinema, on the one hand, and avant-garde jazz on the other. The second wave, characterized by a personal, experimental, and avant-garde mode, created a space for black, feminist, creative, and critical filmmaking. McCullough claims Zora Neale Hurston as her primary inspiration while Shirley Clarke, Julie Dash, and Maya Deren influenced her avant-garde film aesthetic.[3] Rituals and the ritualistic; music, especially avant-garde jazz and world music; and the city of Los Angeles (signified by the freeway), are the dominant preoccupations of McCullough's films.

McCullough saw the creative process as itself ritualistic, noting that in all African societies, arts and rituals are related, and ritual objects are often art objects. Thus, in her film, *Shopping Bag Spirits and Freeway Fetishes: Reflections on Ritual Space* (1981), she interviews African American artists, poets, and musicians to explore why and how they use ritual in their art. The first interview is a recording of artist David Hammons, junk art specialist and provocateur, at work. Here he is seen creating an art-object / earthwork from bric-à-brac thrown aside on the freeway. The result is a work called the "spirit catcher" that he claims catches the loosely floating energies around the freeway, and harks back to ritualistic objects found in African societies.[4] *Shopping Bag Spirits* also features a conversation with Betye Saar, about how the affinity for the ritualistic emerges from McCullough's self-critique vis-à-vis her anxious relationship to her own Catholic faith. In *Freeway Fetishes,* Senga Nengundi and other artists, including McCullough herself, Hammons, and Maren Hassinger, in nylon mesh headdresses, stand beneath a freeway overpass and enact a ritualistic dance while *Fragments* (McCullough, 1981) a ten-minute "montage of magic-centered imagery" reexamines this theme.[5] Hailing from a musical family herself, McCullough explores her affinity for music, especially avant-garde jazz, in her documentaries: *The World Saxophone Quartet* (1980) on jazz saxophonists Hamiet Bluiett, Oliver Lake, Julius Hemphill, and David Murray; and *Horace Tapscott: Music Griot* (1992). *Horace Tapscott* is as much a musical life of Los Angeles's Central Avenue as it is an oral history of the L.A. native and jazz legend..

In this essay, I focus on McCullough's 1979 film, *Water Ritual #1: An Urban Rite of Purification*, a four-minute-long film that David E. James notes is an "inter-artistic work that combines collage, the avant-garde jazz of the Los Angeles native Don Cherry, and themes of history, folklore, magic, and the specificity of black feminism".[6] To what genre does McCullough's avant-garde film *Water Ritual #1* belong? In posing this question I am not trying to find the fit for the film in a generic system. Rather, by suggesting that *Water Ritual* belongs to the *city symphony* genre I am challenging the premises of the genre and its utopian celebration of the modern city. Scott MacDonald's essay, "The City as Motion Picture", has laid the groundwork for an expanded definition of the city symphony to take into account transforming urban realities. Here I am pushing his reconstruction of the genre still further to include a film that does not readily lend itself to being named a city symphony. *Water Ritual* lacks the technological sophistication, the visual play, the artwork, and the sheer diversity of images associated with the city symphony. In inserting this film into the generic system of the city symphony I attempt to question received notions of the city from visualizations in avant-garde works – to ask what is the city? How does it work? Who does it work for? And whom does the city reject and marginalize?

I. The City Symphony and Avant-garde cinema

> "For all its ado of workmen and factories and swirl and swing of a great city, *Berlin* created nothing".[7]

The city symphony, a genre/subgenre that had its flowering in the '20s, synchronous with early modernity, was variously inflected by filmmakers of later decades, and progressively reflected the anxieties and failed promises of the city. The city symphony is far from dead; as a genre it is kept alive by scholars and curators alike. When Walter Ruttmann made his *Berlin: Symphony of a Big City* in 1927, a genre or subgenre called the "city symphony" did not yet exist. In fact, it was used retrospectively to include the earliest avant-garde works of Mikhail Kaufman and Julius Jaenzon's *New York 1911* (1911), Paul Strand and Charles Sheeler's *Manhatta*[8] (1921), and Ilya Kopalin's *Moscow* (1927).[9] Ruttmann's *Berlin*, Alberto Cavalcanti's *Rien que les heures* (1926), and Dziga Vertov's *Man with a Movie Camera* (1929) – together, these three films form the canon in the generic system of the city symphony. Jean Vigo's *A propos de Nice* (1929), a biting satire on the parasitic Parisian leisure class; Joris Ivens's *The Bridge* (1928), on the construction of the Rotterdam rail bridge; and the dreamy *Rain* (1929), a day in the life of a rain shower in Amsterdam, are also versions of the city symphony. Ruttmann himself contributed to the genre with his later films on Düsseldorf, Stuttgart, and Hamburg. In the '30s, there appeared a series of what was referred to as the New York City symphonies, "largely imitative of and less impressive than the triad of European city symphonies".[10] *A Bronx Morning* (1931), Jey Leyda's tribute to Eugene Atget; Irving Browning's *City of Contrasts* (1931), a new realist montage of the city's contrasts; Herman Weinberg's *A City Symphony* (1930), about two separated lovers - the woman who is identified with nature and the man with the city; Lewis Jacob's *City Block* (1934) and *As I Walk* (1939). In the '40s and '50s, Rudy Burckhardt (*The Pursuit of Happiness*, 1940) and Larry Jordan (*Visions of a City*, 1937) were also creating city symphonies.[11]

The features of the city symphony film began to crystallize in the late '20s: with the city itself the protagonist, films in this genre were choreographed depictions of a day in the life of the modern city, from before dawn until after dusk, with the mood evocative of the city or of the filmmaker's own subjectivity. Often abstract modernist works constructed on the basis of musical theory, diverse images of the city are linked by their formal characteristics and pattern creation. The city symphony form began as a celebration of the modern city and modernity - a point that has been critiqued about Ruttmann's *Berlin*. By representing "the swing and swirl" of the metropolis, itself in the eye of stormy discussions about mechanization, modernity, urbanization, and soulless cultures, Ruttmann's film, opening within a year of Fritz Lang's dystopic vision of urbanity in *Metropolis*

(1926), seemed to bypass these debates, foregrounding via its avant-garde and experimental brilliance a euphoric sense of the modern metropolis.[12]

It is this perhaps misplaced euphoria that MacDonald attempts to address in his essay, "The City as Motion Picture: Notes on Some California City Films",[13] where he traces the city symphony genre and its transformations necessitated by changing urban realities of Los Angeles and San Francisco.[14] Through an analysis of the works of filmmakers Dominic Angerame: *Continuum* (1987), *Deconstruction Sight* (1990), *Premonition* (1995), *Course of Events* (1997), and Pat O'Neill: *Water and Power* (1989), MacDonald's essay reconsiders the city symphony tradition away from the canon and suggests how representation alters with new subjects, subjectivities, and histories.[15] To this list I will also add McCullough's *Water Ritual.* The immediate occasion for McCullough's *Water Ritual,* as pointed out earlier, was the construction of the I-105, or Century Freeway. In the following section, I first outline a brief history of the freeway. Then, I draw from archival records maintained by the US Department of Transportation to outline the particular and contested history of the Century Freeway.

II. The freeway and urban history

> "For the ashes are part of us, no matter how straight and smooth we make our beaches and freeways, no matter how fast we drive."[16]

In "Paris: Capital of the 19th Century",[17] Walter Benjamin's flâneur observed the city as it was transformed by Baron Hausmann's gigantic projects, which blasted boulevards through medieval Parisian slums. It was believed that the greatly accelerated traffic flow made possible by the boulevard would unify the city, stimulate local business and employment opportunities, and improve legibility and military control. The boulevards also created public spaces such as cafés, malls, etc., where the city's people intermingled and exchanged ideas. This in turn created a fast-paced public life and a public that ideated on its own fastness, and 19th century Parisians were forced to give up their old ways as they rushed into the arms of modernity.

Unlike the Parisian boulevard, which encouraged the intermingling of people, the 20th-century American freeway followed Robert Moses's (self-proclaimed heir to Baron Haussman, "demolition artist" of the 19th century) famous dictum that people and cars don't mix.[18] Berman describes the building of the Cross Bronx Expressway in New York City as a definitive moment in the experience of modernity.[19] Here was Moses "hacking his way with a meat ax"[20] through the crowded metropolis, displacing populations and preparing way for the New. The sheer gigantism of the freeway has always appealed to the machismo of empire builders since Adolf Hitler built the first autobahn in the 1930s. At the 1939 World's Fair in New York City, visitors to the Futurama exhibit, sponsored by General Motors, were treated to a spectacular display of Norman Bel Gedde's vision of the Metropolis of the future. When they left they were handed buttons that said, "I have seen the future".[21] Indeed, this future of fourteen-lane super-highways on which cars traveled at 100 mph seemed to hold out a gigantic promise to a nation emerging from the dark period of the civil war. Reyner Banham, who famously learned to drive in order to read Los Angeles in the original, includes the freeway in his four ecologies. His book, *Los Angeles: the Architecture of Four Ecologies* (2009), is in part, a utopian celebration of the freeway.

If Paris was Benjamin's capital of the modernist century, then Los Angeles is the paradigmatic postmodern capital whose mythography is dominated by the automobile, the freeway, and Hollywood.[22] Edward Soja famously termed Los Angeles "the post-fordist, post-modern global city".[23] If the Parisian boulevard wedged 19th century Paris into upper and lower class neighborhoods, then the extreme geographical displacement of minorities in Los Angeles can be traced to freeway construction in the mid-20th century, which physically enforced social divisions in ways that were mostly symbolic before.[24] Thus, the initial euphoria around the construction of the freeway was followed by a backlash as migration to the suburbs, enabled by the ubiquitous automobile, increased at an alarming rate, and more and more of the city's core was eaten away by the freeway itself. In Los Angeles, this massive suburbanization, or white flight, emptied the traditional downtown, leaving only a decaying financial and retail center. And Los Angeles's core was transformed into what Mike Davis in his dystopian prophecies for Los Angeles has called the "noir city" characterized by decay, racial and class segregation, high crime rates, and homeless people.[25] Thus, on the one hand, the wealthy and middle classes are pushed farther into the suburbs both psychologically and physically, into what William Fulton has described as "cocoon citizenship" that precludes citizens from actively assuming responsibility towards creating sustainable cities.[26] On the other hand, white flight leaves behind a trail of minorities, a significant portion of which are African Americans and Latinos trapped in the inner cities creating a permanent urban underclass.[27]

The Century Freeway and the Master Plan of Freeways

If the 1958 "Master Plan of Freeways and Expressways" were implemented in its entirety, then the Southern California planner's Utopia would have been in Los Angeles where "no resident would live further than four miles from a highway".[28]

The Century freeway, connecting LAX to the Interstate 605 in Norwalk, was included in the wish list of the Masterplan in 1959, along with the Beverly Hills and Pacific Coast Freeways. Property acquisition for the paving of the freeway began in earnest by January 1970. Eventually, six thousand parcels of land were acquired from traditionally low-income neighborhoods of the city and county of Los Angeles, Hawthorne, Inglewood, Compton, Lynwood, Paramount, South Gate, Downey, and Norwalk. The freeway displaced nearly 21,000 individuals, a "significant percentage of whom were non-white, and an even larger number had relatively low incomes".[29] The US Department of Transportation, engineers, and policy makers justified land acquisition by claiming that the land values in these areas were depressed anyway. Besides, they claimed that construction of the freeway would provide urban renewal in the form of jobs to the corridor residents.

Highways are routed through the "path of least resistance"[30] - low income neighborhoods where political clout is less, and monetary incentives greater. Unlike its predecessor, the Chavez Ravine project, which dislocated entire Hispanic populations to make way for Dodger Stadium, the Century Freeway is unique in that it is celebrated not so much for its fast lanes as for its collateral social programs, such as reallocation of the displaced, and for the affirmative action goals of employment of women and minorities. These social programs, the result of the *Keith v Volpe Consent Decree*[31] (described as the most creative moment in environmental history), however, remained a paper tiger, and social goals were far from achieved. It is in this background that McCullough created her film *Water Ritual*. In the next and final section of the paper, I analyze the film in some detail, highlighting its generic features as city symphony and its departures from the genre.

III.

Water Ritual: Inner-city Symphony[32]

> "... the place where we shot was ... by the 105 freeway ... where the people ... their house had been destroyed ... properties had been sold, and this whole wasteland existed that was preparing for the 105 freeway ... this looks like someplace that could be a shack or shanty in some, you know, someplace or housing for someone in some other third world country. But it was sitting there, you know, and you have the broken glass, wound up looking – when the light was reflected, had this, you know, really jewel quality, you know, about it. And you just had, just pieces of things around that were just really pretty amazing. And then, you know, you'd be there, and every now and then you'd see a kid walk by, you know? And it was like, this could be anywhere. This could be in another country, but this is L.A."[33]

Hollywood's response to the decay at the urban core caused by the freeway, has been to glamorize the decay itself: "The decay of the city's old glamour has been

Figure 39. "*Water Ritual #1: An Urban Rite of Purification.*"

inverted by the entertainment industry into the new glamour of decay".[34] The inner city's or the "gritty city's" retort has been a creative upsurge – hip-hop, graffiti, Blaxploitation film. McCullough's film is an atypical example – it is an avant-garde response that has by turns been called psychic, spiritual, mystical, and political. Jan Christopher Horak describes the film's "cathartic coming out into Africanicity"[35] as an explicitly political act.[36] McCullough herself sees this in continuity with her community:

> ... I lived in a community where that was going on all the time. I lived in a community of people basically who, a lot of them were dressed in traditional clothing, they had an affinity for traditionally African music, and the musicians who were coming out who basically had world influences in their music, and that was an extension of it.[37]

The film opens with a dark screen while the audio track registers African chants, cymbals, and the sound of rain and forests, in a world music tradition, a musical genre in which Don Cherry actively participated. It is not coincidental that Cherry provided the music for this film. Cherry belonged to the group of "jazz guerrillas",[38] who Davis describes as the "underground within the underground".[39] Their marginalized status can be attributed to the racialized LA music scene as well as the repression of modernist expressions in art in the US around that time.[40] The employment of a marginalized tradition of music already sets the film in opposition to the early city symphonies. Only compare Edmund Meisel's upbeat jazz score for Ruttmann's *Berlin* showings.

The first visual on screen is an art-deco gate framed in close up. Against this is an African-African American woman (played by Yolanda)[41] in a headdress[42] who walks out to the center of the frame and holds on to the railings of the gate, with outstretched arms. We then see a long shot of the gate, the woman, and the freeway (a reference to the actual 105 freeway and a signifier of the city). At this point, the sound track merges Cherry's trumpet with the sound of a car horn, and it is only now that we realize that this is no historical gate but a contemporary Los Angeles South Central house in ruins. No virtuosity here, only a simple cut that connects past to present, and a film about the present resonates with the depth of history. The camera then shows us a close-up of the woman who seems to be waiting, looking out, yearning – her face registering neither hope nor despair.

The woman then sits down with her legs stretched out and gathers toward her a collection of objects that are at first indistinguishable but are revealed as a piece of steel from a wrecked car, bits of broken glass, the remnants of a palm frond, a coconut shell filled with cornmeal (McCullough thought of cornmeal as survival food) a splinter of a phonograph record of a Stevie Wonder album – *Songs in the Keys of Life*, and stones, pebbles, and rocks from the railroad track for a "circle of protectiveness", and an ebony "fertility kind" of statue.[43] McCullough loved to work with found objects and this was her way of working them into her films in a process that can be best described as ritualistic.[44]

This is a ritual site of a woman rendered homeless by the city. The objects are then shown in close-up, and among them we see African statues associated with fertility rites. At this point there is a tracking shot of the woman's legs, on which is superimposed a tracking shot of a tract of dry land/desert. No elaborate tricks here – a simple dissolve connects the woman with the African diaspora.[45] The woman then gathers dust in her hands, blows away the dust, and chants an ancient ritual that may connote her links to her Saharan desert of origin. Urbanization and migration have made the urban home a place of belonging more important than it was in the past. At the same time, the processes of urbanization have rendered some people, especially those of the African diaspora, homeless. Thus, diasporic people are twice alienated: first the big city allured them with promises of a better future than the one they could hope for in their countries of origin, and then the big city let them down to render them homeless again.

The next part of the film is a panning shot of an empty stretch of abandoned houses (signifier of the neglected city) among the crabgrass. Cherry's trumpet is muted here, and the African chants that we hear at the beginning of the film are accentuated, evoking forests and African origins. We see a pair of sandaled feet treading the grass as if looking for a spot – a sacred spot for a ritual? The camera then cuts to the body of the woman. She is fully naked and her back is turned to the camera. She emerges out of a demolished house and walks towards the camera while a voice over chants: "let the rite of purification begin". We then see her squat, her back towards the camera, as if to urinate, and then we see her actually urinate.[46] Her squatting posture mimics African fertility statuettes. The big city has no place for her, and an intensely private act becomes a public ritual. The camera lingers on the "water ritual" and then cuts to her face, again the same face registering neither hope nor despair. Gwendolyn Foster notes:

> In the short film, an African woman refigures the deteriorating urban environment with a female fertility statue. In the purification ritual the woman reclaims her environment, her body, her soul.[47]

Purification rituals are performed in three situations: when the body and soul need to be cleansed after they have come into contact with pollutants; in a preemptive move to avoid contact with possible pollutants; or to achieve a higher state of purity. The last is McCullough's own route as she saw ritual as "a means by which a people can overcome their frustration with the society".[48] For her, ritual is tied intimately with the establishment of identity as well as mastery of the environment. In her introduction to *Water Ritual*, she says: "This 16 mm film is not a complete film but a filmic exercise to practice my affinity for rituals. I realized that I would use ritual in some way in my film and video art".[49] McCullough explains ritual as "a symbolic action" that helps "me release myself and move from one space and time to another".[50] David E. James, in *The Most Typical Avant-Garde*, explains it thus:

> Her rituals resonate around her personal and territorial assertion; as if to dispel or refertilize the history of repression and debasement that has made a ruin of her house, the Africa she invokes with such drastic assurance is implicitly proposed as a source of the renewal of nature but also the renewal of culture – the cynosure of a previously unimaginable autonomous and magical African American cinema that might forever flourish in the ashes.[51]

So the ritual in the film is not a formal or prescribed ritual, nor is it a document of an actual ritual; rather it is a "montage of various ritualistic elements".[52] It is for McCullough an intuitive thing, and the ritual objects used in the film are not based on historical rituals or research, though they had a practical use. For example, the fertility statue helped to evoke the female element, of understanding herself as mother and lover, and approaching a culture that she couldn't totally verbalize but could feel intuitively.[53]

Thus, in the film, an African-American woman rendered homeless by the city

Figure 40. "*Water Ritual #1: An Urban Rite of Purification.*"

masters her situation by connecting to a mythical African past through symbolic action or ritual. The city that we see in the film is not the youthful dynamic protagonist of the early city symphonies. Rather it is the decayed, alienating, and empty city. In fact the film has two protagonists – the city and the woman displaced by the city. Like the early city symphonies, *Water Ritual* tells the story of a "day in the life of", of a dead city, where nothing happens, and of an isolated woman who carries out her daily routine. Arguably, this is the face of the new city symphony, where the city itself fades into the background as the site of decay, and what is foregrounded is the individual displaced by the processes of urban development. Often this face is the face of the woman of color. No longer can one be in cinematic raptures over the city as in the early days of the city symphony. The new city symphony has to save its virtuosity to tell the story of the inner cities. In other words, the city symphony has become the *inner city symphony.*

Notes

1. The second wave included Billy Woodberry, Julie Dash, Alile Sharon Larkin, Zeinabu irene Davis, and Jacqueline Frazier. The first wave included among others Charles Burnett, Haile Gerima, Ben Caldwell, Larry Clark, Jamaa Fanaka, Pamela Jones, and Abdosh Abdulhafiz. For more details on the second wave see Masilel Ntongela, "Women Directors of the Los Angeles School", in *Black Women Film and Video Artists*, ed. Jacqueline Bobo (New York: Routledge, 1998), 21–41.

2. David James, *The Most Typical Avant Garde: History and Geography of Minor Cinemas in Los Angeles* (Berkeley: University of California Press, 2005), 327. For an analysis of the Los Angeles School of Black Filmmakers, see ibid., 327–335.
3. Barbara McCullough in *LA Rebellion: Oral History Interviews*, UCLA Film and Television Archive, 2011, transcribed by Kelly Lake, as told to Jacqueline Stewart, Jan-Christopher Horak and Robyn Charles, for a description of some of these influences.
4. David Hammons in *Shopping Bag Spirits.*
5. From the Catalogue description, *Third World News Reel.*
6. James, *The Most Typical Avant-Garde*, 335.
7. John Grierson, commenting on *Berlin: Symphony of a City* in "First Principles of Documentary", in *Imagining Reality*, ed. Kevin MacDonald and Mark Cousins (London: Faber and Faber, 1996), 97–102.
8. A seven-minute portrait of New York City based on a Walt Whitman poem.
9. Erik Barnouw, *Documentary: A History of Non-Fiction Film* (Oxford: Oxford University Press, 1993), 73.
10. Scott MacDonald, "The City as Motion Picture: Notes on some California City Films", *Wide Angle* 19.4 (1997): 109–130.
11. MacDonald, "The City as Motion Picture: Notes on some California City Films"; Erik Barnow, *Documentary*; and *Lovers of Cinema: The First American Film Avant-Garde, 1919–1945*, ed. Jan-Christopher Horak (Madison: University of Wisconsin Press, 1995), 267–286.
12. "The City as Cinematic Space: Modernism and Place in *Berlin, Symphony of a City*", in *Place, Power, Situation and Spectacle: A Geography of Film*, ed. Stuart C. Aitken and Leo E Zonn (Maryland: Rowman and Littlefield Publishers Inc., 1994), 211, has a detailed discussion on the genre and its limitations.
13. See note 10.
14. Not just Los Angeles and San Francisco, New York City has also been the subject of recent city symphonies like Peter Hutton's *New York Portraits* (1990), Jem Cohen's *Lost Book Found* (1996), and Ernie Gehr's *Side/Walk/Shuttle* (1991).
15. MacDonald, "The City as Motion Picture: Notes on some California City Films".
16. Marshall Berman, *All That is Solid Melts Into Air: The Experience of Modernity.* (New York: Penguin Books, 1982), 312.
17. Walter Benjamin, "Paris Capital of the 19th century", in *The Arcades Project*, ed. Howard Eiland and Ken McLaughlin (Cambridge: Harvard University Press, 1999), 14–26.
18. Berman, *All That is Solid Melts into Air.*
19. Ibid., 294.
20. Ibid.
21. Justin Fox, "The Great Paving; How the Interstate Highway System helped create the modern economy", *Fortune*, 26 January 2004, 1.
22. Los Angeles is the subject of much theorization in the works of Mike Davis, et al., who belong to the LA School: "an emerging current of neo-Marxist researchers (mostly planners and geographers) sharing a common interest in the contradictory ramifications of urban 'restructuring' and the possible emergence of a new 'regime of capital accumulation'". See Mike Davis, *The City of Quartz: Excavating the Future of Los Angeles* (New York: Vintage Books, 1992), 84.
23. Allen J. Scott and Edward J. Soja, *The City: Los Angeles and Urban Theory at the End of the Twentieth Century* (Berkeley: University of California Press, 1997) for various theoretical perspectives on the city.
24. Janet Abu-Lughod, *New York, Chicago, Los Angeles: America's Global Cities* (Minneapolis: University of Minnesota Press, 1999).
25. Mike Davis, *The City of Quartz.*
26. William Fulton, *The Reluctant Metropolis: The Politics of Urban Growth in Los Angeles* (Baltimore, MD: Johns Hopkins University Press, 1997), 333.
27. See William Julius Wilson, *The Truly Disadvantaged: The Inner City, the Underclass, and Public Policy* (Chicago: University of Chicago Press, 1987) for an exposition of this idea.
28. Drussila van Hengel, "Citizens Near the Path of Least Resistance: Travel Behaviour of Century Freeway Corridor Residents" (Ph.D. diss., University of Irvine, 1996), 47.
29. Records of the US Department of Transportation, Federal Highway Administration, 1979, The Century Freeway Collection, Special Collections, Regional History Archives, Doheny Memorial Library Documents of the Department of Transportation, Los Angeles.

30. Ibid.

31. The freeway construction did not go entirely unopposed. In 1972 the Center for Law in the Public Interest, NAACP, the Sierra Club, the Environmental Defense Fund, and the Hawthorne Freeway Fighters, filed an injunction against officials involved in the freeway construction, contending that the State and Federal highway agencies had not met the requirements of the National Environmental Policy Act (NEPA) and the California Environmental Quality Act (CEQA), and also violated the Fourteenth Amendment to the Constitution by displacing minority members and poor without adequate replacement housing.

32. First person accounts of the film are culled from the interview with McCullough in *LA Rebellion: Oral History Interviews*, UCLA Film and Television Archive, 2011, transcribed by Kelly Lake, as told to Jacqueline Stewart, Jan-Christopher Horak, and Robyn Charles.

33. McCullough in *LA Rebellion: Oral History Interviews*.

34. Davis, *The City of Quartz*, 275. Davis cites films like *Independence Day* (1996), *The Crow: The City of Angels* (1996), and *Escape from LA* (1996) as examples of films that glamorize urban decay.

35. James, *The Most Typical Avant-Garde*, 335.

36. McCullough in *LA Rebellion: Oral History Interviews*.

37. Ibid.

38. The "jazz guerillas" included Eric Dolphy, Red Mitchell, Billy Higgins, and Charlie Haden. They were led by Ornette Coleman, who tried to perpetuate a "free jazz" tradition expanding the 1940s efforts of Charlie Parker and Dizzy Gillespie. In the late '50s the LA music scene was dominated by an almost entirely white "cool jazz" tradition, and the "hard bebop" was marginalized. Davis, *City of Quartz*, 62–64.

39. Ibid., for a discussion of the LA jazz scene.

40. Ibid., 64.

41. The character is based on a real-life friend whom McCullough used to know. After a complete mental breakdown, this friend – "a beautiful flower of a person" – regressed to a primal state. McCullough describes the shocking memory of the friend who was naked in a bare room and all of a sudden urinated on the floor… "She looked as if she were in the process of exorcising herself of some energy she couldn't control. Everything she did was highly ritualized. She engaged in unconscious symbolic action by creating a circle around herself within which she withdrew for protection. She made gestures like a priestess signaling a protective spirit. She spoke in tongues", Interview with Jackson, Elizabeth in *Black Film Review* and McCullough, *LA Rebellion: Oral History Interviews*.

42. In Julie Dash's *Daughter of the Dust*, she shows how the headdresses of African women are complex ethnic and identity markers.

43. "The statue was probably bought at Pier One or some place like that" – McCullough in *LA Rebellion: Oral History Interviews*.

44. See McCullough in *LA Rebellion: Oral History Interviews* for a detailed description of these objects.

45. McCullough describes this connection with African origins as a kind of "cosmic consciousness", in *LA Rebellion: Oral History Interviews*.

46. "… originally, this was supposed to be about a woman having a period and from the blood that fell to the ground, a flower came. And from that flower came this multi-colored hue of children who were like small children …", McCullough in *LA Rebellion: Oral History Interviews*.

47. Gwendolyn Foster, *Women Filmmakers of the African and Asian Diaspora: Decolonizing the Gaze, Locating Subjectivity* (Carbondale: SIU Press, 1997), 248–249.

48. McCullough in *LA Rebellion: Oral History Interviews*.

49. Interview. DVD of *Water Ritual* (1979), Third World Newsreel, 1990.

50. Ibid.

51. James, *The Most Typical Avant Garde*, 335.

52. Jan Christopher Horak in *LA Rebellion: Oral History Interviews*.

53. McCullough in *LA Rebellion: Oral History Interviews*.

24 Not Just a Day Job: Experimental Filmmakers and the Special Effects Industry in the 1970s and 1980s

Julie Turnock*

West Coast experimental filmmakers' participation in the special effects boom of the late 1970s is a little-known and much misunderstood phenomenon. A perception persists that the 1970s special effects industry "gutted" the experimental optical animation community, exploiting them for their labor and sidetracking them from their art.[1] Elsewhere, I have argued that the intensification of special effects practice in the late 1970s initiated a technological, aesthetic, and narrative shift in feature filmmaking as significant as the introduction of sound in the late 1920s.[2] My research has also revealed the influence of experimental filmmaking on late 1960s and 1970s special effects-heavy feature filmmaking, especially the science fiction extravaganzas like *2001: A Space Odyssey* (1968), *Star Wars* (1977), *Close Encounters of the Third Kind* (1977), and *Blade Runner* (1982). Furthermore, it is clear that the impact of West Coast experimental filmmaking went far beyond lending these science fiction

* This essay was completed in part with the support of a Mellon/ACLS Early Career Fellowship, and a longer version appeared in *Film History* (October 2014). A significant amount of material from this paper came largely from interviews, both conducted by myself and by those at the Academy and the Iota Center, and I want to thank Mark Toscano and Stephanie Sapienza in particular for facilitating the interviews I conducted, and also making the transcripts of the oral history project available to me. Sincere thanks also to David James, Adam Hyman, Allyson Field, and Jonathan Knipp.

films transitory psychedelic visuals representing alien worlds. More specifically, I argue that in the 1970s, experimental filmmakers, both directly as labor and indirectly as inspiration, *taught* popular filmmakers like George Lucas, Steven Spielberg, and Ridley Scott and their teams, strategies for organizing and mobilizing the elaborately designed composite mise-en-scène. Or, in other words, they provided the technological, aesthetic, and conceptual scaffolding for creating the infinite and complex worlds desired for these science fiction films. Moreover, these filmmakers took skills and inspiration from their day jobs back to their own work.[3]

In the 1970s and through the 1980s, many filmmakers both closely and loosely associated with West Coast experimental film put their talents to work in various aspects of the special effects industry. These include such well-known artists as Pat O'Neill, John and James Whitney, and Jordan Belson; as well as Adam Beckett, Robert Blalack, Betzy Bromberg, Chris Casady, Larry Cuba, Roberta Friedman, Peter Kuran, Richard Winn Taylor, and Diana and David Wilson, and many others.[4] Many of them founded or free-lanced for independent optical, title, and effects houses as well as on feature film projects and ads. In fact, much of the optical line on *Star Wars* taught at or were recent graduates of the California Institute of the Arts, known as Cal Arts, where artists such as O'Neill and Beckett trained them primarily in cutting edge optical printing techniques.[5] This kind of workforce is a change from decades past when studio effects personnel followed an apprenticeship system under strict union rules. So-called "closed shop" regulations would have barred most of these artists from work in the studios, except in rare cases.[6] A famous exception included Hitchcock's specially commissioned title sequence for *Vertigo* (1958), completed by John Whitney. However, in addition to his experimental work, Whitney and his brother James also founded an independent optical company, called Motion Graphics, which produced a great deal of commercial work for films and television.

More experimental filmmakers in the special effects business meant a change in approach to effects, as well as a change in aesthetics. Previously, effects hewed to what might be called a functionalist aesthetic, where all elements are in the right perspective and are as unobtrusive as possible, forming a seamless backdrop for the actors in the foreground. However, the 1970s effects artists brought their less conventional art school training to bear for a new kind of special effects production. Additionally, "film school generation" feature filmmakers like Francis Ford Coppola, George Lucas, and John Carpenter were well aware of trends in experimental filmmaking, thanks to courses and workshops at USC and UCLA.[7] Due in part to influential theories of media immersion by writers and theorists such as Gene Youngblood (drawing from Buckminster Fuller, Slavko Vorkapich, Marshall McLuhan, and many others, as well as eastern philosophy and avant-garde art) many understood visual technologies as a possible gateway to "expanded" kinds of experiences, helped along by music and psychotropic drugs.[8] Whether the aesthetic goal was transcendence in the case of Belson and James Whitney, or intellectualized room for play like John Whitney, technologically-mediated abstract imagery had arrived as a broad imaging trend, one that was attractive to feature filmmakers who wanted to deploy the kinesthetic illusion of movement, as well as possibilities of representing fantastic impossible worlds.[9] Of course, at the same time, these narrative feature filmmakers like Lucas and Spielberg streamlined or eliminated the notion of chance and unpredictability the experimentalists courted, presenting their imagery in a popular, accessible form, and also narratively motivating them in the diegesis; for example, as laserbeams or UFO illumination. For many, this streamlining and recontextualizing impulse is exactly the source of their harsh critique of these films.[10] However, it is worth acknowledging that the appropriation of experimental techniques and imagery by films like *Star Wars* and *Close Encounters* in part has helped this experimental movement endure beyond Los Angeles, and has made it more readily accessible for the revived interest for later generations.

Further, despite a misconception that feature filmmaking in general and Lucas in particular "gutted" the Los Angeles experimental scene by distracting the filmmakers with day jobs, experimental filmmakers on the whole view the situation entirely differently. As interviews with artists testify, experimental artists' relationship with the industry cannot be characterized simply as one of exploitation and appropriation. Rather, over and over, many artists claim their day job not only provided them with a steady paycheck, but also offered inspiration for their own work.[11] With this relationship in mind, this essay is not going to argue that experimental filmmakers in the special effects business, through their infiltration, subverted or transformed in any straightforward manner the film industry that was trying to co-opt them and their work. Rather, the situation is much more complicated.

Why did feature filmmaking need a large influx of optical printing experts in the mid to late 1970s? Optical printing is a composite technique in which elements from two or more film strips (one, for example, with a character on a balcony in the foreground, the other with the Eiffel Tower in the background) are joined through an optical printer. The simplest optical printer consists of a projector casting film consisting of one composite element directly into the lens of a camera holding film with the other element. The optical printer operator lines up the composites and matches them frame by frame. This can be simple and straightforward, in the case of a background Eiffel Tower painting matted into a live-action foreground. Or it can be complex, in the case of the opening fly-over of *Star Wars*, where multiple elements (model space ship, 2-D planet artwork, star background, laser animation elements, etc.) entail multiple passes through the printer.

Although various optical printing composite processes had been in use since the late 1910s and early 1920s, as a feature film special effect technique in the studio production hierarchy, "opticals" had been marginalized in favor of rear screen projection since the late 1930s. This is largely because rear screen composites were completed on the set, in the presence of the director, principal actors, and cinematographer, and did not require lengthy or complex post-production.[12] Starting in the 1940s and 1950s, studios tended to outsource their optical printing assignments to independent optical and title companies.[13] Most feature films required only a few optical shots per film, so outsourcing proved most economical. These jobs included matting in title sequences, adding clouds to a blank sky for composition, filling in tops of buildings or ceilings, or compositing in matte paintings. By the 1950s, most studios had only the slimmest of optical departments, if any.[14] All in all, until the late 1970s, optical printing, in the vast majority of cases, involved simple composites that did not require multiple elements or complex equipment.

The startlingly convincing example of Stanley Kubrick's science fiction tour de force *2001: A Space Odyssey* in 1968 (which emphasized optical and contact printing over rear projection for its composite techniques), emboldened filmmakers like Lucas and Spielberg to attempt more stylistically and technically ambitious, special effects-intensive projects.[15] What these productions especially required were a great number of creative and skilled artists to build imagined environments through layers of photographic and animated elements largely on the optical printer bed. *Star Wars* and *Close Encounters* would require huge crews of optical printing experts, not to mention model makers, matte painters, etc. Those with longstanding expertise in the studio era were largely retired or recently deceased, or re-employed by the studios for the just-petering-out disaster cycle. Therefore, the science fiction films of the late 1970s had to recruit first of all out of the independent optical business for their supervisors (Douglas Trumbull for *Close Encounters,* and his protégé John Dykstra for *Star Wars* from Trumbull's independent optical house, and as well as department heads like Dennis Muren from Graphic films and Richard Edlund from Westheimer), and then hire recent graduates of film programs that placed a strong emphasis on optical printing, which in the Los Angeles area was primarily Cal Arts.[16] Finally, to a great degree inspired by *2001* and abstract films shown at psychedelic happenings, young people were entering art and film programs in unprecedented numbers, learning what had been the primarily moribund subject of optical printing techniques.[17]

In specific terms, how did this crossover between the experimental and the industrial sectors happen? It is an economic fact of life that most artists must maintain a day job, or, as the case may be, a night job. It is not entirely coincidental that many of the newly-minted graduates of the recently formed school Cal Arts made a good living in the also newly hot area of special effects in the late 1970s and early 1980s. First of all, many big effects projects were "staffing up" at that time, and as an independent production, *Star Wars* needed a great deal of independent, out sourced labor.[18] One of the most influential teachers at Cal Arts was Pat O'Neill, whose specialty was the kind of optical printing and duplication work that was becoming valuable to the film industry at this time. Furthermore, as founder of independent optical company Lookout Mountain Films, he was a prominent example to his students as an artist who free-lanced in the optical, title, and effects business. Although by his own account, O'Neill mostly completed simple, fairly mechanical composites to order, he occasionally was able to complete projects with more creativity involved. For example, the striking opticals on Melvin Van Peebles's *Sweet Sweetback's Baadasssss Song* of 1971 (in particular the vibrant, distorted-color sequences of Van Peebles as Sweetback running through Los Angeles's industrial backdrops) were a rare example of O'Neill being called upon for what might be called "expressive" effects.[19] O'Neill also claimed to have been strongly influenced in his own work by Classical Hollywood era special effects master Linwood Dunn's very popular series of presentations in art and film schools starting in the 1960s and through the 1970s, that many gave many young art and design school students the idea that special effects might be a viable career path.[20] According to many of his Cal Arts students, O'Neill's quiet authority influenced a great many of his students, and loosened the hold on some of the "purist" rhetoric that demonized work in the movie industry as "selling out", which infused Cal Arts in its early days, and is a prejudice that still often appears.[21]

O'Neill, and many other experimental artists such as Betzy Bromberg and Robert Blalack have insisted that their professional skills developed and improved through work-for-hire in the industry, and did not act as a detriment to their avant-garde work. On the contrary, they often cite their stint in the industry as enhancing their skill set, technological expertise and problem solving skills.[22] As Bromberg has said:

> Honestly, the benefit is probably greater aesthetically and creatively for the experimental filmmaker, and what they can end up, for the person who has the stamina to do both. [...] Honestly, I feel like what was tapped out of me was a lot of time, energy, skill, but every drop of skill that the industry got out of me, I got twice as much for my own films. I can look at the caliber of my filmmaking. [...] That's what is so fabulous about it, that it's this huge realm of knowledge, and you're learning more and more and more over time. To me to watch a Pat O'Neill film, his aesthetic has developed with his skills, and why shouldn't it?[23]

In fact, it should be no surprise that experimental artists in the special effects trade used their animation and aesthetic skills and sensibilities in their day jobs, and that the problem solving and repetition would lead to a more refined and sophisticated skill set they put to work on their own films.

Perhaps most importantly, experimental filmmaking has had an influence on popular filmmaking that goes well beyond an historical account of labor in the film industry. Again, I argue that in the 1970s, West Coast experimental filmmakers *taught* popular filmmakers strategies to rethink the representation of impossible worlds, the illusion of movement, plays with immersion, and the desired gasp of "I've never seen that before" amazement. Mainstream filmmakers like Lucas, who were well aware of the avant-garde, adapted these techniques for a photorealist mise-en-scène and fantasy diegesis.[24] When Gene Youngblood published *Expanded Cinema* in 1970, he positioned experimental filmmaking and its adjacent happenings as the future of media, and more grandly, the new true nature of technologized and mediated human experience. This kind of rhetoric was as important to the future directors coming out of USC and UCLA, like Lucas, Bob Abel (of the innovative Obie-winning ad production company Bob Abel and Associates), John Carpenter, and others, as those coming onto the effects workforce from Cal Arts.

Adopting Youngblood's terminology, largely in order to emphasize the importance of experimental filmmaking, elsewhere I call this approach the Expanded Blockbuster.[25] This is how I characterize many young filmmakers' strategy for refreshing the tired and bloated Hollywood roadshow productions of the *Star!* (Robert Wise, 1968) and *Doctor Doolittle* (Richard Fleischer, 1967) variety. Instead, the expanded blockbuster is the seemingly oxymoronic intellectual popular film. Taking a cue from 1960s New Hollywood, and in particular Kubrick's *2001*, it was a film that would ideally be equal parts sensually exciting, intellectually stimulating, and moneymaking.[26] As I have argued elsewhere, while it may seem unlikely from a contemporary vantage point, this is exactly the type of film that *Star Wars* strove to be.[27] The hugely influential 1970s *Star Wars* model of diegetic world building, in part pioneered and modeled by abstract experimental West Coast filmmaking, has persisted to become dominant in contemporary, digital CGI filmmaking, not to mention other areas of visual culture like video gaming and installation and video art.

These claims are keeping in mind, however, that it is also well known within the special effects and experimental communities that these experimentally trained filmmakers rarely got a chance to let go and really use their most creative work in their day job. Therefore, although I maintain that experimental filmmaking "taught" mainstream film these new approaches to special effects that would eventually spread throughout the industry and become even more prominent in CGI filmmaking, on the practical level, it was very much a case of uneven development, foggy influences, and often a willful misunderstanding of the experimental impulses for unintended purposes. Feature directors and producers like Lucas wanted the creativity of these Cal Arts graduates, but within limits. Furthermore, the experimental filmmakers had to adapt their skill set to fit feature filmmaking, and find narratively appropriate motivation for their imagery.[28] For example, as stills of his unused explosions demonstrate, Adam Beckett produced a great deal of creative and dynamic effects. Apparently, producers consistently rejected the especially colorful and energetic explosions as too much in Beckett's own "psychedelic" style, and not in keeping with the overall desired look of the film.[29]

As I have already stated, many of the core special effects team on *Star Wars* trained in the filmmaking program at Cal Arts. Others of the outside contractors hired to complete the ambitious special effects program were involved in experimental filmmaking as well. It is especially hard to gauge the direct impact of these rather low-level workers because both sides strenuously downplay their influence. Reinforcing Beckett's comments, experimentalists insist that Lucas was "a square" and he consistently rejected the more "out there" material.[30] Moreover, the experimental filmmakers are nearly completely left out of the official ILM histories.[31] However, we can look at special effects traditions before, and also see the work in the strange, visually hybrid creature that is *Star Wars* itself, and nevertheless discern a radically different approach to staging and integrating special effects sequences in a mainstream narrative film.

A significant portion of the impact of films like *Star Wars* but also *Close Encounters*, and later *Blade Runner* derives from a combination of technological, aesthetic, and spectator effects prevalent in 1970s West Coast (and elsewhere) experimental filmmaking, including such filmmakers as Jordan Belson, John and James Whitney, Pat O'Neill, Norman McLaren, and Scott Bartlett.[32] Both special effects work and experimental filmmaking shared techniques stemming from nearly identical technologies, including multi-plane animation, computer as-

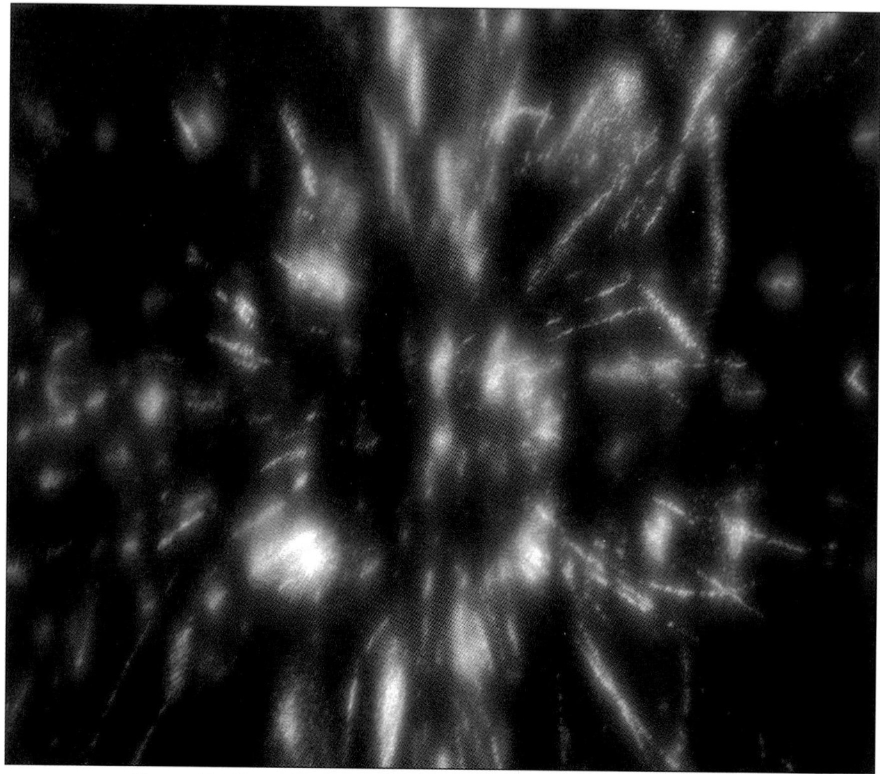

Figure 41. Unused explosions for *Star Wars* animated by Adam Beckett.

sisted camera technologies, high contrast mattes, rotoscoping, and optical reprinting.[33] Also in both cases, these techniques were exploited for the aesthetic effects of kineticism, "all-over" design, ray tracing, after images, rhythmic patterning, and vortex effects, among others. Generally, on the body of spectator, the combined effects result in, for example, mild visual disorientation, a sensation of transcending your body, absorption in the diegesis, and to a certain degree, intellectual engagement in the process formed by unusual juxtapositions. Of course, these effects are typically more sustained in time and more structurally integral in experimental films than in feature films. The trick of feature filmmakers is that they were able to harness these wildly varied techniques and purposefully diffuse effects into a (mostly) narratively coherent, photorealistically realized fictional diegesis. In other words, a traditionally recognizable feature film format enhanced with a renewed approach to absorption and fascination: the expanded blockbuster.

Looking at a Jordan Belson film like *Allures* or a James Whitney film like *Lapis*, one cannot help but notice the visual similarities between the neon-like streaks

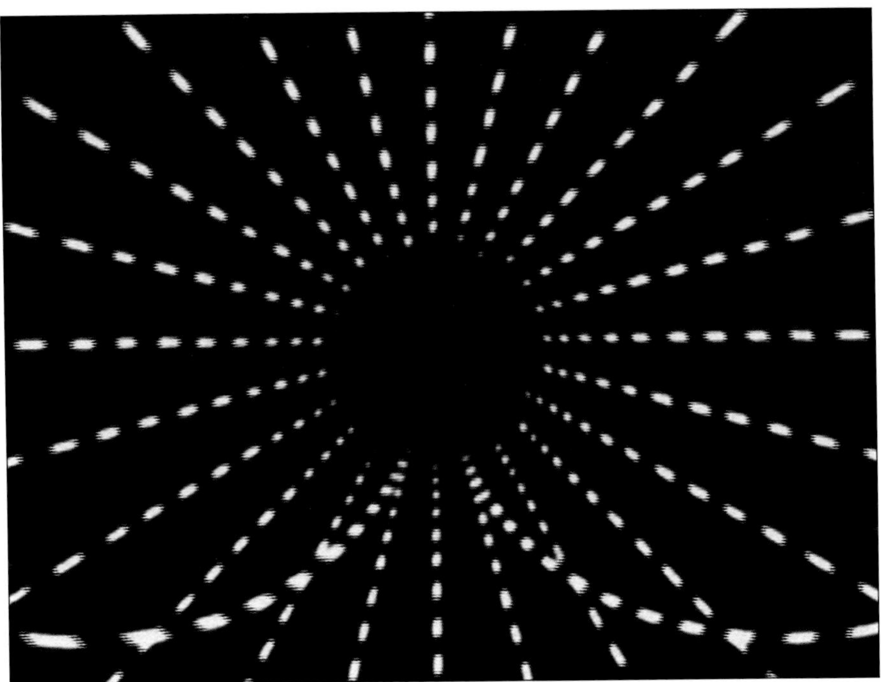

Figure 42. Vortex effect in Jordan Belson's *Allures*.

and points of light and the kind of rotoscoped effects in *Star Wars* light sabers and jumps to light speed. However, the influence goes far beyond sharing a similar roughly contemporaneous look. Namely, how the illusion of movement is initiated and how on and off screen space are conceptualized into, borrowing a term from abstract expressionism, an "all-over" effect. Previously, as in *Forbidden Planet* (1956), or *Conquest of Space* (1956), the special effect focus had been squarely on moving miniature space ships convincingly, typically slowly and horizontally, through a star field. Instead, for example, in the famous opening fly over in *Star Wars*, special effects technicians created a wholly artificial space, combining techniques (photographed motion control spaceship movements, rotoscoped laser blasts, multi-plane animation elements, etc.) in part derived from traditional special effects and animation techniques, but known to them "re-freshed" through experimental filmmaking. The goal is to stage the fast moving space ships in depth, into the screen space at a diagonal canted axis, creating a novel (for feature filmmaking) sense of artificial kinetic dynamism, with the graphic punch of hand-animated elements layered on top.

Also in *Star Wars*, as in the famous jump to hyperspace, the animation's overall composition within the frame heightens the kineticism and dynamizes the picture

Figure 43. 1950s special effects in *Forbidden Planet*.

plane by both multiplying the overall number of moving points, and then streaking them into an illusionistic vanishing point. In both cases, the strobing of the frame and the vibrating streaking mobilizes the eye, adding a layer on top of the "documentary" look of the photography and the "used future" of the production design that Lucas was aiming for in the principal photography.[34]

Again, this tactic was a change from previous special effects work, which the production regarded as supplementary to principal photography. Instead, 1970s filmmakers approached special effects as integral to the overall design of the film's principal photography and editing. They were concerned with an overall design and movement of the effects work within individual shots or sequences, in order to generate certain kinds of emotional and kinetic effects. What mainstream feature filmmaking learned from West Coast experimental film was to level the hierarchy, and blur the distinction, between principal and post-production material. With more and more contemporary productions built primarily in post-production, this proved to be a shift with enormous consequences to the production timeline.

Perhaps most importantly for later mainstream filmmaking, the example of West Coast experimental filmmaking also significantly transformed the way filmmakers conceived of and built spatial relations within the frame. Previously, special effects compositing, and especially science fiction spaces, understood their space as consisting of a perspectival series of planes. These could be viewed statically, either as a matte painting with a series of planar black holes to fill in, or as miniatures filmed to look as though they were moving horizontally across star fields.[35] Furthermore, in traditional studio-era effects, in order to fit the composite parts together in post-production, the camera on the set had to be locked down, with as few composited elements as possible.[36]

However, experimental filmmakers and special effects artists of the 1970s understood the screen space as "global" or spherical rather than planar. The combination of multi-plane animation techniques and motion control, computerized camera techniques (both, to a great degree pioneered and elaborated by experimental filmmakers like the Whitneys) created a possibility for more kinds of movements across different axes. Special effects artists, with the example of experimental animation, moved action through the space (as in McLaren-style multi-plane animation, or Whitney-style computer assisted movement), and staged action along an extended so-called "z axis". A famous example of this is the opening flyover of futuristic Los Angeles in *Blade Runner*, where a mixture of miniature model work, 2D flat artwork, and multi-plane animation glides the viewer into the action of the diegesis. This effect and others like it created the illusion of movement towards a distant vanishing point to establish a sense of forward momentum, all of which generate an immediate and usually fast-paced sense of immersion. It is also often used in opening sequences of films (see also, *Star Trek: The Motion Picture*, 1979), to quickly acclimatize the viewer to the artificial world presented. Filmmakers eventually motivated all of this technical and aesthetic energy towards incorporating special effects into an increasing percentage of feature films' total shots, crafting the kind of all-encompassing diegetic environments of contemporary blockbuster cinema. In the case of *Blade Runner*, *Star Wars*, and many others, this meant prioritizing expandable environments to experience, as much as stories to be staged and narrated.

In sum, certainly experimental filmmakers' direct, hands-on influence over the final look of the film in the special effects business was fairly limited, and artists on the job were considerably circumscribed in what they were allowed to innovate, except in rare cases. However, the aesthetic and technological models presented by experimental filmmaking impacted mainstream filmmaking much more profoundly than is usually acknowledged. Certainly, the mainstream industry exploited the talents of experimental filmmakers, but experimental filmmakers received something in return by making use of the industry equipment, gaining important technical finesse, and taking their money. Experimental filmmakers to a great degree get the final word, and maybe share an inside joke, from seeing their techniques on screen as ghostbusting, starfighting, and alien visitation. Perhaps this is not exactly what they had in mind for lasting career impact, but maybe it is not that far off either.

Practitioner Interviews conducted by the author and by Iota oral history project:

Betzy Bromberg (independent filmmaker and special effects technician), interviewed by the author, Tujunga, CA, 9 July 2007.

Chris Casady (independent filmmaker and special effects technician), interviewed by Mark Toscano, Hollywood, CA, Los Angeles Filmforum Alternative Projections: Oral Histories, 4 December 2009.

Chris Casady, interviewed by the author, Hollywood CA, 23 June 2010.

Larry Cuba (independent filmmaker and special effects technician), interviewed by Andrew Johnston, Hollywood, CA, Los Angeles Filmforum Alternative Projections: Oral Histories, August 2010.

Syd Dutton (co-founder Illusion Arts), interviewed by the author at the Illusion Arts offices, Van Nuys, CA, 25 July 2006.

John Dykstra, ASC (special effects supervisor on *Star Wars*, and founder of Apogee, Inc, independent effects house), interviewed by the author, Los Angeles, CA, 26 July 2006.

Peter Kuran (independent filmmaker and special effects technician), interviewed by the Author, Beverly Hills, CA, 5 August 2011.

Pat O'Neill (independent filmmaker and freelance special effects technician), interviewed by the author, Pasadena, CA, 19 July 2007.

Bill Taylor, ASC (co-founder Illusion Arts, independent effects house), interviewed by the author at the Illusion Arts offices, Van Nuys, CA, 25 July 2006.

Richard Winn Taylor (Abel and Associates employee, computer animation pioneer), interviewed by the author, Marina del Rey, 18 July 2007.

John Whitney Jr (independent filmmaker and producer, computer animation pioneer),interviewed by the author, Hollywood, CA, 20 July 2007.

Notes

1. A recent write-up in *LA Weekly* for the conference this volume is based upon spreads this misunderstanding. See Doug Harvey, "Hollywood's Soft Psychedelic Underbelly: Filmforum's 'Alternative Projections' symposium draws a line from avant-garde to *Avatar*", *LA Weekly*, 11 November 2010.
2. Julie Turnock, *Plastic Reality: Special Effects, Technology, and the Emergence of 1970s Blockbuster Aesthetics* (New York: Columbia University Press, 2014).
3. In my *Film History* (October 2014) version of this essay, entitled, "The True Stars of *Star Wars*?: Experimental Filmmakers the in 1970s and 1980s Special Effects Industry", I explore more specifically the particular contributions these experimental filmmakers brought to mainstream productions like *Star Wars*. This essay takes a broader view of experimental filmmakers' relation to the industry and their own work.
4. See interview list.
5. O'Neill interview, Casady Iota Interview.

6. Taylor and Dutton Interview.
7. The USC Cinema Department Student Guide from the 1960s at the USC cinema library lists courses and professors, but unhappily, not syllabi with film screenings.
8. Gene Youngblood, *Expanded Cinema* (New York: EP Dutton and Co, 1970).
9. See Andrew Johnston, "Pulses of Abstraction: Episodes from a History of Animation", (PhD diss., University of Chicago, 2011). Dissertations & Theses @ CIC Institutions, ProQuest.
10. As Peter Biskind put it:

    Lucas's genius was to strip away the Marxist ideology of a master of editing like Eisenstein, or the critical irony of an avant-garde filmmaker like Bruce Conner, and wed their montage technique to American pulp. Peter Biskind, *Easy Riders, Raging Bulls* (New York: Simon and Schuster, 1998), 343.
11. O'Neill and Bromberg interview. Roberta Friedman, personal remarks, 12 November 2010.
12. Of course there were famous exceptions, especially in the 1950s alien invasion cycle. However, it is worth noting that more often than not, the optical effects in those films, such as *The War of the Worlds* (1953) were completed by independent optical houses.
13. Turnock (2014).
14. Ibid.
15. Kubrick's film never meant to create a sustainable model for special effects production, but instead was an extended experiment in the long-standing effects belief that with unlimited time and money, you could do anything with special effects. After *2001*, Kubrick's effects team (including Douglas Trumbull) disbanded and only much later were the lessons and trial and error of *2001* tried again in more economically sustainable form for *Star Wars* and *Close Encounters*. See Turnock (2014).
16. Turnock (2014).
17. Ibid.
18. Legends of the formation of ILM (such as Mark Cotta Vaz and Patricia Rose Duignan, *Industrial Light and Magic: Into the Digital Age*, New York: Del Ray Books, 1996) concentrate on the core ILM team, led by John Dykstra at the original ILM facility in Van Nuys. However, by the final months of production, Lucasfilm needed to farm out a great deal of optical work in order to complete the film on time. As Adam Beckett, experimental animator and core ILM rotoscope artist on *Star Wars* put it, "... just about every optical house in town worked on *Star Wars*". Paul Mandell, "Adam Beckett: Animation and Rotoscope Design", *Cinefantastique* 7.1 (1978): 19. Even signature visuals such as the glow of the light sabers were farmed out to Van Der Veer opticals, according to Beckett in the same interview. The practice at ILM of hiring outside contractors to complete special effects continued through *Return of the Jedi* in 1983, but by then, ILM was able to complete most of their work in-house. For more on this, see Turnock (2014).
19. O'Neill interview (op.cit.).
20. O'Neill, Dutton, Casady interviews. Also see Stephen A Kallis, Jr., "Motion Picture 'Magic' Demonstrated in Boston", *American Cinematographer* (February 1972): 188, for a description of Dunn's presentations. The Academy Pickford Center's Linwood Dunn Collection also has several versions of Dunn's various presentation reels, some with his recorded voice speaking over the clips.
21. As Bromberg said, "The experimental film community can look down on people who work in the industry. There's a whole thing. Students look down on industry a lot of times. Which to me is insane." Casady expresses similar sentiments.
22. O'Neill, Bromberg, Casady interviews, and remarks by Robert Blalack in interview with Diane and Stan Levine, "Film/Video School Focus", *Cal Arts Alumni News* (Summer 1998).
23. Bromberg interview.
24. For more on Lucas's statements about his favorite avant-garde filmmakers, see many of the interviews in Sally Kline (ed.). *George Lucas: Interviews* (Jackson: University of Mississippi Press, 1999), as well as Will Brooker, *Star Wars* (BFI: London, 2009).
25. Turnock (2014).
26. Ibid.
27. Ibid.
28. For example, see Mandell, op.cit.: 18–21.
29. Some moving image footage of these explosions was shown at the Academy tribute screening to Beckett, *Infinite Animation: The Work of Adam Beckett,* at the Academy's Linwood Dunn Theater, 17 August 2009.
30. Richard Winn Taylor, Casady, Dykstra, interviews.

31. That is, the authors were or are employees of Lucasfilm. See, for example, Cotta Vaz and Duignan (1996); Pamela Glintenkamp, *Industrial Light and Magic: Creating the Impossible* (New York: Abrams, 2011); Thomas G. Smith, *Industrial Light & Magic: The Art of Special Effects* (New York: Ballantine, 1988). These Lucasfilm sponsored histories make little or no reference to the experimental filmmaking background of any of their core staff, and also do not reference the sizable outsourced personnel for the original *Star Wars* trilogy.
32. Reviewers such as Vincent Canby, Stanley Kauffmann, Roger Ebert, and Pauline Kael, refer to these films' visual, graphic, and visceral impact. See Turnock (2014).
33. See, for example, articles in journals such as the issue dedicated largely to the artist technicians on *Star Wars*: *Cinefantastique* 7.1 (1978). Also, the *American Cinematographer* series of articles on the special effects of *Star Wars* (July 1977), and *Close Encounters* (January 1978). Special effects fan magazine *Cinefex* has very detailed technical articles on the making of *The Empire Strikes Back* (Cinefex 3, 1980), as well as articles on *Blade Runner*, *Close Encounters*, and many others.
34. "Behind the Scenes of *Star Wars*," *American Cinematographer* (July 1977): 701.
35. Surprisingly, studio special effects before 1968 rarely took advantage of animation's multiplane animation stands to provide a "z-axis" into space. After Kubrick used multiplane animation and slit scan photography in the "Star Gate" sequence to create movement into the perspectival deep space distance, that technique became more common. Combined with motion control movement, the post-1970s film frame featured many more axes to move virtual cameras through.
36. See Richard Rickitt, *Special Effects: The History and Technique* (New York: Billboard Books, 2000); and Raymond Fielding, *The Technique of Special Effects Cinematography.* (New York: Hastings House Publishers, 1968); as well as Turnock (2014).

25 Storm, Stress, and Structure: The Collaborative Cinema of Roberta Friedman and Grahame Weinbren

Juan Carlos Kase*

> An idea comes to me clear and sharp. However it appears as a single unit, like a mass of hair, straw and scraps of fabric, stuck together with mud, gum and all kinds of gook. The characteristics of this ball of matter are its density and its indivisibility. [...] Often one bit emerges still entangled with others, and what looks like an individual idea or a unitary stream is really itself a complex of thoughts and ideas that themselves cannot be individuated.
> – Grahame Weinbren, 2005[1]

Though they have not been effectively integrated into the dominant narratives of the American avant-garde, the collaborative projects of Roberta Friedman and Grahame Weinbren represent pioneering experiments with form, authorship, and ideology within the independent cinema of the 1970s and early '80s. Over roughly ten years, the pair produced an extensive filmography of conceptually rich, exploratory works.

They began their creative work together around 1969, when, while students at the University of Buffalo (Friedman, an undergraduate student in English and intermedia; Weinbren, a graduate student in philosophy), they made *Three*

* I would like to thank David E. James, Roberta Friedman, and Grahame Weinbren for the comments, corrections, and suggestions that they have shared, all of which have improved this essay. I would also like to thank Mark Toscano (and the Academy Film Archive) for making a number of rare films by Friedman and Weinbren available for viewing, and for providing filmographic details of the artists' collaborations.

Rituals for Two Percussion, Projections, and Lights (1969–70), a film/performance event sponsored by the Rockefeller Foundation, with a soundtrack by Lejaren Hiller (who had recently collaborated with John Cage on the epic *HPSCHD* [1969]). After absorbing the rich film culture in Buffalo, learning about experimental cinema from Hollis Frampton (among others), and interacting with new music composers and performers, the couple relocated to Los Angeles in 1972. There, Friedman enrolled at CalArts as a graduate filmmaking student and Weinbren took a position teaching philosophy in the Humanities department. While at CalArts they made *Amusement Park Composition & Decay* (1973), *California Institute of the Arts 1973* (1973), *California Institute of the Arts 1974/75* (1974), and Friedman's MFA thesis film, *The Making of Americans* (1973–74). These works collectively demonstrate a conceptual playfulness and a technical finesse, including a virtuosic control of optical printing, animation, and other post-production techniques (which collectively indicate the influence of teacher Pat O'Neill).

After finishing their stint at CalArts, Friedman and Weinbren worked on an array of hybrid performance works, such as *Cross Sections* (1975), for two 16mm projectors; *Between the Lines* (1976–77), for film, tape, and solo musician, commissioned by Real Artways; *For Norma and Her Voices* (1977), composed for film and choral group, commissioned by The New Verbal Workshop; *Crotchets and Contrivances* (1977), with music by Carey Lovelace, performed by frequent collaborator, trombonist Jim Fulkerson; and *Vicarious Thrills* (1978–79), another hybrid performance/film work featuring Fulkerson, which was presented at the London Film Festival.

Throughout the mid-to-late 1970s in Los Angeles, Friedman and Weinbren collaborated on some of their most accomplished freestanding film works, including *Bertha's Children* (1976), a technical marvel of split-screen optical printing about Friedman's extended family; *Future Perfect* (1978), an elaborate image/sound experiment in algorithmic and mathematical structures that demonstrated the marked influence of avant-garde musical composition; *Murray and Max Talk About Money* (1979), a virtuosic study of sync-sound cinema, Cagean organizational strategies, and montage (to be discussed in some detail here); and *Margaret and Marion Talk About Working* (1980), a transitional production in geographic terms, having been shot in New York and completed in Los Angeles. The multi-part *Cheap Imitations* series was a playful group of films based on flawed descriptions and intentionally imperfect imitations of other movies, which they began towards the end of their Southern California residency. This cycle of films begins with *Cheap Imitations Part I: Méliès - India Rubber Head* (1980), with David Wilson as Méliès, and ends with *Cheap Imitations VI: Terms of Analysis* (1982–1983), which Friedman and Weinbren made in New York City after the couple permanently relocated there in 1981 (following a bi-coastal period from 1978–81). The artists' last major collaboration of those years was a different sort of project: a massive, pioneering multimedia experiment in interactive art, *The Erl King* (1983–85), which straddled an array of media forms including film, video, and computer technologies.[2] The Los Angeles Museum of Contemporary Art presented the interactive installation of *The Erl King* as part of the exhibition, "The Temporary Contemporary" from 1986–87, and the Whitney Museum in New York included it in its Biennial of 1987.

In assessing the history of Friedman and Weinbren's fertile collaborative relationship, their unwaveringly singular films – including *Murray and Max Talk About Money* and *Vicarious Thrills* – pose significant challenges to straightforward summary because of their distinctive, idiosyncratic amalgamations of unprecedented conceptual structures and uncommon audio-visual rhetorics. Yet their work is not without precedent: their films' theoretical and formal ties to a rich field of artistic experimentation belie a profound understanding of conceptual art, avant-garde music, documentary cinema, philosophy, and performance. Friedman and Weinbren's collaborations collectively comprise a range of filmic test cases and aesthetic-conceptual investigations, realized as experiments with dense thickets of artistic association, which often suggest underlying patterns in their construction, though they do not always reveal their generative organizational systems in upfront or obvious ways. Instead, these works depend upon a hybrid mode of authorship that blends labor-intensive organizational practices with other less controlled structures, such as the incorporation of live, improvised performance, arbitrary patterning, or organizational strategies determined by chance. In addition to their use of opaque, sometimes seemingly paradoxical artistic techniques, these films often utilize other methodologies that further complicate their analysis, including significant, yet partially occluded elements of ideological critique, documentary contingency, and conceptual humor.

Murray, Max, Money

Perhaps the most singular achievement of Friedman and Weinbren's collaborations is an uncommon work of documentary practice that utilizes organizational patterns derived from Cagean principles in order to pose formal and philosophical questions about labor, craft, performance, time, and money. Friedman and Weinbren shot the film with a professional crew using sync-sound equipment and thus made a work with a technical polish not typical of the artisanal production mode generally associated with experimental cinema.[3] The film revolves around interviews with two subjects, each of whom seems to be talking primarily about labor and money. However, the dialogue is fragmented and difficult to discern, even hyperbolically so.

The filmmakers deliberately obfuscate meaning, reference, and signification by utilizing a rigorous and relentless editing structure that shreds its content into brief slivers of sound and image. Friedman and Weinbren have broken up and reordered the interviews into collections of related words and ideas. Throughout the systematic restructuring of these interviews, the filmmakers kept sound and image in sync, even though the viewer rarely sees the lips of the film's onscreen subjects. Instead, a fluidly dollying camera explores the space of the studio without particular attention to the film's documentary subjects. As is sometimes the case with Andy Warhol's wandering camera (as in *The Chelsea Girls* [1966], for example), the cinematography here seems more concerned with the representation of space than with the film's human subjects. Interspersed between these fragments of conversation, Friedman, who is the interviewer, quotes Cage, including repeated catchphrases such as, "Things are always going wrong". As Friedman interviews Murray and Max (the subjects whose last names are never mentioned), behind them, against a large blank wall, a man (artist-filmmaker David Wilson) paints large swathes of bright, often primary colors. Over the course of the film the viewer can follow his painting process as a mode of tracking time.

The film communicates a deliberate, even forceful systematicity, though its organizational principles are, as in Cage's music, not readily apparent to the viewer or listener. The often arbitrary structuring within the work triggers a desire for comprehension, a need to decode the work's organizational principles or, in this case, to mentally reconstruct the fractured interviews that are shredded, broken down, and reorganized through the film's editing process. Weinbren explains that, "We thought that the shooting tactic was so simple, obvious and straightforward that the immediate viewer response would be to reconstruct the production of the film in one's mind as one watched it. We even made it easy by painting a guide to the sequence of colors along the bottom of the wall." Thus, one could track the progression of the film through the arbitrary development of the painter's labor rather than the content of the onscreen interviews.

Weinbren provides some further keys to the film's ornate construction by explaining that Friedman wrote a script for the work, though it was far from any sort of conventional screenplay: "The script consisted of various provocation strategies, along the lines of a John Cage score. e.g. in one section Roberta's script

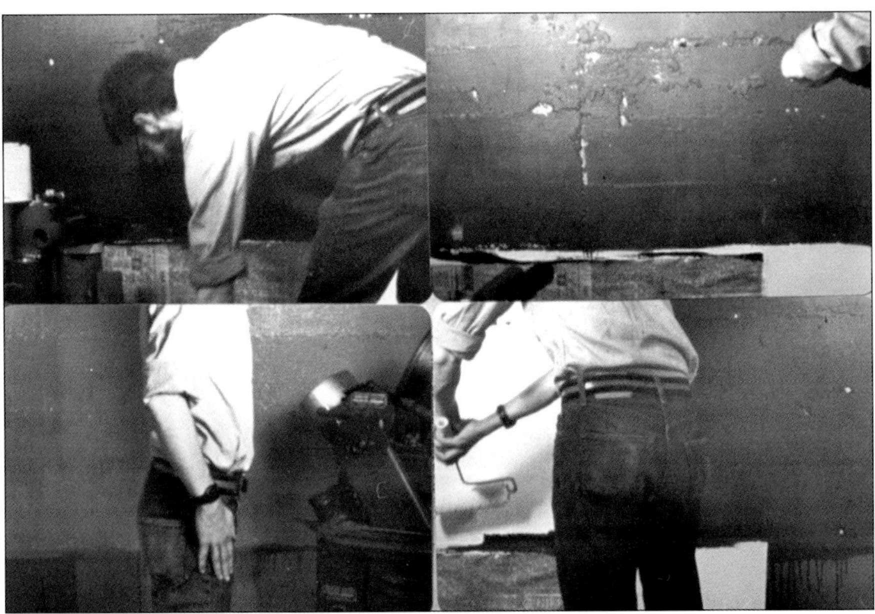

Figure 44. Still from *Murray and Max Talk About Money* (1979). David Wilson paints large swaths of color across the wall, tracking the film's temporal evolution.

was 'I didn't understand what you just said. Can you repeat it?' This phrase was repeated 3 times after Murray's (or Max's) answer. Another strategy involved highlighting an article in *The New York Times* so that words appeared in different colors."[4] Throughout the process of the film's production, the subjects were carefully directed, though Friedman did not guide them in conventional dramatic terms. She explains, "I created the text for *Murray and Max* by excerpting articles about work and money and highlighting words for them to say loudly (red = loud) or softly (yellow = soft voice)".[5] The text that they generated through these processes was then further modified through an astoundingly labor intensive approach to double-system editing in which the filmmakers radically reorganized their materials while keeping the strands of image and sound in perfect synchronicity. Weinbren further explains the organizational principles of the film:

> Then when the film was developed and synced, it was edited by the following method. First all Roberta's questions were removed. Then the film was organized by categories, e.g. all Murray's yeses and noes were grouped, and all Max's (not intermixed); all the "ums" and "ers"; all the texts from the newspaper; all the texts mentioning the word "work"; the word "money"; jobs; investment; etc. We paid no attention to the image, but kept it in synch for every edit – so the sound led the picture, which became more or less aleatorically, organized along Cagean lines. [6]

As these detailed explanations demonstrate, *Murray and Max Talk About Money* involved an incredibly elaborate production practice. However, rather than enhancing the spectacle of the film and giving the viewer greater access to its central narrative conceits, the editing process here consistently and relentlessly blocks the viewer's access to the object of his or her stare. This is a work that continuously and unrelentingly frustrates the conventional documentary experience of spectatorial contact with its subjects. Instead of bringing us into closer proximity with Murray, Max, and their topic of discussion, we are reminded of the constructedness of filmic representation and its basis in the material particularities of the cinematic apparatus. In their unflinching interrogation of the processes of mediation and representation, Friedman and Weinbren – like UK-based structuralist/materialist filmmakers Malcolm LeGrice and Peter Gidal – unmoor the camera and its observational associations from the texture of realist contingency, and destabilize the underlying mechanisms of spoken language and visual reference.

The pornography of the visible

> We are always interested in constructing ways of evoking the pleasures of cinema without implicitly accepting an ideology – of passivity, manipulation, and repressed violence – that we would explicitly reject. Can there be films that remain cinematic without indulging in one form of pornography or another? *Murray and Max* ... is, in part, a proposal, a blueprint, for such a form of cinema.
> – Grahame Weinbren[7]

In his introduction to *Signatures of the Visible* (1992), Fredric Jameson suggests that there is something about cinema that is inescapably exploitative. He writes, "The visual is essentially the pornographic, which is to say that it has its end in rapt, mindless fascination. … Pornographic films are thus only the potentiation of films in general, which ask us to stare at the world as though it were a naked body".[8] There is something in Jameson's totalizing claim that echoes Weinbren's suggestion concerning cinema's role as pornographic observation. Regardless of how we understand this rhetorical linkage between cinema and pornography, if most commercial cinema promises some kind of access to a sexualized visual spectacle of pleasure – which is what Weinbren and Jameson suggest – what *Murray and Max …* offers is something else. In its fragmented, montagist documentary form, it forges an attack on linguistic intelligibility and visual access. It systematically denies admittance to the realm of the diegesis. Instead, we are given a tightly packed articulation of the ways in which a film can be carefully constructed, judiciously manipulated, and rigorously assembled in order to deny almost any kind of contact with the spectacle of human presence. The fact that Friedman and Weinbren made the film using a professional sound crew and elaborate dolly system makes its willful occlusion of audio-visual access all the more perverse. This perversion amounts to an incredible frustration of the goals

Figure 45. Still from *Murray and Max Talk About Money* (1979). Friedman and Weinbren's eccentric visual composition occludes both of the film's onscreen subjects almost completely.

of pornography, defined in its broadest sense. It also forces the viewer to contemplate the work's economy, in both figurative and literal senses, to reflect on the relationship that the film itself forges between actual labor and its meaning. Friedman quotes Cage, saying, "Like ordinary work, meaningless work can make you sweat if you do it long enough".

Murray and Max … is also about art, implicating the artist and his or her labor in the economic processes of exchange that circumscribe the social construction of meaning. Against the rhetorical backdrop of this hyperbolically fragmented conversation about money and labor, David Wilson continuously rolls vivid swaths of paint on the cement wall behind the film's talking heads. On one level Wilson's gestures mark time between the heavily edited passages of conversation that we hear on the soundtrack. On another level, these actions also represent the labor of art. However, through them we do not gain any kind of access to a structuring artistic sensibility. Wilson's back is turned to us – as Jackson Pollock's was in Hans Nameth's notorious footage of the artist at work – and we are denied any simulated spectacle of artistic subjectivity.[9] Artistic presence has been displaced from a gestural guarantee of identity to the baroque complexity of the work's extreme aesthetic eccentricity. This is a labor-intensive sync-sound film, which is, well, about labor. But it is also about art, how it is made, how it relates to the mechanisms of exchange, and how it might or might not relate to visual pleasure, culminating in a conceptual inscrutability that feels elegant and perfect in its peculiarity.

Through such strategies of multi-tiered rhetoric, internal contradiction, and cognitive dissonance, Friedman and Weinbren create works that do not speak directly or univocally, but with an unlikely mixture of representational roughness and conceptual precision. In Friedman's words, these works produce an unusual, hybrid film experience: "You got sort of a rough and raw quality, combined with a very formal quality".[10] A number of their collaborative works contain a crowded aesthetic layering of concepts, references, and ideas that is both overdetermined and unresolved. This intentional aesthetic crosstalk becomes even louder in their filmic collaborations that directly address social and economic considerations.

Vicarious Thrills (1979) and occluded pornography

In *Vicarious Thrills*, Friedman and Weinbren collaborated on a performative reconditioning of sexually explicit found footage within an uncommon essay film that foregrounds the mechanical apparatus, the material of the medium, and the referential content of moving image photography. It is a playful experiment with pornography that we can now only see in its silent form, despite the fact that Friedman and Weinbren generally showed *Vicarious Thrills* in traveling shows around the US and Europe accompanied by live performance from the trombonist Jim Fulkerson.

In the first section of the film, we observe some aspect of film production; it seems that we may be witnessing the construction of the film that we are actually watching.[11] This portion of the work shows a man using a zoom lens to re-photograph a projected film off of a screen at the left of the frame. Our primary attention is given to the manipulation and stroking of the long zoom lens, slowly and carefully finessed by a woman (Friedman) who stands to the side of the cameraman. This is a long take, shot in fast motion (so less light is needed). The room is basically dark with sidelights illuminating the screen.

Then, after we see the footage of the technicians shooting, the second section of the film begins. Here we are shown dangling pieces of 16mm film as the camera slowly moves from one strand to the other, bringing each one in and out of focus while traversing the space virtually through the shifting magnification of its zoom lens. In these first two sections of the film, our attention is drawn to the long-take contingency of filmmaking as performance. We are also exposed to the materiality

Figure 46. Still from second section of *Vicarious Thrills* (1979). The found footage filmstrip hangs loosely in front of the camera, shifting in and out of focus, and giving only fleeting visual access to the sex acts that it displays.

of the celluloid in its unprojected, serialized, still form, as it dangles loosely in front of the camera.

In the third section of the work, we finally see the footage from the first portion now being projected and looped. Here we can most clearly see the sex acts depicted in the found footage film fragments, though they have been transformed and reconstituted in significant ways, using dramatic, unnatural zooms that create an unusual range of compositional frames. Images are flipped upside down and inverted. The movements of the performers are modified, showing their sex acts in slow motion. Here we too are made aware of film's materiality, albeit in a filmic, not a profilmic context (as in section two). This is the inverse of section one in that time is distended, rather than compressed, and we are brought closest to the unique observational pleasures that film can provide as a direct source of prurient sexual stimulation. In this section of the film, the viewer can clearly discern vaginal penetration and fellatio, whereas the filmmakers actively obscured the sex acts through the material manipulation in the work's first two sections. Here at the film's conclusion the images of sexual activity are also scratched, degraded, colored, and chemically modified, ultimately stunting visual access to the pornographic spectacle.

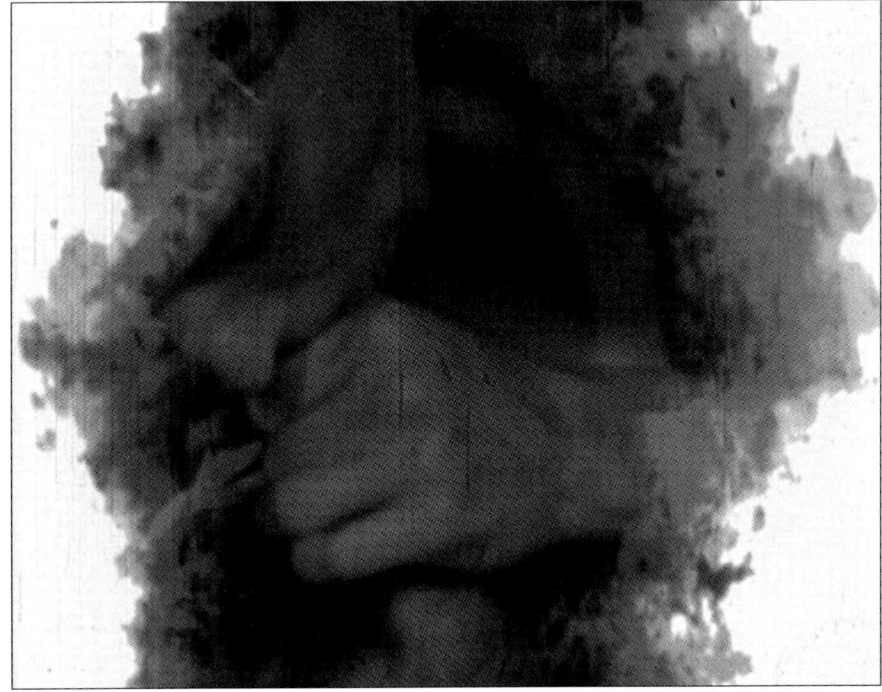

Figure 47. Still from the final section of *Vicarious Thrills* (1979). The viewer briefly glimpses the sexual content that is the film's elusive topic.

Each of these three sections provides a different kind of contact with film's potential for prurience, but in ways that are unresolved and, for the sake of sexual pleasure, unsatisfactory. Each section could be understood to be more intimate and closer to some notion of film's essence, to some privileged filmic ontology: as profilmic performance, as material substrate, as the projection of images in motion. Nevertheless, through the denaturalization of the medium in each of these sequences, the visual experience of sexual pleasure is frustrated.

What does this work say about the representation of sexuality? What is its status vis-à-vis visual pleasure? To simply describe it as some form of straightforward critique of pornographic representation would be too simple, particularly considering the comic and obvious phallic imagery of the manually caressed zoom lens that opens the film. In addition, to add an extra level of playful symbolism, when the work was performed in public, it was accompanied by the live performance of Fulkerson on trombone, an instrument that depends on the undulating protrusion of its hard metallic extension.

Like Bruce Conner's *Marilyn Times 5* (1973), Andy Warhol's *Couch* (1964), or Carolee Schneemann's *Fuses* (1965), *Vicarious Thrills* presents explicit sexual activity in an unconventional setting, mediated carefully and consciously by an active artistic intelligence. In these works, the filmmakers expanded the rhetorical function of their prurient footage and redirected it in a multitude of conceptual directions. As the filmmakers have described it, no matter how it is modified, broken down, or reconstructed, this imagery continues to exert some kind of sexual evidence and, ultimately, a social consideration. Yes, it also shows us the filmic apparatus: we see sprocket holes, rephotographed film, and the careful manipulation of a zoom lens. But we cannot escape the illusionistic content of the images themselves, as contained within strands of an amateur film featuring the explicit representation of group sex. In addition to being overdetermined by a range of complex and unusual formal strategies, the works of Friedman and Weinbren also interact with a network of representational, political, and social concerns.

Mapping the trends, returning to history

In a recent reevaluation of the historiography of the avant-garde and his own place within it, Weinbren argues that the work of the 1970s and '80s requires a more nuanced understanding than it has generally received. He suggests that, in that era, aesthetic transparency and consistency had lost their grasp on artistic practice. Filmmakers challenged these older, classical values by proposing revised creative models that were not hierarchical or didactic in structure or purpose: "Filmmakers who emerged in the early to middle 1970s tended to reject the strategy of centering their work on a single idea and forcing other ideas into subsidiary relationships". To Weinbren, these artists saw new opportunities to "liberate many ideas to float together simultaneously, supporting or contradicting each other in a fabric composed of multiple weights and weaves".[12] Weinbren draws the reader's attention to a kind of cinema that can "perform multiple functions simultaneously".[13] Friedman describes her collaborations with Weinbren in similar terms: "We have so many ideas that we try to pack into just this one little strand. We did work I think that's very layered."[14] The conceptual and formal breadth of their work is a difficult thing to imagine if one is not familiar with the films of Friedman and Weinbren. How precisely might such a cinema work? How might it cohere? Or not?

Like most artists who came of age in the 1960s and '70s, Friedman and Weinbren resisted the ideals of aesthetic purity that were promoted by art critic Clement Greenberg and perpetuated by his influential legacy of medium-specificity. They preferred Cage, an artist who was fundamentally incomprehensible to Greenberg (as well as to film critic P. Adams Sitney, despite recent attempts by the latter to recuperate the composer in exclusively Emersonian terms).[15] In their openness to arbitrary and uncontrolled events, the works of Friedman and Weinbren satisfy the definition of experimental art advanced by Cage, an artist who, like Warhol, left a wake of influence across the whole landscape of the postwar avant-garde by redrawing the boundaries of authorial inscription. In 1957, Cage argued that a truly experimental art would require untested practices and strategies, as well as new notions of what artistic authorship entails. In his words, the use of aleatory and unpredictable structures create work in which, "the word 'experimental' is apt, providing it is understood not as descriptive of an act to be later judged in terms of success and failure, but simply as of an act the outcome of which is unknown".[16] The filmic collaborations of Friedman and Weinbren perfectly encapsulate Cage's goals for an art that is untested, exploratory, and literally experimental.[17] Friedman and Weinbren's discussions of the heterogeneous, polyvalent film work resonate loudly with Cage's own notion that, "Art's a way we have for throwing out ideas – ones we've picked up in or out of our heads. What's marvelous is that as we throw them out – these ideas – they generate others, ones that weren't even in our heads to begin with."[18]

* * *

In order to situate the geographical trends of experimental cinema in the 1970s in context, I present a short quotation that addresses the way in which the New York avant-garde of that era has been understood and historicized from without. In 1978, Bay Area filmmaker Robert Nelson described the aesthetic rigor of New York's avant-garde cinema in that decade, and evoked a particularly vivid and colorful image of the era:

> I think New York, it reminded me of what I imagined Egypt to be like at the height of some majestic dynasty. Because, the artistic formalism, the formalism everywhere, in every expression, even on TV, was very exciting. [...] once I got there, the film [of mine] looked to me in the context of that formalism in New York, it looked to me like something a gypsy brought in on a blanket and rolled out on the sand, like a bunch of hairy handmade objects that were all sort of laying there. That was the reaction I had to my film, in New York. That it looked very hairy.[19]

Nelson's description does not represent a unique opinion. To most California filmmakers and critics working within experimental film communities in the 1970s, it was agreed: what was happening in New York represented, quite simply, a different state of affairs.[20]

A number of scholars have tried to identify and assess the highly mannered formalism and conceptual, even mathematical purity that both excited and confused Robert Nelson during his visit to the New York film community in the 1970s. From critic P. Adams Sitney, we have inherited the descriptive category of "Structural Film", a phrase that he first used in print in the summer of 1969 when he was twenty-four years old.[21] In Sitney's writing about trends in the avant-garde, he made an audacious attempt to corral a variety of films into one group based on isomorphic technical similarities, including a fixed camera position, the flicker effect, and loop printing. In more general terms he would categorize this group of films as ones in which "the shape of the whole film is predetermined and simplified, and it is that shape which is the primal impression of the film. [...] The structural film insists on its shape and what content it has is minimal and subsidiary to the outline."[22]

Though Sitney's category has some minor heuristic value – as Hollis Frampton said, "It worked a little" – its critical legacy has exerted much more intellectual influence than it should have.[23] From its very inception, Sitney's terminology met with overwhelming disagreement from almost all filmmakers who were either directly or indirectly associated with his category.[24] George Maciunas, a Fluxus artist (as well as the frequent layout designer of *Film Culture*, the journal in which Sitney first published his critical formulation), argued that the young critic's critical failures were, at least partially, a function of social factors including "cliquishness and [his] ignorance of filmmakers outside the *Coop* or *Cinematheque* circle".[25] Despite these objections, "Structural Film" has dominated the understanding of the American avant-garde in the 1970s. The fact that this categorical descriptor persists is evidence that we – as film scholars, critics, artists, and historians – should diversify the historical record in order to recognize greater material detail and a wider range of under-recognized, under-historicized films that do not satisfy the basic categories presented by this young critic over forty years ago. In addition, new timelines are needed in order to accommodate the diversity of trends and tendencies that do not gel with the dominant narratives of avant-garde film history.

In a reconsideration of the relation between the cinema of Southern California and the so-called "Structural Film" of New York, critic Paul Arthur argues in support of a more diverse historical model of this era, one that is not defined according to the presumed dominance of certain trends associated with Sitney's term. Arthur suggests that to conceive of experimental film history in the 1970s in simple binary terms – poised between the formalism of the "Structural Film" and a poetic, personal film of a Brakhagean cinema – is to do a disservice to the philosophical range of the artistic field (more generally) and to the work of Southern California (more specifically):

> The local avant-garde [of Los Angeles] has, in fact, remained outside the pull of either a staunchly personal, existential esthetic or an analytic, self-reflexive practice becoming some-

> thing like a *third stream of development*. There are admittedly in New American Cinema *as many third-streams* as there are unified polemical stances. [emphasis added][26]

It is in the context of the structural film debate – or better said – in its wake, that I turn to the theoretical writings of Grahame Weinbren. In an essay from 1979, titled "Six Filmmakers and an Ideal of Composition", Weinbren assessed certain trends in the cinema of Southern California. He argued that a regional strain of cinema had taken hold in which, "The form and content of the work are to be subsidiary to an overriding conception. [...] This can occur when there are no arbitrary or subjective decisions to be made, everything being determined in advance by an outside mechanism." Such an "ideal of composition" is one in which filmmakers deal with "logical consequences" and "algorithm[s] for the construction of a work".[27] On one interpretative level, Friedman and Weinbren's collaborations embody a set of creative strategies similar to those of conceptual artists like Sol Lewitt, who famously claimed that a work of art need not be constructed by its author's hand. In his words, "The idea becomes a machine that makes the art".[28]

In search for an impersonal, automatic model of construction, Weinbren conceived of a kind of conceptual work in which the creative agent would be removed from the manufacture of the project and replaced by a pre-determined system or algorithm. (A remarkable example of such a method can be found in the complex mathematical matrix of Friedman and Weinbren's, *Future Perfect.*) Such works create an impression "as if someone else, or nothing, had created it".[29] It is important to recognize that in the hands of these filmmakers, this kind of strategy takes on a significantly different rhetorical meaning than it would in, say, the work of Michael Snow or Paul Sharits. In the films of Friedman and Weinbren, such strategies follow distinctive paths and represent dissimilar philosophical functions from seemingly related work produced in Canada and on the East Coast. Simply put, their works are generally more playful, arbitrary, ambivalent, and, ultimately, Cagean, than the filmmakers canonized by Sitney. Weinbren suggests looking for an interpretative alternative because "there is a wealth of material to uncover in the independent cinema" and new historiographic approaches and "different digging techniques will bring different concepts to the surface".[30]

Weinbren's critical writing suggests that appropriate evaluative categories cannot be based upon isomorphic structural similarities, such as the ones that Sitney uses to link the unlikely bedfellows of Bruce Baillie's Zen hippie tableau, *Still Life* (1966), and the stroboscopic assault of Tony Conrad's *The Flicker* (1965). As Weinbren writes, in a more recent evaluation of Sitney's categorization, his work was "erecting fences between filmmakers who belong in the same yard, and herding together some who ought to be kept fields apart. [...] Sitney's techniques of literary analysis domesticated the raucous films that were its subject".[31] One of the major shortcomings of this category was the overwhelming emphasis on medium specificity, which suggested that, if these systemic, self-aware films were about anything, they were about cinema itself. On the contrary, a number of the reflexive, seemingly formalist films of the 1970s – whether made in New York, Montreal, San Francisco, or Los Angeles – are sometimes actually about things and concern specific topics, including sex, violence, and money.[32] Weinbren's collaborations with Friedman challenge the singularity of Sitney's "Structural Film" and its associated set of critical values by following an unpredictable aesthetic trajectory through crosswise shifts of association beyond established formal, conceptual, or ideological boundaries. Far from being a shortcoming, the conceptual polyvalence of Friedman and Weinbren's films contributes immeasurably to their unique audio-visual pleasures and their quietly raucous intellectual experiments.

In recent interviews for the Alternative Projections oral history project, Friedman and Weinbren expressed their frustration with the historiography of experimental film, particularly as it relates to work of the 1970s and '80s.[33] By comparing filmmakers from Southern California with more dominant, established, and well known names from New York's avant-garde community, critics and scholars have induced a kind of geographic flattening, a historical reduction and simplification that is also traumatic, in historiographic terms. Such selective reification – of canonized New York "Structural Film" – wipes out those texts that simply do not satisfy the inherited patterns of the dominant critical teleologies. The quirky systematicity, the thematic intricacy, and the sublime strangeness of a work like *Murray and Max Talk About Money* would be leveled, critically speaking, by any effort to define it in relation to Sitney's inapt historical model from almost forty years ago. As Paul Arthur argued, "there are many third streams", and as Grahame Weinbren wrote, "there are different ways of digging".[34]

It is only by reassessing film history, with an awareness of the blank pages that fall between chapters and movements as we have inherited them, that we can be more receptive to the fresh aesthetic experiences that the past has to offer. When considering insufficiently documented art forms, artists, and movements such as Southern Californian avant-garde cinema of the 1970s, it is essential that any responsible historian do his or her best to provide the most catholic evaluation of the history being assessed without using terminological shortcuts. To be more direct, selective canon building is particularly detrimental when it occurs well outside the register of popular awareness or democratic consensus.

Notes

1. Grahame Weinbren, "Post Future Past Perfect", in *Experimental Film and Video*, ed. Jackie Hatfield (Eastleigh, UK: John Libbey Publishing, 2006), 3–4.
2. In the early 1990s, they collaborated on another interactive, multi-media work, titled *Sonata* (1991–93), directed by Weinbren and produced by Friedman. More recently, in the new millennium, the two artists have begun to work together again, and have completed the video work *Bertha's Grandchildren* (2011).
3. Friedman recently summarized the unfamiliar aesthetic territory that their work explored by suggesting that it "looked too slick for New York" and "for California filmmakers, it was too structural". Author's telephone conversation with Friedman, 3 March 2014.
4. Author's email correspondence with Weinbren, 15 August 2011. I have made minor changes to the orthography and punctuation of all email correspondence, e.g. changing "M&M" to "Murray and Max".
5. Author's email correspondence with Friedman, 3 March 2014.
6. Author's email correspondence with Weinbren, 15 August 2011.
7. Weinbren in "Filmmaker's Cooperative Catalog",, http://film-makerscoop.com/rentals-sales/search-results?fmc_filmid=3426, accessed 31 March 2014.
8. Frederic Jameson, *Signatures of the Visible* (New York: Routledge, 1992), 1.
9. See Nameth's film, *Jackson Pollock 51* (1951).
10. Interview with Roberta Friedman, "Alternative Projections Oral History Project, 19 January 2010", http://www.alternativeprojections.com/oral-histories/, accessed 31 March 2014.
11. As in David Wilson's *Dead Reckoning* (1980), the film begins by showing us the recording apparatus as it films the movie that we will eventually see projected later.
12. Weinbren, "Post Future Past Perfect", 13.
13. Ibid., 9.
14. Interview with Roberta Friedman, "Alternative Projections Oral History Project, 19 January 2010", http://www.alternativeprojections.com/oral-histories/, accessed 31 March 2014.
15. See P. Adams Sitney, *Eyes Upside Down: Visionary Filmmakers and the Heritage of Emerson* (Oxford: Oxford University Press, 2008). One systematic way to track Sitney's reading of Cage is to follow his citations of the composer through the index to *Eyes Upside Down*. It is remarkable how forcefully Sitney situates Cage within the legacy of American transcendentalism, denying his modernity by completely ignoring the formal innovations that tie him to Duchamp and Warhol as the 20th century's most successful protagonists in the separation of art from the egocentric tendencies of romanticism.
16. John Cage, "Experimental Music: Doctrine", in *Silence: Lectures and Writings by John Cage* (Middletown, CT: Wesleyan University Press, 1961), 13.
17. Most scholars and historians have failed to recognize the potency of Cage's influence on the history of experimental film. The films of Friedman and Weinbren encourage a historiographic corrective to this oversight.
18. John Cage, "Diary: Audience 1966" in *A Year From Monday: New Lectures and Writings by John Cage* (Middletown, CT: Wesleyan University Press, 1969), 51.
19. Robert Nelson quoted in Scott MacDonald, *Canyon Cinema: The Life and Times of an Independent Film Distributor* (Berkeley: University of California Press, 2008), 307.
20. In 1975 English filmmaker and theorist Peter Wollen argued that the New York avant-garde filmmaking sensibility had always been as distinct from the West Coast as it was from London. He wrote, "there is a sense in which avant-garde Co-op film-making in Europe is closer to New York than Californian film-making is, and the leading New York critics and tastemakers – Sitney, Michelson, etc. – are not appreciated in San Francisco any more than they are in London". Peter Wollen, "The Two Avant-Gardes", *Studio International: Journal of Modern Art* 190 (November/December 1975), 171.
21. P. Adams Sitney, *Film Culture* 47 (Summer 1969): 1.
22. Ibid.
23. Frampton quoted in MacDonald, *Canyon Cinema*, 268.
24. One of the few people who accepted Sitney's category of "Structural Film" was Tony Conrad. Art historian Branden Joseph articulates Tony Conrad's shifting responses to Sitney's category, and ultimately concludes that, "By 1972,

Conrad would come to embrace *The Flicker*'s reception as a structural film as one of several legitimate understandings". See Joseph, *Beyond the Dream Syndicate: Tony Conrad and the Arts After Cage* (New York: Zone Books, 2008), 300.

25. George Maciunas, "Some Comments on Structural Film by P. Adams Sitney" in *Film Culture Reader*ed. P. Adams Sitney (New York: Cooper Square Press, 2000), 349.
26. Paul Arthur, "The Western Edge: Oil of L.A. and the Machined Edge", *Millennium Film Journal* 12 (Fall/Winter 1982–83): 21.
27. Grahame Weinbren, "Six Filmmakers and an Ideal of Composition", *Millennium Film Journal* 3 (Winter–Spring 1979): 40.
28. Sol Lewitt, "Paragraphs on Conceptual Art", *Artforum* 5.10 (June 1967): 79–83.
29. Weinbren, "Six Filmmakers": 40.
30. Ibid., 41.
31. Weinbren, "Post Future Past Perfect", 6–7 .
32. A powerful counterexample to the conceptual purity of Sitney's so-called "Structural Film" is the work of Paul Sharits. In films such as *Piece Mandala/End War* (1966), *T, O, U, C, H, I, N, G* (1968) and *Epileptic Seizure Comparison* (1976), Sharits addresses violence, sexuality, and bodily trauma in all their visceral, somatic excess. Despite the academic undergirding of the works they are not the anemic, bloodless projects of an exclusively intellectual cinema. They are unwieldy, horrific, and affectively arresting.
33. See interviews with Grahame Weinbren from 19 February 2010, and Roberta Friedman from 19 January 2010, accessed 31 March 2014, http://www.alternativeprojections.com/oral-histories/
34. Arthur, "The Western Edge", 21; Weinbren, "Six Filmmakers", 40.

26 Nun Notes and Deviant Longings

Erika Suderberg

The development of the women's movement is, in my opinion, at least as important as the discovery that the earth is round.
– Helke Sander

I'm an experienced woman; I've been around… well, all right I might not've been around, but I've been ... nearby.
– Mary Richards in The Mary Tyler Moore Show

My head is like a radio set ... my nightmares don't project my dreams.
–The Slits, "FM" (1976)

Until all women are lesbians there will be no true political revolution.
– Jill Johnston

The US is out of Vietnam. Patty Hearst goes rogue and underground. Anita Bryant declaims, "I don't hate the homosexuals, but as a mother, I must protect my children from their evil influence". The homosexuals don T-shirts emblazoned with "Anita Sucks Fruits" and cease consumption of Florida orange juice. Mary Tyler Moore as Mary Richards in the *Mary Tyler Moore Show* (1970–77) is a character that is single, independent, childless, ebullient, and pursuing a career. *Mary Hartman, Mary Hartman* has a volatile year on TV, filled with dysfunctional unabashed weirdness, a star who says she shot the whole thing coked out of her mind, and a devoted following of fans who relished the explosion of the American dream in primetime. Sonny and Cher divorce but reunite on camera for the sake of the show. The Queen of England, in her tiara, dances with President Ford. Ford then loses to Jimmy Carter. The underage *Runaways* form and release a cherry bomb, whilst in England, members of *The Flowers of Romance* and *The Castrators* start *The Slits* and encounter a backlash against their chosen moniker. Their first LP is adorned with a picture of them bare breasted in loincloths anointed in mud. Steve Jobs and Steve Wozniak roll out the Apple 1 which looks like a typewriter tethered to a remainder bin at Radio Shack. And Radio Shack sells you the *Bicentennial Everything System* for $499. The TV grid hosts *The Bionic Woman, All in the Family, Donny and Marie, Charlie's Angels* and *M*A*S*H*. Barbra Streisand decides it's a good idea to remake *A Star Is Born*. Both Alix Dobkin's *Living With Lesbians* and Patti Smith's *Horses* are released. David Bowie falls to earth in androgen confusion. Billie Jean King has an affair with a woman and struggles in public to repair her marriage while battling Bobby Riggs at ping-pong on an episode of *The Odd Couple. The Flying Nun* is still healthily in syndication as Matsushita introduces the VHS home video cassette recorder. Sony's Betamax dies a quick death. Two Vikings land on Mars, while the US, China, and the USSR are busy with underground nuclear testing. George Bush becomes director of the C.I.A. Elections in Vietnam are held for a National Assembly to reunite the country. The Supreme Court upholds a woman's right to unemployment benefits during the last three months of pregnancy. Alice Paul's 1923 Equal Rights Amendment (ERA) again fails ratification. 1976 is a rocky schizoid trail, an incongruous timeline that tastes of gumbo and speaks of untold repercussions and remainders resplendent as signposts for our current day. It serves also as a scene setting apparatus for nuns, deviants, and queer shape-shifting sisters from all environs.

Consider this text, dear reader, as modest preliminary, observational notes, reheated manifestos, and incantatory rants about a 1976 Los Angeles, as location and utopist projection, and its collusion with nascent queer Feminist Video, a text born of archival longing recently stoked anew by current occupations and the promise or invocation of a radical future. I saw Nancy Angelo's and Candace Compton Pappas's *Nun and Deviant* several years after its bicentennial birth in 1976 but at precisely the right time to add it to my lavender backpack of compasses, banned books, pre-riot girl pinups and anti-anti-porn porn. These current skeletal observations are partially under the control of a younger self, planted in an iced Minnesota plotting an escape to California – an entity vying for control with an older self, longing for radical possibilities and hopeful intercessionary lessons to apply to the current assimilationist morass. 1976 means many things to many people – primarily to these co-mingled selves: the first year without war in Vietnam, a black lesbian in Congress with a voice of Texas steel, and the overt, unapologetic machinations conceived by homegrown terrorist cells, punk, disco, and the *Lavender Menace* erratically caught in a strobe oscillating wildly between two, possibly three, Marys: *Mary Hartman, Mary Hartman*, Mary Richards (MTM), and of course Mother Mary. I was busily dancing in gay male leather bars to the disco revolution, less-so at flannel-clad dyke bars and with all-out delight to Prince, when he was an almost one-man band of fluctuating gender references. Minneapolis had a healthy, grainy counter cultural milieu scented by Pillsbury and wrapped by 3M. Perhaps this but activates a fevered recovered dream. Something had to activate to an impressionable lass spending sub-zero nights watching MTM re-runs, unsuccessfully selling *The Young Socialist* on street corners, watching experimental film and dancing until dawn. All the Marys watch over the current re-telling with bemused calm and hopeful surveillance: pretend performers, all but feminist saints, clearing a crooked path that connects disorganized religion, art, the Midwest, pilgrimages to California, and a women's movement finally challenged by a loud lavender menace no longer content to be scapegoats nor demure quietly for the heterosexual feminist revolution.

The video artifact *Nun and Deviant* posited some specific challenges and laid out promises that had repercussions in nascent alternative media production and performance art apart, but not unaware of, narrative lesbian film history (scant as it appeared), intertwined with an embryonic experimental presence. This is a presence centered solely on the capable shoulders of Barbara Hammer, who single-handedly must have shown her work in and attended every woman's film festival in the 1970s while teaching baby dykes how to shoot in her living room. Hers was a surgical strike upon the criminal paucity of images of the unpunished, happy, or let's face it *living* lesbian. The experimental film world of the period afforded Hammer and only Hammer a hard won and, at times I imagine, lonely platform. In the 1970s, international women's collectives organized festivals, but the female queer voice was effectively muted under an avalanche of centrist feminist homophobia, legislative homophobia-enforced invisibility, poverty, naturalized hetero normatively, and fear.[1] Exposure to such work outside the major US and Canadian urban regions resided in Women's Art Collectives, University Film Clubs, struggling experimental film venues, and, on an international scale, in year-long touring programs of Feminist film from Western Europe. If you did not reside in Chicago, New York, San Francisco, or Los Angeles, mythologies were born and circulated before you ever laid eyes on the actual work. *Nun and Deviant* entered my own airspace in politically progressive Minneapolis through an ad hoc screening at Women's Art Resources of Minnesota (WARM), which was a collective organized specifically to give women space to exhibit, talk, and strategize.[2] WARM's existence dovetailed nicely into a subsequent 1977 US tour funded by the Goethe Institute of West German Feminist film, including the first US screenings of the work of Helke Sander, Helga Reidemeister, Jutta Brückner, and Helma Sanders-Brahms under the auspices of *Frauen und Film*, the German Feminist Film journal co-founded by

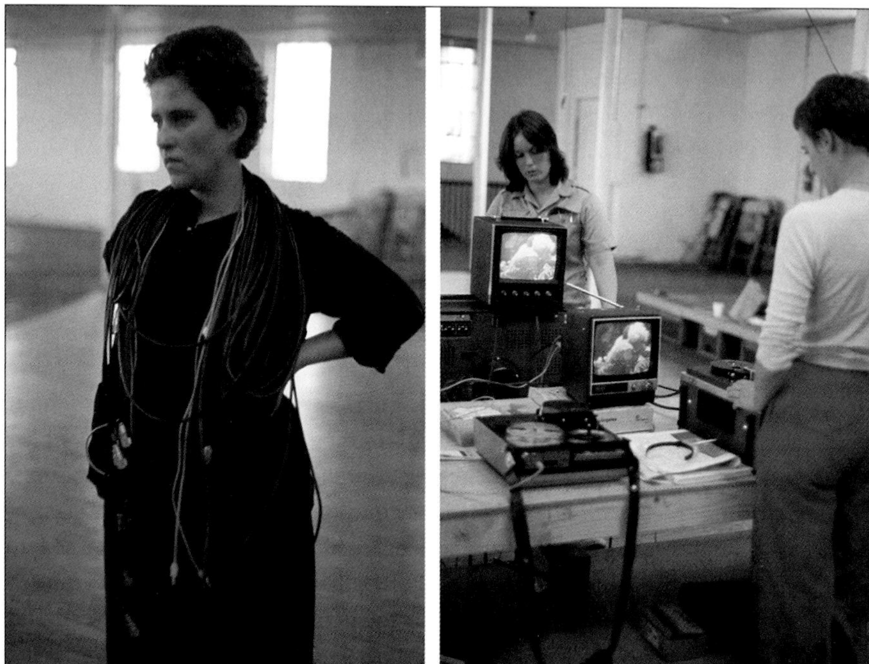

Figure 48. Left: Nancy Angelo, Summer Video Program, Woman's Building, Los Angeles, 1976. Right: Kate Horsfield and Candace Compton Pappas, Summer Video Program, Woman's Building, Los Angeles, 1976. Photos by Sheila Ruth.

Sander in 1974 and which preceded the US's *Camera Obscura* by a decade. The tour introduced a generation to *The All Around Reduced Personality (Die allseitig reduzierte Persönlichkeit – Redupers,*1977), which, along with Yvonne Rainer's *Film About a Woman Who ...* (1974) and Barbara Hammer's *Dyketactics* (1974) and *Women I Love* (1979), sculpts the territory into which *Nun and Deviant* and its performance-art driven nucleus is born.[3] Upon leaving a screening of the Goethe tour at the University of Minnesota, I was convinced, perhaps for the first time, that women directors actually existed and made radical work unencumbered by financial support and mega markets, and some of them looked decidedly queer. In my haphazardly developing consciousness, this revelation suggested only two possible destinations upon exiting the Midwest: Los Angeles or Berlin; Los Angeles because it nurtured the Woman's Building and taught women how to use the means of production in a production-laden town and offered access to equipment and community. The militancy of women teaching each other how to make work outside the academy, film school, and Hollywood (but also sometimes inside Hollywood), places the Woman's Building squarely into foundational counter culture aspirations that continue to deliver in myriad ways.

In the messy, impoverished, and funky digesting belly of the TV industry, alternative video production programs like the Summer Video Workshop (1976) and L.A. Woman's Video Center nestled within the ever-morphing framework of the Women's Building (WB, 1973–1991) and its creative and scrappy nurturing of multiple educational programs, groups, exhibitions, concerts, consciousness-raising groups (C.R.), publications, and creative agendas in the late 1970s and early 1980s.[4] Sheltering under its auspices were projects, collectives, and workshops including: the Feminist Studio Workshop (1973–1981), the Lesbian Art Project, (affectionately known as LAP (1977–78), the Women's Graphic Center, the Natalie Barney Collective (1977), the theater piece "An Oral History of Lesbianism" (1979), the Feminist Art Workers (1976–79), the Waitresses (1978–80) with Lily Tomlin as an occasional guest server, and the Sisters of Survival (1981–85). This was a legacy that produced myriad kinfolk and bad girl daughters everywhere, and was accompanied in institutional sisterhood by the Feminist Art Program, which was founded by Judy Chicago and Miriam Schapiro. The Feminist Art Program originated at California State University, Fresno, and later migrated to the California Institute of the Arts (CalArts) which ambitiously produced the multi-media "Womanhouse" in 1972.[5] Many of these progeny went on to become sleeper agents employed in diverse locations all the way from San Fernando porn factories to HBO executives and teachers of impressionable youth.

Unlike the game-changing battle, begun by East Coast headliners like the *Lavender Menace* (formed to combat mainstream feminism's professed horror of all things lesbianic), the Woman's Building integrated Sapphic leaders early and often. It benefited from a "can do" attitude directed at the necessity of constructing alternative and separatist women's spaces inclusive of, if not dominated by, dykes. From a complete program of studio classes, a graphic production center, writing workshops, and video instruction, archiving & production, it was less about gaining a seat at Feminism's banquet and more about using that seat to mess with expectations, while providing a steady stream of extra-institutional contact hours. The question of how to build voice and agency, and what to do with that visibility, was the linchpin of the space and the moment. It was intrinsically coupled with a nervy DIY aesthetic salted with inspirational Marxist precepts of controlling the means of production. The Woman's Building, wholly unconcerned with the dominant art world, which it identified as irrelevant, sexist, homophobic and exclusionary, knitted together women from broadcast television, Wicca, the margins of the Hollywood industry, independent theater, the poetry scene, lesbian separatists, stand up comedy, and the nascent West Coast women's music industry.[6]

The raw jaggy mess that early video was (control tracks wandering hither and yon), does remind one of the portapak's nature to act best as an overgrown tape recorder, perhaps explaining the move by poets and studio-constricted artists to give it a whirl, divorced from films' technological, financial, and historical demands. Video's birth is not so much an offshoot or warped stepdaughter of experimental film as it is the awkward spawn of experimental tape music, studio practice, and performance art, sprinkled with bits of broadcast television exceptions like Norman Lear's *The Jeffersons* (1975–85) and *Mary Hartman, Mary Hartman* (1976–78). These are disruptive inoculations into the grid, akin to cupcake jimmies disguising strychnine. Video history can be charted in lockstep with the development of the Sony corporation, studio-bound artists and poets who "canned" performances, *and* composers who overlaid the tenants of audiotape splicing onto video, all blithely ignoring and/or bypassing experimental film histories and strategies. Tape composers, corporate engineers, performers, surveillance technicians, activists, and composers in search of immediate replay form the armature of early video's field of vision. Folded into this ever-morphing mêlée are various riffs from standup comedy, Feminist consciousness-raising groups (C.R.), the Gay Liberation Front, *EST*, and the alternative theater. *Nun and Deviant* channels, complicates, and juggles all these shifting modalities. Performance-based video has its roots in the transfer of poets and visual artists, ensconced in their studios and glued to their writing tables – busting out the reel to reel. From Lynda Benglis's chilly *Female Sensibility* (1973) (a lesbo tale for another day) to Vito Acconci's *Red Tapes* (1976), the studio door is slightly cracked open, and the dematerialization of the art object takes a small step toward the cliff's edge. Marvelous, dreadful, dull, silly, and fabulous experiments in performance, installation, dance, and broadcast video emerge and turn into today's rubble boxes of magnetic filings, ephemera of which we can make whatever we desire. Magic entropic dust bunnies.

The ability of video portapaks to be *reasonably* portable, capable of instant playback and long running times, made it the receptacle of choice for performance and/or durational works for which film was prohibitive both technically and conceptually. That video should be a contingent fit with burgeoning Women's Art centers makes sense as it was quickly understood that unlike film production (even at the consumer level of Super-8 film), the means of production, projection (sharing), and distribution could be accessible to all women. Teaching a video skill set could be akin to the arming of a populace with self-made images. In reviving *Nun and Deviant*, I admit a prodigal return to sites of possibility and desire, a connection to the implicit promise of video and a naming or unearthing of queer possibilities. This is fueled by my own fascination for nuns of all persuasions and – the word *sexual* that is *always* implied *before* the word deviant and the erotic implications of the word "nun". In title alone one would want to claim tribal affiliation. In re-viewing, the work-nagging questions re-surface. What would a radical rethinking of deviance look[7] like beyond current mediated retread puppetry – a puppetry within which you can count the representations of queer women on one hand with most of the fingers of that hand submerged in the drecky trough of assimilationist capital wherein bobs *The L Word* and *Ellen* franchises? Granted, I bask in convenient hindsight – a little as if the promise of 1976 was a horizon of possibility within which multiple marginalized cultures learned how to name themselves unabashedly, forged some deliciously perverted templates and, rocketed by.

Nun and Deviant was a collaborative work between Nancy Angelo and Candace Compton Pappas, who both helped found and run the video workshop at the Woman's Building. This production and teaching collective included Kate Horsfield, who later helped begin the Video Data Bank in Chicago, and Jerri Allyn, a co-founder of the Waitresses and the Sisters of Survival and the current head of ACT: Artists, Community and Teaching program at the Otis College of Art and Design in Los Angeles. *Nun and Deviant* marks the commitment to tape of an ongoing performance persona "Sister Angelica Furiosa" developed by Angelo in multiple collaborative and solo works under the auspices of the Feminist Art Workers, including "Nothing to Say" and "The Swinging Nun" (1977), and in collaboration with Cheri Gaulke in "The Passion" (1979). Sister Furiosa eventually entered the anti-nuclear order the Sisters of Survival, founded by Nancy Angelo, Jerri Allyn, Anne Gauldin, Cheri Gaulke, and Sue Maberry in 1981.[8] She is a nun with a venerable history.

The *Nun and Deviant* begins with a series of negotiations both as internal monologues (voice over) and as a dialogue between the two artists as they morph into their respective personae. They help each other transform while asking crucial V.O. questions about making work:

> Can this tape possibly be of significance and meaning to an audience? I am afraid of being misunderstood. Boring. I am afraid of caring more about this work than Candace does. She feels displeased. Distant. I wonder what she is thinking? I want to draw her out of her silence. I am overly solicitous, overly protective of her. I want everything to be absolutely perfect for her. (Nancy, can I have my comb? Where is it?) Pause. She needs something! I don't know if I need anything. I'm being so strong. Can I prove myself? Am I too responsible? I have to be careful of her feelings. This has to be perfect.

They sit at the table in the alley and exchange items, glances at the mirror. The deviant takes cues from James Dean, dons a baseball jacket and slicks back her short hair telegraphing dyke code, gender nicely bent. She is camouflaging her

Figure 49. Nancy Angelo and Candace Compton Pappas. *Nun and Deviant*, 1976.

artist in order to unleash possibilities of courage, forthrightness, unapologetic chutzpah ... a true delinquency resplendent in drag. The nun needs help with her wimple. Each articulates the process of transformative collaboration as not only activating permissive and empowered personae, but as a way to use the work process itself to unpack the intricacies of themselves as artists and friends. They struggle to understand their position via à vis each other but also by investigating, by *doing in public* what is not allowed. What does playacting do; what do artists do? What do women do? What does art do?

> Being the nun and the deviant is divine permission. While the deviant takes care of the nasty, sordid, seamy parts of life, the nun has permission to remain aloof, pure, holy. I have permission to explore melodrama and fantasy. I feel vulnerable and strong as an artist; as a deviant I feel ugly, uncomfortable. Working with a nun gives me protection and permission. I can be whatever I want.
>
> I can say whatever I want. I can be loved.

Both the nun and deviant check to see if the other is complete, and then move toward their close-up. The deviant resembles today's boi, boy but not boy, tomboy not a man, not drag exactly but a queer chameleon. The nun looks like any nun except she is angry, and her address of disdain, doubt, and fury – nose pressed against lens so to speak – eggs the audience on and implicitly implicates all of us in the vagaries of gendered power relationships and concomitant failures at confronting our own complicity. The nun's voice is different from her artist's voice, which is characterized by quiet consideration of the feelings of the artist/deviant. The deviant moves from bragging about what she "did for the revolution" into apology and vulnerability, a tomboy revealing a soft center and armored exterior. Each fully-costumed character takes turns occupying upstage to speak intimately with us, using the close-up of the lens space for position, platform, and regard. Our nun marches up to the camera, rosary flying in the wind.

> Are you there? Can you hear me? Listen to me: I am fed up. I am fed up. Don't foist your expectations of nun-ness on me! I'm not the nun you want me to be. I am not the nun you think I am. Don't expect me to take care of you! Don't expect me to take care of all your problems, to make you feel good, absolve you of your guilt.

Because we have seen them in an ersatz downstage/backstage dressing each other

Figure 50. *Nothing To Say*, Feminist Art Worker's. Nancy Angelo's "Sister Angelica Furisosa" performance persona 1977.

and then transforming from creators to characters, we are eased into the theatrical, let in on the secret and invited to play. The stage, an alley that occasionally is interrupted by a delivery truck, is makeshift, derelict, faceless, activated only by energized and energizing chameleons.

The nun's initial monologue is back staged or upstaged by the deviant smashing plates on the back of the alley wall, forming a soundtrack of controlled explosion. Not surprisingly, the nun on the lam, upon relinquishing upstage to the deviant, takes up the smashing duties. They squint into the lens to make sure we are there. The deviant offers evidence.

> One night Chris Mancini and Bob Spot called me and they said let's commit a crime. I said sure. We went and committed grand theft. We stole electric typewriters and mimeograph machines from the Barrant Park Elementary School. For the Revolution. We took them to a house that belonged to a Stanford student who was in SDS and they had machine guns there. I wasn't scared; nope, I wasn't scared. I've committed grand theft for the revolution. Yup and I've shoplifted. I shoplifted everything, everything I could in high school. Everything I could get my hands on.

To deploy the term deviant is to track into a hidden language. This deviant places herself as perhaps a boy, a juvenile, kin to a rebel with no cause, except her/his gender flake won't allow a single read. This boi is tired of being a good girl and says as much. Deviant is a label that can be followed by any number of modifiers, but really implies a queering attached to any normative label: a good girl teetering into a multitude of unsanctioned dimensions – queer, fat, oversexed, too smart, lesbian, androgynous, too tall, polymorphous perverse, just plain perverse, insane, troubled, bad to the bone, evil – a deviation from a hyper fabricated "normal". This American "normal" is an oddly sourced hybridity of Wally Beaver, Levittown, and Valium. Our nun figure suggests a back-story of rumored lesbian tendencies, porno set-ups, repression, and educational power that she too is trying to simultaneously accept and reject while diverting the daydreams of the societal good girl. The characters' direct address makes it clear that all containers hold traps. In this alley ids will be blown.

Eventually the deviant insists that he/she isn't really that bad, and the nun expresses her weariness at being a good cop. Costume makes playacting transparent; we are not convinced that this a real nun or a real deviant (already an out-of-date term recomputed as a code for queerness). Beginning the tape with dress up and identity dialogue, as well as negotiations about power dynamics and exchange, places the work in an experimental rubric, an artifact, if you will, of performative chance-taking unencumbered because of an empowering cloak of assumed character as agent of release and camouflage.

> I am a nun of my own design. I've survived. I've survived lots of things. I've survived a lifetime of illness. Weakness. Unhappiness. Suicide. Death. I've made it. I am strong. Resilient. I'm making it. I'm a nun of my own design. Following my own definition. I'm creating my life, as I want it to be.

The nun smiles and covers up the lens with the lens cap. Personae are put away. The lens is uncapped for the credits, written in chalk on the street, while both artists clean up piles of smashed plates. Good girls may clean, but the intimation is always that bad girls can return unannounced at any moment.[9]

I am impatient for Queer back-stories, impatient in having to continue to forage for radical dyke history. If pushed I will make it up, draw connections that I fabricate from the thinnest of threads, strain to conjure the back-story into visibility. Fairytale, revision, or projection, these images can handle all I invest in them. I need to steep in this nostalgic and irrational glow in order to brew an antidote to *The Real L Word* and its product placement wedding contract devoid of content and politics, a void of melodrama and self absorption unable to move anywhere outside its own circle jerk where "Real" is unclear and gasping for air. For me it is more than possible to desire the nun *and* the deviant as they suggest myriad reconfigurings of being, of possibilities to be tried on. Playacting becomes a tool of re-mapping. If both the nun and the deviant share your bed, are you the object of conversion, or are they?

Why can't we make a revolution? Why can't we posit cultural production that is not solely marked by the market and our grateful complacent neo-liberal bend over – tossing out any dream of morphing oppositional structures? *Nun and Deviant* returns me – at least momentarily – to a certain possibility. When I came across the image of Nancy Angelo with a nest of cables around her neck I added her without asking permission to my pantheon of heroines located just to the left of Patti Smith's *Horses*. Accepting the invitation into the tent of deviancy, I will follow an angry nun. What *Nun and Deviant* means to me – is perhaps also of importance to others. Jill Johnston departed the planet while I was in the midst of thinking about a world of nuns with assault weapons and deviants in quiet contemplation, awash in a sea of portapaks, costumes, conversions, and conversations. In archive diving I found a photograph of a bespangled hip hugger-clad Johnston at the Woman's Building the year *Nun and Deviant* was made. She, like our nun and deviant, was kin, beloved, and lover to mess makers everywhere (who only sometimes deign to clean up), a courtly jester coyote starring in my own overheated bicentennial dream. I am heartened that all these people temporarily occupied the same space/time continuum, at least one night long ago. Jill, Nancy, and Candace populate a possibility confirmed in longing hindsight, and dreamed in an ongoing ecstatic delirium that simply cannot, for present day sanity's sake, terminate. There is something about a nun, about a deviant, that can never be safely corralled or defined as they continue to shimmer between boundaries.

Notes

1. For a no holds barred and bracing account of this battle, consult Barbara Hammer, *HAMMER! Making Movies Out of Sex and Life* (New York: The Feminist Press at CUNY 2010).
2. WARM was founded in 1973 and is currently alive and kicking with a vibrant exhibition and mentorship program.
3. Marc Silberman, "Film and Feminism in Germany Today Part 1: From the Outside Moving In", *Jump Cut* 27 (1982): 41–42. For a more detailed introduction to the women's movement in West Germany, see *New German Critique* 13, Special Feminist Issue (Winter 1978). For an overview of this generation of women filmmakers in West Germany, see *Camera Obscura* 6 (Fall 1980).
4. The Woman's Building was founded in 1973 by Judy Chicago, Arlene Raven, and Sheila Levrant de Bretteville. For a history of the WB and video in terms of video practice see Alexandra Juhasz, "A Process Archive: The Grand Circularity of Woman's Building Video", in *Doin' It in Public: Feminism and Art and the Woman's Building*, eds. Sondra Hale and Terry Wolverton (Los Angeles: Otis College of Art and Design, 2011), 97–121.
5. See Johanna Demetrakas wonderful film, *Womanhouse* (1974), which includes the installation and performance pieces as well as interviews with the participants.
6. See Terry Wolverton, *Insurgent Muse: Life and Art At The Woman's Building* (San Francisco: City Lights, 2002), and the WB's digital archive lovingly overseen by Sue Maberry and housed at Otis College of Art and Design in Los Angeles.
7. For a brief overview of video art and technology in its heyday, see the introduction to Michael Renov and Erika Suderburg's *Resolutions: Contemporary Video Practices* (Minneapolis: University of Minnesota Press, 1995).
8. Video histories of many of these artists, collectives, programs, and activists connected to the WB in Los Angeles and the Feminist Studio Workshop. It hosts as wonderful interviews with many of the main culprits deserving of sainthood in our partially factual tale can be found here: http://www.otis.edu/ben-maltz-gallery/womans-building-video-her-stories.

9. For a contextualization of *Nun and Deviant* see Cecilia Dougherty, "Stories From A Generation: Video Art at the Woman's Building", in *Doin' It in Public: The Woman's Building In Contemporary Culture*, ed. Hale and Wolverton (Los Angeles: Otis College of Art and Design, 2011), 303–325.

27 Currents Direct and Alternating: *Water and Power* and Other Works by Pat O'Neill

Grahame Weinbren

Almost all the water used by the inhabitants of Greater Los Angeles is brought in. With around four million people in the city itself, and close to fourteen million if the neighboring urban areas are included, this is no small undertaking. If the extensive system of dams, pumps, and conduits were to fail, the area would revert quickly to the condition of a desert. The *Los Angeles Department of Water and Power* (LADWP) is the utility company that manages the distribution of water and also electrical power. In 2003, the LADWP provided more than 200 billion US gallons of water through 7,226 miles of pipe, 48% of it from the northern mountain ranges.

While Pat O'Neill's film *Water and Power* incorporates many images of the Los Angeles water and power systems from the Basin up to the Sierra Nevada mountains, it is not quite right to think of the water and power infrastructure as the "subject" of the film, in the sense that a documentary has a subject. *Water and Power* does not provide any factual data about the LADWP, as, for example, does Ross Spears's documentary *The Electric Valley* (1983), about the Tennessee Valley Authority. As a major part of the background of the film, the public utilities network of Los Angeles might be thought of as an aspect of the film's unconscious. It affects and sometimes determines what is on the screen, just as the "unconscious" in Freud's terminology is a shorthand metaphor for the systematic production of ideas and mental images out of lost memories and desires, in that the repressed material never becomes the unfiltered object of thought. So although *Water and Power* is intricately connected with the region that Pat O'Neill has inhabited his entire life and whose geography, landscapes, and cityscapes, as well as its culture and industry, have inspired him, the film's inspiration is not its subject. Like many works of art, the film points only indirectly to the material that triggered it. The massive water and power systems of Greater Los Angeles occasionally surface in the film, like forgotten incidents dredged up during psychoanalysis.

To put it more generally, the concept of "subject" does not quite apply to the film. There is always something inexplicable about a Pat O'Neill work, a sense of forces that hold its disparate elements together; but, like gravity, these forces are felt but remain unstated and unseen, elusive to formulation or conceptualization. This paper hopes to address a double question about O'Neill's films: What unifies them, what transforms them from a collage of disconnected elements into a satisfying whole? And what, beyond this question, is the nature of the enigma that characterizes each of his films? One's impression is that in the layered material there is always something held back, something that it ought to be possible to uncover and expose, but, like a repressed trauma, constantly resists.

Each of O'Neill's films is an independent work, emphasizing some issues over others. In many cases a specific film is clustered around a single concept. *Downwind* (1972), for example, presents different types of exhibition, from a cat show to museum curiosities, from gogo girls to natural wonders, all allegories for display, exhibition or spectacle. *Decay of Fiction*'s (2002) reference is the Hollywood *film noir*, appropriating its structural elements, its costumed actors playing fictional characters with scripted dialogue and expressive musical scoring; the film binds these elements within a sophisticated visual and conceptual framework. Some of O'Neill's films are organized by structural tropes. Each of the seven scenes of *Saugus Series* (1974), for example, consists of a single image without edits, incorporating three or four components that, in the real world of physics, geometry, and logic, are incompatible, but combine in each scene into a coherent, if impossible, unit. The central concepts change from film to film, and of course there is a substantial development, evolving interests, and an increasing sophistication of technique, technology, and aesthetics over the artist's fifty year career. But at the same time O'Neill, like many great artists, is drawn repeatedly to particular images, subjects, methodologies, and visual styles, which recur throughout the explicit themes of his films.

Taking *Water and Power* as a base starting point, this paper reviews certain leitmotifs, styles, concerns, approaches, and investigations that re-appear in the

O'Neill oeuvre. However, the particular distinction of an O'Neill film lies in the interaction of a multiplicity of types of investigation that are rarely, if ever, incorporated in single works of other cinema artists. Each film combines materials that usually characterize very different aesthetic approaches, bringing them together in ways that are unique and brash.

One of O'Neill's recurring devices is a kind of impropriety, a defiance of conventional values, most obvious in the films produced in the 1960s and 70s, but present in later works as well. *Downwind* opens with an episode, hardly more than a gesture, of rapid copulation by a pair of rhesus monkeys, the male aggressively staring into the camera as if challenging the viewer to adopt a moral position towards his display of sexual prowess. Another example is the opening scene of *Foregrounds* (1978), which shows O'Neill sitting calmly in the center of what appears to be his back yard. At first viewing, one is distracted by the antique car and lush vegetation in the complex, calm scenario, failing to notice the huge phallic formation in the arrangement of rocks and scraggly undergrowth in the foreground of the image.

Another type of brazenness throughout the O'Neill oeuvre is the incorporation of images from popular culture, low-end advertising, cartoons, high-school educational films, and daytime network television. O'Neill is hardly the only artist to incorporate subversive and lowbrow elements. Outrageous subversion, often sexual but also political and iconoclastic, is characteristic of a number of well-known West Coast artists (Mike Kelley, Paul McCarthy, and Robert Heinecken to name but three). Though often highly sophisticated in technology and craft, their iconoclasm is rarely, if ever, accompanied by an exploration of formal or structural properties of the artist's chosen medium. O'Neill frequently combines both "funkiness" (to use the vernacular) or "abjectness" (a more fashionable term) with refined aesthetic explorations. For example, his films frequently include formal investigations into the visual logics of the cinema image. Later in this paper I will cite several examples of O'Neill's unflagging interest in the interplay between the material flatness and the perceived depth of the cinematic image. However, one can find oneself ignoring these explorations, captivated by the films' playful irreverence. Or vice versa.

Yet it must be emphasized that any attempt at reductive analysis of an O'Neill film is a recipe for failure; the pleasures one finds in these works are inseparable from their excesses. Confronted with multiple factors simultaneously, factors that are often contradictory or inconsistent but always intertwined and phenomenologically interconnected, the viewer must navigate through images, concepts, and stylistic traits that do not support one another and require different kinds of attention, all the while caught up in a fast-flowing cinematic current. It is like navigating the rapids of a rock-strewn river while attempting a scientific categorization of its ecology. Focusing on one concern can be a distraction from others – yet O'Neill's films are equally a demonstration of the capability of the human mind to hold logically incompatible ideas simultaneously – as in the disavowal of the fetishist discussed with relish by Freud and others: "I know perfectly well, but ..."

This skeletal preamble is presented by way of warning: that a descriptive analysis of Pat O'Neill's films is necessarily reductive and, as Gödel demonstrated of arithmetic, fundamentally incomplete, largely because of the very qualities that I will attempt to describe in the following descriptive analysis.

I. *Water and Power*: Opening Section

At the beginning of *Water and Power* there is a sequence of three scenes that exemplify qualities that characterize much of O'Neill's work. The images share a common base: the variations in light and shadow generated by the periodic orbits of the sun or the moon in relation to the earth, transformations of illumination beyond human control.

The first scene consists of a translucent window filmed over a period of hours, soft light modeling the textures of its uneven surface. The plane of the window is parallel to the camera plane, so the window reiterates the cinema screen, forming a second projection surface within depicted space. Several hours, perhaps an entire day, is compressed into a minute or two. For much of the scene, the light source, presumably the sun, is behind the glass, visible both by transmission and through its illumination of the pebbled glass.

Also a record of effects of the sun's motion, the second scene is more complicated. In this case the light source itself is not visible, but registered in the shadows of door and window openings generated by the changing light on the wall behind a plain desk and chair. The image echoes the previous scene, the far interior wall similarly parallel to the camera plane, and again functioning as an avatar for the actual projection screen. The presentation of the wall as a cinema screen is reinforced by another quality. At first it is semi-transparent like dirty glass, as if we can see through it to clouds scudding across the sky, their rate of speed exactly matching that of the movement of the shadows of the door and window. After a short period the transparency abates and the wall becomes opaque, revealing its stained surface, its abandonment and dereliction, ravaged by time like the cobbled window of the first shot.

The third scene is a direct image of a light source, in this instance the moon, its motion across a dark sky accelerated, referring directly to the orbit of an astronomical body and the effect of its travel on the objects it illuminates and the shadows it generates.

Instantaneously and effortlessly, the viewer takes in all these aspects of the three scenes. As is often true of visual experience, the verbal description of it is prolix and enervating, the details absorbed by visual perception grossly exceeding what can be captured in words. With O'Neill's films the labors of description are heightened by the fact that one cannot fall back on story or documentary "content" as a shorthand indicator of perceptual experience. The films are primarily audio-visual explorations, difficult if not impossible to pin down in language. Their power is in the experience.

Notwithstanding its resistance to a semantic or narrative analysis, *Water and Power* is a coherent work. Variations on, or at least relatives of the three images described, occur throughout the film. The sense of unity and continuity of the film is determined by the repetition of these elements. In order to lay a foundation for an analysis of O'Neill's work, I'll start by indicating some general characteristics of the three scenes, qualities that frequently re-appear not only in *Water and Power*, but throughout the O'Neill oeuvre.

Common to the three scenes is the travel of light and shadow marking the passage of time in an interior or exterior, abandoned, ravaged, or ruined architectural space. The man-made structure is often set against a natural environment, which can be centuries or millennia older, but never in a state of dereliction. This combination is a staple of O'Neill's films since the early 1970s. *The Decay of Fiction* (2002), for example, includes numerous splendid images of accelerated natural light movement through neglected, half-ruined spaces. The single location, and indeed the primary protagonist of the film, is the Ambassador Hotel in its fading magnificence on the verge of demolition, while its gardens and the lush vegetation of the (constantly watered!) Southern California environment is not affected by the hotel's dilapidation. Half a decade before *The Decay of Fiction*, *Trouble in the Image* (1997) includes a prescient example of a luxurious bathroom, now lapsed into disrepair, filmed at a slow frame rate so that the light crossing it as the day passes creates changing highlights and shadows, which invest the simple architecture of the room with an elegance and a nostalgic beauty. A window functions like a projection screen within the room, revealing a dynamic natural landscape that cannot possibly be the actual view through the window.

Low frame-rate recording, often identified as the "time-lapse effect", is used not only to capture natural change in architectural spaces, too slow to be perceptible

Figure 51. Seated Figure, *Water and Power*.

in real time, but also as a means of defining the terrestrial qualities of broad exterior locations, both in cityscapes and in the great desert landscapes of the Western United States. In the latter, the movement of natural light emphasizes dimensional surface topographies, transforming mountains and buildings into sculptural objects. *Saugus Series* (1974) and *Sidewinders Delta* (1976) both include many examples of this phenomenon. Notable are those filmed in Monument Valley and other iconic western landscapes.

This leads to the second quality of the three scenes at the beginning of *Water and Power* and characteristic of the O'Neill oeuvre: challenges to physics and natural law. In this case it is the mercurial opacity of the interior architectural wall, the landscape beyond it partially visible for a period and then obscured. This quality might be more generally described as a portrayal of a world characterized by alternative laws of optics, in which, in this example, the transparency of solids is a variable property like temperature. Variable transparency of a man-made structure first occurs in a scene of *Sidewinders Delta* in an image of a small house in the desert, its walls semi-transparent to a distant mountain range, but opaque to traffic that passes on the highway between the house and the mountains. A different challenge to natural law, in this case botany, is the "anti-chameleon" cactus, also in *Sidewinders Delta,* whose color, rather than matching that of the illuminating light bulb as it changes hue, is its contrary: when the light-bulb turns red, the cactus turns green, purple elicits yellow, and so on.

A third general quality is the sense of continuity from one image to the next: the three *Water and Power* scenes depict in three different ways the motion of light from the sun or moon, and there is in each case a careful match between the characteristics of movement (i.e., direction and speed) within each image but also from one image to the next. The illusion of continuity produced by these matching motions, an effect familiar in many genres of cinema, appears throughout *Water and Power.*

The fourth general quality can be best described with Clement Greenberg's expression "all-over composition".[1] One of the distinctive visual traits of O'Neill's films is the utilization of the entire available screen area, without investing one segment with more significance than another. There is no hierarchy of screen space, challenging standard practice of composition for the screen. In the second *Water and Power* shot described above, the fleeting shadows draw attention to one area after another. Unlike mainstream cinema, in which there is usually a specific area of interest that renders the remainder of the screen "background", O'Neill works like a modernist painter, the picture plane becoming a surface of overall composition.

As described so far, the exploration of cinematic territory in the first three scenes of *Water and Power* is unified and coherent ... as long as we ignore the accompanying soundtrack. A dramatic track lifted from a Hollywood film, probably of the 1940s, endows the abandoned space with a melancholic tension. The sound is a fragment of a first-person narrative occurring in a room, perhaps a hotel room, and we take for granted that it is the very room currently on screen. An unseen character delivers a guilt-ridden monologue, with dramatic suspense music heightening the already high drama of his anxiety. The rhythm of the speech and music, drawn out and tinged with desperation, magically matches the movement of light in the room. The visual qualities described above remain primary components of the viewer's experience. But though there is a rhythmic and tonal resonance between the image and the soundtrack, each requires a different mode of viewing. The inclusion of the narrative element in the audio requires a different type of spectatorship, that of engagement with a story. We are thrust into an arena of inconsistency, unable to settle into one mode of perception or another.

Throughout *Water and Power*, in earlier works, and playing a central role in the later *The Decay of Fiction*, narrative fragments are included, sometimes spoken, sometimes in text on screen. Compelling though these story-fragments are, they rarely deliver the particular satisfactions of narrative, such as identification, character and plot development, and closure. However, this lack is not by any measure a negative aspect of the films, disappointing or incoherent, but rather suggests that narrative has an unusual function in the O'Neill oeuvre, as a counterpoint to the lush visuality of the works. I'll return to this point later.

The rhythmic clatter of a train's metal wheels along the rails accompanies the third shot, the moon's travel across a dark sky. The sound effectively matches the lunar motion, but modifies one's perception of it. Again, one is caught in a space of inconsistency – the desire to indulge in the pleasure of the moon's travel as a natural phenomenon, but jogged into a contradiction, experiencing the motion as mechanical, the planet driven not by the mysterious force of gravity but by the prosaic action of a motor. The moon has been transformed from an element of nature to an element of cinema. This is a template for one of O'Neill's basic strategies, used throughout his work and in a number of different ways. In summary, it involves destabilizing the comfort of settling into a scene and appreciating it as a visual exploration of cinematic properties, an unfolding narrative, or a mild challenge to upright values. A single scene can contain all these elements, clashing against one another. We are on edge. Each interpretation is immediately undercut by incompatible alternatives. We are caught in the phenomenology of an enigma.

II. *Water and Power:* Performance and Narrative

Much of *Water and Power* incorporates individuals performing for the camera, paralleling standard narrative filmmaking practice. We see musicians, costumed performers, a painter's nude model, and individuals undertaking repetitive actions that have no clear intention other than that of creating presence and movement for the camera. These images are often shot at an under-cranked speed with extended shutter times, so that they produce streaking traces of light, with each frame of the film marking time *periods* rather than *instants*. These traces emphasize the passage of time as much as the pro-filmic events. The pure visuality of these shots overwhelms the sense of the screen as a window into situations and events. O'Neill's interactions with the tropes of narrative cinema serve both to acknowledge his recognition of the tradition as an aspect of his work and to indicate his separation from that tradition. His films also frequently contain archival scenes from Hollywood films, presented both as objects of ridicule and as layers in the multiple semi-abstract composites of movement and light. While the abstraction is partly undercut by the theatrical quality of the movies from which they are drawn, these qualities are never completely obliterated even when subjected to substantial manipulation. Thus one senses the specter of Hollywood hovering over much of O'Neill's work.

Actors and musicians performing for the camera and in appropriated scenes from Hollywood films are not the only images of humanity that appear in *Water and Power*. There are street scenes, shot, presumably, without the crowds in them aware that they are being filmed, for example, from a camera position in a window above the street. A dynamic throughout the film is between things (people, objects, scenarios) designed, placed, or created to be filmed, and those that O'Neill finds like a documentarian, and sometimes records with the same techniques of severe under cranking and long exposure times for each frame so that, when projected, time is accelerated and light-stains are produced. The two kinds of image are frequently combined, and we get a sense of the two major cinematic traditions, descendants of the Lumière brothers and Méliès, coming together in a single frame, another type of internal contradiction that the viewer is invited to navigate. It is not that O'Neill is either questioning the truth value of documentary photography, or pointing at the indexical photographic underpinning of narrative construction. On the contrary, he is emphasizing and taking advantage of the contrast between the two approaches and again placing the viewer in an unstable equilibrium of reception.

The same considerations apply to the fragments of narrative included, both in text on screen and on the soundtrack. They are in one way a reference to the Hollywood movie and an invitation to experience the work through the filter of narrative cinema, although with a denial of its usual satisfactions. O'Neill accepts that he is making use of the same medium as Hollywood, but without the criteria of success of that culture. (This applies even more emphatically to *Decay of Fiction*). There are also references to the modernist tradition in visual art (consider the famous Brassai photograph of Matisse with his nude model); it is as if O'Neill is placing his work at the meeting point of these opposing cultures and forging out of these two bases a new center-point for art in which the medium is the moving image.

The broader program in which O'Neill is invested is at bottom a proposal for an art of film that is distinct from the accepted experimental film tradition. As part of this investigation, he uses himself as a subject to suggest the nature of the enterprise, as a way of portraying the character of the artist who makes the kind of art to which he is committed. There are self-portraits throughout the oeuvre – often shown as hooded, naked, battered, and buffered by forces beyond his control, temporarily blinded or in an ecstatic semi-conscious dance. It is a portrayal of a character akin to Silenus, a figure in well-known works by Peter Paul Rubens and his one-time studio assistant Anthony Van Dyck.

Silenus is a minor Bacchic character of Roman mythology, to whom Virgil pays an undue amount of attention, endowing him with symbolic significance for artistic production.[2] In a drunken stupor, Silenus is awoken by two shepherds and a nymph, who bind him with vines, smear fruit juices on his forehead, and force him to sing. Out of a semi-conscious, ecstatic state, Silenus produces compelling tales, one after another, about the creation of the world and the interactions of the gods and man. Virgil and Rubens were both rational and productive artists, the former known as an obsessive editor of his writing, the latter as a canny businessman. In short, neither was a stream-of-consciousness virtuoso in the mold of Silenus. Svetlana Albers interprets Rubens's portrayal of Silenus as empathetic: "[...] in his identification with the disempowered, fleshy, drunken singer Silenus, Rubens evokes a desire for access to a potent, ecstatic mode of creating".[3] But it is a mode of creating that was most likely not available to Rubens as the most successful artist of his time, an entrepreneur and director of a major studio employing over one hundred artists.

Like Rubens, Pat O'Neill ran a successful business for a number of years. His practice with the optical printer involves precise calculations and careful settings – one small error can invalidate many hours of work. At the same time, O'Neill's irrational images must be conjured up in the kind of ecstasy that one imagines for the half-inebriated Silenus. These images of the naked, clumsy, dancing artist, played by himself, speak to the double-nature of O'Neill's approach, based on two irreconcilable visions of the artist's practice. In contrast to the artist as an inspired semi-conscious Silenus, we often meet O'Neill through his hands, hands that either manipulate the image or form an element of it. A simple example is in *Sidewinder's Delta*, in which O'Neill shakes persimmon-laden branches on a table in front of him until the fruit separates. In *Downwind*, the artist's cotton-gloved hands snap like a flamenco dancer's, apparently conducting the cuts and flashes of the scene behind; and in the opening scene of *Saugus Series* an ink-covered thumb traces a wobbly line in front of melting painted rectangles, which at the end of the scene become a rock-strewn lake. Thus two types of self-portrait of the artist appear throughout the work – the craftsman dependent on the deliberate work of his hands, and, in contrast, the inspired weaver of tales and images beyond his control, but wondrous, captivating, transformative, and requiring labor and craft for their realization. Between exerting total control and operating out of the forces of the unconscious, the model of the artist for O'Neill is a binary, inconsistent image, the two opposite vectors communing without settling. It should be emphasized that O'Neill's primary presentation of his position and his identity in relation to the films is as an *artist* – not a filmmaker or a director, producer or "member of a team", and depicting himself as both inebriated storyteller and craftsman dependent on skillful hands reinforces this reading.

III. *Water and Power:* Depiction / Representation

The great British aesthetician Richard Wollheim forcefully argues that one of the deep pleasures of painting as an art is in the two-fold nature of seeing: in a painting we see both the surface of the canvas as well as the depth depicted, relying on the many manners by which marked surfaces represent (perspective, color, focus, obtrusion, etc.), and this experience of "seeing surface *as* depth" is fundamental to understanding how art operates on us.[4] Attempts to discover double-aspect seeing in the cinematic image is one of the repeated themes of the O'Neill oeuvre. Again and again in his films we find images that, if stilled, would rest perceptually on the surface of the screen – silhouettes, blocks of color, non-depictive particle fields. His hypnotic 1967 film *Screen* is practically a demonstration of the inescapable dimensionality of the cinematic. The image consists entirely of rapidly moving film grain, yet despite its radical non-depictiveness it is impossible not to see the agitated surface as defining a recessive space. The speckles simply do not cohere on the plane of the projection screen, as they would if they were painted on it, but, to our eyes, occupy a space behind the screen plane. A later scene in *Water and Power* is composed of a number of elements that are pure surface: red, yellow, blue, and black undifferentiated blocks of color. Yet we cannot see them except as existing in a dimensional depictive space. The circle, describing an elliptical pattern, can only be seen as moving closer and further, even without any other indications of the z-axis, such as changes in light or focus.

Perceptual psychology accounts for this phenomenon through the proposal that cinematic motion is indistinguishable from real motion – to our eyes it *is* actual motion, not a picture or illusion of motion, unlike, for example, volume and spatial relationships on the screen which are *representations* of these properties of the real world. Cinema motion is, to the human eye, real motion. The eminent researcher J. J. Gibson took pains to demonstrate that one of the most efficient ways we comprehend depth in the world is by means of movement.[5] If cinematic motion is real for the perceptual system, the perception of depth, which depends on the perception of motion, will share in this sense of reality. Thus the third dimension, the z-axis, is inescapable in the cinematic image, as O'Neill demonstrates with great aplomb in multiple examples.

This is the very investigation inherent to the works of the late modernist painters, and it activates the same deep satisfactions. Except that, again, these investigations in O'Neill's work are always in tension: with the subject matter, the soundtrack, and the context of the images. Here is the greatness of O'Neill – a simple demonstration of these psycho-perceptual effects would be limiting and educational. His technique is to embed such demonstrations within his other concerns, which do not by any means support a formalist modernist outlook, and indeed, as I am arguing here, conflict with such an outlook in many ways. It is at this juncture that we are at the central enigma of the O'Neill work, in the fact that we cannot settle on one familiar mode of seeing at the expense of others. The combinations of multiple genre-crossing explorations are the works' distinction.

IV. The Consolidation of *Water and Power*

Given the knots of contradictory forces pulling at the viewer, what holds *Water and Power* together? What makes it a film, rather than a series of sketches?

Returning to the opening of this essay, the most obvious candidate is in the particularity of the several subjects addressed, which resurface throughout the film: water and power as metaphors, as abstract qualities, and as utilities necessary for the great urban environments of Southern California; performances especially for the camera (by musicians, the nude model, simple actions repeated, such as the man who repeatedly walks towards his own shadow, O'Neill himself dancing like a bear, and the strangest, three actors costumed as lazy light bulbs); city images shot from different levels and at different scales; natural phenomena of the Western United States; derelict architectural structures, self-portraits – these themes are the "subjects" of the film, insofar as that term applies. Images of these subjects are woven into a single fabric together with repeated interstitial elements: rooms bathed in changing light, fragments of narrative, the sun's or moon's trajectory either directly or abstracted into looping curves.

Repeating techniques and technologies are applied separately and in combination to these images: time lapse, computer controlled camera movement, layering and embedding of disparate images one on another, the continuation of movement from shot to shot.

The tripartite structures described at the beginning of this essay are a fundamental architectural form throughout the work, both in sets of three shots and reiterated in images composed of three elements in an uneasy combination. The sense of the triptych endows the film with coherence, even if the viewer is not consciously aware of the structure – it plays at a lower level of consciousness.

Finally there is the overall arc of the work – the accelerating montage, whereby all the elements introduced throughout the film tend to pile up and accumulate as the film progresses towards its finale – which is, as we might expect, a bookend, a variation on the first image described, a shallow room, its walls mildewed and decayed, now with a campfire burning in the center of the floor. With this final image *Water and Power* leaves the viewer with a satisfying sense of closure: the culmination of a journey replete with disjunctive chords that play against one another but are finally resolved in a return to a variation on the image with which it began.

Notes

1. Clement Greenberg, "The Crisis of the Easel Picture" (1948), *Art and Culture: Critical Essays* (Boston: Beacon Press, 1961 & 1985), 155: " ... the all-over, 'decentralized,' 'polyphonic' picture that relies on a surface knit together of identical or closely similar elements which repeat themselves without marked variation from one edge of the picture to the other. It is the kind of picture that dispenses with beginning, middle, end ... "
2. Virgil, *Eclogue VI*, "The Song of Silenus". http://www.poetryintranslation.com/PITBR/Latin/VirgilEclogues.htm#_Toc533239267, accessed 17 January 2014.
3. Svetlana Albers, *The Making of Rubens* (New Haven: Yale University Press, 1995), 153.
4. Richard Wollheim, *Painting as an Art* (Princeton, NJ: Princeton University Press, Bollingen Series, 1990).
5. James J. Gibson, *The Ecological Approach To Visual Perception* (Hove, UK: Psychology Press, Taylor and Francis Group, 1986).

PART III
SCREENINGS

28 *Alternative Projections* Screening Series

Adam Hyman

Introduction

From the start, the screening series for *Alternative Projections* was the anchor of the whole project. Pacific Standard Time was geared towards exhibitions, and the Filmforum exhibition was this series, with the research, papers, and oral histories all supporting the films and providing a resource for critics, scholars, and filmmakers to learn more about the films. In our original proposal, we estimated that we would present sixteen different programs. We ended up presenting twenty-eight different shows, including one marathon, and even had two additional programs curated that we couldn't fit in the calendar! In sum, artists made a large number of interesting films in Los Angeles from 1945 to 1980, far more than are widely-known.

We committed ourselves to focusing on short films, including only two works that might be defined as features, Stanton Kaye's *Georg* and Chick Strand's *Soft Fiction*, due to the importance of each. We also decided not to have any single-filmmaker screenings, instead emphasizing themes, approaches, or groups. Our choice and *Alternative Projections*'s strong archival component allowed us to go deeper within the period we were covering, 1945–1980, than did Filmforum's earlier series, *Scratching the Belly of the Beast* (1994). We rediscovered and presented a great many films that hadn't been seen in decades, often located by personal relationships or by the discovery of old program notes that made us curious. It took many hours of viewing by Mark Toscano, our guest curators, and myself of the films we located or knew in order to devise these programs, and to define some contexts that we felt would enrich their viewing. As you can see, we included some films in more than one screening to demonstrate how all these films could be approached in multiple ways. Full notes for the series, including individual film descriptions, can be found at http://www.alternativeprojections.com/screening-series/, and an ever-growing filmography of works made in LA is at http://alternativeprojections.com/data/films.php.

Our series was preceded by a REDCAT screening dedicated to films by Chick Strand. Although it was not part of our series per se, it felt related to it, paying tribute to this incredible and influential artist whom we lost just a few years ago. Our kickoff weekend in October 2011 included two great shows, one of early experimental work, including several classics, and another of animation from Cal Arts in the 1970s. I felt that we were really onto something good when, after the fourth show, *Early Abstractions*, filmmaker Peter Mays commented to me that he thought it was "the best screening he had ever seen". That show was entertaining, presented multiple works that people had little knowledge of, and demonstrated a clear historical moment of artistic practice that evolved over time.

Another of many highlights through the year was the Punk show at MOCA in January 2012, a full house, almost rowdy with anticipation, and giddy with delight at some of the wonders we found from the later 1970s. At one point we had a technical break between films, and filmmaker Eugene Timiraos started declaiming free verse to the crowd. Musicians, artists, and curious fans all had a great time at a screening that can't be repeated.

The true highlight of the series was the many guests, artists who had made films in the 1950s, '60s, and '70s, all still lively and thoughtful. Some came from a distance, but many are still based in Southern California. A few, now deceased, were represented by family members or former partners. Many of the artists changed their lives and aren't making media art anymore, and it was wonderful to welcome them and their films "back into the fold", as it were. The notes below list the many guests. We'd like to thank all of them again for honoring us with their attendance. Filmforum videotaped all of our post-show Q&As, and those can be found on the "LAFilmforum" YouTube channel.

Many people deserve great thanks for this series, most importantly my lead programming partner, Mark Toscano. Mark has the great benefit of living with these films, always seeking out more, in his preservation work at the Academy Film Archive, and was able to bring many films to the project that might otherwise have remained unfound.

We collaborated with multiple venues over the twenty-eight shows, and we'd like to thank many people for working with us and making it possible to bring so many great films back in the public eye. Our primary screening venue is the Egyptian Theatre in Hollywood, run by the American Cinematheque. Barbara

Figure 52. Mark Toscano working on film preservation at the Academy Film Archive.

Smith, Gwen Deglise, Grant Moninger, and Paul Rayton have made it possible for us to screen films properly there since 2000. Beyond that, our greatest thanks go to curatorial contributors Christine Panushka, Abraham Ferrer, Rani Singh, Jerri Allyn, Alex Juhasz, Rita Gonzalez, Jesse Lerner, Ben Caldwell, Stephanie Sapienza, Terry Cannon, and David James. Additional thanks go to the venues and organizations that collaborated with us: Steve Anker and Berenice Reynaud at REDCAT; Hadrian Belove and Bret Berg at Cinefamily; Shinae Yoon and Rukshana Singh with Visual Communications; Kris Kuramitsu and the Japanese American National Museum; Jim Kirst and the Downtown Independent Theatre; Aandrea Stang, Catherine Arias, and Jeffrey Deitch of MOCA; Bernardo Rondeau at LACMA; KP Pepe and Outfest; Meg Linton and Sue Maberry of the Otis College of Art and Design; May Haduong and the Academy Film Archive; Mark Quigley, Todd Wiener, Steve Hill, and the UCLA Film & Television Archive; Samuel Prime and UCLA Melnitz Movies; Dino Everett, Alex Ago, Dana Knowles, and the USC School of Cinematic Arts; Lisa Marr, Paolo Davanzo, and Rick Bahto of the inestimable Echo Park Film Center; and Gloria Gerace and Leila Hamidi of Pacific Standard Time.

Hundreds of films of interest might still be lost from these decades, thrown in a box by a student after a few screenings, to be forgotten and discarded years later, or perhaps still in an unlabeled can waiting to be rediscovered. But as a result of these programs, many remarkable films came out of closets or from under beds, and a healthy subset of those have now made their way to the Academy Film Archive or the UCLA Film & Television Archive for proper storage and preservation. Most of these films are not just historical curiosities, but retain all their original power and ability to inspire. We hope more people will seek these out, and will also locate more to send our way for future preservation.

Program Notes

Program One. Dream States: The Avant-Garde Of The 1940s And 1950s[1]

Original screening 9 October 2011

The Los Angeles Filmforum is pleased to launch our film screening series *Alternative Projections: Experimental Film in Los Angeles, 1945–1980,* which will include over twenty-four shows between now and May 2012. *Alternative Projections* is Filmforum's exploration of the community of filmmakers, artists, curators, and programmers who contributed to the creation and presentation of experimental film and video in Southern California in the postwar era. Film series curated by Adam Hyman and Mark Toscano, except as noted, and with contributions by David E. James, Christine Panushka, Terry Cannon, Ben Caldwell, Stephanie Sapienza, and more.

The American Avant-Garde film started coming into its own in Los Angeles during and after World War II, at first influenced by several key films from Europe, particularly Jean Cocteau's *Blood of a Poet,* along with influences from psychoanalysis and surrealism. We start our series with the classic Maya Deren film, *Meshes of the Afternoon*, generally considered the seminal American Avant-Garde film, made on North Kings Road above the Sunset Strip. The works tonight are mostly from the 1940s, often invoking dream states and elements of surrealism.

Meshes of the Afternoon. Maya Deren (1943, b/w, 14 min.)

Juliet. Man Ray (ca. 1940, digital [orig. 8mm], b/w, silent, 3.5 min.)

Salvador Dali sequence from Hitchcock's *Spellbound* (1945, DVD [orig. 35mm], 3 min.)

Fireworks. Kenneth Anger (1947, 35mm, [orig. 16mm], b/w, 15 min.)

House of Cards. Joseph Vogel (1947, b/w, 16 min.)

On the Edge. Curtis Harrington (1949, b/w, 6 min.)

Psyche (Du sang, de la volupté et de la mort, part 1). Gregory Markopoulos (1947, 25 min.)

What is a Man? Sara Kathryn Arledge (1958, 9 min.)

Program Two. Animation of the Unconsciousness: CalArts and the Teachings of Jules Engel

10 October 2011, at Roy and Edna Disney/CalArts Theater (REDCAT), 631 West 2nd Street.

Co-presented by REDCAT. Curated by Christine Panushka.

Guests: Christine Panushka, Sky David (formerly Dennis Pies), Lisze Bechtold, Steve Socki.

Founded and directed by Jules Engel (1909–2003), the CalArts Film Graphics Program (later called "Experimental Animation") sought to push the boundaries of animation. Through his teaching, and the example of his own work, Engel fostered the emergence of a new form of animation – freewheeling, transgressive, and imaginative. What happens when an animator follows a line, a patch of color, or a shape into the unconscious? What wild images would emerge; how could one image lead to another? What can we learn about art and the human condition from these brave forays into the unknown depths of the mind? Such were the questions posed by Engel's own films – *Shapes and Gestures, Wet Paint, Hors d'Oeuvres* – and by the students carrying his legacy: Kathy Rose (*Mirror People*), Adam Beckett (*Flesh Flows*), Sky David (formerly Dennis Pies, *Aura-Corona*), Henry Selick (*Phases*), Lisze Bechtold (*Moon Breath Beat*), and others.

California Institute of the Arts 1974/75. Roberta Friedman and Grahame Weinbren (1974, 3.5 min.)

Shapes and Gestures. Jules Engel (1976, 7 min.)

Wet Paint. Jules Engel (1977, 3 min.)

Hors d'Oeuvres. Jules Engel (1978, 4 min.)

Dream of the Sphinx. James Gore (c. 1970–71, silent, 24fps, 4 min.)

The Letter. James Gore & Adam Beckett (c. 1971, silent, 24fps, 2 min.)

Flesh Flows. Adam Beckett (1974, 6.5 min.)

Mirror People. Kathy Rose (1974, 5 min.)

A Film for Log Hill Dogs. Diana Wilson & David Wilson (1974, silent, 24fps, 2 min.)

Painting/Movie. Barbara Stutting (1973, 7.5 min.)

Well Birds. Howard Better (1978, b/w, 3 min.)

The Gameroom. Dorne Huebler (1978, 4 min.)

Aura-Corona. Sky David (formerly Dennis Pies) (1974, 4 min.)

Blue Star Mine. Susan Elmore (1977, 4 min.)

Phases. Henry Selick (1978, digital [orig. 35mm], 5.5 min.)

Animal Crackers. Mark Kirkland (1978, DVD [orig. 16mm], 2 min.)

Moon Breath Beat. Lisze Bechtold (1980, 35mm, 5 min.)

Water Cycle. Steve Socki (1981, 5 min.)

Figure 53. "Animation of the Unconsciousness: CalArts and the Teachings of Jules Engel," 10 October 2011, at REDCAT. Left to right: Christine Panushka, Steve Socki, Sky David, and Lisze Bechtold.

Inside Out. Howard Danelowitz (1979, 10 min.)

Pencil Booklings. Kathy Rose (1978, 35mm, 13 min.)

Program Three. Industry Town: The Avant-Garde and Hollywood[2]

16 October 2011

Guests: Peter Mays, Bruce Yonemoto, Norman Yonemoto.

Many experimental works have explicitly played with the dominant film industry (Hollywood and beyond), parodying its forms or structures of manufacture or utilizing images from classic and not-so-classic films as the raw material for new creations. We'll start the show with one of the earliest examples of commentary on the Hollywood quest, and perhaps the first made with a expressionist bent in Los Angeles, *The Life and Death of 9413: A Hollywood Extra*. Its importance is such that we have included it despite it coming from before 1945.

We continue through the decades with ever evolving approaches to the industry, practice and lifestyle of Hollywood. *Puce Moment* and *Zebra Skin Clutch* (Kenneth Anger and Cynthia Maughan) both look at a woman and their relationship to the fabulous styles of starlets, revealing the influence of celebrity and fashion. In *Death of the Gorilla*, Peter Mays manipulates footage filmed off late night television to create his own colorful collage of form and wonder. George Lucas's *6-18-67* starts from the position of a standard movie "making of" short and subverts it into a meditation on landscape and beauty. By the time we reach the 1970s, the conceptual investigations of art of the time find appropriate parallels. John Baldessari's *Title* breaks down some of the essential elements of screen-plays, language, and acting. *Based on Romance* utilizes storytelling traditions of melodrama but locates the scenes in the art world of the time.

The Life and Death of 9413: A Hollywood Extra. Robert Florey, Slavko Vorkapich & Gregg Toland (1928, 16mm [orig. 35 mm] b/w, silent, 24fps, 11 min.)

*Puce Moment. (*Kenneth Anger, 1949, 6 min.)

The Loves of Franistan. Jules Schwerin (1949, b/w, 9 min.)

Death of the Gorilla. Peter Mays (1966, 16 min.)

6-18-67. George Lucas (1967, DVD [orig. 16mm], 5 min.)

Title. John Baldessari (1971, digital [orig 16mm], b/w & color, 20 min.)

Metro-Goldwyn-Mayer. Jack Goldstein (1975, 2 min.)

Cue Rolls. Morgan Fisher (1974, 5.5 min.)

Zebra Skin Clutch. Cynthia Maughan (1977–78, b/w, 2 min.)

Based on Romance. Bruce and Norman Yonemoto (1979, video, 24.5 min.)

Program Four. Film/Music/Forms – Early Abstractions of the 1940s and 1950s

23 October 2011

Guest: Delmore Scott (Companion of Curt Opliger)

A key strain of experimental filmmaking in Los Angeles, predating World War II but continuing and greatly expanding after it, was the abstract film, usually (but not always) created through animation. Other examples evolved from a dance film tradition but chose to use the human figure as something approaching an abstract form. The preeminent practitioner of "visual music" or abstract animation before the war in Los Angeles was Oskar Fischinger, whose work influenced generations of filmmakers who were inspired to integrate aspects of color, rhythm, and motion. As World War II ended, two additional key figures emerged, the brothers John and James Whitney, who built their own ingenious and elaborate devices to produce unforeseen abstract work that continues to amaze.

Beyond the canonical Whitneys and Fischinger was a multiplicity of lesser known, in some cases nearly forgotten, L.A. artists who engaged in their own varieties of moving abstraction. These artists produced a dazzling array of work in numerous distinct modes: optically-manipulated dance performance, hand-drawn animation, multi-plane stop motion, live action sculptural environments, and even the microphotography of crystals in flux. Filmmakers such as Sara Kathryn Arledge, Flora Mock, Curt Opliger, Elwood Decker, and Lynn Fayman created highly developed and articulated works that greatly deserve rediscovery.

John and James Whitney Home Movie / 3 Untitled Films. John and James Whitney (c. 1941–43, silent, 24 fps, 8 min.)

Moonlight Sonata. Frank Collins and Donald Meyer (1948, 7.5 min.)

Film Exercises #4 and #5. John and James Whitney (1945, 13 min.)

Introspection. Sara Kathryn Arledge (1947, 8 min.)

Color Fragments. Elwood Decker (1948, silent, 24 fps, 11 min.)

Sophisticated Vamp. Lynn Fayman (1951/1958, 4 min.)

Mahzel. John Whitney (c. 1949, b/w, 3 min.)

Title sequence from Hitchcock's *Vertigo*. John Whitney and Saul Bass (1958, digital [orig. VistaVision 35mm], 3 min.)

Paper Moon. Flora Mock (1949, digital [orig. 16mm], 4 min.)

Phantasmagoria. Curt Opliger (1946/49, digital [orig. 8mm], b/w, silent, 5.5 min.)

Prelude. Curt Opliger (1950, 3 min.)

Crystals. Elwood Decker (1951, silent, 24fps, 2.5 min.)

Yantra. James Whitney (1957, 7 min.)

Program Five. Distributing the Avant-Garde: The Creative Film Society

30 October 2011

Guests: Angie Pike, Dan McLaughlin

Film historian Anthony Slide, while writing an appraisal letter for the film collection of late 1960's film distributor Creative Film Society (CFS), stated that "Any student researching the rise of the independent and experimental American film in the 1960s and 1970s would find this collection invaluable, and it is unlikely that a collection of this scope exists elsewhere. It is in many ways a tribute to a filmmaking experience that has disappeared." The Creative Film Society was founded in 1957 by Robert Pike, with the intention of "consolidating the efforts of the individual West Coast film artists in terms of aiding closer communication of ideas, films and equipment, as well as distributing the finished works of the members". The CFS was one of the key distribution organizations of the Los Angeles avant-garde film movement in its time. According to David E. James, CFS played "a major role in publicizing experimental film and in bringing the

Los Angeles avant-garde film communities together". Founder Robert Pike and later Angie Pike distributed a wide array of works: well known comedy shorts, student experiments, short documentaries, unusual cartoons, racy "underground" films, and rarified abstract films. (Notes by Stephanie Sapienza)

Tonight we feature selections from the CFS collection – a mix of visionary student work, rarities and canonical films, leaning towards some of the animation work.

The Critic. Mel Brooks and Ernie Pintoff (1963, 35mm, 4 min.)

God Is Dog Spelled Backwards, or 3000 Years of Art History in 3 ½ minutes. Dan McLaughlin (1963, 3.5 min.)

Mobile Static. Helmut C. Schulitz (1969, 6 min.)

Carnival. Donald Bevis, Jim May and Herb Hertel (c.1955, 8 min.)

The Unicycle Race. Robert Swarthe (1966, 35mm, 7.5 min.)

The Further Adventures of Uncle Sam. Dale Case and Robert Mitchell (1970, 35mm, 12 min.)

Furies. Sara Petty (1977, 35mm [orig. 16mm], 3 min.)

One Hundred and Eight Movements. Peggy Wolff (1972, 7 min.)

Waiting. Flora Mock (1952, digital [orig. 16mm], 12 min.)

The Towers. William Hale (1955/2010, digital [orig. 16mm], 13 min.)

Microsecond. Dan McLaughlin (1970, 5 min.)

Wu Ming. James Whitney (1977, silent, 24fps, 17 min.)

Program Six. Asco: Chicano Cinema and Agnes Varda's *Mur Murs*

11 November 2011, at Bing Theater, LACMA, 5905 Wilshire Boulevard, Los Angeles

Co-presented by the Los Angeles County Museum of Art (LACMA).

Introduced by Rita Gonzalez and Jesse Lerner

This evening's program is part of *Asco: Elite of the Obscure, A Retrospective, 1972–1987*, an exhibition that traces the remarkable trajectory of the art group and showcases their intermedia art practices that continuously refused to respect categories and distinctions and sought to transgress limitations and shatter preconceptions and stereotypes. Asco blurred the lines of various media, merging performance, photography, muralism, and film. As was the case for many Los Angeles based artists working with media, Asco lived in the shadow of Hollywood, feeding off its productions but also striving to create a counter-vision out of their own lived realities.

Asco's invention of *No Movies*, or film stills for non-existent films, allowed the group to appropriate the spectacle of Hollywood even as the critiqued the absence of Chicanos in the mass media. The group did use film occasionally when they had access to Super 8 and 16 millimeter cameras, but their engagement with media was greatly enhanced with the advent of public access media and portable video equipment. In their *No Movies* and in performances such as "Walking Mural" and "Instant Mural", Asco extended and exploited what film scholar David E. James has called "the liminal zone between the mural movements and movies proper".

Agnes Varda's *Mur Murs* is a documentary that the filmmaker made in 1981 about murals and muralists in Los Angeles. The film includes footage of Tai-chi done in front of Margaret Garcia's "Two Blue Whales" on Venice Boulevard, footage of the likes of Judy Baca and Kent Twitchell, as well as Asco contributing a wild tableau vivant, staged on the back wall of Self-Help Graphics in East Los Angeles.

Program notes by Rita Gonzalez and Jesse Lerner, drawn in part from the curators' essays in the exhibition catalogue for *Asco: Elite of the Obscure*, eds., C. Ondine Chavoya and Rita Gonzalez (Los Angeles: Los Angeles County Museum of Art, 2011).

Asco Performance Compilation. (1972–74, video [orig. Super 8mm], 10 min.)

Blessed Bag Bombers. Harry Gamboa Jr. with Asco (1982, video [orig. slides and audio cassette], 5 min.)

Blanx. Harry Gamboa Jr. (1984, video, color, 8 min.)

Mur Murs. Agnes Varda (1981, digital, [orig. 35mm], color, 80 min.)

Program Seven. Doin' It on Tape: Video from the Woman's Building

13 November 2011

Co-presented by the Otis College of Art and Design.

Guests: Jerri Allyn, Kathleen Forrest, Alexandra Juhasz, Cheri Gaulke, Leslie Labowitz-Starus, Suzanne Lacy, Sue Maberry, Susan Mogul.

The Woman's Building was a public center for women's culture in Los Angeles from 1973–1991, and housed the Feminist Studio Workshop, a two-year program for women in the arts accredited by four colleges and universities; the Summer Art Program, a two-month intensive course; a Continuing Education Program (courses in video, creative writing, performance art, graphic arts, fine arts, art history, women's studies, self-defense, professional art practices, and more were offered quarterly); the Women's Graphic Center; galleries; performance space adjacent to a café and thrift store; *Chrysalis: A Magazine of Women's Culture*; Sisterhood bookstore; a feminist travel agency, and the Los Angeles Women's Video Center (LAWVC). The LAWVC was cofounded at the

Woman's Building by Nancy Angelo, Candace Compton Pappas, and Annette Hunt in 1976, and joined by Jerri Allyn in 1977.

Tonight's show, *Doin' It on Tape: Video from the Woman's Building*, is hosted by Jerri Allyn and Dr. Alexandra Juhasz. They will introduce the video excerpts that they've selected from LAWVC's archives now housed at the Getty Research Institute. Highlighting work from 1971–1986, this presentation includes excerpts from documentary features and raw footage that touches on women artists in Southern California circa 1968–1973, feminist education, lesbian art, the goddess in the city of angels, violence against women and women fighting back, art collectives, exhibitions, and activism. These works were made by many of the leading artists of the era. Featured artists include: The LAWVC Collective, Cheri Gaulke, Starr Goode, Suzanne Lacy, Leslie Labowitz-Starus, Susan Mogul, Sheila Ruth, Jane Thurmond, and more. Much of this work has not been seen in twenty years or more!

This screening is organized in conjunction with the exhibition *Doin' It in Public: Feminism and Art at the Woman's Building* on view at Ben Maltz Gallery, Otis College of Art and Design.

All screenings on video.

L.A. Women's Video Center (LAWVC), Childcare Public Service Announcement, produced by Jerri Allyn, Nancy Anglo, Candace Compton Pappas, Annette Hunt (1977, 1 min.)

LAWVC, Mother and Lesbian Daughter Public Service Announcement, produced by Jerri Allyn, Nancy Angelo, Candace Compton Pappas, Annette Hunt (1977, 1 min.)

LAWVC Homosexuality Public Service Announcement, produced by Jerri Allyn, Nancy Angelo, Candace Compton Pappas, Annette Hunt (1977, 00:30 sec.)

LAWVC, Lesbian Occupations Public Service Announcement, produced by Jerri Allyn, Nancy Angelo, Candace Compton Pappas, Annette Hunt (1977, 1 min.)

My Friends Imitating Their Favorite Animals. Candace Compton Pappas (1979, 15 min.)

FSW (Feminist Studio Workshop) Video-letter. Susan Mogul (1975, 33 min.)

lalala workshop (Los Angeles League for the Advancement of Lesbians in the Arts or Lesbian Artists Living And Loving Amazons). Shirl Buss (1976, 9:23 min.)

1893 Historical Handicrafts Exhibition, The Woman's Building at the Chicago World's Fair. LAWVC (1976, 26 min.)

Signed by a Woman. Sheila Ruth & Jan Zimmerman (1976, 60 min.)

Opening night at the Woman's Building (Spring Street). Sheila Ruth (1975, 30 min.)

Judy Chicago in 1976. Sheila Ruth (1976, 23 min.)

Constructive Feminism: Reconstruction of the Woman's Building. Sheila Ruth with Annette Hunt and Diana Johnson (1976, 32 min.)

Scenes Never To Be Seen Beyond This Scene: The Hidden Eye Takes a Long Look at the FSW 1975–1976. (1976, 31 min.)

Kate Millet. Claudia Queen and Cyd Slayton (1977, 11 min.)

First Day FSW. LAWVC (1980, 62 min.)

Our Lady of L.A. Kathleen Forrest, Cheri Gaulke, and Sue Maberry (1982, 30 min.)

Eclipse in the Western Palace. Cheri Gaulke (1976, 20 min.)

I Love L.A. Jane Thurmond (Jane Krauss) (c. 1973–1991, 5:27 min.)

Nun and Deviant. Nancy Angelo and Candace Compton Pappas (1976, 20 min.)

So You Want to be a Waitress? The Waitresses (Jerri Allyn, Leslie Belt, Chutney Gunderson, and Denise Yarfitz) (1978, 25 min.)

Learn Where Meat Comes From. Leslie Labowitz and Suzanne Lacy (1976, 15:37 min.)

Record Companies Drag Their Feet. Leslie Labowitz and Suzanne Lacy with LAWVC (Jerri Allyn, Nancy Angelo, Candace Compton Pappas and Annette Hunt) (1977, 18 min.)

In Mourning and In Rage. Leslie Labowitz and Suzanne Lacy with LAWVC (Jerri Allyn, Nancy Angelo, Candace Compton Pappas and Annette Hunt) (1977, 30 min.)

Program Eight. Alarms from the 60s: Experiments in Political Expression[3]

20 November 2011

Guests: Stanton Kaye, Bill Norton, Penelope Spheeris.

Independent filmmakers have often used the medium as a way to comment on the political and social issues of the day. The growing counterculture of the 1960s with its activist and rebellious youth saw a great expansion in political work, often didactic or straightforward documentaries. But some filmmakers took the form and the commentary in new directions.

Stanton Kaye's legendary, award-winning *Georg* is an affecting, formally inventive narrative that follows a German émigré in America seeking to escape the encroaching militarism that threatens his family's existence. The film unfolds as a series of diaristic sequences supposedly assembled after the protagonist's death as a found audiovisual document, a formal approach that was a great influence on Jim McBride's *David Holzman's Diary*, and countless other films that followed.

In counterpoint to Kaye's experimental *verité*-fiction, Bruce Lane's distilled three-minute epic *unc.* crystallizes a whole generation's paranoia and disgust at old-fashioned American militarism and patriotism. Bill Norton's hilarious and unnerving *Coming Soon* uses the form of a WWII Hollywood movie trailer to dissect the absurdity and inhumanity of the War in Vietnam. Christina Hornisher's controversial and intense *And on the Sixth Day* cuts harshly to the bone of man's inhumanity to man in 1960s America. And Penelope Spheeris brilliantly and soberly suggests the inevitable next step in the government's intensifying lockdown on free expression and socio-political dissension in *The*

National Rehabilitation Center, an early mockumentary that at the time was responding to the McCarran Act but that has disturbing connections to the present issues raised by the Patriot Act and political imprisonment.

Coming Soon. Bill Norton (1966, 5 min.)

The National Rehabilitation Center. Penelope Spheeris (1969, b/w, 12 min.)

unc. Bruce Lane (1966, 3 min.)

And On The Sixth Day. Christina Hornisher (1966, b/w, 6 min.)

Georg. Stanton Kaye (1964, b/w, 50 min.)

Program Nine. Wallace Berman's Underground[4]

3 December 2011 at the Armory Center for the Arts, 145 North Raymond Avenue, Pasadena

Curated by Rani Singh and David E. James with Mark Toscano

Screening in conjunction with the Armory Center's exhibition, *Speaking in Tongues: The Art of Wallace Berman and Robert Heinecken, 1961–1976*

Guests: Toni Basil, Tosh Berman, George Herms, Russ Tamblyn.

In the mid-1960's, Wallace Berman inspired and communed with a close-knit circle of actors and artists, who screened their underground films domestically among a group of Topanga Canyon bohemians. These films were influenced by Berman's spiritualist and radically amateur concepts of art that nevertheless thrived in the intersection among art, Hollywood, and the institutions of the semi-commercial underground. Among this expanded circle in Topanga were Dennis Hopper, Russ Tamblyn, Toni Basil, Dean Stockwell, George Herms, Bruce Conner, and Robert Alexander. The evening will include several films made by the artists in this community, along with a conversation among the guests, and perhaps a performance.

Artifactual: Films from the Wallace Berman Collection. Wallace Berman (1956–66, compiled 2007, digital [orig. 8mm and 16mm], silent, 33.5 min.)

A Dance Film Inspired by Jim Morrison. Toni Basil (1968, digital [orig. 16mm], 2 min.)

Breakaway. Bruce Conner (1966, b/w, 5 min.)

First Film. Russ Tamblyn (c. 1966, [orig. 8mm], silent, 18 fps, 8 min.)

Rio Reel. Russ Tamblyn (c. 1968, silent, 18 fps, 6 min.)

Selections from *Topanga Rose.* George Herms (1960s, digital [orig. 16mm], 22 min.)

Figure 54. "Wallace Berman's Underground" on 3 December 2011, at the Armory Center for the Arts. Left to right: Russ Tamblyn and George Herms.

Program Ten. Community Visionaries: Visual Communications and the Dawn of Asian Pacific American Cinema

4 December 2011 at the Downtown Independent Theater, 251 S. Main Street, Los Angeles

Co-presented by Visual Communications.

Curated by Abraham Ferrer, Adam Hyman, and Mark Toscano.

Guests: Alan Kondo, Duane Kubo, Robert Nakamura, Eddie Wong.

In the course of media art in Los Angeles, the late 1960s and 1970s brought a rise in the possibilities of media access for minority groups that generally did not have access to the tools of cinema or control of how they were presented in mass media. Much of this critical work came out of the Ethno-Communications program at UCLA, formed in 1970, which worked to bring in African American, Asian American, Chicano, and Native American students. The remarkable work of the African American students is the focus of the L.A. Rebellion series at the UCLA Film & Television Archive, also part of Pacific Standard Time. This program highlights the documentary-focused early years of Visual Communications (VC), an organization created by a group of visionary Asian American filmmakers, educators, and activists from the Ethno-Communications program.

VC's founders – Duane Kubo, Robert Nakamura, Alan Ohashi, and Eddie Wong – incorporated the organization in 1970 on the heels of a groundbreaking photographic exhibition about Japanese American internment assembled by Nakamura and Ohashi entitled "America's Concentration Camps". (The modular exhibit, popularly referred to as "The Cubes Exhibit", is currently on display at the Japanese American National Museum as part of their show "Drawing the Line: Japanese American Art, Design & Activism in Post-War Los Angeles".) The foursome envisioned Visual Communications as a filmmakers' collective that sought to re-represent the history and culture of Asian Pacific Americans, to use media for social change, and to train future generations of Asian Pacific American filmmakers. The first such organization in the United States, VC continues to engage in community-based filmmaking through training, education and filmmaker support initiatives, public screening and exhibitions programs including the annual Los Angeles Asian-Pacific Film Festival, and film/video preservation activities. VC is also home to one of the largest repositories of photographic and moving image archives on the Asian Pacific experience in America. http://www.vconline.org/

Manzanar. Robert Nakamura (1971, [orig. Super 8mm], 8 min.)

Wong Sinsaang. Eddie Wong (1971, b/w, 12 min.)

City City. Duane Kubo & Donna Deitch (1974, 12 min.)

I Told You So. Alan Kondo (1974, b/w, 18 min.)

Cruisin' J-Town. Duane Kubo (1975, 24 min.)

Program Eleven. Dangerous Ideas: Political Conceptual Work in Los Angeles, 1974–1981

8 January 2012 at the Ahmanson Theater at MOCA, 250 S. Grand Ave., Los Angeles

Co-presented by the Museum of Contemporary Art (MOCA).

Guests: Amy Halpern, Tom Leeser, Dennis Phillips.

In the political hotbed of the 1970s, some artists merged conceptual approaches practiced in video or film with their political concerns in an explicit manner. These artworks play with basic elements of media creation and perception, while at the same time addressing the troubled times covered by the MOCA show, *Under the Big Black Sun: California Art 1974–1981*. This afternoon we'll primarily screen film work from that period, works viewed far less often than some more well-known works on video which can be viewed in the exhibition.

Figure 55. "Dangerous Ideas: Political Conceptual Work in Los Angeles, 1974–1981," 8 January 2012, at MOCA. Left to right: Dennis Phillips, Tom Leeser, and Amy Halpern.

Nine Scenes. David James (1980, 13 min.)

Vicarious Thrills. Roberta Friedman & Grahame Weinbren (1979, silent, 24fps, 9.5 min.)

Cigarette Burn. Amy Halpern with Nancy Halpern Ibrahim and Yves Marton (1978, b/w, 9 min.)

Opposing Views. Tom Leeser (1980, 12.5 min.)

The Broken Rule. Ericka Beckman (1979, 16mm [orig. Super 8mm], 19 min.)

Possibilities of Activity: Part I; The Argument. Dennis Phillips & Anthony Forma (1975, b/w, 29 min.)

Program Twelve. Strange Notes and Nervous Breakdowns: Punk and Media Art, 1974–1981

12 January 2012 at the Ahmanson Theater, MOCA, 250 S. Grand Ave., Los Angeles

Co-presented by the Museum of Contemporary Art (MOCA).

Guests: Eugene Timiraos, Paul Allen Newell, Johanna Went, Mark Wheaton, Rene Daalder, Bradley Friedman.

Punk and the Do It Yourself aesthetic were born in the late 1970s. Most scholarship on punk film and video has focused on works from New York and

San Francisco, but Los Angeles also was home to a rich scene of such media. In conjunction with *Under the Big Black Sun: California Art 1974–1981*, Los Angeles Filmforum presents this amazing collection of rarely screened performances by punk bands of the era, performance art, and D.I.Y. works. We'll be seeing performances from the early days by The Screamers, X, Suburban Lawns, Black Flag, Los Plugz, Johanna Went, and more.

A key source of the video for tonight was the video class taught by Shirley Clarke at UCLA in the late 1970s. Clarke was a pioneer of American independent film and video art, under-recognized but very influential. Among her students represented tonight were Cynthia Gianelli, Paul Allen Newell, Eugene Timiraos, and Bradley Friedman, as well as a variety of other media art makers. Without her class, and the equipment made available through it, much of the punk scene would have been even less documented than it was.

All on video except as noted.

Never Mind the Sex Pistols, Here's the Bullocks. Cynthia Gianelli and Paul Allen Newell (1979, b/w, sound, 30 min.)

Monologue on Camping. Eugene Timiraos (1979, 3 min.)

I'm Comin' Over – X. Eugene Timiraos (1979, 2 min.)

La Bamba – Los Plugz. Eugene Timiraos (1980, 3 min.)

Let's Have a Party and *Walking in the Sand* – The Go-Gos Play Live. Richard Newton (1979, video [orig. Super 8mm], 3 min.)

I Wanna Hurt – The Screamers. Live in Hollywood. Rene Daalder (1979, 9 min.)

Johanna Went. New Wave Theater (1980, 6:30 min.)

Revenge, Jealous Again and Interview – Black Flag. New Wave Theater (c. 1980, 3.5 min.)

The Black Train – Gun Club. New Wave Theater (c. 1980, 3 min.)

I'm going out in the RAIN. Richard Newton (1978, video [orig. Super 8mm], 3.5 min.)

Gidget Goes to Hell – Suburban Lawns. Jonathan Demme & Jack Cummins (ca. 1980, 3 min.)

Cardinal Newman – Nervous Gender. Michael Intriere (1981, 3 min.)

Paul Is Dead with David Byrne. Eugene Timiraos (1980, 1 min.)

Can't Make Love – Wall of Voodoo. Eugene Timiraos (1980, 3.5 min.)

Can't Find My Mind – The Cramps. Eugene Timiraos & Bradley Friedman (1981, 3.5 min.)

Stunt Dykes – The Anti-Sex League. Bradley Friedman (1980, 4 min.)

Eva Braun – The Screamers. Bradley Friedman (1981, 11.5 min.)

Peter Ivers talks. New Wave Theater. (ca. 1980, 2 min.)

Program Thirteen. Psychedelic Visions & Expanded Consciousness

18 January 2012 at the Cinefamily, 611 N Fairfax Avenue, Los Angeles

Co-presented by Cinefamily.

Guests: Beth Block, David Lebrun, Peter Mays, Pat O'Neill

Hyperkinetic experimental film and animation in the late '60s and early '70s both echoed and informed the volcanic psychedelia that defined those years – and the filmmakers featured in tonight's show created challenging, gorgeous work during that era through obsessive mastery of groundbreaking techniques. Chick Strand's solarized synchronicities, Pat O'Neill's optically-printed densely haptic experiments and Adam Beckett's infinite ecstatic morphs all manage to alter minds, both addled and unaided. The care that went into the films of tonight's sizeable collection of visionaries cannot be overstated, and their influence is a testament to the potent revolutions that originated in obscurity, but still resound in our collective consciousness.

Les AngeS Dorment. Felix Venable (1965, b/w & color, 9 min.)

Lapis. James Whitney (1966, 9 min.)

Waterfall. Chick Strand (1967, 3 min.)

Evolution of the Red Star. Adam Beckett (1973, 7 min.)

Binary Bit Patterns. Michael Whitney (1969, 3 min.)

Terminal Self. John Whitney Jr. (1971, 8 min.)

Coming Down. Pat O'Neill (1968, 4 min.)

Pulse. Peter Spoecker/B.Y.M. Productions (1969, b/w, 9 min.)

Aether. Daina Krumins (1972, 4 min.)

Twelve (The First Three Parts ...). Beth Block (1977, 9 min.)

Easyout. Pat O'Neill (1972, 9 min.)

Tanka. David Lebrun (1976, 9 min.)

The Star Curtain Tantra. Peter Mays (1969, 14 min.)

Program Fourteen. Los Angeles Observed

21 January 2012 at the Cinefamily, 611 N Fairfax Avenue, Los Angeles

Co-presented by Cinefamily.

Guests: Thom Andersen, Baylis Glascock, John Vicario.

If Thom Andersen's 2003 video essay *Los Angeles Plays Itself* explored the way that filmmakers have trained thousands of lenses upon the city's fragmented topography over the course of a century, tonight's program uncovers how alternate visions of Los Angeles were executed by multiple generations of experimental filmmakers. Andersen's own contribution to the oeuvre, 1966's *Olivia's Place*, will be screened alongside an eclectic roster of unconventional documentaries, avant-garde ethnographies and rare films that capture landscapes turned on their fractured heads. A selection of archival and restored prints showcase artist Gary

Beydler, Hollywood maverick Joseph Strick, *The Exiles* director Kent MacKenzie, and other artists whose takes on their local surroundings were carried out with a palpable awareness of truth's often lovely precariousness in non-fiction.

Muscle Beach. Joseph Strick & Irving Lerner (1948, 35mm, b/w, 9 min.)

City City. Duane Kubo & Donna Deitch (1974, 12 min.)

Bunker Hill 1956. Kent MacKenzie (1956, b/w, 18 min.)

Olivia's Place. Thom Andersen (1966/74, 6 min.)

Shoppers Market. John Vicario (1963, 22 min.)

Film Exercise Number One. Baylis Glascock (1962, 5 min.)

Venice Pier. Gary Beydler (1976, 16 min.)

Program Fifteen. Visions, Memory, and a Machine: Optical Manipulations

28 January 2012 at the Cinefamily, 611 N Fairfax Avenue, Los Angeles

Co-presented by Cinefamily.

Guests: Pat O'Neill, Beth Block.

The optical printer played a crucial role not only in the Hollywood special effects industry, but in certain strains of experimental cinema as well. Perhaps because of its co-habitation with America's commercial film production center, Los Angeles artists, more than those of any other experimental film community, produced a substantial body of work that engaged with this versatile and powerful re-photography device.

Pat O'Neill is one of Los Angeles's true avant-garde masters, creating beautiful, moody, always surprising films with floating mattes, variable film speeds, ghostly layering, wry wit, and masterful soundtracks, all working together to form a fractured almost-narrative, a reflection on the lost spaces and times of our city. It is a testament to his influence that all the other filmmakers in this program (not to mention countless others not represented here) were at one time students or assistants of Pat's.

Playing with memory, landscape, animation, humor, and more, these films will delight you with their stunning, transformative, and often bizarre visions and stories.

Saugus Series. Pat O'Neill (1974, 18 min.)

Throbs. Fred Worden (1972, 7 min.)

Heavy-Light. Adam Beckett (1973, 7 min.)

Saturn Cycle. David Wilson (1975, 16 min.)

Film Achers. Beth Block (1976, 8 min.)

Figure 56. Pat O'Neill (front center) in the audience, before *Wallace Berman's Underground* repeat screening, on 7 January 2012, at Cinefamily.

Project One. David Lourie (1968, 14 min.)

Foregrounds. Pat O'Neill (1978, 14 min.)

Babobilicons. Daina Krumins (1982, 35mm [orig. 16mm], 16 min.)

Program Sixteen. Outsiders Observe Los Angeles

4 February 2012, at Echo Park Film Center, 1200 N Alvarado Street, Los Angeles

Guest: David Lamelas.

Although it's perhaps a cliché that most folks you meet in Los Angeles aren't actually from here, many artists have not surprisingly been interested to bring that "outsider" perspective to their work as they explore the unique urban landscape of the City of Angels. Earlier this season, we presented a screening of films which appraised the city a bit more on its own terms, through the searching, subjective eye of the filmmaker. But the view of Los Angeles as seen through someone maintaining a certain distance, perhaps skeptical, definitely curious, is a crucial one for a city that some might say is defined by notions of insiders and outsiders.

The program begins with San Francisco icon Ben Van Meter's extremely rarely seen *Me & Bruce & Art*, which documents a trip he and artist Bruce Conner made to Los Angeles to explain Underground Film on *The Art Linkletter Show*. This will be followed by *The Desert People*, in which David Lamelas examines the questionable authority of "documentary" form, and its relationship to constructed narrative, first person testimony, and even oral folk traditions.

On 9 January this year, we lost the great Robert Nelson, and are very happy to present his experimental travelogue *Suite California Part 1* in its original version, for the first time in decades here in Los Angeles. The second half of the program will also feature Nelson's last completed film, *Special Warning*, which was finished by him in 1999 from footage generated while teaching at Cal Arts in the early 1970s.

Me & Bruce & Art. Ben Van Meter (1968, 5.5 min.)

The Desert People. David Lamelas (1974, 48 min.)

Special Warning. Robert Nelson (1999, b/w & color, 5.5 min.)

Suite California Stops & Passes Part 1: Tijuana to Hollywood Via Death Valley. Robert Nelson (1976, b/w & color, 46 min.)

Program Seventeen. Sex Roles & Rules: Gender, Liberation, and Sexuality

12 February 2012

Guests: Richard Newton and Penelope Spheeris.

Films and videos exploring the definitions, meanings, representations, and interactions of women and men. Storytelling about past experiences; performances; documentary ahead of its time, social conflicts. Yes, plenty of nudity and adult behavior as well. There are a large number of great works that focus on these themes. These are a few highlights.

Now Show Yours. Richard Newton (1977, digital [orig. Super 8mm] 2.5 min.)

Bondage Boy. Chris Langdon (1973, 5 min.)

Bondage Girl. Chris Langdon (1973, 5 min.)

Female Sensibility. Linda Benglis (1973, video, 14.5 min)

Water Ritual #1: An Urban Rite of Purification. Barbara McCullough (1979, 35mm [orig.16mm], b/w, 6 min.)

Hats Off to Hollywood. Penelope Spheeris (1972, 22 min.)

Soft Fiction. Chick Strand (1979, b/w, 54 min.)

Program Eighteen. Rock & Roll Experiments

15 February 2012, at the Cinefamily, 611 N Fairfax Avenue, Los Angeles

Co-presented by Cinefamily.

Guests: Toni Basil, Gail Zappa.

This selection of films from the 1960s and '70s shows that music and cinema in Los Angeles ran parallel and frequently intersecting courses of rapid aesthetic development during this period, resulting in works of brilliant and ecstatic creative innovation that BULGE almost obscenely with the energy of the era. Filmmakers lived, explored, channeled, and booglarized the rock music and culture of the period, a symbiosis perhaps most vividly on display here in the twin kaleidoscopes of Frank Zappa's ridiculously rare and frantic *Burnt Weeny Sandwich* and Thom Andersen's spine-tinglingly affecting - - - - - - - - - -.

In this show, we'll see prototype music shorts, rapid-fire visualizations, heartfelt tributes, absurdist homages, experiments in portraiture, and even learn how to eat persimmons, every minute of it pungently infused with the vibrations and vexations of that mysterious and bewitching force we call rock 'n' roll.

The Gypsy Cried. Chris Langdon (1973, b/w, 3 min.)
Coming Down. Pat O'Neill (1968, 4 min.)
4x8=16. Christina Hornisher (1966, 3 min.)
Two Faces Have I. Chris Langdon (1973, b/w, 3 min.)
Truly Right. Bill Norton and Steve Rosen (1967, 3 min.)
Angie. Deirdre Cowden and Adam Beckett (1976, 4 min.)
Kinky. Jim Joannides and Maurice Bar-David (1966, digital [orig.16mm], 3 min.)
A Dance Film Inspired by Jim Morrison. Toni Basil (1968, digital [orig.16mm], 2 min.)
The Emperor. George Lucas (1967, b/w, 24 min.)
The Last of the Persimmons. Pat O'Neill (1972, 6 min.)
Burnt Weeny Sandwich. Frank Zappa (1969, digital [orig.16mm], 18 min.)
- - - - - - - - - -. Thom Andersen and Malcolm Brodwick (1966–67, 12 min.)

Program Nineteen. Tricky Poses and Taxing Conditions: Performance and Media

19 February 2012

Guests: Sam Erenberg, Susan Mogul, Richard Newton, Allan Sekula.

Much early video work captured performance events in real time, utilizing this capability of video and its distribution. Some works went further, to analyze the nature of performance for media; replicating performances from past performances; and confronting the challenging space created by bodies. Less well known are films that also made these investigations. All films that have people in them in some way involve performance; these selections raise questions about the nature and purpose of performance, and also playfully look at how the camera, filmmaker, and projectionist also perform their roles.

Projection Instructions. Morgan Fisher (1976, b/w, 4 min.)

Performance Under Working Conditions. Allan Sekula (1973, video, b/w, 20 min.)

Pulling Mouth. Bruce Nauman (1969, b/w, silent, 8 min.)

Ma Bell. Paul McCarthy (1971, video, b/w, 7 min.)

Frozen & Buried Alive. Cynthia Maughan (1974–75, b/w, 1.5 min.)

Trajectory. Sam Erenberg (1977, HD [orig. Super 8mm], 4.5 min.)

Big Tip, Back Up, Shout Out. Susan Mogul (1976, b/w, video, 10.5 min.)

Nun and Deviant. Nancy Angelo, Candace Compton Pappas (1976, b/w, 20.5 min.)

A Glancing Blow. Richard Newton (1979, 35 mm [orig. Super 8mm], 3 min.)

Cheap Imitations 1: Méliès - India Rubber Head. Grahame Weinbren and Roberta Friedman (1980, b/w, 5.5 min.)

I'm Too Sad To Tell You. Bas Jan Ader (1971, digital [orig. 16mm], b/w, silent 24 fps, 3.5 min.)

Program Twenty. Material Concerns

4 March 2012

Guests: Pat O'Neill, Craig Rice.

One of the key concerns of experimental film, in the tradition of all modern art, is the stuff of film itself: how it is made, what it is made of, what are the basic elements of the camera, the celluloid, and the projector. In experimental film, focusing on the materials and procures of filmmaking has come to be known as structuralist filmmaking, with a hey-day from the late 1960s through the mid-1970s, but continuing in much work today. These are several classic examples made in Los Angeles, with precise control over the instruments of filmmaking, the depth of good art, and (more often than not) a fair dose of wit.

Screen. Pat O'Neill (1969, digital [orig. 16mm], silent, 24 fps, 4 min.)

Accident. Jules Engel (1973, b/w, 3 min.)

Venusville. Chris Langdon and Fred Worden (1973, 10 min.)

Photogrammetry Series. Louis Hock (1977, 8 min.)

Pasadena Freeway Stills. Gary Beydler (1974, silent, 24 fps, 6 min.)

Future Perfect. Roberta Friedman and Grahame Weinbren (1978, 11 min.)

Stasis. David Wilson (1976, 8 min.)

Picture Without Sound. Susan Rosenfeld (1976, silent, 24 fps, 4.5 min.)

I Kiss the Dear Fingers So Toil-Worn For Me. Craig Rice (1981, 16mm, b/w, silent, 24 fps, 7 min.)

Standard Gauge. Morgan Fisher (1984, 35 min.)

Program Twenty-One. The L.A. Rebellion: Boundary-Breaking Shorts

11 March 2012

Curated by Ben Caldwell and Adam Hyman.

Guests: Charles Burnett, Ben Caldwell.

The early 1970s was a very important time for people of color artist/filmmakers at UCLA. After the arrival of future MacArthur Grant winner Charles Burnett in 1967 and Ethiopian filmmaker Haile Gerima the following year, there emerged a significant black independent movement. The students developed a fecund, cosmopolitan, and politically-engaged movement that came to be unofficially known, as essayist Ntongela Masilela dubbed, the Los Angeles School of Black Filmmakers or "L.A. Rebellion".

The first wave of these filmmakers also included Larry Clark, John Reir, Ben Caldwell, Pamela Jones, Carol Blue, Abdosh Abdulhafiz, Tommy Wright, Barbara-O, Charles David Brooks III, and Jamaa Fanaka. The second continued the remarkable cinematic work with Julie Dash, Sharon Larkin, Barbara McCullough, Bernard Nicolas, Billy Woodberry, Jacqueline Frazier, Adisa Anderson, and Zeinabu irene Davis. The program includes some of the short films by these makers pursuing less conventional modes of storytelling.

Hour Glass. Haile Gerima (1971, digital video, b/w & color, 14 min.)

A Day in the Life of Willie Faust, or Death on the Installment Plan. Jamaa Fanaka (as Walt Gordon) (1972, digital [orig. 8mm], 20 min.)

Medea. Ben Caldwell (1973, digital [orig. 16mm], 7 min.)

Four Women. Julie Dash (1975, 7 min.)

Water Ritual #1: An Urban Rite of Purification. Barbara McCullough (1979, 35mm [orig.16mm], b/w, 6 min.)

Daydream Therapy. Bernard Nicolas (1977, digital video [orig. 16mm], b/w & color, 8 min.)

I & I: An African Allegory. Ben Caldwell (1979, 16mm in-progress preservation, 32 min.)

The Horse. Charles Burnett (1973, 14 min.)

Program Twenty-two. Crosstown Rivals: Films from UCLA and USC in the 1960s[5]

12 April 2012, at the James Bridges Theater, Melnitz Hall, UCLA, Los Angeles

Co-presented by UCLA Melnitz Movies.

Guests: David Lebrun, Penelope Spheeris.

Enthused by the possibilities of "underground" film, energetic students at Los Angeles's leading universities made a healthy amount of work using alternative

Figure 57. The L.A. Rebellion: Boundary-Breaking Shorts, 11 March 2012, at the Egyptian Theatre. Left to right: Allyson Field (film historian), Ben Caldwell, Charles Burnett, and Ross Lipman (archivist and filmmaker).

approaches in the 1960s. This work gained notoriety in the mass media, with an article in *Time* magazine, among others. The most well-known filmmaker to come out of this period is George Lucas, but we'll also be looking at remarkable student works by Penelope Spheeris, David Lebrun, Paul Golding, Robert Abel, John Milius, Burton Gershfield, Bruce Green, and Rob Thompson. Politically and socially activated works, experimenting in animation, collage, documentary, and narrative, topped by two unusual science fiction films from Spheeris and Lucas.

Visiting from USC:

Wipeout. Paul Golding (1965, b/w, 3 min.)

Pulp. Bruce Green (1967, b/w, 8 min.)

Marcello, I'm So Bored. John Milius (1966, 9 min.)

Herbie. Paul Golding and George Lucas (1965, b/w, 3 min.)

Electronic Labyrinth: THX 1138 4 EB. George Lucas (1967, 15 min.)

Home at UCLA:

Freightyard Symphony. Robert Abel (1963, DVD [orig.16mm], 6.5 min.)

Les angeS Dorment. Felix Venable (1965, b/w & color, 9 min.)

S.W.L.A. Rob Thompson (1971, b/w & color, 6 min.)

Synthesis. Penelope Spheeris (1968, 16mm [orig 8mm], 7 min.)

Now That The Buffalo's Gone. Burton Gershfield (1967, 7 min.)

Sanctus. David Lebrun (1967, b/w, 18 min.)

Program Twenty-Three. Bright Ideas: Conceptual Art Films

22 April 2012

Guests: Thom Andersen, Susan Rosenfeld.

Los Angeles was one of the centers of Conceptual Art production, as reflected by multiple Pacific Standard Time exhibitions. Where sculptural and installation manifestations of Conceptual Art are more widely known, film and video also served as media for these sorts of explorations – works in which the concept preceded the work, and for which one could theoretically conceive the work with the rules themselves.

Metro-Goldwyn-Mayer. Jack Goldstein (1975, 2 min.)

Melting. Thom Andersen (1965, 5 min.)

Four Short Films. John Baldessari (1972–73, digital [orig. Super 8mm], silent, 5.5 min.)

Picture and Sound Rushes. Morgan Fisher (1973, b/w, 11 min.)

Thin Premises. Chris Langdon (1973, 5 min.)

The Gypsy Cried. Chris Langdon (1973, b/w, 3 min.)

Subject. Ken Feingold (1974, 5.5 min.)

After 10 Minutes Lines. Roberta Friedman (1976, b/w & color, 15.5 min.)

Murray and Max Talk About Money. Roberta Friedman and Grahame Weinbren (1979, 15 min.)

Dead Reckoning. David Wilson (1980, 9 min.)

Now Playing. Susan Rosenfeld (1983, silent, 24fps, 7 min.)

Program Twenty-Four. Same Sex/Different Sex: Queer Identity and Culture[6]

29 April 2012

Co-presented by Outfest.

Guests: Penelope Spheeris, Linda Spheeris.

From the 1950s through the 1980s, underground film was an avenue for artistic self-expression for lesbian and gay artists, and also occasionally provided a way for LGBT people to see representations of themselves without persecution. But the cultural climate changed dramatically over the decades, with the closeted screenings for friends of the earlier period changing to public screenings and well-advertised events. For example, in 1957 and 1964, the exhibitors at the

Coronet Theater and the Cinema Theater, respectively, were each arrested by the Los Angeles Police for exhibiting obscene works, and both times the police were primarily targeting films with homoerotic (but not explicit) content – *Fireworks* by Kenneth Anger and *Voices* by John Schmitz in 1957; *Scorpio Rising* by Anger in 1964. Both times the exhibitor was originally convicted, and then the conviction was overturned in Los Angeles County Superior Court.

By the late 1960s, after various court cases (up to the US Supreme Court), such police action was no longer prevalent. The 1970s and 1980s brought the rise of identity politics, creating new venues for self-expression. There soon resulted healthy numbers of works with Queer Identity and culture as the subject by makers such as Pat Rocco, and multiple artists from the Woman's Building – documentaries; fantasies; activist works; news reporting; experimental films – a full range of media art showing the lives and conflicts and creativity of LGBT artists – a point of view not found in mainstream media of the time.

This program starts with a little-known work from 1962, made by Robert Chatterton, who was also a prominent underground film exhibitor. Taylor Mead, on one of his occasional visits to Los Angeles, acted in two films by Chatterton, including *Passion in a Seaside Slum*. Brought to our attention by Marc Siegel in the Alternative Projections symposium in 2010, Filmforum arranged for the preservation of *Passion in a Seaside Slum* with the generous support of the National Film Preservation Foundation and the Film Foundation. This is the premiere screening of this new print. We are also screening a remarkable short documentary made by Penelope Spheeris; classics by Kenneth Anger and Chick Strand; lesbian public service announcements from the Woman's Building in the 1970s; a light romp from the key figure of Pat Rocco, and one from the filmmaker, critic, and archivist William Moritz, a key figure for experimental film in Los Angeles for over three decades.

Passion in a Seaside Slum. Robert Wade Chatterton (1962, [orig. 8mm], silent, 18 fps, 32 min.)

Kustom Kar Kommandos. Kenneth Anger (1965, 3.5 min.)

The Game and How the Game Was Made. Pat Rocco (1969–70, DVD [orig. 16mm], 10.5 min.)

Lesbian occupations – public service announcements (PSAs). Los Angeles Women's Video Center. (1970s, video, each PSA 30–60" secs.)

Fever Dream. Chick Strand (1979, b/w, 7 min.)

I Don't Know. Penelope Spheeris (1970, b/w, 18 min.)

Slow Morning Rain. Bill Moritz (1970–78, video [orig. 16mm], b/w & color, 30 min.)

Program Twenty-Five. Numbers, Patterns, and Shapes: Later Abstractions of the 1960s and 1970s

3 May 2012, at the Cinefamily, 611 N Fairfax Avenue, Los Angeles

Co-presented by Cinefamily.

Guests: Larry Cuba, Louis Hock, Pat O'Neill, Sara Petty, Michael Scroggins, John Whitney Jr.

Last October as part of "Alternative Projections", we presented "Early Abstractions of the 1940s and 1950s", which charted an evolution of imagery from filmed sculptural shapes to abstract images created by animation, creative photography, and even early optical printers. Tonight, we continue looking at this evolution with more remarkable abstract films from the 1960s and '70s. As in the earlier show, John and James Whitney continue as key figures, but working separately. John Whitney's 1967 *Experiments in Motion Graphics* introduces the possibilities of computer animation, soon to be deeply explored in, among others, the masterful, and too-little-seen *Matrix III*. The classic films *7362* by Pat O'Neill and *Kitsch in Synch* by Adam Beckett reveal some of the transformative and transcendental possibilities of film printers. Jules Engel's *Train Landscape* and Sara Petty's *Furies* provide bold examples of traditional animation, while Louis Hock's remarkable *Light Traps* uses imagery of neon tubing to give us the cinematic equivalent of a Rothko. Michael Scroggins worked with pioneering video manipulation following his legendary work in light show liquids. Departing strongly from John Whitney's example, Larry Cuba explored computer animation in a more pure, medium-specific manner, working with the expansive aesthetic possibilities achievable from a minimalist approach. The program concludes with what is perhaps James Whitney's least-seen work, and his final film, *Kang Jing Xiang*, which, following his untimely death in 1982, was completed by William Moritz and Mark Whitney.

Experiments in Motion Graphics. John Whitney (1967–68, 12 min.)

Matrix III. John Whitney (1972, 10 min.)

Kitsch in Synch. Adam Beckett (1975, 5 min.)

Train Landscape. Jules Engel (1974, 3 min.)

Light Traps. Louis Hock (1975, silent, 18fps, 8 min.)

7362. Pat O'Neill (1967, 11 min.)

3/78 (Objects and Transformations). Larry Cuba (1978, digital [orig.16mm], b/w, 6 min.)

Furies. Sara Petty (1977, digital [orig. 16mm], 3 min.)

Two Space. Larry Cuba (1979, digital [orig. 16mm], b/w, 8 min.)

Recent Li. Michael Scroggins (1980, video, 5 min.)

Kang Jing Xiang. James Whitney (1982, silent, 24 fps, 13 min.)

Program Twenty-Six. Moving Pictures: Painting, Photography, Film

12 May 2012, at Echo Park Film Center, 1200 N Alvarado Street, Los Angeles

Guests: Ben Caldwell, Sam Erenberg, Sylvia Morales, Eugene Timiraos.

Movies are made up of many still images, moving rapidly through a projector. And they are among the two-dimensional pictorial arts, along with painting and photography. And here's a show bringing these ideas front and center, with lively deconstructions of movies into stills; commentaries on the "death" of painting; explorations into the possibility of making moving paintings; and intense explorations into the meaning of still images in the creation of identity of a people.

Walking Forward-Running Past. John Baldessari (1971, video, b/w, 13 min.)

Production Stills. Morgan Fisher (1970, 11 min.)

Pasadena Freeway Stills. Gary Beydler (1974, silent, 24 fps, 6 min.)

Abacus. Lyn Gerry and Estelle Kirsh (1980, silent, 24 fps, 5 min.)

The Last Statement of Painting. Sam Erenberg (1970, digital [orig. Super 8mm], silent, 9 min.)

The Last Statement of Painting II. Sam Erenberg (1970, digital [orig. Super 8mm], silent, 4 min.)

Painting Face Down – White Line. Paul McCarthy (1972, video, b/w, 2.5 min.)

Whipping the Wall with Paint. Paul McCarthy (1975, video, b/w, 2 min.)

Dada Knows Best. Eugene Timiraos (1979, video, 11.5 min.)

Medea. Ben Caldwell (1973, digital, [orig. 16mm], 7 min.)

Chicana. Sylvia Morales (1979, 23 min.)

Program Twenty-Seven. The Alternative Projections Marathon

18 May 2012, at Echo Park Film Center, 1200 N Alvarado Street, Los Angeles

"Alternative Projections" has featured over twenty-six shows since October 2012. For the penultimate experience, we celebrate with an incredible range of films and videos that we haven't squeezed into other screenings, with frequent breaks for socializing!

Guests: Richard Newton, Michael Scroggins.

Reel One: Ceremonies and Divinations

Anselmo. Chick Strand (1967, 4 min.)

Filament (*The Hands*). Amy Halpern (1975, b/w, silent, 24 fps, 6 min.)

The Divine Miracle. Daina Krumins (1973, 6 min.)

Christopher Tree (aka *Spontaneous Sound*). Les Blank (1968, 9.5 min.)

The Assignation. Curtis Harrington (1953, 7.5 min.)

Keinbahn. Lyn Gerry (1976, 5 min.)

Eclipse Predictions. Diana Wilson (1982, 3.5 min.)

Hand Held Day. Gary Beydler (1974, silent, 24fps, 5.5 min.)

Reel Two: Studies and Observations

Home Movies – Bunker Hill. Laure Lourié (ca.1940, b/w, silent, 24 fps, 7 min.)

Fall From Palisades. Richard Newton (1973, digital [orig. Super 8mm], b/w, 4.5 min.)

Thomas, A Man. Richard Newton (1970, digital [orig. Super 8mm], b/w, silent, 3.5 min.)

Peach Landscape. Amy Halpern (1973, silent, 24fps, 5 min.)

Interview with an Artist. Chris Langdon (1975, b/w, 11.5 min.)

Down Wind. Pat O'Neill (1973, 15 min.)

Studies in Chronovision. Louis Hock (1975, silent, 24fps, 22 min.)

Reel Three: Consumption and Capitalism

TV Commercial – Muntz TV. Oskar Fischinger (1952, b/w, 2 min.)

Grand Central Market. William Hale (1963, digital [orig 16mm], b/w, 10 min.)

Dressing Up. Susan Mogul (1973, video, b/w, 7 min.)

Full Financial Disclosure. Chris Burden (1976, video, 1 min.)

Cluck. Celia Shapiro (1978, video, 16.5 min.)

A Budding Gourmet. Martha Rosler (1974, b/w, 18 min.)

Reel Four: Information/Transformation

Destiny Edit. Michael Scroggins (1972–1975, video, 7.5 min.)

Rumble. Jules Engel (1975, b/w, 3 min.)

Sausage City. Adam Beckett (1974, 5 min.)

.... David Wilson (ca.1973–74, 4 min.)

Vital Interests. Beth Block (1981, b/w, 15 min.)

Protective Coloration. Morgan Fisher (1979, video, 13 min.)

Berta's Children. Roberta Friedman and Grahame Weinbren (1976, 7 min.)

Glass Face. Gary Beydler (1975, silent, 24fps, 2 min.)

Stanfield Family Home Movie – Hollywood Blvd., Downtown L.A. (1930, b/w, silent, 18 fps, 6 min.)

Reel Five: Good Night

Mirror. Gary Beydler (1974, digital [orig. Super 8mm], silent, 24fps, 6 min.)

Our Lady of the Angels Part 1: Entrance Entrance. Chris Regan (1976, b/w, 15 min.)

Nightcats. Stan Brakhage (1956, silent, 24fps, 9 min.)

Elasticity. Chick Strand (1975, 25 min.)

Sleeping Dogs Never Lie. Pat O'Neill (1978, b/w & color, 9 min.)

Program Twenty-Eight. L.A. Filmworks: The State of the Art in Los Angeles, 1980

20 May 2012

Guests: Betzy Bromberg, Terry Cannon, Tom Leeser, Craig Rice, William Scaff, Keith Ullrich.

In the early 1980s, Filmforum's Terry Cannon assembled a few mixed shows for touring of experimental films by Los Angeles filmmakers. Along with *Filmforum Film*, a document of Filmforum in 1980, selections from these shows, and maybe some additional treats, provide a fitting conclusion to Alternative Projections, revealing the state of the art in Los Angeles, circa 1980. We'll have a great mix of films, with experimental, animated, conceptual, and documentary works, followed by a celebratory reception!

Zulu As Konoe. Craig Rice (1980, b/w, 5 min.)

Renée Walking/TV Talking. Tom Leeser (1980, 10 min.)

Rose for Red. Diana Wilson (1980, 3 min.)

The Dream Trilogy Part 1: Searching for Planes. William Scaff (1977, Super 8mm, 15 min.)

The Dream Trilogy Part 2: In This Trembling Shadow. William Scaff (1979, Super 8mm, 15 min.)

Soothing the Bruise. Betzy Bromberg (1980, 21 min.)

Filmforum Film. Craig Rice (1980, b/w, 4 min.)

Notes

1. Written by Adam Hyman and Mark Toscano unless noted, these program notes accompanied the programs screened under the rubric, "*Alternative Projections: Experimental Film in Los Angeles, 1945–1980*", between 9 October 2011, and 20 May 2012. They have been somewhat abbreviated and standardized, but complete versions, including sources for the films and videos and some illustrations, may be seen at http://alternativeprojections.com/screening-series/. Unless otherwise noted, all screenings took place at Filmforum's regular venue, the Spielberg Theater at Grauman's Egyptian Theatre, 6712 Hollywood Boulevard, Los Angeles. Unless otherwise noted, all works were 16 mm, color, with sound.
2. This program, minus *Puce Moment* and *The Loves of Franistan*, was repeated on 14 January at Cinefamily. Guests: Morgan Fisher, Peter Mays, Bruce Yonemoto.
3. This program was repeated at Cinematheque 108, University of Southern California (USC) on 1 December 2011.
4. This program was repeated 7 January 2012, at Cinefamily, minus *Artifactual: Films from the Wallace Berman Collection*, and adding *Aleph*, Wallace Berman (1956–66, silent, 6 min.) and *Pas De Trois*, Dean Stockwell (1964, 16mm b/w transferred to video, 8 min.) in an edit by Bruce Conner. Guests: Toni Basil, Tosh Berman, George Herms, and Russ Tamblyn.
5. This program was repeated 19 April 2012, at Cinematheque 108, USC, with the halves of the program reversed.
6. This program played twice on 29 April. The first screening, at 5 pm, did not include *Slow Morning Rain*. The second run, at 7:30 pm, did include it.

Notes on the Contributors

Ken Eisenstein is writing his dissertation on Hollis Frampton at the University of Chicago. He taught at Mount Holyoke College from 2010–13 and is currently at Bucknell University.

Josh Guilford is a Ph.D. candidate in the Department of Modern Culture and Media at Brown University, where he is completing a dissertation on the New American Cinema. He is also co-curator of the Providence, RI-based experimental film and video series Magic Lantern Cinema.

Veena Hariharan is currently Assistant Professor of Cinema Studies at the School of Arts & Aesthetics, Jawaharlal Nehru University, New Delhi. She completed her Ph.D. from the Critical Studies Division of the School of Cinematic Arts, University of Southern California, Los Angeles. Her dissertation *Private Modernities: The "I" in Contemporary Indian Documentary and Visual Culture* focuses on colonial home movies and the first-person documentary in contemporary India. Her research interests include transnational cinema, cinemas of the south, home movies and amateur film, and documentary and avant-garde cinemas. Veena's publications include "The Twice-Lived Fragment of Time: Memory, Time-travel and the Photographic Image in Chris Marker's *La Jetée*" in *Journal of the Moving Image*; and "At Home In the Empire: The Colonial Home Movies of Edgar S. Hyde" in *Bioscope* (forthcoming).

Alice L. Hutchison writes on contemporary visual arts and is based between New Zealand and Los Angeles.

Juan Carlos Kase has published in *Discourse: Journal for Theoretical Studies in Media and Culture*, *Millennium Film Journal*, and *The Moving Image*. He has written a chapter on the observational cinema and minimalist music of Phill Niblock for a forthcoming anthology, which will be the first to assess the artist's wide-ranging intermedial output. He is currently completing revisions on his manuscript, *A Cinema of Anxiety: American Experimental Film in the Realm of Art (1964–76)*, which considers the work of experimental filmmakers in relation to a range of confrontational actions in art and media of the era. His ongoing research concerns the overlapping aesthetic, historical, and political registers of experimental cinema, documentary, art history, performance, and popular music within American culture. He is Assistant Professor of Film Studies at the University of North Carolina Wilmington.

Alison Kozberg is a Ph.D. candidate in the department of Critical Studies in the USC School of Cinematic Arts. Her research focuses on modern and contemporary art, experimental film, and the history of Los Angeles. She was head researcher for Los Angeles Filmforum's Alternative Projections project.

Based in Columbus, Ohio, **Tim Lanza** has been the caretaker of the Rohauer Collection for the past 19 years, distributing the films in the library for Theatrical, Home Video, and Television markets throughout North America and in Europe and Asia. He has contributed to and worked with archives such as the Library of Congress, the British Film Institute, the George Eastman House, and the U.C.L.A. Film and Television Archive on the restoration and preservation of a number of films in the Collection, as well as having programmed special public film programs, such as the "Tom Verlaine and Jimmy Rip: Music for Film" program that played in North America and Europe.

Jesse Lerner is a filmmaker based in Los Angeles. His short films *Natives* (1991, with Scott Sterling), *T.S.H.* (2004) and Magnavoz (2006) and the feature-length experimental documentaries *Frontierland/Fronterilandia* (1995, with Rubén Ortiz-Torres), *Ruins* (1999) *The American Egypt* (2001), *Atomic Sublime* (2010), and *The Absent Stone* (2013, with Sandra Rozental) have won numerous prizes at film festivals in the United States, Latin America and Japan. He has curated projects for the Mexico's *Palacio Nacional de Bellas Artes*, the Guggenheim Museums in

New York and Bilbao, and the Robert Flaherty Seminar. His books include *F is for Phony: Fake Documentary and Truth's Undoing* (with Alexandra Juhasz), *The Shock of Modernity* and *The Maya of Modernism*.

Ross Lipman is a Senior Film Preservationist at the UCLA Film & Television Archive, where his many restorations include Charles Burnett's *Killer of Sheep*, Kent Mackenzie's *The Exiles*, Barbara Loden's *Wanda*, the Academy Award-winning documentary *The Times of Harvey Milk*, and works by Charlie Chaplin, Orson Welles, Shirley Clarke, Kenneth Anger, and John Cassavetes. He was a 2008 recipient of Anthology Film Archives' Preservation Honors, and is a three-time winner of the National Society of Film Critics' Heritage Award. His essays on film history, technology, and aesthetics have been published in numerous books and journals. Lipman is also an independent filmmaker whose works have screened internationally and been collected by museums and institutions including the Oberhausen Kurzfilm Archive, Budapest's Balazs Bela Studios, and Munich's Sammlung Goetz.

Matt Reynolds is Assistant Professor of Art History and Visual Culture Studies at Whitman College. He is currently working on a book-length project exploring the role of the visual arts in the ongoing Hollywood Redevelopment Project.

Marc Siegel is an Assistant Professor in the Department of Theater, Film, and Media Studies at the Goethe University in Frankfurt. He recently edited a special issue of the journal *Criticism* on the work of Jack Smith (forthcoming) and co-edited a German anthology on synchronization and the arts, *Synchronization der Künste* (Munich: Fink Verlag, 2013). His curatorial projects include numerous film series, as well as the festivals "Camp/Anti-Camp: A Queer Guide to Everyday Life" (Berlin/Frankfurt, 2012), "LIVE FILM! JACK SMITH! Five Flaming Days in a Rented World" (Berlin, 2009) and the exhibition "George Kuchar" (Berlin Biennial, 2010).

Erika Suderburg is a filmmaker and writer. She is co-editor with Michael Renov of *Resolutions: Contemporary Video Practices* and editor of *Space Site Intervention: Situating Installation Art,* both published by the University of Minnesota Press, which also published *Resolutions 3: Global Networks of Video* co-edited with Ming-Yuen S. Ma in 2012. She has made seven feature length films and myriad short works that have been screened internationally. Currently she is on the faculty of the University of California, Riverside in the Department of Media and Cultural Studies.

Julie Turnock is Assistant Professor of Media and Cinema Studies at the University of Illinois, Urbana/Champaign, in the College of Media. She is the author of *Plastic Reality: Special Effects, Art and Technology in 1970s US Filmmaking*, and has been a Whiting Fellow and an Andrew W. Mellon / ACLS Early Career Fellow. She has published on special effects in *Cinema Journal, Film History, New Review of Film and Television Studies* and *Popping Culture* (2010). Additionally, Julie has research, writing, and teaching interests in silent film, spectacle, experimental film, melodrama, and animation, among others.

Grahame Weinbren is a filmmaker and media artist, editor of the *Millennium Film Journal,* and a faculty member in the graduate division of the School of Visual Arts.

Index